Compulsory Jurisdiction in International Law

To the memory of Vilmos Peschka,
the great Hungarian legal philosopher

Compulsory Jurisdiction in International Law

Vanda Lamm

Professor of International Law, Hungary and member of the Institut de Droit International

Edward Elgar

Cheltenham, UK • Northampton, MA, USA

Published by
Edward Elgar Publishing Limited
The Lypiatts
15 Lansdown Road
Cheltenham
Glos GL50 2JA
UK

Edward Elgar Publishing, Inc.
William Pratt House
9 Dewey Court
Northampton
Massachusetts 01060
USA

A catalogue record for this book
is available from the British Library

Library of Congress Control Number: 2014938804

This book is available electronically in the ElgarOnline.com Law Subject Collection, E-ISBN 978 1 78347 321 2

MIX
Paper from
responsible sources
FSC www.fsc.org FSC® C013056

ISBN 978 1 78347 320 5

Typeset by Columns Design XML Ltd, Reading
Printed and bound in Great Britain by T.J. International Ltd, Padstow

Contents

Preface

There was a long path traversed from the various conceptions, being naive and illusory, regarding the compulsory judicial settlement of interstate disputes to the creation of the first permanent international judicial forum of a universal character, i.e. the Permanent Court of International Justice. Its Statute, by the provisions of the optional clause, finally introduced a system, up until then unknown, of partial obligatory international adjudication based on the full observance of the voluntary acceptance of the Court's jurisdiction.

That system consists of a network of unilateral declarations in which states assume an obligation, in addition to those specified by the Court's Statute, to the effect that they oblige themselves to submit their disputes with other states – also having made such declarations – to the decision of the Permanent Court of International Justice, and since 1946 to the International Court of Justice.

This system, since its establishment, has been the subject of controversy, especially because it could not fulfil the expectations regarding a worldwide system of obligatory international adjudication. Nevertheless, it has great merits and it has contributed to the peaceful settlement of international disputes.

The book offers a wide-ranging survey of the development of the optional clause system, the theoretical and procedural aspects of unilateral declarations of acceptance, the different reservations added to these declarations and it seeks to find solutions to the improvement of the system.

The author wishes to express her gratitude to Professor András Bragyova, who was kind enough to read the first draft of the book, special thanks must also go to Frank Orton, former Swedish judge and ombudsman for his encouragement and support. Sincere thanks are due to Judit Elek, head of the Library of the Centre for Social Sciences (Hungarian Academy of Sciences), who helped in collecting the respective literature and to Anthony Vago for checking the manuscript's English. Finally, immense gratitude goes to Edward Elgar Publishing Ltd for publishing the book and Ben Booth, Chloe Mitchell and Bryan Campbell for their very helpful and constructive approach.

Abbreviations

AFDI	Annuaire Français de Droit International
AJIL	American Journal of International Law
AVR	Archiv des Völkerrechts
BYIL	British Yearbook of International Law
Cal L R	California Law Review
Can YB Int'l L	Canadian Yearbook of International Law
Chinese J I L	Chinese Journal of International Law
Colum J Transnat'l L	Columbia Journal of Transnational Law
EJIL	European Journal of International Law
Fordham Int'l L J	Fordham International Law Journal
Ga L Rev	Georgia Law Review
Geo L J	Georgetown Law Journal
ICJ	International Court of Justice
ICLQ	International and Comparative Law Quarterly
JDI	Journal du Droit International
Ky L J	Kentucky Law Journal
Law & Prac Int'l Courts & Trib	Law and Practice of International Courts and Tribunals
LoN	League of Nations
NYIL	Netherlands Yearbook of International Law
ÖzöR	Österreichische Zeitschrift für öffentliches Recht
PCIJ	Permanent Court of International Justice
RCADI	Recueil des Cours, Hague Academy of International Law
RDILC	Revue de Droit International et de Législation Comparée
RGDIP	Revue Général de Droit International Public
Rev Colomb Derecho Int	Revista Colombiana Derecho Internacional
Rev BDI	Revue belge de droit international

Span Yrbk Int'l L	Spanish Yearbook of International Law
UNCIO	United Nations Conference on International Organization
US Dep't St Bull	U.S. Department of State Bulletin
VJIL	Virginia Journal of International Law
Wm & Mary L Rev	William & Mary Law Review
ZaöRV	Zeitschrift für ausländisches öffentliches Recht und Völkerrecht

Table of cases

PERMANENT COURT OF INTERNATIONAL JUSTICE

Contentious Cases

Advisory Opinions

INTERNATIONAL COURT OF JUSTICE

Contentious Cases

Advisory Opinions

Arbitral Awards

1. A short history of the arbitral settlement of interstate disputes until the establishment of the PCIJ

I OVERVIEW OF THE ARBITRAL SETTLEMENT OF INTERSTATE DISPUTES BEFORE THE HAGUE PEACE CONFERENCES

Time and again in the centuries-old history of interstate relations there have emerged ideas arguing that states have to submit their disputes for third party settlement, especially to adjudication as an alternative to war. Such conceptions can be traced to old legends, according to which disputes between states or sovereigns were settled by arbitration. The records that have come down to us suggest that in more than one case bitter disputes were submitted to arbitration and the majority of arbitral awards were executed by the parties. In other words, it seems that recourse to arbitration was for centuries a rare but successful means of settling interstate disputes.

Arbitration between ancient Greeks was rather widespread. Relying on cases treated by various authors, Taube estimates that over five hundred years, from the 7th to the middle of the 2nd century B.C., the number of cases settled by arbitration between the city-states (*polis*) ran to about 110.[1] Some sort of arbitration was practised in theory by the Senate between allies (*socii*) in the Roman Empire, but one cannot speak of genuine arbitration at the time of the Roman Empire as Rome sought to have even the institution of arbitration serve its own expansionist aspirations.[2] As Nicolas Politis rightly points out 'Rome considered itself

---

[1] Cf. Michel de Taube, 'Les origines de l'arbitrage international antiquité et moyen age' in *Collected Courses of the Hague Academy of International Law*, 1932 (Recueil Sirey 1933) tome 42, IV, 14.

[2] On arbitration in the Graeco-Roman word see *id.*, 24–56.

as the arbitrator of the world, accepted to be judge, but not to be justiciable'.[3]

In the Middle Ages, the arbitral settlement of disputes between souvereigns was relatively frequently used and serving as sole arbitrators were, besides the Pope, sovereigns, kings, emperors and, not infrequently, certain institutions, law professors and lawyers acting on their behalf.

By the 18th century, arbitration had practically disappeared from interstate relations, a fact which seems to be strange and incomprehensible, especially because the retreat of arbitration was witnessed precisely in the decades subsequent to the Peace Treaty of Westphalia, even though the foundation of contemporary international law was, in point of fact, laid by that Treaty.

The idea of international arbitration was throughout centuries closely linked to different – rather illusory – projects of federation between states of the 'civilized' world, often with plans for 'perpetual peace' related thereto.[4] Among the various projects for 'perpetual peace' and the related plans for a federation of European states, the greatest influence was undoubtedly exerted by Abbe Saint-Pierre's work, 'Projet pour rendre paix perpétuelle' (1713).[5] The influence of Saint-Pierre's plan was

---

[3] '… se considérant comme arbitre du monde, elle acceptait d'être juge, non justiciable'. Nicolas Politis, *La Justice Internationale* (2nd edn, Librairie Hachette, 1924), 27.

[4] Such a conception was formulated in Pierre Dubois's work, '*De recuperatione Terrae Sanctae*', probably of 1306, in the proposal of King George of Pogebrady of Bohemia and his advisor (the humanist, Antonio Marini from Geneva) concerning the alliance of Christian States in the second part of the 15th century, and in the perceptions of King Henry IV of France and presumably his Minister Sully about a federation of European States. For more detail, see, Ernst Reibstein, *Völkerrecht, eine Geschichte seiner Ideen in Lehre und Praxis* (Karl Alber, 1958); and Jacob Ter Meulen, *Der Gedanke der Internationalen Organisation in seiner Entwicklung* (Martinus Nijhoff 1917) Vol. I, 99–339. One could also mention Émeric Crucé from the 17th century whose work remained practically unknown to later centuries. Émeric Crucé proposed the establishment of a permanent congress composed of representatives from all sovereigns, regulating the differences between them. However, the gravest questions touching sovereignty and independence should be settled by arbitration. According to Crucé, once arbitration was admitted to these disputes, it could not be rejected for disputes of lesser importance. See Émeric Crusé, *Le nouveau Cynée* (Réimpression du texte original de 1623 avec introduction et traduction anglaise par Thomas Willing Balch, Lane and Scott 1909).

[5] Charles Irénée Castel de Saint-Pierre, *Projet pour rendre paix perpétuelle* (Publisher Chez Antoine Schouten, Marchand Libraire MDCCXIII) (Open Librarie).

enormous both in his own time and afterwards.[6] One should also mention the famous perpetual peace project of the great philosopher Immanuel Kant.[7]

In connection with the peace plans of the 17th and 18th centuries, the French author Michel Revon is right in noting that all these plans share the imperfection of being vague, utopian and having no practical meaning.[8]

A much more realistic view than those of the aforementioned authors is struck by such classics of international law as Grotius and Vattel. By citing historical examples, according to Grotius, wars could be evaded by arbitral decision as well.[9]

---

[6] Cf. Ter Meulen (1932), 180–221. Thus, for example, both Rousseau and Leibnitz dealt extensively with Saint-Pierre's work. See also Jean-Jaques Rousseau, *A project for perpetual peace* (Thomas Nugent (tr.) M. Cooper 1761). Rousseau's abridgement of Saint-Pierre's work; and Wilhelm Gottfried Leibniz, *Observations sur le Projet de paix perpétuelle de l'abbé de Saint-Pierre*, précédées de la lettre de Leibniz à l'abbé de Saint-Pierre du 7 février 1715. (Presses universitaires de Caen 1993).

[7] Immanuel Kant, *Perpetual peace: A Philosophical Sketch* (1795), (translated with introduction and notes by Marie Campbell Smith, M.A.; Preface by Professor Latta. (1st edn), George Allen & Unwin Ltd., The MacMillan Company, 1903) 218. Kant's essay on *Perpetual peace* takes the form of an international treaty, with the author's comments and an Appendix.

[8] Michel Revon, *L'arbitrage international*: Son passé. – Son présent. – Son avenir (Librairie nouvelle de droit et de jurisprudence 1892) 144.

[9] Grotius writes:

> The office of deciding wars and putting an end to the contentions of armies was assigned, according to Starbo, to the Druids of the Gauls, and upon the testimony of the same writer, it formed a part of the priestly functions among the Iberians.
>
> Surely then it is a mode of terminating their disputes, balancing their powers, and settling their presentations worthy to be adopted by Christian Kings and States. For if, in order to avoid trials before judges who were strangers to the true religion, the Jews and Christians appointed arbitrators of their own, and it was a practice recommended and enjoined by St. Paul, who much more sought such a practice to be recommended and enforced, to gain the still nobler end of preventing the calamities of war.
>
> These and many other reasons of no less importance might be advanced for recommending to Christian powers general congresses for the adjustment of their various interests, and for compelling the refractory to submit to equitable terms of peace.
>
> Hugo Grotius (Hugo de Groot), *On the Law of War and Peace* (Tr. from the original latin De Jure Belli ac Pacis and slightly abridged by A.C. Cambell, A.M., Batoche Books 2011) 235.

Vattel writes that, 'When sovereigns cannot agree about their pretensions and are nevertheless desirous of preserving or restoring peace, they sometimes submit the decision of their disputes to arbitrators chosen by common agreement.'[10] He emphasises that, 'Arbitration is a very reasonable mode, and one that is perfectly comfortable to the law of nature, for the decision of every dispute which does not directly interest the safety of the nation.'[11]

The great English author, jurist and philosopher Jeremy Bentham in his essay, 'A Plan for an Universal and Perpetual Peace', points very rightly to the advantages of third party settlement by saying that 'Establish a common tribunal, the necessity for war no longer follows from difference of opinion. Just or unjust, the decision of the arbiters will save the credit, the honour of the contending party.'[12]

The idea to settle interstate disputes by adjudication was markedly present in the works of writers of the second half of the 19th century, owing not least to the fact that arbitral settlement of disputes between states had become rather frequent during that century and in the last two decades of the century more arbitral awards were rendered than those put together in the first part of the century.[13] The modern era of arbitration

---

10 Emmerich de Vattel, *The Law of Nations, or the Principles of Natural Law* (Tr. from the French by Joseph Chitty, Esq. Based on the 1797 edition, republished by T.&J.W. Johnson 1853) Book II, § 329.

11 *Id.*

12 Jeremy Bentham, 'The Principles of International Law' Essay 4, in *The Works of Jeremy Bentham* (published under the superintendence of his executor, John Bowring, vol. II. William Tait, Simpkin, Marshall & Co., MDCCCXLIII), 552.

13 The following figures can be mentioned in support of this statement. The number of arbitral awards was

1 between 1801 and 1810
about 17 between 1811 and 1820
about 5 between 1821 and 1830
about 7 between 1831 and 1840
about 7 between 1841 and 1850
about 23 between 1851 and 1860
about 25 between 1861 and 1870
about 28 between 1871 and 1880
about 46 between 1881 and 1890
about 61 between 1891 and 1900

Cf. A.M. Stuyt, *Survey of International Arbitrations 1794–1970* (Sijthoff, Oceana 1972) 6–237.

dates back to the Jay's Treaty of 1794,[14] and later on to the Alabama Arbitration in 1871–72, a successful settlement of a harsh dispute between the United States of America and the United Kingdom arising from the American Civil War.[15]

During the 19th century, there were numerous plans for establishing international tribunals and some authors were arguing not only for such forums but for the introduction of a general obligation of states to recourse to arbitration for the settlement of certain disputes. The most notable among them were plans of Dudley Field (American lawyer and member of the US Congress),[16] the Moscow professor Kamarowsky,[17] and Mérignhac from France, who developed similar principles which were adopted later at the First Hague Peace Conference.[18] Also concerned with projects of a permanent international court of arbitration

---

[14] After the Treaty of Paris (1783), which ended the American War of Independence, the relations between the United States and Great Britain deteriorated. On 19 November 1794, the Treaty of Amity, Commerce, and Navigation (Jay's Treaty) was signed, which among other things, provided for the establishment of three mixed claims commissions for dispute settlement. The first arbitral commission dealt with the delimitation of which river was under the name of St. Croix mentioned in the Treaty of Paris. The second commission's task was to deal with claims with respect to debts owed by American citizens (or residents) to British creditors contracted before the peace. The third commission had to settle the claims of American citizens against Great Britain regarding the illegal seizure of ships and cargos. The mixed commissions consisted of an equal number of members (two or four) appointed by each of the two states, plus an umpire chosen by them or drawn by lot. The mixed commissions decided many claims to the satisfaction of the parties.

[15] The Alabama Claims were a series of claims for damages by the United States against Great Britain for the assistance given to the Confederation during the American Civil War and especially for the violation of neutrality by allowing the construction in Britain of the warship Alabama, which caused significant damage to the US Navy and merchant marine. The arbitration tribunal, composed of five arbitrators, decided the case on 14 September 1972.

[16] Cf. David Dudley Field, *Project d'un Code International:* Proposé aux diplomates, aux hommes d'État, et aux jurisconsultes du droit international (Albéric Rolin tr., Pédone-Lauriel, Adolphe Hoste 1881) 880.

[17] Cf. Leonide Kamarowsky, *Le tribunal international* (Serge de Westman (tr.), G. Pedone-Lauriel 1887).

[18] According to Mérignhac, one day there will be a permanent international forum whose decisions will be sanctioned by international forces. Cf. Alexandre Mérignhac, *Traité théorique et pratique de l'arbitrage international* (L. Larose Éditeur 1895) 516.

were the Universal Peace Congresses, the Interparliamentary Union, the Institut de Droit International and the International Law Association.[19]

A rather clear and – one might safely say – still valid statement about international arbitration during the 1880s was made by the Russian Professor Friedrich Fromhold Martens[20] to the effect that, regarding the future of international arbitration, it was necessary to distinguish hopes and realities and international arbitration was not the way to go in all international disputes in which the political element was paramount.[21] In the author's view, international arbitration is a viable path in the case of less significant disputes, particularly concerning questions of a legal nature and in cases where the rights of the parties can be clearly identified.[22]

II THE RESULTS OF THE HAGUE PEACE CONFERENCES

The establishment of an arbitral tribunal was discussed in detail at the First Hague Peace Conference in 1899, convened at the initiative of the Russian Tsar Nicholas II, with the purpose of elaborating on proposals for the reduction of armaments and discussing peace with the object of preventing armed conflicts between nations.

At the First Hague Peace Conference, several proposals regarding arbitration and methods of pacific settlement of interstate disputes were presented,[23] and the majority of delegates agreed that the settlement of disputes by international arbitration was important and desirable, but the

---

[19] Cf. Dr Hans Wehberg, *The Problem of an International Court of Justice* (The Clarendon Press 1918) 132–40.

[20] Later on F.F. Martens was one of the leading figures of the Hague Peace Conferences in 1899 and 1907.

[21] Cf. F. de Martens, *Traité de droit international* (Alfred Léo (tr.), Librairie Marescq Ainé 1887) vol. 3, 154–5.

[22] *Id.* 155.

[23] Draft proposals were submitted by Great Britain, Italy, Russia and the United States. Those drafts drew heavily upon the customary law on arbitration that was available at the end of the 19th century, as well as upon the drafts prepared by the Institut de droit international (see Resolution of the Institut de droit international adopted at the Session of 1875 at The Hague termed, 'Projet de réglement pour la procédure arbitrale international') and the Interparliamentary Union. The starting point for the negotiations was furnished by the Russian and British drafts, which were debated in a so-called special Committee of Examination.

The documents produced by the Russian, British, American and Italian delegations, see *The Hague Peace Conferences of 1899 and 1907 and International*

debate was rather sharp about the arbitral tribunal to be established and mainly about whether states were under obligation to submit their disputes to that forum. During the negotiations, concrete proposals on obligatory arbitration were formulated in certain cases,[24] provided that neither the vital interests nor the national honour of states were affected. Recourse to arbitration in other matters was to be subject exclusively to the discretion of states, and the parties' consent to such recourse was to be required in each case.[25]

The negotiations produced a draft proposing the introduction of compulsory international arbitration in a number of cases.[26]

Arbitration. Reports and Documents. (Compiled and edited by Shabtai Rosenne, T.M.C. Asser Press 2001) 89–113.

[24] It was the Russian proposal that went furthest towards the introduction of obligatory arbitration.

[25] According to the Russian draft, subject to obligatory arbitration would be all legal matters which, arising in disputes between states, did not affect the vital interests and the national honour of states. The Russian draft specified two classes of international disputes subject to obligatory arbitration, notably pecuniary claims to recover for unlawful injuries on the one hand and, on the other, the interpretation or application of certain non-political conventions, chiefly treaties known as 'universal unions' like the one exemplified by the Treaty of 1874 on the Universal Postal Union, which in Art. 16 provides obligatory arbitration for the solution of all differences concerning the interpretation or application of that treaty. Cf. Rosenne (2001) 47.

[26] Under the terms of the draft,

> Arbitration is obligatory between the high contracting Powers in the following cases, so far as they do not concern the vital interest or national honour of the States in controversy:
>
> I. In case of disputes concerning the interpretation or application of the conventions enumerated herein:
>
> (1) Postal, telephone, and telegraphic conventions.
> (2) Conventions concerning the protection of submarine cables.
> (3) Conventions concerning railroads.
> (4) Conventions and regulations concerning means of preventing collisions of vessels at sea.
> (5) Conventions concerning the protection of literary and artistic works.
> (6) Conventions concerning the protection of industrial property (patents, trade-marks, and trade-names).
> (7) Conventions concerning the system of weights and measures.
> (8) Conventions concerning reciprocal free assistance to the indigent sick.
> (9) Sanitary conventions, conventions concerning epizooty, phylloxera and other similar scourges.
> (10) Conventions concerning civil procedure.

The draft appeared to be acceptable to the majority of delegates, but upon the second reading the German delegate came out against the adoption of the text, as in the German Government's view the experience to date was not sufficient to support the introduction of compulsory arbitration in connection with the conventions enumerated in the draft. According to the German delegation, 'a too rapid introduction of obligatory arbitration into international law might present more dangers than advantages from the point of view of peace among nations.'[27] Thereupon the Russian delegate submitted another draft proposing the introduction of compulsory adjudication in a still smaller number of questions. However, the delegates were still unable to reach an agreement and in place of enumerating various conventions, they adopted an article containing a twofold provision. The first refers to treaties which already provide a resort to arbitration, the second one is a declaration reserving the right to conclude new agreements extending obligatory arbitration to cases which they deem possible of submission thereto.[28]

The result of the negotiations was a text which later on appeared as Articles 15–19 in the Convention for the Pacific Settlement of International Disputes. That was a compromised text, reflecting the principle of voluntary arbitration, postulating that each State decides in its sovereign capacity whether a dispute should be submitted to arbitration or not. However, in Article 19 there was a reference to treaties stipulating obligatory arbitration, providing that the contracting parties may conclude new agreements with a view to extending arbitration to other cases they consider suitable for arbitration.

At the First Hague Peace Conference, regarding the establishment of an arbitral tribunal, the outcome was also a compromised solution, although a permanent machinery was adopted and an agreement was reached on the establishment of the Permanent Court of Arbitration.[29] What was not a real court but a list of jurists, designated up to four judges by each contracting party to the 1899 Convention for the Pacific

---

(11) Extradition conventions.

(12) Conventions for delimiting boundaries so far as they touch upon purely technical and non-political questions.

II. In case of disputes concerning pecuniary claims arising for damages when the principle of indemnity is recognized by the Parties.

[27] Report to the Conference from the Third Commission on Pacific Settlement of International Disputes. See Rosenne (2001) 48.

[28] *Id.* 48.

[29] On the Permanent Court of Arbitration and on cases decided by it see, James Brown Scott (ed.) *The Hague Court Reports* (OUP 1916) cxi, 664.

Settlement of International Disputes, from among whom, in concrete disputes, the members of each arbitral tribunal might be chosen. Nevertheless, one can say that with the establishment of the Permanent Court of Arbitration, international tribunals have become a constant institution of international law, and the judicial settlement of international disputes is no longer a sporadic phenomenon in interstate relations. Thus, one can agree with Hershey that 'its importance lay rather in what it held out by way of promise for the future than of actual achievement'.[30]

At the Second Hague Peace Conference in 1907, the question of obligatory arbitration and the conclusion of a convention on that subject were lengthily discussed. Several proposals were submitted by delegates with respect to the class of disputes to be subject to obligatory arbitration and regarding the revision of the 1899 Convention for the Pacific Settlement of International Disputes in this respect.[31] The Conference nevertheless reached no agreement on matters that were to be subject to obligatory arbitration without reserve nor the creation of a permanent tribunal, finally very few amendments were adopted to the provisions on international arbitration of the 1899 Convention.[32] Among others, as a result of the Second Peace Conference, one can refer to a declaration concerning obligatory arbitration in which, it was stated that:

> while reserving to each of the Powers represented full liberty of action as regards voting, enables them to affirm the principles which they regard as unanimously admitted: It is unanimous:
>
> 1. In admitting the principle of obligatory arbitration.
> 2. In declaring that certain disputes, in particular those relating to the interpretation and application of the provisions of international agreements, may be submitted to compulsory arbitration without any restriction.

Rather interesting is that the document goes on by saying that the Conference was '... unanimous in proclaiming that, although it has not

---

[30] Amos S. Hershey, 'Convention for the Peaceful Adjustment of International Differences' (1908), 2, *AJIL*, 29, 30.

[31] See Report to the Conference from the First Commission on the Revision of the Convention of 1899 for the Pacific Settlement of International Disputes. See Rosenne (2001) 223–399.

[32] The Convention for the Pacific Settlement of International Disputes prepared in 1899 was amended and enlarged, especially with regards to the commissions of inquiry, and a new chapter was added for facilitating appeal to arbitration by summary procedure. On the amendments regarding arbitration see Table 1.1 below.

yet been found feasible to conclude a Convention in this sense, nevertheless the divergences of opinion which have come to light have not exceeded the bounds of judicial controversy …'[33]

The negotiations at the Second Hague Peace Conference in 1907 about obligatory arbitration and about various categories of disputes to be subject thereto showed that the states agreed only in principle with obligatory arbitration in so far as it involved no concrete commitment and they were reluctant to assume any further concrete obligation already accepted at the First Peace Conference in 1899.

Notwithstanding, one could say that the Second Hague Peace Conference was a success and in the final analysis, an important step towards the introduction of general international arbitration had been made. Most experts were of the opinion that it was possible for the general introduction of obligatory arbitration to be achieved only gradually and that the peace conferences had made a considerable step to reaching that goal.[34]

---

33 Final Act of the Second International Peace Conference, 1907. See Rosenne (2001), 411.

34 While discussing the development of international arbitration and the judicial settlement of international disputes one should mention also the Central American Court of Justice, established by five Central American states (Costa Rica, El Salvador, Guatemala, Honduras and Nicaragua) which functioned between 1907 and 1917. The Court had jurisdiction not only for interstate disputes, but over certain cases of international character between a government and an individual who was a national of another state. During its existence of ten years, ten cases came before the Court, of which five cases were brought by individuals. According to many authors it was 'a matter of regret that this experiment in the administration international justice was so short-lived, and that the convention of 1907 was not revised and renewed in 1917'. On the Central American Court of Justice, see Manley O. Hudson, 'The Central American Court of Justice' (1932) 26, *AJIL*, 759, 785.

Table 1.1 Relevant provisions of the two Hague Conventions for the Pacific Settlement of International Disputes

Convention of 29 July 1899	Convention of 18 October 1907
Title IV. International Arbitration	Part IV. International Arbitration
Chapter I. The System of Arbitration	Chapter I. The System of Arbitration
Art. 15 ' International Arbitration has for its object the settlement of differences between States by judges of their own choice, and on the basis of respect for law.'	Art. 37 'International arbitration has for its object the settlement of disputes between States by Judges of their own choice and on the basis of respect for law. Recourse to arbitration implies an engagement to submit in good faith to the Award.'
Art. 16 'In questions of a legal nature, and especially in the interpretation or application of International Conventions, arbitration is recognized by the Signatory Powers as the most effective, and at the same time, the most equitable, means of settling disputes which diplomacy has failed to settle.'	Art. 38 'In questions of a legal nature, and especially in the interpretation or application of International Conventions, arbitration is recognized by the Contracting Powers as the most effective, and, at the same time, the most equitable means of settling disputes which diplomacy has failed to settle. Consequently, it would be desirable that, in disputes about the above-mentioned questions, the Contracting Powers should, if the case arose, have recourse to arbitration, in so far as circumstances permit.'
Art. 17 'The Arbitration Convention is concluded for questions already existing or for questions which may arise eventually. It may embrace any dispute or only disputes of a certain category.'	Art. 39 'The Arbitration Convention is concluded for questions already existing or for questions which may arise eventually. It may embrace any dispute or only disputes of a certain category.'
Art. 18 'The Arbitration Convention implies the engagement to submit loyally to the Award.'	
Art. 19 'Independently of general or private Treaties expressly stipulating recourse to arbitration as obligatory on the Signatory Powers, these Powers reserve to themselves the right of concluding, either before the ratification of the present Act or later, new Agreements, general or private, with a view to extending obligatory arbitration to all cases which they may consider it possible to submit to it.'	Art. 40 'Independently of general or private Treaties expressly stipulating recourse to arbitration as obligatory on the Contracting Powers, the said Powers reserve to themselves the right of concluding new Agreements, general or particular, with a view to extending obligatory arbitration to all cases which they may consider possible to submit to it.'

2. The legislative history of the optional clause and its conception

I DRAFTING THE STATUTE OF THE PERMANENT COURT OF INTERNATIONAL JUSTICE

Even before the end of World War I, negotiations between states started on the post-war political landscape, and it was already decided in those days to set up an international organization. The different conceptions included the idea that there should be an international court of justice created to decide interstate disputes within the framework of the international organization that was to be established. The related plans of more detail had not yet been drawn up, and the first proposals submitted to the Paris Peace Conference touched marginally on the question of an international court, generally in connection with the pacific settlement of disputes.

So far as we know, the establishment of a permanent 'judicial body' was first brought up in the British draft of 20 January 1919, but no concrete proposal concerning the court to be set up was contained in that document either.[1] The resolution adopted at the 25 January 1919 plenary session of the Preliminary Peace Conference, approving the principle of the League of Nations, made no reference to a court, but decided to establish, for the study of the constitution of the League of Nations, a commission to be composed of fifteen members, with the five great powers (British Empire, France, Italy, Japan and United States of America) respectively represented by two members each and five members elected to represent all the powers with special interest.[2]

The Commission on the League of Nations started to work on 3 February 1919 and had before it three drafts – an American, a French and

---

[1] Cf. Chapter II of the British Draft Convention. For this document, see David Hunter Miller, *The Drafting of the Covenant* (G.P. Putman's Sons 1928) vol. II, 106–16.

[2] For the resolution, see Minutes (English) of the Commission on the League of Nations. *Id.* 229. The elected members were from Belgium, Brazil, China, Portugal and Serbia.

an Italian – relative to the future organization.[3] The Commission decided to take the so-called Hurst-Miller Draft, presented by President Wilson of the United States, as the basis for its deliberations. Article 12 of that document provided that the Executive Council of the future organization was to formulate plans for the establishment of a Permanent Court of International Justice. Under the Hurst-Miller Draft, the Court 'will be competent to hear and determine any matter which the parties recognize as suitable for submission to it for arbitration …'. In accordance with the aforementioned proposal, a drafting committee worded the articles of the League of Nations Covenant relating to the future international court and submitted it to the Preliminary Peace Conference.[4] During the consultations on the Commission's draft, several amendments were proposed until finally, on 28 April 1919, the Preliminary Peace Conference adopted the text which was to form Articles 13 and 14 of the Covenant of the League of Nations.[5]

These Articles Read as Follows: Article 13

1. The Members of the League agree that, whenever any dispute shall arise between them which they recognize to be suitable for submission to arbitration or judicial settlement, and which cannot be satisfactorily settled by diplomacy, they will submit the whole subject-matter to arbitration or judicial settlement.

---

[3] For the drafts, see Miller (1928) 231–55.

[4] On the elaboration of the Covenant's provisions relating to the Permanent Court of International Justice, see Manley O. Hudson, *The Permanent Court of International Justice,* 1920–1942, (Arno Press 1972) 93–112, and Antonio Sánchez de Bustamante y Sirvén, *La Cour Permanente de Justice International* (Paul Goulé (tr.), Librairie Recueil Sirey 1925) 80–95.

[5] It may be of interest to note that on 9 May 1919 the German delegation put forward a counter-proposal dealing with, inter alia, the international court to be established. That delegation, which on previous occasions, including the Hague Peace Conferences, had come out against the introduction of obligatory international adjudication, but now suggested that the court should be invested with compulsory jurisdiction over disputes of a legal nature and should also have jurisdiction over complaints of private persons in certain cases. That motion was not discussed in more detail and Germany was told that its proposal would be submitted to the Council of the League of Nations for fuller consideration when preparing the draft relating to the establishment of the court. The case also happened with the Austrian counter-proposals of 23 June 1919 relating to, inter alia, Arts. 12, 13 and 14 of the Covenant.

For the German Draft see Miller (1928) 744–61.

2. Disputes as to the interpretation of a treaty, as to any question of international law, as to the existence of any fact which, if established, would constitute a breach of any international obligation, or as to the extent and nature of the reparation to be made for any such breach, are declared to be among those which are generally suitable for submission to arbitration or judicial settlement.
3. For the consideration of any such dispute, the court to which the case is referred shall be the Permanent Court of International Justice, established in accordance with Article XIV, or any tribunal agreed on by the parties to the dispute or stipulated in any convention existing between them.
4. The Members of that League agree that they will carry out in full good faith any award or decision that may be rendered, and that they will not resort to war against a Member of the League which complies therewith. In the event of any failure to carry out such an award or decision, the Council shall propose what steps should be taken to give effect thereto.

Article 14

1. The Council shall formulate and submit to the Members of the League for adoption, plans for the establishment of a Permanent Court of International Justice. The Court shall be competent to hear and determine any dispute of an international character which the parties thereto submit to it. The Court may also give an advisory opinion upon any dispute or question referred to it by the Council or by the Assembly.

A closer scrutiny of the quoted provisions basically admits two conclusions. On the one hand, after World War I the majority of states agreed on the need to set up an international court of justice – that was the Permanent Court of International Justice – and to take effective measures in pursuance of that goal.[6] On the other hand, states have never really held such clearly enunciated views on the Court's jurisdiction and – although the Covenant lent itself to various interpretations with respect to the jurisdiction of the future court – one thing remains certain, namely that the said instrument did not provide for the compulsory jurisdiction, i.e. for the possibility of bringing a case against another state without the latter consenting to the proceedings. That is why one could look upon the

---

[6] As is known, the Covenant formed part of the post-First World War Peace Treaties (of Versailles, Saint Germain, Trianon, Neully), and thus, by signing and ratifying them, some 27 states gave consent to the establishment of the court. The United States was not among them as it did not ratify the instrument. Cf. Alexander Pandelli Fachiri, *The Permanent Court of International Justice*: Its Constitution, Procedure and Work (Reprint of the 2nd edition 1932, Scientia Verlag 1980) 1.

Covenant article on the jurisdiction of the Permanent Court of International Justice as representing some sort of a retreat from the results of the Second Hague Peace Conference, since in 1907 the Powers expressed approval of compulsory arbitration in a declaration[7] which had not been opposed, at least not openly, even by those states that had essentially disagreed with a wide introduction of international adjudication.

By the terms of the Covenant, the Council of the League appointed a ten-member Advisory Committee of Jurists, representing different civilizations and legal systems, to elaborate on a draft concerning a court referred to in the Covenant.[8] The Advisory Committee of Jurists met at The Hague from 16 June to 24 July 1920.[9]

During the Committee's deliberations, one of the liveliest debates was provoked by the Court's jurisdiction, notably regarding the question of

---

[7] Cf. Final Act of Second Hague Peace Conference in Rosenne (2001) 412.

[8] Among the members of the Committee of Jurists were numerous famous experts of international law of the time, such as Baron Descamps (Belgium), Albert de Lapradelle (France), Lord Phillimore (Great Britain), and Elihu Root (United States). The other members of the Committee included Minéichirŏ Adatci (Japan), Rafael Altamira (Spain), Clovis Bevilaqua (Brazil), who was later replaced by Raoul Fernandes, Francis Hagerup (Norway), Bernard C.J. Loder (Netherlands) and Arturo Ricci-Busatti (Italy).

[9] For the negotiations of the Advisory Committee of Jurists and those regarding the Optional Clause, see *Cour Permanente de Justice Internationale* (hereafter: C.P.J.I.), *Comité Consultatif de Juristes.* Procès Verbaux des Séances du Comité. La Haye, 1920; Fachiri (1980) 1–11. Lorna Lloyd, 'A Springboard for the Future': A Historical Examination of Britain's Role in the Shaping the Optional Clause of the Permanent Court of International Justice (1985). 79, *AJIL*, 28, 28–45; O. I. Spiermann, 'Who Attempts Too Much Does Nothing Well': The 1920 Advisory Committee of Jurists and the Statute of the Permanent Court of International Justice' (2002) 73, *BYIL*, 187, 187–259.

According to the speech delivered by Léon Bourgeois at the opening of the Committee's meetings, the Committee had to find answers essentially to the following six questions:

- How should the Permanent Court be organized?
- How should its members be appointed?
- What will be their number and status?
- In what country and in what town will the seat of the Court be fixed?
- What will be its rules of procedure, both in the matter of preliminary pleadings and of judgment?
- What will be, finally, the limits of its competence?

Cf. C.P.J.I., *Comité Consultatif de Juristes … op. cit.* 7.

whether or not to confer compulsory jurisdiction on the court.[10] The controversy was due – in no small measure – to the members of the Advisory Committee of Jurists giving different interpretations of Article 14 of the Covenant. The majority held that the Covenant conferred a priori compulsory jurisdiction on the court to be established, while Adatci of Japan, who opposed compulsory jurisdiction, was of the opinion that the Covenant deliberately intended to limit the competence of the Court to cases submitted to it by the parties.[11]

The Advisory Committee of Jurists finally arrived at a solution and in Article 34 it agreed that the Court may hear and determine without any special convention disputes between states which are Members of the League of Nations, if such disputes are of a legal nature.[12] The Committee unanimously adopted that position and was quite quick – in the space of six weeks – in preparing by 24 July 1920, the Draft Scheme for the establishment of the Permanent Court of International Justice. That document was sent to the Council of the League of Nations in the form of a report drawn up by de Lapradelle, a member of the Committee and essentially served as a commentary on the various draft articles.[13] At the time, the Committee was of the view that by the elaboration of the Draft Scheme or, as was put by the Advisory Committee of Jurists itself, by the establishment of the Permanent Court of International Justice, states made a significant step in the direction indicated by the declaration adopted at the Second Peace Conference, according to which 'certain disputes, in particular those relating to the interpretation and application of the provisions of international agreements, may be submitted to

[10] Compulsory jurisdiction was favoured chiefly by Loder of the Netherlands and was opposed most strongly by Adatci of Japan. Cf. Spiermann (2002) 210.

[11] Cf. C.P.I.J. *Comité Consultatif de Juristes … op. cit.* 541–2.

[12] Draft Art. 34 reads as follows:

> Between States which are Members of the League of Nations, the Court shall have jurisdiction (and this without any special convention giving it jurisdiction) to hear and determine cases of a legal nature, concerning:
>
> a. the interpretation of a treaty;
> b. any question of international law;
> c. the existence of any fact, which, if established, would constitute a breach of an international obligation;
> d. the nature or extent of reparation to be made for the breach of an international obligation;
> e. the interpretation of a sentence passed by the Court.

[13] For the report, see C.P.I.J. *Comité Consultatif de Juristes … op. cit.*, 693–746.

compulsory arbitration without any restriction'.[14] Although the Draft Scheme was subsequently amended by the Council and the Assembly of the League, it remained the basis, and contains, broadly speaking, the system of the Court as was set up.

Draft Article 34, worded by the Advisory Committee of Jurists *undoubtedly envisaged the introduction of compulsory jurisdiction by providing that disputes of a legal nature arising between Members of the League of Nations could be submitted to the court without any special agreement.* According to the reasoning of the Committee, this did not mean that such disputes were to be brought before an international court without the consent of states, since the jurisdiction of international tribunals had always been based on a treaty and, according to the interpretation of the Advisory Committee of Jurists, the Statute of the Permanent Court should be such a treaty. Under the Draft-Scheme, any dispute, in addition to those of a legal nature (in respect of which compulsory jurisdiction was intended to be introduced), could be submitted to the Court on the basis of a general or special agreement between the parties.[15]

The report of the Advisory Committee of Jurists evoked a lively debate at the Council of the League of Nations. The Council transmitted the Draft Scheme first to the member states of the League, which returned rather reluctant dismissive replies concerning the introduction of compulsory jurisdiction.

The Council of the League of Nations entrusted the French jurist, Léon Bourgeois, with preparing the report on the future court. The report presented by Léon Bourgeois was approved by the Council on 27 October 1920.[16] The document stated that the adoption of the draft articles elaborated by the Advisory Committee of Jurists on compulsory jurisdiction would in reality be a modification of Articles 12 and 13 of the Covenant. In order to avoid modifying the Covenant, the Council proposed amending the articles submitted by Committee of Jurists and omitting the proposal for the introduction of compulsory jurisdiction. As an explanation of that Council's action, one can read the following:

---

14 Cf. Para. 2. Final Act of the Second Peace Conference in Rosenne (2001) 411.

15 Cf. second section of Art. 34.

16 The report presented by Léon Bourgeois, see *League of Nations, Permanent Court of International Justice*, Documents concerning The action taken by the Council of the League of Nations under Art. 4 of the Covenant and The adoption by the Assembly of the Statute of the Permanent Court, 45–50.

> … (t)he Council will, no doubt, consider that it is not its duty, at the moment when the General Assembly of the League of Nations is about to meet for the first time, to take the initiative with regard to proposed alterations in the Covenant, whose observance and safe keeping have been entrusted to it.[17]

In view of this, the Council suggested substituting in the draft scheme, in place of Articles 33 and 34, the following Articles:

Article 33

'The jurisdiction of the Court is defined by Articles 12, 13 and 14 of the Covenant.'

Article 34

> Without prejudice to the right of the parties according to Article 12 of the Covenant to submit disputes between them either to judicial settlement or arbitration or to enquiry by the Council, the Court shall have jurisdiction (and this without any special agreement giving it jurisdiction) to hear and determine disputes, the settlement of which is by Treaties in force entrusted to it or to the tribunal instituted by the League of Nations.

In November 1920, the Council, with that amendment and some minor alterations, submitted the Draft Scheme to the Assembly, which referred the document to the Third Committee of the Assembly for consideration.[18] The Third Committee set up a Sub-Committee of ten members to examine the Draft Scheme in detail and report to the Committee.[19]

The Third Committee and the Sub-Committee continued the debate on jurisdiction, and several amendments were submitted to the Draft Scheme. Some states, e.g. Italy, proposed an amendment to the draft which was tantamount to virtually ruling out compulsory jurisdiction *in toto*.[20] On the other hand, Argentina presented a version of the text which would clearly have led to the introduction of compulsory jurisdiction between the member states of the League.[21]

---

17 *Id.* 47.

18 Cf. *Id.* 54–60.

19 Five members of the subcommittee, Adaci, Fernandes, Hagerup, Loder, Ricci-Busatti, took part in the work of the Committee of Jurists as well; the other members were: Joseph Doherty (Canada), Henri Fromageot (France), Max Huber (Switzerland), Sir Cecil Hurst (Great Britain), and Nicolas Politis (Greece).

20 Cf. Bustamane (1925) 105.

21 Cf. *Id.* 105–106.

The opponents of compulsory jurisdiction were mainly delegates of the great powers, while the proponents thereof were mostly representatives of the smaller states. The great powers hinted at their intention to conclude, after signing the Statute, bilateral treaties specifying the class of disputes and the range of states for which they would recognize as compulsory the jurisdiction of the court. In other words, as is pointed at by Waldock, they wanted on no account to commit themselves in advance under the Statute to either a class of legal disputes or certain states with which they would bind themselves in accepting the Court's jurisdiction.[22] Incidentally, some authors assert that the debates made it quite clear that inclusion of compulsory jurisdiction in the Statute would have resulted in a number of states refraining from accession to the Statute of the Permanent Court of International Justice.[23]

In the Sub-Committee, the debate over compulsory jurisdiction had reached a rather critical point when the Brazilian delegate Fernandes came forward with the idea of incorporating an optional clause in the Statute of the future court. Originally, Fernandes had proposed the inclusion of two versions of the articles on the jurisdiction of the court, one on compulsory jurisdiction and the other on voluntary jurisdiction, with states entitled to make a declaration, on accession to the Statute, as to the version of the court's jurisdiction which they chose to accept.[24]

With an eye to the proposal of the Brazilian jurist, the much-disputed Articles 33 and 34 of the draft statute were combined into Article 36 of the Statute of the Permanent Court of International Justice, containing the widely known formula called the 'optional clause'. This formula, which will be discussed in detail at a later point,[25] enables states – when adhering to the statute of the future court – to exercise the option of accepting its jurisdiction as compulsory *ipso facto* without special agreement in certain classes of legal disputes.

---

22 C.H.M. Waldock, 'Decline of the Optional Clause' (1955–56) 22 *BYIL*, 244.

23 Cf. Edward Lindsey, *The International Court* (T.Y. Crowell 1931) 98–9.

24 Thus there will be a so-called 'Temporary Provision' providing that, 'In ratifying the Assembly's decision adopting the Statute, the Members of the League of Nations are free to adhere to either of the two texts of Article 33. They may adhere unconditionally or conditionally to the Article providing for compulsory jurisdiction, a possible condition being reciprocity on the part of a certain number of Members, or of certain Members, or, again, of a number of Members including such and such specified Members.'

25 See para. III of this Chapter.

As has been mentioned, the optional clause was inspired by Fernandes of Brazil, with most of the sources referring to him as the 'father' of the clause. Nevertheless, the Fernandes formula was not completely new, for it had first appeared in a Swiss proposal at the Second Peace Conference at The Hague.[26] The author of that document was the young professor Max Huber from the University of Zürich,[27] who had participated as a member of the Swiss delegation at the Second Hague Peace Conference.[28]

In the light of the above considerations, the provisions on the Court's jurisdiction read as follows:

> The jurisdiction of the Court comprises all cases which the parties refer to it and all matters specially provided for in treaties and conventions in force.
>
> The Members of the League of Nations and the states mentioned in the Annex to the Covenant may, either when signing or ratifying the protocol to which the present Statute is adjoined, or at a later moment, declare that they recognize as compulsory *ipso facto* and without special agreement, in relation to any other Member or state accepting the same obligation, the jurisdiction of the Court in all or any of the classes of legal disputes concerning:
>
> (a) the interpretation of a Treaty;
> (b) any question of International Law;
> (c) the existence of any fact which, if established, would constitute a breach of an international obligation;
> (d) the nature or extent of the reparation to be made for the breach of an international obligation.
>
> The declaration referred to above may be made unconditionally or on condition of reciprocity on the part of several or certain Members or States, or for a certain time.

Under the quoted provisions, the Court's jurisdiction is not compulsory, but states may by unilateral declaration undertake to recognize as

---

[26] For the Swiss proposal, see *Deuxième Conférence Internationale de la Paix*. La Haye 15 juin–18 octobre 1907. Actes et documents. (Martinus Nijhoff 1909) tome II., 888–90.

[27] Cf. Dietrich Schidler, 'Max Huber – His Life' (2007) 18, *EJIL*, 69, 88.

[28] This proposal was essentially related to an Amendment of the Convention of 1899 for the Pacific Settlement of Disputes, its article, which can be seen as the antecedent of Fernandes's proposal, reading as follows: 'The signatory Powers may, subject to reciprocity, accept compulsory arbitration in all or some of the matters mentioned above, and may, through the intermediary of the International Bureau based in The Hague, communicate such matters to the other Powers signatory to the present Convention'.

Deuxième Conférence Internationale de la Paix … op. cit., 888.

compulsory the jurisdiction of the Court in relation to states having made a similar declaration. Thus the jurisdiction of the Court rests clearly on the will of the parties and, by the terms of the article, the states may express their consent to the Court's jurisdiction in a compromise made after the dispute had arisen, in a jurisdictional clause of a treaty, or in a declaration of acceptance (of compulsory jurisdiction, also termed as 'optional clause declaration').

The Third Committee's document and the report were brought before the Assembly of the League of Nations which after debate, by a resolution of 13 December 1920, unanimously approved the draft Statute of the Permanent Court of International Justice, and decided on a separate legal instrument with respect to the signature and ratification of the Statute, i.e. the Protocol of Signature.[29] Thus the Members of the League of Nations were to adopt the Statute in the form of a Protocol duly ratified and declaring their recognition of the Statute.[30] That Protocol was done at Geneva on 16 December 1920[31] and was ratified by the majority of the Members of the League of Nations before 5 September 1921, so the Statute entered into force on that day. Many believed that with the establishment of the Permanent Court of International Justice, the 1907 Hague Peace Conference had come to bear fruit, albeit compulsory jurisdiction had not been introduced.[32] At any rate, the regime of Peace Treaties can be said to have been instrumental in, among other things, establishing the Permanent Court of International Justice, which came to be 'a true court of international justice which means that it ought to decide questions according to international law rather than on grounds of compromise or expediency as may properly be done by a tribunal of arbitration'.[33] No question, it was still impossible to achieve the introduction of a system of general compulsory jurisdiction, but some progress had certainly been made in this domain as well. The

---

29 The resolution, see *PCIJ* Series D. No.1, 4.

30 The resolution provided also that the Protocol shall be open for signature by non-member states enumerated in the Annex to the Covenant. The purpose of that provision was to permit the United States of America and some other non-member states to 'adhere to the Statute.' Cf. Hudson (1972) 124.

31 The Protocol of Signature, see *PCIJ* Series D. No.1., 5.

32 Cf. Manley O. Hudson, 'The First Year of the Permanent Court of International Justice' (1923) 17, *AJIL*, 15, 15–28. In a similar sense, see Ernest Lémonon, 'La Cour Permanente de Justice International' (1922) 49, *JDI*, 761, 771–3.

33 Cf. John Eugen Harley, *The League of Nations and the New International Law* (OUP 1921) 32–3.

proponents of the judicial settlement of international disputes believed 'that the future will bring compulsory jurisdiction between States'.[34]

II THE SAN FRANCISCO CONFERENCE: NEW COURT BUT NO BREAK IN THE CHAIN OF CONTINUITY WITH THE PAST

During World War II, when politicians and experts began dealing with the plan to set up a new international organization, which was later to be the United Nations, there emerged again various conceptions about the need to establish an international judicial forum with compulsory jurisdiction. On this score, it is worthwhile to cite a study of 1943 by Hans Kelsen, who advocated the compulsory adjudication of international disputes, writing that 'the next step on which our efforts must be concentrated is to bring about an international treaty concluded by as many states as possible – victors as well as vanquished – establishing an international court endowed with compulsory jurisdiction'.[35] The eminent Austrian expert held that all parties to the treaty 'shall be obliged to renounce war and reprisals as means of settling conflicts and to submit all their disputes without any exception to the decision of the court and to carry out its decisions in good faith.'[36]

The first of the official documents with respect to the creation of the United Nations, addressing the question of a judicial forum of the world organization, was that of the Dumbarton Oaks Proposals for a General International Organization which in Chapter VII referred to the need for an international court within the new international organization to be established.[37] It was also stated that the court should be the principal

---

[34] Cf. B.C.J. Loder, 'The Permanent Court of International Justice and Maintenance of Peace' (1921–1922) 2, *BYIL*, 6, 26.

On the activities of the Permanent Court, see Ole Spiermann, *International Legal Argument in the Permanent Court of International Justice*: The Rise of the International Judiciary. Cambridge Studies of International and Comparative Law (CUP 2005).

[35] See Hans Kelsen, 'Compulsory Adjudication of International Disputes' (1943) 37, *AJIL*, 37, 3, 397.

[36] *Id.*

[37] It is to be noted that unofficial documents had already addressed questions relating to international adjudication. Thus, among others, a committee of experts in London had studied the Statute of the Permanent Court of International Justice in 1943, and had indicated the provisions to be amended, as well as the nature of amendments. The members of that committee were purely in their personal

judicial organ of the new organization, with its statute which could be either the same as that of the Permanent Court of International Justice – with some modifications – or a new one based on that of the Permanent Court, and annexed, being a part of the Charter of the new Organization, the members of the Organization becoming *ipso facto* parties to the Statute of the Court.[38] A few rather important questions on which the delegates' views were sharply divided were left to further discussion, namely those points concerning the issues of whether to establish a new court or whether to adapt the Permanent Court to the new situation, the number of judges, the method of their nomination and to what extent

---

capacity and not in the name of their government, it included R.M. Campbell (New Zealand), R. Cassin (France), E. Colban (Norway), G. Fitzmaurice (United Kingdom), A. Gros (France), F. Havlicek (Czechoslovakia), G. Kaeckenbeeck (Belgium), G. Schommer (Luxembourg), E. Star-Busmann (Netherlands), C. Stavropoulos (Greece) and B. Winiarski (Poland). For the committee's report, see Report of the Informal Inter-Allied Committee on the Future of the Permanent Court of International Justice, 10th February, 1944. See *AJIL*, 39, 1., Supplement Official Documents (Jan. 1945), 1–56.

[38] The *Dumbarton Oaks Proposals for a General International Organization* in Chapter VII, under the title *An International Court of Justice* provided that:

1. There should be an international court of justice which should constitute the principal judicial organ of the Organization.
2. The court should be constituted and should function in accordance with a statute which should be annexed to and be a part of the Charter of the Organization.
3. The statute of the Court of International Justice should be either: (a) the Statute of the Permanent Court of International Justice, continued in force with such modifications as may be desirable; or (b) a new statute in the preparation of which the Statute of the Permanent Court of International Justice should be used as a basis.
4. All members of the Organization should *ipso facto* be parties to the statute of the International Court of Justice.
5. Conditions under which states not members of the Organization may become parties to the Statute of the International Court of Justice should be determined in each case by the General Assembly upon recommendation of the Security Council.

Documents of the United Nations Conference on International Organization, San Francisco, 1945. United Nations Information Organization, London, New York, 1945 (hereafter *UNCIO Documents*) vol. III, 11–12.

compulsory jurisdiction should be incorporated into the new statute of the court.[39]

A further elaboration of the draft statute of the new court was put into the hands of a Committee of Jurists consisting of representatives from 44 states. From 9–18 April 1945 the Committee of Jurists met in Washington, with the American, Hackworth, as Chairman and the French, Basdevant, as Rapporteur thereof.[40]

On the table of the Committee of Jurists lay a great variety of proposals for the amendment of both Chapter VII of the Dumbarton Oaks Proposals and the Statute of the Permanent Court, and during the deliberations several suggestions were made concerning the introduction of compulsory jurisdiction. However, the Committee members felt that the introduction of compulsory jurisdiction was a political matter, a reason why no decision was taken on that and many other important issues, leaving the final decision to be made by the San Francisco Conference with respect to elaborating the Charter of the new World Organization. Incidentally, as was pointed out by Hambro, the Committee of Jurists whose task 'was technical and not a political one, decided not to take a definite position on this matter of principle, but proposed two alternatives for Article 36'.[41] This notwithstanding, the problem of compulsory jurisdiction was one of the most controversial issues during the said negotiations, and the introduction of compulsory jurisdiction was opposed chiefly by the United States and the Soviet Union.[42]

---

39 For a more detailed discussion of these topics, see Shabtai Rosenne, *The Law and Practice of the International Court*, 1920–2005 (fourth edition with the assistance of Yaël Ronen, Martinus Nijhoff Publishers 2006) vol. I., 52–5.

40 For the deliberations of the Committee of Jurists, see Ruth B. Russel – Janette E. Muther, *A History of the United Nations Charter* (The Brooklings Institution 1958) 865–75.

41 Edward Hambro, 'Some Observations on the Compulsory Jurisdiction of the International Court of Justice'(1948), 25, *BYIL*, 133, 138.

42 In the case of the United States it was recalled that the accession by the United States to the Statute of the Permanent Court had been blocked by the Senate at the time, although the Statute did not provide for the compulsory jurisdiction of the Court, and concern was expressed about possible senatorial rejection of the Court's compulsory jurisdiction. Cf. Russel-Muther (1958) 877–8.

As for the Soviet Union, Moscow was known to have traditionally shown a negative attitude to international adjudication, as is well illustrated by the statement of Maxim Litvinov, later People's Commissar for Foreign Affairs, at The Hague on 12 July 1922 and which has often been quoted ever since. He said that 'It was necessary to face the fact that there was not one world but two, a

During deliberations of the Committee of Jurists, it was proposed (by Egypt) that the Court's compulsory jurisdiction should be made as a general rule and that, in addition, every state should be entitled to withdraw from it. The Committee itself was not in full agreement with that nor other proposals, thus in its *Report on Draft of Statute of an International Court of Justice referred to in Chapter VII of the Dumbarton Oaks Proposals* there were presented two alternative texts relating to the court's jurisdiction.[43] One contained the Statute of the Permanent Court of International Justice with a few minor changes of a technical nature in the wording and no change with respect to jurisdiction. The other version provided for the compulsory jurisdiction of the Court in Article 36 of the Statute, without giving the option by which each of the states would be free to take or not take.[44] As is stated in the Report which the Committee of Jurists presented to the San Francisco Conference,

> … it did not seem certain, nor even possible, that all the nations whose participation in the proposed International Organization appears to be necessary, were now in a position to accept the rule of compulsory jurisdiction, and that the Dumbarton Oaks Proposals did not seem to affirm it; some, while retaining their preference in this respect, thought that the counsel of prudence was not to go beyond the procedure of the optional clause inserted in Article 36, which has opened the way to the progressive adoption, in less than 10 years, of compulsory jurisdiction by many States which in 1920 refused to subscribe to it.[45]

The subject matters of the judicial forum were addressed by Commission IV of the San Francisco Conference and the question of jurisdiction was on the agenda of Subcommittee D of Committee IV/1. During the deliberations of the Subcommittee, renewed attempts were made, chiefly by New Zealand with support from Australia and Mexico, to adopt a version of Article 36 of the Statute which would have been tantamount to the introduction in principle of compulsory adjudication, applicable to all

---

Soviet world and a non-Soviet world. Because there was no third world to arbitrate, … Only an angel could be unbiased in judging Russian affairs …' (Conference at The Hague, 26 June–20 July 1922. Minutes and Documents, p. 126.) Quoted in T.A. Taracouzio, *The Soviet Union and International Law* (The MacMillan Company 1935, Kraus Reprint Co. 1972) 296.

43 See *UNCIO Documents*, vol. XIV, 821–53.

44 For the part of the Committee's report dealing with the optional clause, see *Id.* 839–42.

45 *Id.* 840.

disputes which the parties refer to the Court, with only two uniform reservations, unless the parties to any particular dispute otherwise agree.[46]

Subcommittee D rejected the New Zealand proposal and, as was stated in its report, came to the conclusion by majority '... that everything being taken into account, the system of optional jurisdiction at the present time would more likely to secure general agreement.'[47] Thus Subcommittee D finally left the provisions on the jurisdiction of the Permanent Court's Statute unchanged, and the Committee IV/1 of the Conference decided by a vote of 31 to 14 to incorporate in the new Statute Article 36, para. 2, of the Statute of the Permanent Court of International Justice.[48] Thus, although the Committee after lengthy debates voted for retaining optional jurisdiction, it unanimously adopted a resolution on the motion of the delegate of Iran 'that the Conference be requested to recommend to all members of the United Nations that they should make declarations adhering to the compulsory jurisdiction of the Court as soon as possible'.[49] This text was adopted by the plenary session of the San Francisco Conference as well.[50]

In light of the pronouncements made at the San Francisco Conference it can be stated that the representatives of the smaller and middle powers stood firm with respect to the introduction of compulsory jurisdiction, since they felt that it would be a great protection to them if they could bring any other state, large or small, into the Court.[51] So it was not entirely without good reason that 15 years later Sørensen, a well-known jurist of Denmark, wrote that the sentiments in favour of compulsory jurisdiction ran higher in 1945 than they had at the time of the establishment of the Permanent Court of International Justice.[52] In spite of the fact that at the San Francisco Conference a considerable proportion of states advocated the introduction of compulsory jurisdiction, the Soviet Union and United States resolutely rejected the related proposals,[53] stressing that should compulsory jurisdiction be introduced they

---

46 For the New Zealand proposal, see *Id.* vol. XIII, 561.

47 Cf. *Id.* 558.

48 Cf. *Id.* 251.

49 Cf. *Id.* 299.

50 The said desire was restated in the UN General Assembly resolution of 14 November 1947.

51 Cf. Russel-Muther (1958) 877.

52 Max Sørensen, 'The International Court of Justice: its Role in Contemporary International Relations' (1960) *International Organization*, 261, 265.

53 Cf. Russel-Muther (1958) 886.

would 'not be able to ratify' or would 'be obliged to withhold their acceptance of the Statute'.[54]

As can be seen, during the negotiations about an international judicial forum in the wake of World War II, just as different views were expressed concerning the compulsory jurisdiction of the future court as there had been at the time of the elaboration of the Permanent Court's Statute and, regarding the substance, the same solution was adopted as in 1920.

The text of the Statute of the International Court of Justice as adopted at the San Francisco Conference showed no great difference from that of the Statute of the Permanent Court and there was no fundamental change with respect to the optional clause either (see Table 2.1 below). Nevertheless, regarding Article 36 of the Statute, the Conference inserted certain amendments, which may be summed up as follows:

(a) Para. 2 of Article 36 was amended. Its former wording said that states might recognize as compulsory the jurisdiction of the Court 'in all or any of the classes of legal disputes', while the new text omitted the word 'any', thus states were no longer entitled to recognize the compulsory jurisdiction of the Court concerning only the disputes under subparagraphs (a), or (b), or (c) or (d) of paragraph 2 of Article 36 which is to say that states are to accept the compulsory jurisdiction of the new Court 'in all legal disputes' under subparagraphs (a), (b), (c), and (d).

(b) The second change was that a declaration accepting the compulsory jurisdiction of the Court may only be made by a state party to the Statute, notably one which has signed and ratified the Statute. While at the time of the Permanent Court a declaring state could not only be a Member of the League of Nations, but a state not being a party to the Statute, provided that the state was mentioned in the Annex to the Covenant.

(c) The declarations should be deposited with the UN Secretary-General.

(d) Paragraph 5 of Article 36, was incorporated in the Statute as a new provision thereof, which passed to the International Court of Justice, the declarations relating to the Permanent Court's compulsory jurisdiction still being in force, thereby expressing the continuity between the two Courts.[55] One cannot downplay this article at all, because at the time it did affect the in-force declarations of some 17 states.[56]

---

54 Cf. *Id.* 886 *et seq.*

55 On this score see Chapter 3.

56 Cf. *I.C.J. Yearbook 1946–47*, 221–8.

Table 2.1 The two statutes on jurisdiction

The Statute of the PCIJ	The Statute of the ICJ
Art. 36	Art. 36
'The jurisdiction of the Court comprises all cases which the parties refer to it and all matters specially provided for in treaties and conventions in force.	1. The jurisdiction of the Court comprises all cases which the parties refer to it and all matters specially provided for in the Charter of the United Nations or in treaties and conventions in force.
The Members of the League of Nations and the States mentioned in the Annex to the Covenant may, either when signing or ratifying the protocol to which the present Statute is adjoined, or at a later moment, declare that they recognize as compulsory *ipso facto* and without special agreement, in relation to any other Member or State accepting the same obligation, the jurisdiction of the Court in all or any of the classes of legal disputes concerning:	2. The States parties to the present Statute may at any time declare that they recognize as compulsory *ipso facto* and without special agreement, in relation to any other State accepting the same obligation, the jurisdiction of the Court in all legal disputes concerning:
(a) the interpretation of a Treaty; (b) any question of International Law; (c) the existence of any fact which, if established, would constitute a breach of an international obligation; (d) the nature or extent of the reparation to be made for the breach of an international obligation.	(a) the interpretation of a treaty; (b) any question of international law; (c) the existence of any fact which, if established, would constitute a breach of an international obligation; (d) the nature or extent of the reparation to be made for the breach of an international obligation.
The declaration referred to above may be made unconditionally or on condition of reciprocity on the part of several or certain Members or States, or for a certain time.	3. The declarations referred to above may be made unconditionally or on condition of reciprocity on the part of several or certain States, or for a certain time.
	4. Such declarations shall be deposited with the Secretary-General of the United Nations, who shall transmit copies thereof to the parties to the Statute and to the Registrar of the Court.
	5. Declarations made under Article 36 of the Statute of the Permanent Court of International Justice and which are still in force shall be deemed, as between the parties to the present Statute, to be acceptances of the compulsory jurisdiction of the International Court of Justice for the period which they still have to run and in accordance with their terms.
In the event of a dispute as to whether the Court has jurisdiction, the matter shall be settled by the decision of the Court.	6. In the event of a dispute as to whether the Court has jurisdiction, the matter shall be settled by the decision of the Court.

The negotiations on the establishment of the International Court of Justice are evidence that the decline and inefficacy of the League of Nations did not affect the Permanent Court of International Justice and did not shake the confidence of states in international adjudication. This was likewise stated in the report of the Washington Committee of Jurists, saying that: '... the Permanent Court of International Justice had functioned for twenty years to the satisfaction of the litigants and that, if violence had suspended its activity, at least this institution had not failed in its task.'[57]

The activity carried out by the Permanent Court of International Justice to the satisfaction of the states is evidenced more clearly by nothing other than the fact that among the institutions created at the time of the League of Nations the Permanent Court was after all one such institution that came to be incorporated and unaltered, as it were, within the system of the new world organization, the United Nations.[58] And as Nasrat Al-Farsy, the rapporteur of Committee IV/1 of the San Francisco Conference, rightly pointed out, 'The creation of the new Court will not break the chain of continuity with the past'.[59] To that, one could add that the international system established by the San Francisco Conference strengthens the position of the Court insofar as the International Court of Justice became a principal organ of the United Nations and the provisions of the Charter served to increase the role thereof in the peaceful settlement of international disputes.[60]

III THE CONCEPT OF THE OPTIONAL CLAUSE

Article 36, paragraph 2, of the Statutes of the two International Courts relating to compulsory jurisdiction is referred to as the 'optional clause' in the literature of international law, which is rather misleading for two reasons. First, because the term 'optional clause' originally appeared as the title of a second section of the 1920 Protocol of Signature.[61] That

---

57 *Id. UNCIO Documents,* vol. XIV, 822.

58 In a similar sense, see J.G. Merrils, 'The Optional Clause Today' (1979) 50, *BYIL*, 87, 88.

59 *UNCIO Documents*, Report of the Rapporteur (Nasrat Al-Farsy) of Committee IV/1, vol. XIII, 384.

60 On this score, see Arts. 92 to 96 of the UN Charter.

61 The Protocol of Signature of the Statute of the Permanent Court of International Justice contained after the section headed 'A, Protocol of Signature', a second section headed 'B, Optional Clause' which reads as follows: 'The

subsidiary document was not an independent instrument but a document attached to the 1920 Protocol of Signature and was designated to serve as a model text for the declarations relating to the acceptance of the jurisdiction of the Permanent Court being compulsory.[62] Second, the term 'optional clause', which is to be found nowhere in the Statute either of the Permanent Court or of the International Court of Justice in the last more than nine decades, was generally used to designate the provisions of the two instruments by which states may recognize as compulsory the jurisdiction of the Courts.[63]

It should be admitted that the optional clause was a fortunate solution in enabling states to recognize, if they so wish, the Court's compulsory jurisdiction on a rather wide range of disputes. Accordingly, it came to serve as a formula which, in the last analysis, introduced compulsory jurisdiction in a form fully respecting the sovereignty of states.

By the terms of Article 36 of the Statutes of the two Courts, the states may, by unilateral declaration of acceptance, recognize as compulsory, in relation to any other state having made a similar declaration, the jurisdiction of the Court in specified categories of disputes. As President McNair points out in his individual opinion submitted in the *Anglo-Iranian Oil Co. case*, the optional clause is that of 'contracting-in', not of 'contracting out'.[64] The optional clause does not by itself impose on states any obligation whatsoever, but provides a basis for states undertaking, by unilateral declaration, obligations additional to those stated in the Statutes with regard to the Court's jurisdiction. It was with this consideration that Kelsen wrote that jurisdiction under Article 36, paragraph 2 of the Statute could not be regarded as 'compulsory' in the true sense of the word, for one could only speak of compulsory jurisdiction if the Statute provided that '... any member of the judicial community,

---

undersigned, being duly authorized thereto, further declare on behalf of their Government, that, from this date, they accept as compulsory *ipso facto* and without special convention, the jurisdiction of the Court in conformity with Art. 36, para. 2, of the Statute of the Court, under the following conditions'.

It should be mentioned that although the Protocol of Signature refers to para. 2 of Art. 36, the paras of Art. 36 were not numbered, which might cause some confusion. See *PCIJ*, Series D, No.1, 6.

62 Cf. Hudson (1972) 451.

63 See Constantin Vulcan, 'La clause facultative' (1947–1948), 18 *Acta Scandinavica Juris Gentium* fasc. 1.30.

64 Cf. *Anglo-Iranian Oil Co. case* (Preliminary Objection), Judgment of 22 July 1952, Individual Opinion of President McNair, *ICJ Reports 1952*, 116.

party to any case whatever, is obliged to recognize the jurisdiction of the Court if the other party refers the dispute to the Court.'[65]

Along with paragraph 2 of Article 36, paragraphs 3 to 5 are also often consigned to the 'optional clause' insofar as they contain further elements concerning the compulsory jurisdiction of the Court. Consequently, the optional clause as laid down in the Statute has in fact a wider notion of the term embracing, apart from Article 36, paragraph 2 of the Statute, all the provisions relating to the procedure for making declarations of acceptance, the validity thereof, etc.

The totality of the declarations of acceptance made under the optional clause *constitute a special regime called the system of compulsory jurisdiction or optional clause system.* The specific features of the system constituted by the optional clause – in the wider sense – and the unilateral declarations made by states, can be summarized as follows:

(a) The declarations made under the optional clause constitute a compulsory jurisdictional system between declarant states. The declarant states accordingly recognize the Court's compulsory jurisdiction in relation, not to the states party to the Statute, but only to those which have also made such a declaration. Any state party to the system and having made such a declaration, may, by unilateral application, institute proceedings against another declarant state, in all disputes covered by both states' declarations.

(b) States making declarations of acceptance, accept the Court's jurisdiction not necessarily with regard to the same range of matters, and they may, by reservations, exclude one or several classes of international disputes from the scope of the Court's compulsory jurisdiction.[66]

(c) The principle of reciprocity applies in the fullest extent to declarations accepting compulsory jurisdiction, meaning that concerning two declarant states the Court has no jurisdiction except in the category of matters covered by the declarations of both states.[67] In other words, a state may not sue another state for a dispute which was excluded by its own declaration of acceptance, even though the other state recognized the Court's compulsory jurisdiction over that dispute.

---

65 Hans Kelsen, *The Law of the United Nations* (Stevens & Sons Limited 1951) 522.

66 On reservations see Chapters 4, 7 and 8.

67 On reciprocity see Chapter 6.

(d) Under Article 36, paragraph 5 of the Statute of the International Court of Justice, the legal effects of the in-force declarations of acceptance made between the two World Wars with respect to the compulsory jurisdiction of the Permanent Court are to pass to the International Court of Justice.

(e) Declarations accepting the compulsory jurisdiction of the International Court of Justice are to be deposited with the Secretary-General of the United Nations, who is to transmit copies thereof to the parties to the Statute and to the Registrar of the Court.[68]

---

68 On the making of declarations see Chapter 3.

3. Declarations accepting the compulsory jurisdiction of the Court

I WHO IS ENTITLED TO MAKE AN OPTIONAL CLAUSE DECLARATION?

The Statutes of the two World Courts contain very few provisions concerning the declarations made under Article 36, paragraph 2 and the texts thereof.

Article 36 of the Statute of the Permanent Court of International Justice is confined to stating that:

> The Members of the League of Nations and the States mentioned in the Annex to the Covenant may, either when signing or of ratifying the Protocol to which the present Statute is adjoined, or at a later moment, declare that they recognize as compulsory *ipso facto* and without separate agreement, in relation to any other Member State accepting the same obligation, the jurisdiction of the Court in all or any of the classes of legal disputes concerning: …

Under Article 36, paragraph 2 of the Statute of the International Court of Justice, 'The States parties to the present Statute may at any time declare that they recognize as compulsory *ipso facto* and without special agreement, in relation to any other State accepting the same obligation, the jurisdiction of the Court …'

The cited paragraphs of the two Statutes seem rather similar at first sight, suggesting that the provisions set forth in the Statute of the Permanent Court were practically reproduced in the Statute of the new Court. However, as was already mentioned in the previous chapter, some changes were effected at the San Francisco Conference to the Statute regarding optional clause declarations and thus there are differences which relate among others to the declaring states.

In effect, under the Statute of the Permanent Court, declarations accepting the Court's compulsory jurisdiction could only be made by states, which had at least signed the Statute, meaning that a state could make a declaration of acceptance even before the Statute had entered into force in respect of that state. By contrast, the Statute of the new Court refers to states that are parties to the present Statute, which allows the compulsory jurisdiction of the new Court to be accepted only by states that are already parties to the Statute, namely those that have signed and ratified the Charter of the United Nations, of which the Statute forms an integral part, or by states that are not members of the world organization but have acceded to the Statute,[1] as Switzerland, Liechtenstein and Nauru did becoming parties to the Statute as non-members of the United Nations, who also concurrently – with the acceptance of the Statute – made their optional clause declarations.

At the time of the Permanent Court, it was in the *Gerliczy case* that the question arose of whether a declaration of acceptance, made by a state which was not listed in the Annex to the Covenant of the League of Nations or which was not a member of the League of Nations, could be deemed to be valid. That dispute was submitted by Liechtenstein against Hungary in 1939, on the basis of declarations of acceptance made by the two states.[2] In that legal dispute, the Hungarian Government questioned the validity of Lichtenstein's declaration of acceptance, for Liechtenstein was not among the states listed in the Annex to the Covenant, nor a member of the League of Nations, having made declaration of acceptance upon the Council's resolution of 17 May 1922.[3] Since the *Gerliczy case* remained pending because of the war, no answer was given to the question relating to a declaration of acceptance made by a non-member state of the League and not listed in the Annex to the Covenant.[4]

More than half a century later, the International Court of Justice was faced with a problem, somewhat similar to that of the *Gerliczy case*, with

---

[1] According Art. 93, para. 2 of the Charter, a non-member state of the United Nations 'may become a party to the Statute of the International Court of Justice on conditions to be determined in each case by the General Assembly upon the recommendation of the Security Council'.

[2] The application was filed with respect to claims espoused by the Government of Lichtenstein on behalf of a Lichtenstein national, Dr Felix Gerliczy; the applicant challenged some judgments of the Hungarian Curia (Supreme Court) saying that these were contrary to international law and in particular to the Convention concluded between Hungary and Romania on 16 April 1924.

[3] A letter of 21 February 1922, by the Court's President led to Council's Resolution of 17 May 1922, which concerned itself with the conditions under which states not Members of the League of Nations nor mentioned in the Annex to the Covenant were entitled to resort to the Court. On this point, see Hudson (1972), 386–7 and 755–6.

[4] The *Gerliczy case* see Manley O. Hudson (ed.), *World Court Reports* (Carnegie Endowment for International Peace 1943) vol. IV, 495–9.

regard to the Federal Republic of Yugoslavia (hereinafter: FRY) in the context of whether it was possible for a declaration of acceptance to have been made by a state whose membership in the United Nations was uncertain, and regarding that membership the opinion of the international community was rather divided.[5]

---

[5] After the disintegration of the former Yugoslavia, the membership of the FRY in the United Nations was uncertain from 27 April 1992, i.e., from the date of its establishment. The problem of Yugoslavia's membership in the United Nations was on the agenda of the General Assembly from 1992. Long debates and a quasi political compromise led to the adoption of a resolution by the General Assembly as a result of a recommendation from the Security Council on 22 September 1992, which stated that the General Assembly:

> 1. Considers that the Federal Republic of Yugoslavia (Serbia and Montenegro) cannot continue automatically the membership of the former Socialist Federal Republic of Yugoslavia in the United Nations; and therefore, decides that the Federal Republic of Yugoslavia (Serbia and Montenegro) should apply for membership in the United Nations and that it should not participate in the work of the General Assembly.

Thereafter, the FRY took part in the activities of only some UN organs. After the downfall of the Milosević regime, the FRY was admitted to the UN on 1 November 2000. During the days of the Milosević regime, the Belgrade Government made a declaration under the optional clause on 25 April 1999 and a few days later, on 29 April 1999, during the NATO air strikes, it instituted ten separate proceedings against ten NATO member states arguing that some of the alleged violations of international law by NATO air strikes against Yugoslavia were deemed to be genocide and violations of the prohibition of the use of force (*Cases concerning Legality of Use of Force*). In each case, the Belgrade Government based the Court's jurisdiction on Art. IX of the *Convention on the Prevention and Punishment of the Crime of Genocide* providing for the Court's jurisdiction, and in the case of six states (Belgium, Canada, Netherlands, Portugal, Spain and United Kingdom) it invoked Art. 36, para. 2 of the Statute along with Art. IX of the Genocide Convention and in two cases (Belgium, Netherlands) it referred to other in-force treaties between the parties.

In May 1999, the Governments of Bosnia and Herzegovina, Croatia, Slovenia and the former Yugoslav Republic of Macedonia objected to the declaration of acceptance of Yugoslavia. According to these states, the declaration had no legal effect whatsoever, because the FRY (Serbia and Montenegro) was not a member state of the United Nations, nor was it a state party to the Statute of the Court, that could make a valid declaration under Art. 36, para. 2 of the Statute of the Court.

Appearing before the Court in the *Cases concerning Legality of Use of Force*, some respondent states[6] argued that according to General Assembly resolution 47/1 of 22 September 1992 – which was adopted on the motion of the Security Council – FRY was not a UN member state, and not a successor to the former Yugoslavia, thus not a party to the Statute, and consequently it couldn't make a valid declaration of acceptance.[7]

For its part, in the first phase of the *Cases concerning Legality of Use of Force*, the Court gave no answer on the issue of the FRY's membership in the United Nations[8] and in connection with the Yugoslav declaration of acceptance, it found sufficient grounds to point out that, in view of the reservation *ratione temporis* (concerning future disputes) included in that declaration,[9] the Court was without jurisdiction even *prima facie*, for, given this limitation, it had jurisdiction only in disputes relating to situations and facts subsequent to the signature of the declaration, whereas the dispute between the parties arose before 25 April 1999 – which was the date of making the declaration of acceptance – for the air strikes by NATO states had already begun earlier on 24 March 1999.[10]

Thus, in the phase of provisional measures, the Court endeavoured to sidestep the question of the FRY's membership in the United Nations as well as the possibility of the FRY having made a declaration of acceptance. That position of the Court was sharply criticized by some members of the Court. According to Judge Kooijmans, the Court's

---

6 Belgium, Canada, the Netherlands, Portugal, Spain and the United Kingdom.

7 The membership in the UN of the FRY was also lengthily discussed in the *Case concerning the Application of the Convention on the Prevention and Punishment of the Crime of Genocide* (Bosnia and Herzegovina v. Serbia and Montenegro), however, in that case the question of the declarations of acceptance were not touched upon because the Court's jurisdiction was based on Art. IX of the Genocide Convention.

8 According to the Court, there was no need to decide on Yugoslavia's membership in the United Nations and whether it was a party to the Statute for the purpose of deciding whether or not it could indicate provisional measures in that case.

9 On these reservations see Chapter 7.

10 Cf. *Case concerning Legality of Use of Force* (Yugoslavia v. Belgium) (Request for the Indication of Provisional Measures), Order of 2 June 1999, *ICJ Reports 1999,* 134–5.

reasoning implied the presumption that the Yugoslavian declaration was valid, at least in the present phase of the proceedings.[11]

One could see that in that stage of the *Cases concerning Legality of Use of Force*, the Court was reluctant to examine whether a state whose membership in the UN was uncertain could make a declaration of acceptance.[12] Such an attitude reflects the Court's view that the declaring state assumes, of its own will, certain surplus obligations regarding the Court's jurisdiction and that the Court should take such obligations into account.

II VARIOUS FORMS AND CONTENTS OF DECLARATIONS OF ACCEPTANCE

The idea that it would be advisable to elaborate a model for declarations of accepting the future Court's compulsory jurisdiction had emerged as early as the deliberations of the 1920 Advisory Committee of Jurists. Consequently, as was already mentioned, a draft or model document for such declarations under the title 'Optional Clause' was attached to the Protocol of Signature of the Statute. The above-mentioned separate document on the declarations of acceptance was designated to encourage and facilitate the making of declarations under the optional clause by providing a framework within which states might cast the limitations which they desired.[13]

Thus, in spite of the existence of a model document regarding the declarations of acceptance, states – recognizing the compulsory jurisdiction of the Permanent Court – paid little attention to it and developed declarations of acceptance with diverse contents and forms in the years following the establishment of the Court.

---

[11] *Id.* 177. Judge Kooijmans wrote: 'How can the Court say that there is no need to consider the validity of Yugoslavia's declaration whereas at the same time it concludes that this declaration, taken together with that of the Respondent, cannot constitute a basis of jurisdiction?'

[12] The dispute about the FRY's membership in the UN was finally ended by the Court's Judgments on *Legality of Use of Force cases* on 15 December 2004. In these cases the Court concluded that between 1992 and 2000, Yugoslavia/Serbia and Montenegro was not a Member of the United Nations, and consequently, was not, on that basis, a state party to the Statute of the Court.

Cf. *Case concerning Legality of Use of Force* (Serbia and Montenegro v. Belgium), Judgment of 15 December 2004, *ICJ Reports 2004*, 291–315.

[13] Cf. Hudson (1972) 450.

According to their text, the following groups of declarations can be differentiated:

- declarations repeating the *chapeau* of Article 36, paragraph 2 of the Statute, or the model document, stating that the declaring state 'recognize as compulsory *ipso facto* and without special agreement, on condition of reciprocity' or 'in relation to any other state accepting the same obligation' the jurisdiction of the Court;
- declarations not only referring to Article 36, paragraph 2 of the Statute, but also enumerating the four categories of disputes listed in that paragraph;
- declarations consisting of a single sentence, quite short and to the point, that the declaring state accepts the jurisdiction of the Court;
- declarations of acceptance incorporated in the instruments of ratification of the Statute of the Permanent Court;
- declarations of acceptance made in the form of a letter sent to the Secretary-General of the League of Nations.

Considering that, as noted previously, the Statute did not provide any consistent form or content regarding the declarations of acceptance, in the practice of the two Courts any form of optional clause declaration became accepted. This was recognized by the International Court of Justice by stating that: 'The Statute of the Permanent Court did not lay down any set form or procedure to be followed for the making of such declarations, and in practice a number of different methods were used by States.'[14]

The Permanent Court of International Justice did not deal with the form of optional clause declarations, however, the International Court of Justice touched upon the subject in several cases. In the *Temple of Preah Vihear case*,[15] in which the Court sought to answer the question whether Thailand's letter of 20 May 1950, addressed to the United Nations Secretary-General in accordance with Article 36, paragraph 2 of the Statute, could to be regarded, in substance and form, as recognizing compulsory jurisdiction under Article 36, paragraph 2 of the Statute,[16] the Court held:

---

[14] *Case concerning Military and Paramilitary Activities in and against Nicaragua* (Jurisdiction of the Court and Admissibility of the Application), Judgment of 26 November 1984, *ICJ Reports 1984*, 404.

[15] On this case, see footnote 73 below.

[16] In its declaration of 30 September 1929, Thailand originally accepted the compulsory jurisdiction of the Permanent Court for a period of ten years; in 1940

> The precise form and language in which they do this (the declaration – V.L.) is left to them, and there is no suggestion that any particular form is required, or that any declarations not in such form will be invalid. No doubt custom and tradition have brought it about that a certain pattern of terminology is normally, as a matter of fact and convenience, employed by countries accepting the compulsory jurisdiction of the Court; but there is nothing mandatory about the employment of this language.[17]

With regard to the contents of the optional clause declarations, the Court stressed that:

> the sole relevant question is whether the language employed in any given declaration does reveal a clear intention, in the terms of paragraph 2 of Article 36 of the Statute, to 'recognize as compulsory *ipso facto* and without special agreement, in relation to any other State accepting the same obligation, the jurisdiction of the Court in all legal disputes' concerning the categories of questions enumerated in that paragraph.[18]

As can be seen, the Court attached no importance to the form of declarations and deemed the intentions of the parties to be the determining fact. Relying on private-law examples, it pointed out that international law 'places the principal emphasis on the intentions of the parties, the law prescribes no particular form, parties are free to choose what form they please provided their intention clearly results from it.'[19] All this was summed up by Sir Percy Spender in that case by these terms: 'No requirement of form are called for paragraph (2) of Article 36. If consent to recognize this Court's jurisdiction in terms of that paragraph is clearly manifested, it matters not in what form the declaration containing that consent is cast.'[20]

Since the establishment of the International Court of Justice, states have been accepting the compulsory jurisdiction of the Court in a

---

and 1950 it renewed the 1929 acceptance by the two other declarations, containing the same conditions and reservations as the 1929 declaration, for additional periods of ten years. In its first preliminary objection in the *Temple of Preah Vihear case*, Thailand advanced the argument, along with others, that in 1950 it had a mistaken view of the status of its earlier declaration of 1940 as it had renewed its declaration of acceptance in respect of a court that no longer existed.

[17] *Case concerning the Temple of Preah Vihear* (Preliminary Objections), Judgment of 26 May 1961, *ICJ Reports 1961*, 32.

[18] *Id.* 32.

[19] *Id.* 31.

[20] *Id.* Sir Percy Spender's individual opinion, 40.

separate declaration with very divergent content and length. Some of the declarations are rather short, whilst the others, as will be discussed later, contain reservations, limitations etc. One can state that in more than ninety years of international practice, since both the two Courts and the international community have recognized as valid declarations of acceptance with any wording, they have provided that the clear consent of the declaring state to the Court's compulsory jurisdiction must be reflected in the declaration itself.

III EMERGENCE OF THE NOTION OF COLLECTIVE DECLARATIONS OF ACCEPTANCE

For nearly seven decades subsequent to the establishment of the Permanent Court, states had made individual declarations of acceptance and it was not until the end of the 1980s that, in the *Case concerning Border and Transborder Armed Actions* (Nicaragua v. Honduras),[21] there arose the notion of collective declarations of acceptance.[22]

In that case, the applicant state, Nicaragua, founded the Court's jurisdiction on Article XXXI of the American Treaty on Pacific Settlement also known as the Pact of Bogotá,[23] signed on 30 April 1948, and its and the respondent state's declarations were made by accepting the

---

[21] The case concerned a legal dispute between Nicaragua and Honduras regarding the alleged activities of armed bands, said to be operating from Honduras, on the border between Honduras and Nicaragua and in Nicaraguan territory.

[22] On this point, see M.E. Buffet-Tchalakoff, 'La compètence de la Cour Internationale de Justice dans l'affaire des 'Actions frontalières et transfrontalières' (Nicaragua-Honduras)' (1989), 93, *RGDIP*, 623–53.

[23] Art. XXXI of the Pact of Bogotá reads as follows:

> In conformity with Article 36, paragraph 2, of the Statute of the International Court of Justice, the High Contracting Parties declare that they recognize, in relation to any other American State, the jurisdiction of the Court as compulsory *ipso facto*, without the necessity of any special agreement so long as the present Treaty is in force, in all disputes of a juridical nature that arose among them concerning:
>
> (a) The interpretation of a treaty;
> (b) Any question of international law;
> (c) The existence of any fact which, if established, would constitute a breach of an international obligation;
> (d) The nature or extent of the reparation to be made for the breach of an international obligation.

jurisdiction of the Court as provided for in Article 36, paragraphs 1 and 2 respectively of the Statute.[24] These two instruments – serving as the basis for the Court's jurisdiction, and offering the possibility of making collective declarations of acceptance that actually arose in connection with them – highlight the specific feature that Article XXXI of the Pact of Bogotá is virtually identical, almost word for word, to Article 36, paragraph 2 of the Statute.[25]

Before the Court, Article XXXI of the Pact of Bogotá was linked by Honduras with declarations of acceptance under Article 36, paragraph 2 of the Statute. According to the Memorial of Honduras, 'this "optional clause" in Article XXXI, contains a jurisdiction which can be more precisely defined by means of a unilateral declaration by all states which are parties to the Pact', notably declarations, under Article 36, paragraph 2 of the Statute.[26] Starting with this, on the basis of the connection between the two documents, Honduras was of the position that any reservation being made to one document is automatically applicable to the other.[27]

---

[24] The Honduran declaration of acceptance was dated 2 February 1948, and was renewed several times, first on 24 May 1954, for a period of six years and on 20 February 1960, for an indefinite period. It was modified by a declaration on 22 May 1986, inserting a paragraph under which the present declaration and the reservations contained therein may at any time be supplemented, modified or withdrawn by giving notice to the Secretary-General of the United Nations. The Nicaraguan declaration of acceptance was made on 24 September 1929 and its legal effect was, according to Nicaragua, transmitted to the International Court of Justice by Art. 36, para. 5 of the Statute. This Nicaraguan declaration of acceptance was the same as that which was at issue in the legal dispute between Nicaragua and the United States of America.

[25] The jurisdictional system of the Pact of Bogotá was discussed at great length in the *Territorial and Maritime Dispute* (Nicaragua v. Colombia). See *Territorial and Maritime Dispute* (Preliminary Objections), Judgment of 13 December 2007, *ICJ Reports 1977.* In their applications several Latin-American states, as the bases of the Court's jurisdiction, were referring to both the Pact of Bogotá and the optional clause. Cf. *Dispute regarding Navigational and Related Rights* (Costa Rica *v.* Nicaragua)*, Certain Activities Carried Out by Nicaragua in the Border Area* (Costa Rica *v.* Nicaragua).

[26] *Case concerning Border and Transborder Armed Actions* (Nicaragua v. Honduras)*, ICJ Pleadings*, vol. I, 65.

[27] *Id.* 74. Honduras relied on this in its objection of the Court's jurisdiction on the grounds that, owing to the reservations appended to its 1986 declaration of acceptance, the Court lacked jurisdiction in the present case on the basis either of the optional clause or of Art. XXXI of the Pact of Bogotá.

In that case, Honduras interpreted Article XXXI of the Pact in two ways. Under the first interpretation, this article must be supplemented by a declaration of acceptance and the Court only had jurisdiction if a declaration of acceptance was also made under the optional clause. The Honduran view was 'that declarations pursuant to Article 36, paragraph 2 were linked to the obligation assumed under Article XXXI of the Pact: these declarations defined the limits within which the State accepted the jurisdiction.'[28] According to the Court, that interpretation was incompatible with the actual terms of Article XXXI, since that article does not subject the recognition of the Court's jurisdiction to any additional declaration made under Article 36, paragraphs 2 and 4 of the Statute.[29] The Court emphasized: 'It is drafted in the present indicative sense, and thus of itself constitutes acceptance of the Court's jurisdiction.'[30] The other Honduran interpretation advanced that Article XXXI of the Pact of Bogotá operates as a collective declaration of acceptance under Article 36, paragraph 2 of the Statute since 'There might be a treaty obligation to make a unilateral declaration under Article 36, paragraph 2; or, alternatively, a treaty provision might be designed as a form of collective declaration for the purposes of Article 36, paragraph 2.'[31]

The Court did not examine this argument; however, it furthermore did not rule out that Article XXXI was to be regarded as a collective declaration of acceptance made under Article 36, paragraph 2.[32] What the Court found decisive was that the declaration was incorporated in the Pact of Bogotá as Article XXXI and thus it could only be modified in accordance with the rules provided for by the Pact itself.[33] Thus the Court did not take any definite stand on whether it was possible or not to

---

28 *Case concerning Border and Transborder Armed Actions* (Nicaragua v. Honduras), *ICJ Pleadings*, vol. I, 55.

29 Cf. *Case concerning Border and Transborder Armed Actions* (Nicaragua v. Honduras), Judgment of 20 December 1988, *ICJ Reports 1988*, 84.

30 Cf. *Id.*

31 Cf. Memorial of Honduras (Jurisdiction and Admissibility), 23 February 1987. *Case concerning Border and Transborder Armed Actions* (Nicaragua v. Honduras), *ICJ Pleadings*, vol. I, 49.

32 In the *Case concerning Military and Paramilitary Activities in and against Nicaragua* (Nicaragua v. United States of America), Nicaragua asserted that Art. XXXI of the Pact of Bogotá constituted a declaration under Art. 36, para 2. Cf. Memorial of Nicaragua (Questions of Jurisdiction and Admissibility) *ICJ Pleadings*, 386.

33 Cf. *Case concerning Border and Transborder Armed Actions* (Nicaragua v. Honduras), Judgment of 20 December 1988, *ICJ Reports 1988*, 84.

accept the Court's compulsory jurisdiction by a collective declaration of acceptance.

To admit Article XXXI of the Bogotá Pact as a collective declaration of acceptance could have entailed interesting consequences. In the first place, the Court's compulsory jurisdiction would have operated not only in the *inter se* relations of the contracting parties to the Pact of Bogotá, but also in relations between the rest of states' parties to the optional clause system. Moreover, it would have raised the question of how such a collective declaration of acceptance is related to individual optional clause declarations made by Latin American states. This problem should not be treated as a speculative one, for several states' parties to the Pact of Bogotá have made individual declarations of acceptance, many of them with reservations appended thereto.[34] Consequently, one should answer the question whether the basis for the Court's jurisdiction is provided for by individual declarations of acceptance or by the Pact of Bogotá as a collective declaration of acceptance in cases where a state party to the optional clause system intends to institute proceedings against a state that is a party to the Pact of Bogotá as well. This may give rise to a problem, particularly when it is borne in mind that certain disputes are excluded from the Court's jurisdiction by reservations appended to individual declarations of acceptance, even though such disputes may still come under the jurisdiction of the Court on the basis of a possible collective declaration of acceptance under the Pact of Bogotá.[35]

---

[34] These are Costa Rica (1973), Dominican Republic (1924), Haiti (1921), Honduras (1986), Mexico (1947), Nicaragua (1929), Paraguay (1996), Peru (2003), Uruguay (1921).

[35] There were other cases as well where the applicant based the jurisdiction of the Court, among others, on Art. XXXI of the Pact of Bogotá and on the declarations of acceptance of the parties. See the *Dispute regarding Navigational and Related Rights* (Costa Rica v. Nicaragua) on the San Juan river. However, in that case the respondent, Nicaragua, had not raised any objections to the jurisdiction of the Court to entertain the case.

On the application of the Pact of Bogotá by the Court in the *Nicaragua case* and in the *Dispute regarding Navigational and Related Rights* see Ricardo Abello Galvis, 'Analyse de la compétence de la Cour internationale de Justice selon le Pacte de Bogotá' (2005), No. 6, *Rev. Colomb. Derecho Int.* 403–41. http://www.javeriana.edu.co/juridicas/pub_rev/international_law/ultimo_numero/11.pdf (accessed 18 September 2013).

IV DEPOSITION AND ENTERING INTO FORCE OF OPTIONAL CLAUSE DECLARATIONS

At the San Francisco Conference, regarding the proposal of the Conference's Committee IV/1, a new paragraph was added to Article 36 (para. 4) providing that 'Such declarations shall be deposited with the Secretary-General of the United Nations, who shall transmit copies thereof to the parties to the Statute and to the Registrar of the Court'.

Thus, the optional clause declarations, which are usually signed on behalf of the declaring state by the head of state, the minister for foreign affairs or the permanent representative to the United Nations, are to be sent to the United Nations' Secretary-General, who must transmit them to the states' parties to the Statute and to the Registrar of the Court for publication in the Court's Yearbooks.[36] The Statute contains nothing more and does not specify the date at which declarations of acceptance enter into force or begin to take legal effect.

According to writers of international law and the Court, Article 36, paragraph 4 essentially refers to two distinct actions that are practically independent of each other. The first one is that the declarations of acceptance are to be deposited by the declaring state with the Secretary-General, which produces its effects from the moment the act is performed by the state concerned; the other one is the duty incumbent on the Secretary-General to convey copies of the declaration to the parties to the Statute and to the Registrar of the Court.

The problems relevant to the deposit of declarations of acceptance with the Secretary-General have been considered by the International Court in several cases. The best-known case in this category is the legal dispute concerning the *Right of Passage over Indian Territory*.[37] Portugal made its declaration of acceptance on 19 December 1955 and submitted an application with the Court against India under the optional clause a few days later, on 22 December 1955. India filed preliminary objections and contended that the filing of the Portuguese application violated the principles of equality and of reciprocity as the Portuguese application had been filed without waiting for a brief period between moment of

[36] The Secretary-General follows the usual practice as depositary of multilateral treaties. See Rosenne (2006) vol. II 729–30.

[37] Portugal instituted proceedings against India on 22 December 1955 concerning the matter of a right of passage over the Indian territory claimed by Portugal to be between its territory of Daman and the Portugal enclaves. The jurisdiction of the Court was based on the declaration of acceptance of the two states.

acceptance by Portugal of the Court's compulsory jurisdiction and the instant of filing of the application, necessary to allow Article 36, paragraph 4 to have appropriate effects, which, under normal circumstances, would have enabled the Secretary-General to transmit the Portuguese declaration to the states party to the Statute, including India.[38]

The Court found that the filing of the Portuguese application on 22 December 1955, was not contrary to the Statute and constituted no violation of India's rights; it specifically stated that:

> by the deposit of its Declaration of Acceptance with the Secretary-General, the accepting State becomes a Party to the system of the Optional Clause in relation to the other declaring States, with all the rights and obligations deriving from Article 36. … A State accepting the jurisdiction of the Court must expect that an Application may be filed against it before the Court by a new declarant State on the same day on which that State deposits with the Secretary-General its Declaration of Acceptance. … The legal effect of a Declaration does not depend upon subsequent action or inaction of the Secretary-General.[39]

The Court pointed out that

> unlike some other instruments, Article 36 provides for no additional requirement, for instance, that the information transmitted by the Secretary-General must reach the Parties to the Statute, or that some period must elapse subsequent to the deposit of the Declaration before it can become effective. Any such requirement would introduce an element of uncertainty into the operation of the Optional Clause system. The Court cannot read into the Optional Clause any requirement of that nature.[40]

Several members of the Court did not concur with these passages of the judgment. In his dissenting opinion, Vice-President Badawi stressed that 'The notification of Declarations to the Secretary-General, or their deposit with him and his obligation to communicate them to other States, are merely intended to take place of direct communication. The Secretary-General is thus a mere depository entrusted with the duty of bringing the Declarations to the knowledge of the other States.'[41] The Vice-President stressed that since the declaration was made on the day of

---

[38] See India's second preliminary objection. www.icj-cij/docket/files/32 (accessed 8 August 2013).

[39] *Case concerning Right of Passage over Indian Territory* (Preliminary Objections), Judgment of 26 November 1957, *ICJ Reports 1957*, 146.

[40] *Id.* 146–7.

[41] *Id.* Dissenting opinion of Vice-President Badawi 155.

that preceding the filing of the application, no one could suppose that the Secretary-General had been able to transmit the declaration to the other states within 24 hours. In his dissenting opinion, ad hoc Judge Chagla argued that Article 36, paragraph 4 of the Statute consisted of two parts, one making it incumbent upon the declaring states to deposit declarations with the Secretary-General, and the other incumbent upon the Secretary-General to transmit copies thereof to states party to the Statute and to the Registrar of the Court. The ad hoc Judge could not understand why the Court's decision had deemed only the first element to be mandatory, for, in his view, it would have been absolutely necessary that a certain period of time should lapse between making the declaration and filing the application.[42]

More than 40 years after its decision in the *Right of Passage case,* the Court was again faced with the problem of the submission of a dispute under the optional clause before the respondent state could have been informed of the applicant's accession to the optional clause system.

This problem arose in the *Case concerning the Land and Maritime Boundary between Cameroon and Nigeria*, because on 3 March 1994, Cameroon made a declaration of acceptance and the Secretary-General transmitted it to the parties to the Statute eleven-and-a-half months later.[43] Consequently, when Cameroon filed an application against Nigeria on 29 March 1994, the respondent state, Nigeria, did not know or was not in a position to know that Cameroon had acceded to the optional clause system. This led Nigeria to conclude that Cameroon 'acted prematurely', and had violated 'its obligation to act in good faith ..., acted in abuse of the system established by Article 36, paragraph 2 of the Statute.' According to Nigeria, the Court when considering the Cameroonian application should have arrived at a different conclusion than that reached in the *Right of Passage* case, which was an isolated one and that it was time the Court revised its findings in this case in connection with making optional clause declarations.[44] It stressed that the interpretation of Article 36, paragraph 4 of the Statute in 1957 should be reconsidered in

---

42 *Id.* 169–70.

43 In 1994, Cameroon instituted proceedings against Nigeria, and asked the Court to determine the question of sovereignty over Bakassi Peninsula and over islands in Lake Chad and to specify the course of the land and maritime boundary between itself and Nigeria. Cameroon founded the Court's jurisdiction on the Nigerian declaration of acceptance of 14 August 1965, and on the Cameroonian declaration of acceptance of 3 March 1994.

44 Cf. *Case concerning the Land and Maritime Boundary between Cameroon and Nigeria, ICJ Pleadings,* vol. I, paras. 1.10 and 1.28.

the light of changes that had since taken place in the law of treaties and in this context it referred to Article 78 of the 1969 Vienna Convention on the Law of Treaties.[45]

In response to that assertion, the Court pointed out the fact that 'the régime for depositing and transmitting declarations of acceptance of compulsory jurisdiction laid down in Article 36, paragraph 4 of the Statute of the Court is distinct from the régime envisaged for treaties by the Vienna Convention'.[46] Then, repeating its findings of the *Case concerning Military and Paramilitary Activities in and against Nicaragua*, the Court emphasized that the provisions of the Vienna Convention on the Law of Treaties may only be applied to declarations of acceptance by analogy.[47]

Indeed, the Court said nothing more, and it examined the Vienna Convention on notifications and communications (Article 78), the exchange of instruments of ratification, acceptance, approval and accession (Article 16) and the entry into force of treaties (Article 24).

The Court found that the provisions of the Vienna Convention did not have the scope that Nigeria inferred on them. Regarding Article 78 the Court observed that this article:

> is only designated to lay down the modalities according to which notifications and communications should be carried out. It does not govern the conditions in which a State expresses its consent to be bound by a treaty and those under which a treaty comes into force, those questions being governed by Articles 16 and 24 of the Convention.[48]

Accordingly, Articles 16 and 24 of the Vienna Convention on the Law of Treaties contain a general rule that, unless otherwise provided for by a treaty, the deposit of the instrument of ratification, accession, approval, etc. establishes the consent of a state to be bound by a treaty and the

---

45 Art. 78 of the 1969 Vienna Convention on the Law of Treaties stipulates:

> Except as the treaty or the present Convention otherwise provides, any notification or communication to be made by any State under the present Convention shall:
>
> … c) if transmitted to a depositary, be considered as received by the State for which it was intended only when the latter State has been informed by the depository in accordance with article 77, paragraph 1(e).

46 *Case concerning the Land and Maritime Boundary between Cameroon and Nigeria* (Preliminary Objections), Judgment of 11 June 1998, *ICJ Reports 1998*, 293.

47 *Id.*

48 *Id.*

treaty comes into force in respect of that state on the day of the deposit. The Court held that these rules of the Vienna Convention corresponded to the solution adopted by the Court in the *Right of Passage case* and that solution should be maintained.[49]

Thus, for its part in the *Land and Maritime Boundary case*, the Court maintained its view as set forth in the *Right of Passage case* and stated again that a declaring state should not be concerned with the actions of the Secretary-General or with his performance or non-performance thereof, specifically mentioning that 'The legal effect of Declarations does not depend upon subsequent action or inaction of the Secretary-General.' Unlike other documents, Article 36 of the Statute prescribes no additional requirement whatsoever, such as the transmission of information by the Secretary-General to reach the parties to the Statute or the entrance into force of a particular declaration after the lapse of a specified period of time.[50] The Court noted that, in contrast to Nigeria's contention, its decision in the *Right of Passage case* could not be regarded as an isolated one as its findings in this case had been reaffirmed by those in the cases concerning the *Temple of Preah Vihear* and the *Military and Paramilitary Activities in and against Nicaragua.*

More recently, in the *Cases concerning Legality of Use of Force* the International Court of Justice had again been confronted with a situation similar to that which Portugal created in 1955 and which brought into the limelight the *Right of Passage case*, namely that circumstance whereby a state filed an application with the Court a few days after its optional clause declaration had been deposited. As it was already mentioned in the spring of 1999, when during the period of air strikes by NATO forces, specifically on 25 April 1999, Yugoslavia deposited its declaration accepting the Court's compulsory jurisdiction and then, four days later, on 29 April, it instituted proceedings before the Court against ten NATO member states separately, 'for violation of the obligation not to use force', and accused these states of bombing Yugoslav territory,[51] and simultaneously with the application, Yugoslavia submitted requests for the indication of provisional measures. In the case of six states (Belgium, Canada, Netherlands, Portugal, Spain, and United Kingdom), the Belgrade Government based the Court's jurisdiction on the optional clause in

---

49 *Id.* 294.

50 *Case concerning Right of Passage over Indian Territory* (Preliminary Objections), Judgment of 26 November 1957, *ICJ Reports 1957*, 146–7.

51 For NATO's military actions in Kosovo, see 'Editorial Comments: NATO's Kosovo Intervention' (1999), 93, *AJIL*, 824–62.

addition to the Genocide Convention and, in the case of some states, on other treaties in force between the parties.[52]

As for the Court's decisions in these cases of greatest interest to our subject is the fact that, in dismissing the Yugoslav request for the indication of provisional measures, the Court did not even touch on the question of Yugoslavia having recognized the Court's compulsory jurisdiction only a few days before the filing of applications. Considering the political background of the applications submitted by the repressive Milosević regime against the NATO states, one could think that if the Court had wished to depart from its earlier legal practice in the least measure, these cases would have offered a good opportunity for it to abandon its position as expressed in the *Right of Passage case*. In all likelihood, the international community would have approved of a finding by the Court that the matter – of whether Yugoslavia was a party to the optional clause system at the time of filing the applications – was under serious question, since Yugoslavia had deposited its declaration of acceptance only four days before and hence its right to submit disputes to the Court under the optional clause was strongly questionable.

In view of the unilateral character of the declarations of acceptance, their deposit with the Secretary-General is a very important element, since it is the task of the Secretary-General to secure the publicity of the declarations and to forward them to the states and to the Registrar of the Court.[53] For this reason it is worthwhile to touch briefly on the Secretary-General's actions connected with declarations of acceptance and chiefly on how similar these actions are to those regarding treaties registered or deposited with him.

In this context, one should examine two of the said functions related to treaties. The Secretary-General's first function is the registration of treaties and conventions concluded by UN member states. This function is a special one, based on Article 102 of the Charter, its essence consisting of securing due publicity for treaties concluded by the members of the Organization.[54] The other function is related exclusively

---

[52] See, e.g. in the case of Belgium, Yugoslavia invoked, as an additional ground of jurisdiction, Art. 4 of the Convention of Conciliation, Judicial Settlement and Arbitration between Belgium and the Kingdom of Yugoslavia, signed in Belgrade on 25 March 1930.

[53] Cf. Bertrand Maus, *Les réserves dans les déclarations d'acceptation obligatoire de la Cour internationale de Justice* (Librairie E. Droz, Librairie Minard,1959) 63.

[54] For more detail on this point, see: Kelsen (1951), 696–705 and Lord McNair, *The Law of Treaties* (Clarendon Press 1961), 178–90. Also, see General

to those treaties of which the Secretary-General is the depositary, being governed by the Vienna Convention on the Law of Treaties.[55]

The Secretary-General's duties related to declarations of acceptance are similar in some measure to those connected with treaties registered with him under Article 102, of the Charter. In both cases, the Secretary-General receives certain documents and transmits them to states. His duties related to declarations of acceptance are practically fulfilled by these actions, but his functions as a depositary of treaties involve much more than this and are much more substantive.

According to the 1969 Vienna Convention on the Law of Treaties, the depositary has the function of examining whether signatures, instruments and reservations are in conformity with any applicable provisions of the treaty, and, if need be, bringing the matter to the attention of the state in question.[56] The Secretary-General as depositary may likewise have a highly important function not only in informing the states – entitled to become parties to the treaty – when the number of signatures, or ratifications, etc. required for the entry into force of the treaty has been received or deposited, but even in some cases determining the date at which the treaty enters into force. However, the situation is much more complicated in the case of treaties which are silent concerning reservations, i.e. treaties whereby it is permissible to make reservations, provided they satisfy the compatibility test.[57]

In the case of declarations of acceptance, the Secretary-General's functions are similar to the above-mentioned practice, being limited to only receiving declarations and transmitting them to the Registrar of the Court and to the parties to the Statute. Declarations henceforward pass out from the Secretary-General's purview, for as mentioned above, the Secretary-General has no additional functions related to declarations of acceptance, owing among other reasons to the fact that reservations or limitations appended to declarations of acceptance need no approval or consent by the other states parties to the optional clause system.

In light of the foregoing, it is understandable why the Court stuck to its position that declarations of acceptance enter into force on the day of

---

Assembly resolution 97 (1) of 14 December 1946 as amended by resolutions 364 B (IV), 482 (V) and 33/141 A.

[55] The depositary's functions are governed by Art. 77 of the 1969 Vienna Convention on the Law of Treaties. See also Summary of Practice of the Secretary General as Depository of Multilateral Treaties. UN ST/LEG./7/Rev.1.

[56] Art. 77, para. 1, subparagraph (d) of the 1969 Vienna Convention on the Law of Treaties.

[57] Cf. Anthony Aust, *Modern Treaty Law and Practice,* (CUP 2002), 129.

deposit with the Secretary-General. The Court's position is justified by the fact that an element of uncertainty would be introduced into the system[58] by accepting, as the date of entry into force of declarations of acceptance, the date of receipt of declarations by the parties to the Statute or parties to the optional clause system, because in that case a declaration would in fact enter into force on different dates, depending on the time at which each state receives the same notification.

If, however, declarations were to become effective after the lapse of a reasonable period of time, as was proposed by many, the question naturally arises as to what that reasonable period – 30 days or 3 months – should be. Yet the example of Cameroon's declaration of acceptance shows that not even a few months is necessarily sufficient for declarations to reach the states parties to the Statute.

With all probability, the dispute regarding the date of the effect of declarations of acceptance recently influenced some states to note in their declarations of acceptance that the document will take effect immediately or from the date of its receipt by the Secretary-General.[59]

V TRANSFERRING THE LEGAL EFFECT OF DECLARATIONS OF ACCEPTANCE MADE AT TIME OF THE PERMANENT COURT

At the San Francisco Conference, when it was decided to set up a new international judicial forum, the question was raised on what was to become of the declarations of acceptance providing for the compulsory jurisdiction of the Permanent Court. As noted earlier, the Conference discussed various proposals regarding the jurisdiction of the new Court and was unable to decide on the fate of declarations in force until an agreement had been reached to maintain the Permanent Court's optional clause system in the new Statute. At that point a paragraph was adopted transferring the legal effects of the declarations which were made to the Permanent Court and still in force. The provision reads as follows:

> Declarations made under Article 36, of the Statute of the Permanent Court of International Justice and which are still in force shall be deemed, as between

---

58 On this point, see the *Case concerning the Land and Maritime Boundary Line between Cameroon and Nigeria,* Judgment of 11 June 1998, *ICJ Reports 1998*, 295–6.

59 See, e.g., the declaration of Djibouti (2005), Ireland (2011) and Timor-Leste (2012).

> the parties to the present Statute, to be acceptances of the compulsory jurisdiction of the International Court of Justice for the period which they still have to run and in accordance with their terms.

This section was incorporated in Article 36, as paragraph 5 and according to it, as was pointed out later by the International Court of Justice itself, the compulsory jurisdiction of the Permanent Court, as well as the declarations of acceptance still in force, passed *ipso jure* on to the new Court. Paragraph 5 is completely clear at first sight, reflecting the aim to see that the declarations of acceptance made between the two world wars do not become void because of the dissolution of the Permanent Court. The apparently clear wording is delusive, however, as the said paragraph permits various interpretations.

When the Permanent Court ceased to exist, the quoted paragraph affected the declarations of acceptance made by some 16 states,[60] a figure which naturally kept decreasing over the years, with as little as six declarations that originally provided for the compulsory jurisdiction of the Permanent Court still being in force at the end of 2013.[61]

The question concerning the validity of declarations of acceptance made to the Permanent Court has been addressed by the International Court of Justice in several cases, of which each involved different aspects of the problems associated with declarations of the inter-war period.

In connection with Article 36, paragraph 5 of the Statute, Rosenne observes that this paragraph operated satisfactorily for the purpose of effecting immediate transformation of declarations accepting the compulsory jurisdiction of the old Court into declarations providing the jurisdiction of the new Court; however, it lost its efficacy after that.[62]

The necessity to interpret Article 36, paragraph 5 of the Statute in the jurisprudence of the International Court of Justice arose for the first time in the *Case concerning the Aerial Incident of 27 July 1955*. Under the optional clause, the Israeli Government instituted proceedings before the Court against Bulgaria with regard to the destruction of an Israeli civilian aircraft belonging to the El Al Israel Airlines Ltd by the Bulgarian anti-aircraft defence forces and for the loss of life and property and all

---

60 Cf. *ICJ Yearbook 1946–47*, 221–8.

61 See the declarations of the Dominican Republic (1924), Haiti (1921), Luxembourg (1930), Nicaragua (1929, amended 2001), Panama (1921) and Uruguay (1921).

62 Rosenne (2006) vol. II 722.

other damage that resulted therefrom.[63] In its response to the application, Bulgaria filed preliminary objections, arguing, *inter alia*, that the Court had no jurisdiction to decide the dispute, because Bulgaria's declaration of 1921 accepting the compulsory jurisdiction of the Permanent Court had ceased to have effect with the Court's dissolution on 18 April 1946 and therefore it had been impossible for the legal effect of the declaration to pass on to the International Court of Justice in 1955, when Bulgaria was admitted to the United Nations.[64]

Thus the Court had to decide whether Article 36, paragraph 5 of the Statute of the International Court was applicable to the 1921 Bulgarian declaration of acceptance.

In dealing with the first preliminary objection, the Court made a distinction between the declarations of acceptance made by states that had both participated in the San Francisco Conference and become members of the United Nations before the dissolution of the Permanent Court on the one hand, and the declarations of states that had become parties to the Statute of the International Court of Justice after the Permanent Court had been dissolved. Article 36, paragraph 5 when considered in its application to the declarations by the states of the first group, effected a simple operation: the declarations of acceptance of the Permanent Court were transformed into acceptances of the compulsory jurisdiction of the new Court. Thus, in the case of these states, Article 36, paragraph 5 maintained an existing obligation while modifying its subject matter.

Contrarily, the position of states of the other group – namely those which did not participate in the San Francisco Conference and were admitted to the United Nations at later dates – were totally different. According to the Court 'the operation of transferring from one Court to the other acceptances of the compulsory jurisdiction by non-signatory States could not constitute a simple operation, capable of being dealt

---

[63] Israel founded the Court's jurisdiction on its declaration of acceptance of 3 October 1956 and on Bulgaria's declaration made on 29 July 1921, which was the occasion for the deposit of its instrument of ratification of the Protocol of Signature of the Permanent Court's Statute. Israel contended that the legal effect of the Bulgarian declaration accepting the compulsory jurisdiction of the Permanent Court had passed to the International Court of Justice by virtue of Art. 36, para. 5.

[64] The Bulgarian Submission, deposited to the Registry on 20 March 1959, consisted of five preliminary objections. The First Preliminary Objection contained the above-mentioned arguments. Cf. *Aerial Incident of 27 July 1955, ICJ Pleadings*, 126–9.

with immediately and completely by Article 36, paragraph 5.'[65] Article 36, paragraph 5 was originally only prescribed for signatory states, and it was without legal force as far as non-signatory states were concerned. The Statute could neither maintain nor transform their original obligation, and the dissolution of the Permanent Court freed them from their obligations regarding the Court's compulsory jurisdiction, as was also the case with Bulgaria's declaration of acceptance of 1921.[66]

The Court's view was that restricting the application of Article 36, paragraph 5 exclusively to those original members of the United Nations was fully in keeping with the aim of this provision. In point of fact, it was foreseeable at the time of adoption of the new Statute that the Permanent Court was to be dissolved in the near future and, as a consequence, the lapsing of declarations accepting its compulsory jurisdiction were in contemplation. The Court pointed out rightly that:

> If nothing had been done there would have been a backward step in relation to what had been achieved in the way of international jurisdiction. Rather than expecting that the States signatories of the new Statute would deposit new declarations of acceptance, it was sought to provide for this transitory situation by a transitional provision and that is the purpose of Article 36, paragraph 5.[67]

According to the Court, if a state became a party to the new Statute long after the dissolution of the old Court, there is no transitory situation to be dealt with by Article 36, paragraph 5.[68] That provision could not in any event be operative as regards Bulgaria until the date of its admission to United Nations in December 1955. However, at that date, the 1921 declaration of acceptance was no longer in force as a consequence of the dissolution of the Permanent Court in 1946 and the acceptance of the compulsory jurisdiction set out in that declaration was devoid of object since the Permanent Court was no longer in existence.

One can see, that in the *Case concerning the Aerial Incident of 27 July 1955*, the Court gave a narrow interpretation of Article 36, paragraph 5 of the Statute, ruling that only the in-force declarations accepting the jurisdiction of the Permanent Court made by those states being represented at the San Francisco Conference were to transfer to the International Court of Justice. The application of that paragraph is 'subject to two conditions: (1) that the

---

[65] Cf. *Case concerning the Aerial Incident of July 27th, 1955* (Preliminary Objections), Judgment of 26 May 1959, *ICJ Reports 1959*, 137.

[66] Cf. *Id.* 138.

[67] *Id.* 139.

[68] *Id.*

State having made the declaration should be a party to the Statute, and (2) that the declaration of that State should still be in force'.[69]

The judgment of the Court in that case drew criticism from many writers of international law. In their joint dissenting opinion Judges Sir Hersch Lauterpacht, Wellington Koo and Sir Percy Spender pointed out that the Court added two further conditions to the applicability of Article 36, paragraph 5 of the Statute, notably: (1) the declarant state must have participated in the Conference of San Francisco; and (2) the declarant state must have become a party to the Statute of the new Court prior to the date of the dissolution of the Permanent Court of International Justice on 18 April 1946.[70] They tried to demonstrate that the operation of Article 36, paragraph 5 was not intended to be limited to states participating in the Conference of San Francisco. They did not question whether the operation of that paragraph to states not represented at San Francisco could not have immediate and automatic effect; however, it was not expressed that those states were excluded from the operation of the paragraph, since their declarations would be transferred to the International Court of Justice when they became parties to the Statute.[71] They emphasized 'to attach decisive importance to the effect of the dissolution of the Permanent Court amounts not only to re-writing paragraph 5; it amounts to adding to it an extraneous condition which it was the purpose of that article to exclude and to disregard'.[72]

The issue of the transfer of declarations of acceptance made at the time of the Permanent Court to the new Court emerged in the *Case concerning the Temple of Preah Vihear* as well. The dispute between Cambodia and Thailand relating to the territorial sovereignty over the Temple of Preah Vihear was submitted to the Court by Cambodia under Article 36, paragraph 2;[73] Thailand protested against the proceedings instituted by Cambodia and raised two preliminary objections.[74]

---

69 *Id.* 144.

70 *Id.* Joint Dissenting Opinion by Judges Sir Hersch Lauterpacht, Wellington Koo and Sir Percy Spender. *ICJ Reports 1959*, 156.

71 *Id.* 178.

72 *Id.* 168.

73 In 1959, Cambodia instituted proceedings against Thailand by alleging violation by Thailand of Cambodia's territorial sovereignty in the region of the Temple of Preah Vihear. The applicant state founded the Court's jurisdiction on, among other things, the combined effect of her own declaration of acceptance on 9 September 1957 and that of Thailand on 20 May 1950, both renewing their respective declarations made to the Permanent Court.

74 For the preliminary objections, see *Case concerning the Temple of Preah Vihear, ICJ Pleadings*, vol. I, 133–49.

In its first preliminary objection, Thailand contended that the declaration of May 1950 renewing its declaration of acceptance of 1929 was invalid as a whole, because the Thai declaration of 1929, which had been prolonged for a term of ten years in 1940, had been terminated upon the dissolution of the Permanent Court on 18 April 1946 and therefore it had been impossible to renew it in 1950.[75] Thailand, for her part, referred to the judgment of the International Court of Justice in the *Case concerning the Aerial Incident of 27 July 1955* and reasoned that her position was the same as that of Bulgaria. Hence, the Government of Thailand argued that when she renewed her declaration of acceptance of 1929 for another ten years, she actually renewed a declaration which was not in force and which could not have a legal effect other than that of recognizing the compulsory jurisdiction of a tribunal that no longer existed.[76]

The Court held that the case of Thailand was different from that of Bulgaria, and furthermore that Thailand, by her declaration of 20 May 1950, had placed herself in a different position from Bulgaria. The 1940 Thai declaration of acceptance had expired, according to its own terms, on 3 May 1950, two weeks before Thailand made her declaration of 20 May 1950. After the lapse of its declaration of 1940, Thailand was completely free to decide whether or not to accept the compulsory jurisdiction of the International Court of Justice. At that date, however, Thailand took a step which Bulgaria did not, namely she addressed a communication – embodying her declaration of 20 May 1950 – to the Secretary-General of the United Nations. 'By this she at least purported to accept, and clearly intended to accept, the compulsory jurisdiction of the present Court'[77] – the Court held in its judgment. Therefore the Court deemed the Thai declaration of 20 May 1950 to be a new declaration of acceptance and that it did not relate to Article 36, paragraph 5 of the Statute.

The liveliest controversy about the continuity of the declarations of acceptance made between the two world wars was aroused by the 1929

---

[75] Originally, by a declaration of 20 September 1929, Thailand had recognized the compulsory jurisdiction of the Permanent Court for a term of ten years and in 1940 and 1950 it had renewed that declaration, with the same conditions and reservations, for additional terms of ten years.

[76] *Case concerning the Temple of Preah Vihear, ICJ Pleadings,* vol. I, 135–9.

[77] *Case concerning the Temple of Preah Vihear* (Preliminary Objections), Judgment of 26 May 1961, *ICJ Reports 1961*, 29.

Nicaraguan declaration of acceptance in the *Case concerning Military and Paramilitary Activities in and against Nicaragua*.[78]

The point here was that on 24 September 1929, Nicaragua, as a member of the League of Nations, signed the Protocol of Signature of the Statute of the Permanent Court of International Justice and concurrently made a declaration of acceptance. However, it did not ratify the Protocol at the time and it was only ten years later, on 29 November 1939, that it notified the Secretary-General of the League of Nations via telegram that the Protocol of Signature of the Statute of the Permanent Court was ratified and the instrument of ratification would be sent in due course. According to the available documents, however, the instruments of ratification had never been received by the League of Nations in Geneva.

For all these reasons, in the *Case concerning Military and Paramilitary Activities in and against Nicaragua*, the United States in its counter-memorial concerning the questions of jurisdiction and admissibility, contended that Nicaragua never ratified the Protocol of Signature of the Statute, never became a party to the Statute of the Permanent Court and consequently the 1929 declaration never came into force.[79] Thus, Article 36, paragraph 5, of the Statute did not operate to pass the legal effects of the Nicaraguan declaration of 1929 to the International Court of Justice, because Nicaragua's declaration was never an acceptance of the Permanent Court's compulsory jurisdiction.[80]

The Court was of the view that at the time the Statute of the new Court came into force the 1929 declaration of Nicaragua 'though valid, had not become binding under the Statute of the Permanent Court'.[81]

> Nicaragua failed to deposit its instrument of ratification of the Protocol of Signature of the Statute of the Permanent Court, was not party to that instrument. Consequently the Declaration made by Nicaragua in 1929 had not acquired binding force prior to such effect as Article 36, paragraph 5, of the Statute of the International Court of Justice might produce.[82]

---

78 On this score, see D.W. Greig, 'Nicaragua and the United States: Confrontation over the Jurisdiction of the International Court', (1991) 62, *BYIL*, 119, 123–65.

79 *Case concerning Military and Paramilitary Activities in and against Nicaragua, ICJ Pleadings*, vol. II, 11–17.

80 *Id.* 18–29.

81 *Case concerning Military and Paramilitary Activities in and against Nicaragua* (Jurisdiction of the Court and Admissibility of the Application), Judgment of 26 November 1984, *ICJ Reports 1984*, 404.

82 *Id.*

In other words, concerning declarations of acceptance made at the time of the Permanent Court, the International Court of Justice made a distinction between the validity and the binding force of declarations. The Nicaraguan declaration was valid but did not have binding force because Nicaragua had failed to ratify the Protocol of Signature of the Statute of the Permanent Court and hence was not a party to the Statute.

It thus seems that the Nicaraguan declaration was not binding although – not being disputed – it could have been had Nicaragua ratified the said Protocol of Signature prior to the establishment of the new Court. In the judgment, it was emphasized that declarations similar to that of Nicaragua 'had certain legal effects which could be maintained indefinitely'. According to the Court, this durability of potential effect of the Nicaraguan declaration derives from the fact that it was made 'unconditionally', i.e. without any limitation whatever, and for an unlimited period.[83] Thus when Nicaragua became a party to the Statute of the new Court, its declaration of 1929 was valid.[84] The Court found that Nicaragua's ratification of the new Statute had the same effect – with respect to its 1929 declaration of acceptance – as if it had ratified the Protocol of Signature of the old Statute.

By recognizing as valid the Nicaraguan declaration of acceptance of 1929 and ruling that it had jurisdiction in the dispute between Nicaragua and the United States, the International Court of Justice stirred enormous controversy, so much so that even the writers discussing that decision of the Court are, as it were, far too numerous to list in the literature of international law.[85] The judgment that was delivered – with regard to jurisdiction and admissibility in the *Nicaragua case* – allowed the proceedings to continue, and in its judgment of 1986 on the merits, the Court found, among other points, that the United States had acted in

---

83 *Id.*

84 *Id.*

85 Washington made no secret of having terminated, on 7 October 1985, its declaration of acceptance of 1946, owing to this decision of the Court.

Among the works in the pertinent literature, see Michael W. Reisman, 'Has the International Court Exceeded its Jurisdiction?' (Editorial Comments) (1986) 80, *AJIL*, 128–34; Joe Verhoeven, 'Le droit, le judge et la violance. Les arrêts Nicaragua c. États Unies' (1987) 91, *RGDIP*, 1159–201; Lori F. Damrosch (ed.), 'The International Court of Justice at a Crossroads' (Transnational Publishers, Inc. 1987) 511.

breach of its obligation under customary international law not to intervene in the affairs of another state, not to use force against another state and not to violate the sovereignty of another state.[86]

On the basis of the three cases discussed above it can be stated that with respect to the application of Article 36, paragraph 5 the Court has attached of paramount importance that the states having made declarations of acceptance at the time of the Permanent Court, should have the continuity of being contracting parties, without interruption, concerning the two Courts' Statutes. In the *Case concerning the Aerial Incident of 27 July 1955* it was emphatic about the fact that a state which had not acceded to the Statute of the new Court by 18 April 1946 was freed from the obligations undertaken in its declaration accepting the compulsory jurisdiction of the Permanent Court and that those obligations could not be revived any more.

The situation with regard to Thailand was different. Thailand's declaration of acceptance made to the Permanent Court had lapsed on 3 May 1950, and it was some two weeks later that Thailand made a declaration to renew its previous one. The Court held that the expiration of Thailand's previous declaration relieved that country from the obligations undertaken in her declaration of acceptance made to the old Court, and that from that time Thailand was free to decide whether or not to make a declaration of acceptance. Within the meaning of the judgment, it was clearly intended by Thailand to accept the compulsory jurisdiction of the new Court, as was indeed expressed in her declaration of 20 May 1950.

Nicaragua's declaration of acceptance involved a special problem, since there was a declaration of acceptance from 1929 which was valid but not in force. In the case of Nicaragua nobody questioned the continuity of being a contracting party to the Statutes of the two Courts. Nicaragua was a founding member of the United Nations, being among the first to duly sign and ratify the United Nations Charter on 7 July 1945, and, upon becoming a party to the Statute of the new Court, had a valid declaration, whose entry into force was subject to a step still missing,

---

86 Cf. *Case concerning Military and Paramilitary Activities in and against Nicaragua* (Merits), Judgment of 27 June 1986, *ICJ Reports 1986*, 146–9.

On this score, see Keith Highet, 'Evidence, the Court, and the Nicaragua Case' (1987) 81, *AJIL*, 1–56; Gary L. Scott – Craig L. Carr, 'The I.C.J. and Compulsory Jurisdiction: the Case for Closing the Clause' *Id.* 57–76; Gordon A. Christenson, Appraisals of the I.C.J.'s Decision: Nicaragua v. United States (Merits). *Id.* 77–100; Michel Pierre Eisemann, 'L'arrét de la C.I.J. du 27 juin 1986 (fond) dans l'Affaire des activités militaries et paramilitaries au Nicaragua et contre celui-ci' (1986) XXXII, *AF DI*, 153–91.

notably ratification of the Protocol of Signature of the Statute of the Permanent Court. According to the International Court that requirement had been satisfied by the ratification of the United Nations Charter, and thus the Nicaraguan declaration of acceptance of 1929 thereupon attained binding force.

When examining the Court's conclusions in the above three cases one can discover at first glance certain contradictions between the three judgments, especially those delivered in the *Aerial Incident case* and the *Nicaragua case*, particularly with regard to the fact that in the *Aerial Incident case* the Court gave a *sensu strictu* (narrow) interpretation of Article 36, paragraph 5 of the Statute, a reason why it refused to recognize the applicability of that provision to Bulgaria's declaration of acceptance of 1929. In the *Nicaragua case*, on the other hand, it relied on that same provision in admitting the continuance of a declaration of acceptance which did not have binding force even between the two world wars. In that case the Court gave an interpretation of Article 36, paragraph 5 of the Statute which covered the application of that provision even to declarations without binding force at the time of the Permanent Court, and Nicaragua's ratification of the new Statute had the same effect as if it had ratified the Protocol of Signature of the old Statute.[87]

In point of fact, the aforementioned contradictions between the judgments are but seeming ones, for in all three cases the Court acted consistently in respect of two questions, (1) namely with respect to the application of Article 36, paragraph 5, it was necessary that the declarant state should have a continuous status as party to the Statutes of both Courts and (2) that this paragraph of the Statute relates 'solely to the cases in which the declarations accepting the compulsory jurisdiction of the Permanent Court would be deemed to be transformed into acceptances of the compulsory jurisdiction of the present Court, without any new or specific act on the part of the declarant State'.[88]

---

87 In the Nicaragua case, the Court took notice of the conduct of states and international organizations as well as the fact that in the Court's publications Nicaragua was among the states accepting the compulsory jurisdiction of the Court, and that was not denied by Nicaragua nor questioned by any state. Thereby, the Court actually accepted the doctrine of 'consent by subsequent conduct', which was sharply challenged by several members of the Court.

88 *Case concerning the Temple of Preah Vihear* (Preliminary Objections), Judgment of 26 May 1961, *ICJ Reports 1961*, 27.

4. Admissibility of reservations to declarations of acceptance

Even the very first declarations of acceptance contained certain clauses that served to place limitations on the obligations that states had undertaken concerning the Court's compulsory jurisdiction,[1] and, as Jochen Frowein points out, from the very beginning it was understood that states may exclude different areas from the operation of the optional clause.[2] In connection with the practice of placing limitations by attaching reservations to the declarations of acceptance, Leo Gross considers it paradoxical that 'in practice states apply both the "contracting-in" (or "opting-in") principle as well as the "contracting-out" (or "opting-out") principle: they "contract-in" by making a declaration of acceptance and they "contract-out" by attaching reservations'.[3]

The limitations or restrictions – included in the declarations of acceptance – are called 'reservations' both in the writings of publicists and practice of the two Courts. This terminology is not the most suitable, chiefly because the said limitations cannot be deemed to be real reservations according to the interpretation used in international law regarding the law of treaties and, as will be discussed later, they differ in many aspects from the reservations made to multilateral treaties.[4] The appearance of reservations in the declarations of acceptance was somewhat 'unexpected' because, in the drafting of the Permanent Court's Statute, the Committee of Jurists did not anticipate any reservation being

---

1 According to available data, the Netherlands' declaration of acceptance in 1921 was the first to contain certain limitations.

2 J.A. Frowein, 'Reciprocity and Restrictions Concerning Different Optional Clauses' in Nisuke Ando, Edward McWinney, Rüdiger Wolfrum (eds), *Liber Amicorum Judge Shigeru Oda* (Kluwer Law International 2002) vol. I, 307.

3 Leo Gross, 'Compulsory Juristiction under the Optional Clause: History and Practice' in Damrosch (1987) 21–2.

4 Cf. Maus (1959), 94.

made by a declarant state concerning the compulsory jurisdiction.[5] On the other hand, however, acceptance with reservations of the Court's jurisdiction should not have been really so 'unexpected', as it can in no way be seen to be a novelty for states to accept with certain conditions the arbitral settlement of international disputes, or attach, a priori, such clauses to arbitral agreements to exclude one or more questions from arbitration. Thus, for instance, arbitration agreements concluded in the 19th century often included clauses to the effect that arbitral settlement was not to apply to questions affecting the 'vital interests', 'national honour', 'independence', etc. of states. At the time this was considered to be a basic assumption so much so that, according to Hans Wehberg, even when not definitely expressed, the clause concerning vital interests is included in all arbitration treaties.[6]

I APPEARANCE OF RESERVATIONS TO DECLARATIONS OF ACCEPTANCE

Article 36 of the Statute of the Permanent Court of International Justice provides that 'The declarations referred to above may be made unconditionally or on condition of reciprocity in relation to several Members or States, or for a certain time'.

In other words, certain limitations, namely reciprocity and limitations of time, were permitted by the Statute itself. In 1930, the eminent British expert of international law, Hersch Lauterpacht, wrote the following with respect to this issue: 'There is no doubt that the Optional Clause does not provide *expressis verbis* for the possibility of reservations being made, but there is no necessity for such an express provision.'[7] As a general rule, a state may qualify any treaty obligation with whatever reservation it deems necessary; as is shown throughout their history, treaties of arbitration constitute no exception in this respect.[8]

In his monograph published in the early 1930s, Fachiri writes that the language of Article 36 referring to certain reservations, does not preclude

---

[5] Cf. Shigeru Oda, 'Reservations in the Declarations of Acceptance of the Optional Clause and the Period of Validity of those Declarations: the Effect of the Schultz Letter' (1989) 59, *BYIL*, 4.

[6] Cf. Hans Wehberg, 'Restrictive Clauses in International Arbitration Treaties' (1913) 7, *AJIL*, 301, 310.

[7] Hersch Lauterpacht, 'The British Reservation to the Optional Clause' (1930) 10, *Economica*, 137, 168.

[8] *Id.*

the admissibility of further reservations in one way or the other.[9] In any case, one can say that the cited paragraph of the Statute forms the legal basis of the states' practice to make limitations or reservations to their declarations of acceptance, placing limitations as to persons, subject matters or periods of time on the obligations they have assumed concerning the Court's compulsory jurisdiction.

The literature of international law from the inter-war period reflected views which – considering that Article 36 of the Statute only contains limitations phrased like 'on condition of reciprocity' or 'for a certain time' – argued the conclusion *a contrario* that no other reservation, condition, limitation or restriction should be joined to declarations of acceptance.[10] That position did not have many advocates, and, to our knowledge, Judge Levi Carneiro was the only member of the two International Courts to maintain the said view.[11] Contrary to this, the prevalent opinion was that Article 36 had no restrictive character in this respect and did not preclude the admissibility of further reservations.[12] Moreover, as a consequence of the efforts to reconcile the idea of obligatory arbitration with certain inalienable sovereign rights of states, it was natural that the idea of implied reserves emerged.[13] Another author argued that, in addition to the admissibility of reservations, if a state was free to accept or not accept the obligations as laid down in the clause, then, in the absence of express provisions, the liberty not to accept the optional clause covers the liberty to place conditions on acceptance.[14]

The disputes about the permissibility of limitations on reservations to declarations of acceptance were *ab initio* rather academic in nature, since states in practice did make use of the possibility to make reservations, attaching to their declarations rather varied limitations and reservations consisting of different contents, not only those which are mentioned in Article 36 of the Statute.[15]

---

[9] Cf. Fachiri (1980) 98.

[10] Cf. Pearce A. Higgins, *British acceptance of compulsory arbitration under the Optional Clause and its implications* (Cambridge 1929); and Brierly, *The Times*, 1 October 1929, quoted by Maus (1959) 85.

[11] Cf. *Anglo-Iranian Oil Co. case* (Preliminary Objections), Judgment of 22 July 1952, Dissenting Opinion of Judge Levi Carneiro, *ICJ Reports 1952*, 154.

[12] Cf. Fachiri (1980), 98–9 and Lauterpacht (1930) 168–9.

[13] Cf. Robert R. Wilson, 'Reservation clauses in agreements for obligatory arbitration' (1929) 23, *AJIL*, 68, 70–71.

[14] Sir John Fischer Williams, 'The Optional Clause (The British Signature and Reservations)' (1930) 11, *BYIL*, 63, 72.

[15] Cf. Robert Kolb, *The International Court of Justice* (Hart Publishing, 2013) 459–63.

The question of the permissibility of reservations was also addressed by the League of Nations.[16] Concerning the proposal of its First Committee and a special subcommittee,[17] the Assembly of the League of Nations, in its resolution of 2 October 1924, expressed the view that the wording of the optional clause was broad enough for states to accede to the clause with such reservations as they deemed necessary.[18]

While interpreting the above-cited provision of the Statute, the First Committee stated that its flexibility authorizes the making of any kind of reservation. Since states are free to accept the Court's compulsory jurisdiction in certain classes of disputes, but not in others, they are all the more free to accept the compulsory jurisdiction in only a fraction of one of those classes.[19]

Since comparatively few states had made declarations of acceptance and some of the declarations had not come into force, the question of reservations to declarations of acceptance was brought forward, among other issues, in the course of preparations for the Disarmament Conference held in 1932 under the auspices of the League of Nations. In the resolution of 26 September 1928, the Assembly emphasized that it wished to remove the obstacles preventing states from adhering to the optional clause system. The Assembly called the attention of states to the possibility of making reservations limiting their obligations either in time or in scope. Furthermore, the resolution stated that 'the reservations conceivable may relate, either generally to certain aspects of any kind of dispute, or specifically to certain classes or lists of disputes, and that these different kinds of reservation can be legitimately combined'.[20]

---

[16] In 1924, the fifth session of the League's Assembly entrusted its First Committee to clarify the terms of Art. 36, para. 2, of the Statute in order to facilitate a more general acceptance of the Court's compulsory jurisdiction. The reason behind that decision was that only a few States had made optional clause declarations and, according to the Assembly, one of the reasons was that they didn't know whether they could insert reservations in their declaration of acceptance.

[17] The members of the subcommittee were Adatci, Apponyi, Loucheur, Erich, Fernandes, Sir Cecil Hurst, O'Bryne, Politis, Rolin, Scialija, Titulesco, de la Torriente, Limburg, and Unden.

[18] Cf. League of Nations, Official Journal, Special Supplement No. 23, Records of the Fifth Assembly, 225.

[19] Cf. Société des Nations, Journal Officiel. Proces-verbal de la lère Commission, 109–10.

[20] For the resolution see League of Nations. Official Journal, Special Supplement No. 64, Record of the Ninth Ordinary Session of the Assembly, Plenary Meetings, 183.

Some authors conceived how that resolution of the League of Nations was an interpretation of the Statute, while others categorically refuted such conceptions.[21] No matter how one looks at the resolution, one thing is sure: it had no binding force but was in fact a political declaration. In any case, after the adoption of the resolution, several states made declarations of acceptance. At the same time, however, the cited position taken by the League of Nations on reservations to declarations of acceptance did have certain 'negative' effects as well, because afterwards states came to make more and more complicated declarations and accept the Court's compulsory jurisdiction with more and more limitations. According to Hudson, the tendency towards a more complicated form of declarations and to multiply the limitations on the jurisdiction recognized was encouraged not only by the above-mentioned 1928 Assembly's resolution but by Article 39 of the Geneva General Act of 1928, which enumerated three classes of disputes that could be excluded by reservations from the scope of application of the treaty.[22]

The efforts exerted by the League of Nations to have the Court's compulsory jurisdiction accepted by as many states as possible remained a topic of discussion even in later decades. In the late 1990s, Judge Kooijmans noted that it was ironic that the League of Nations, by encouraging the acceptance of the Court's compulsory jurisdiction, endorsed the making of reservations to the declarations of acceptance (although Article 36, paragraph 3 of the Statute does not authorize declarant states to make such reservations), thereby weakening the system which it intended to strengthen.[23]

---

[21] According to Maus, the interpretation by the League Assembly of the Statute in principle has no legal force because the Assembly of the League of Nations was not empowered to amend or to interpret the Statute. The Statute was a separate international treaty independent of the Covenant, one that had to be ratified separately, while the Member States of the League of Nations were not under obligation to accede to the Statute. In reality, the competence to interpret the Statute was vested either in the Court itself or the conference of States signatory to the Protocol of Signature of the Statute of the Permanent Court. Cf. Maus (1959) 19.

[22] Hudson (1972) 467–8.

[23] Cf. *Fisheries Jurisdiction case* (Jurisdiction of the Court), Judgment of 4 December 1998, Separate opinion of Judge Kooijmans, *ICJ Reports 1998*, 489.

II FREEDOM TO ATTACH RESERVATIONS TO DECLARATIONS OF ACCEPTANCE

Regarding the question of reservations to declarations of acceptance, the San Francisco Conference identified itself fully with the practice established at the time of the Permanent Court, although ideas were voiced about the need for certain changes.

During the debate of Subcommittee D of Committee IV/1 of the San Francisco Conference, Canada proposed that there should be incorporated in Article 36, paragraph 2 a list of permitted reservations, with liberty to add others. On the other hand, Australia argued that there should be added an exhaustive list of *permitted reservations*, along the lines of that adopted in the Geneva General Act of 1928. However, both proposals were rejected by the Subcommittee.[24]

In its report to Committee IV/1 of the Conference, Subcommittee D stated the following in connection with reservations to declarations of acceptance:

> The question of reservations calls for explanation. As is well known, the article (i.e. Article 36, – V.L.) has consistently been interpreted in the past as allowing States accepting the jurisdiction of the Court to subject their declarations to reservations. The Subcommittee has considered such interpretation as being henceforth established. It has therefore been considered unnecessary to modify paragraph 3, in order to make express reference to the right of the States to make such reservations.[25]

After the International Court of Justice had been established, states continued the practice of making reservations to declarations of acceptance and even 'invented' additional reservations that became more and more complicated. As will be discussed later, several of these 'new' reservations place many more limitations on the Court's compulsory jurisdiction than did the reservations to inter-war declarations of acceptance, with no small part of them finding a loop-hole of escape from the Court's jurisdiction. For that matter, among the post-1945 declarations of acceptance there are very few in which, similar to those declarations of acceptance of compulsory jurisdiction made by Latin American states between the two world wars, a state accepted the Court's jurisdiction without any limitation.

---

[24] Report of Subcommittee D to Committee IV/1 on Art. 36 of the Statute of the International Court of Justice. *UNCIO Documents*, vol. XIII, 558.

[25] *Id.* 559.

In connection with the various reservations, the question rightly arises as to what this can be traced to and what lies at the root of more and more complicated reservations.

In our view, there are three reasons for this trend.

The first reason is, as was very wittily stated in the report of the 1964 Tokyo Congress of the International Law Association, 'almost every State has some skeletons in its closets and might not wish to have them exposed before the Court.'[26] In addition, the report goes on to say, states undoubtedly believe certain difficulties to be surmountable by reservations, but are usually afraid they might have forgotten something important or that in the future there might arise some new problems that are not covered by specific reservations. This fear of unforeseen consequences tends to prompt states either to refrain from making a declaration accepting compulsory jurisdiction or to attach sweeping, open-ended reservations to their declarations.[27]

The second reason is related to the development of international law. The advancement of science and technology requires more and more domains to be governed by international law; however, because of the uncertainty of the new norms and state practice, some states prefer to exclude these issues from the scope of their declaration of acceptance.

The third reason can be traced back to the fact that states have 'learnt' from the jurisprudence of the Court in previous cases, in the sense that they have 'elaborated' new reservations, on the basis of the opinions formulated by the Court in its judgments, in order to prevent a similar situation occurring in the future. This is best exemplified by the reservations that sought to ward off 'surprise applications', which became widespread after the Court had delivered its judgment on the preliminary objections in the *Right of Passage case*.[28]

For that matter, the problem of reservations to declarations of acceptance has been repeatedly addressed by the United Nations as well. One of the most important of the relevant documents is Resolution 3232 (XXIX) on Review of the role of the International Court of Justice, which the General Assembly adopted by consensus on the basis of the proposal of the Sixth Committee. In that resolution, the General Assembly recognized 'the desirability that States study the possibility of accepting, with as few reservations as possible, the compulsory jurisdiction of the International Court of Justice in accordance with Article

---

[26] *International Law Association,* Report of the Fifty-first Conference, Tokyo, 1964, 87.

[27] *Id.*

[28] For more detail, see Chapter 7, Section II.

36, of the Statute'. That appeal and other similar ones met with little response, and states continued the practice of making reservations to their declarations of acceptance, with some declarations containing so many and so diverse limitations that, with some exaggeration, now the question arises, as it were, which of the disputes come, under Article 36, paragraph 2 of the Statute, within the compulsory jurisdiction of the Court in respect of a particular state.

Most authors on international law recognize the freedom to make reservations, and only occasionally can one meet with views claiming that under the new Statute no reservation to or limitation on declarations of acceptance is admissible in addition to those phrased like 'on condition of reciprocity' and 'for a certain time', notably those mentioned in the Statute.[29]

Such views are based on the fact that the provisions of the new Statute on the optional clause have been slightly amended, as was already mentioned, by omitting the word 'any' from the phrase 'in respect of all or any classes of legal disputes' in Article 36, paragraph 2. This amendment, as Waldock points out, did not impair the right to make reservations to the declarations of acceptance in the same way as existed in the days of the Permanent Court of International Justice.[30] It's true that '... while it is no longer open to a state, in accepting compulsory jurisdiction under the Optional Clause, to differentiate between the classes of legal disputes listed in the Clause, it may still, in other ways, differentiate between categories of disputes with respect of which it accepts the Clause. It may still, by limitations, reservations and conditions, except large categories of disputes from its acceptance of compulsory jurisdiction'.[31]

The view concerning the inadmissibility of reservations not mentioned in the Statute was revived by Pakistan in the *Case concerning Aerial Incident of 10 August 1999*. In that dispute, the application that was submitted by Pakistan, instituting proceedings against India in respect of a dispute relating to the destruction of a Pakistani aircraft, was based on Article 36, paragraphs 1 and 2 of the Statute and the declarations of

---

[29] According to Thévenaz, besides the limitations mentioned in the Statute, one more reservation is admissible, that is, States may, under Art. 95 of the Charter, exclude from the scope of their declarations of acceptance those differences the solution of which they have previously entrusted to other tribunals. Henri Thévenaz, 'La nouvelle Cour internationale de Justice' (1945), 20, *Die Friedens-Warte,* 406, 411.

[30] Waldock (1955–56) 249.

[31] *Id.*

acceptance of the two states. In response to the application, India submitted preliminary objections invoking, *inter alia,* the so-called 'Commonwealth reservation' to its declaration of acceptance regarding the exclusion of disputes in respect of any state which 'is or has been a Member of the Commonwealth of Nations'.[32] Countering this, Pakistan argued that nothing but the reservations mentioned in the Statute may be made to declarations of acceptance. Limitations other than those stated in the Statute are regarded as 'extra-statutory', which was in excess of the conditions permitted under Article 36, paragraph 3 of the Statute, thus according to Pakistan, the Indian reservation is inapplicable and the Commonwealth reservation cannot be invoked against Pakistan.[33]

In connection with the so-called 'extra-statutory' reservations going beyond the conditions fixed in Article 36, paragraph 3 of the Statute, the Court observed that Article 36, paragraph 3 had never been regarded as laying down in an exhaustive manner conditions under which states may accept the compulsory jurisdiction of the Court. On this ground, the Court rejected the Pakistani argument that the Commonwealth reservations should be regarded as 'extra-statutory', because it contravened Article 36, paragraph 3 of the Statute.[34]

In view of the foregoing it can be stated that the positions placing limitations on making reservations to declarations of acceptance may be considered as isolated, the majority view being that, according to the generally accepted interpretation of the Statute, states have the right to attach various limitations, reservations or conditions to their declarations under the optional clause. As regards the different reservations and their relationship with the Statute, James Crawford comes to the conclusion that, since Article 36, paragraph 3, suggests that no other conditions were intended than those mentioned in the Statute, the 'process by which reservations came to be accepted is a striking case of interpretative development of Article 36 by subsequent practice'.[35]

The permissibility of reservations to declarations of acceptance and the freedom in formulating the contents thereof are similarly proved by the fact that cases are rather rare in which a state has protested against

---

[32] On this reservation, see Chapter 7, Section III.

[33] *Case concerning the Aerial Incident of 10th August 1999. ICJ Pleadings*, Memorial of the Government of Pakistan on Jurisdiction, Paras. D-E, see www.icj-cij.org/docket/files/119/8308 (accessed 13 October 2013).

[34] *Case concerning the Aerial Incident of 10th August 1999* (Jurisdiction of the Court), Judgment of 21 June 2000, *ICJ Reports 2000*, 29–30.

[35] James Crawford, 'The Legal Effect of Automatic Reservations to the Jurisdiction of the International Court' (1979), 50, *BYIL*, 63, 79.

the declaration of acceptance by another state or the limitations contained therein. One such rare case occurred in the mid-1950s, when Sweden protested against the reservation included in the Portuguese declaration of acceptance of 19 December 1955, which provided that 'The Portuguese Government reserves the right to exclude from the scope of the present declaration, at any time during its validity, any given category or categories of disputes, by notifying the Secretary-General of the United Nations and with effect from the moment of such notification.'[36] That objection had little effect, as is best evidenced by the fact that in the *Right of Passage case* the Court did not even consider the Swedish objection to the reservation included in the Portuguese declaration of acceptance, although it examined the validity of the Portuguese declaration.

In point of fact, objections by other declarant states to reservations to declarations of acceptance have only been raised in concrete cases where states have tried, in the form of preliminary objections, to challenge reservations invoked by the opponent party.

The question of the limits and the permissibility of certain reservations arose in the jurisprudence of the International Court in several cases, including – first of all in the 1950s – the *Case of Certain Norwegian Loans,* the *Interhandel case,* the *Right of Passage case*, and recently the *Case concerning Fisheries Jurisdiction* (Spain v. Canada). It should be emphasized that the legal problems emerging in these cases were not the same. In the *Case of Certain Norwegian Loans*[37] and the *Interhandel*

---

[36] For the Swedish declaration, see *Right of Passage over Indian Territory, ICJ Pleadings*, vol. I, 217. In its declaration, Sweden stated that

> in its opinion the cited condition in reality signifies that Portugal has not bound itself to accept the jurisdiction of the Court with regard to any dispute or any category of disputes. The condition nullifies the obligation intended by the wording of Art. 36, para. 2, of the Statute where it is said that the recognition of the jurisdiction of the Court shall be 'compulsory *ipso facto*'. For the stated reason, the Swedish Government must consider the cited condition as incompatible with a recognition of the 'Optional Clause' of the Statute of the International Court of Justice.

[37] The dispute was around certain Norwegian loans issued on the French and other foreign markets in the 19th century. These loans were floated between 1885 and 1909, but the bonds contained a gold clause. The convertibility into gold of notes of the Bank of Norway had been suspended on various dates since 1914 and a Norwegian law of 1923 provided for the postponement of payments where the creditor refused to accept payment in Bank of Norway notes on the basis of

case[38] the so-called Connally reservation (or subjective reservation of domestic jurisdiction) was the subject of the debate, a reservation which, according to most writers of international law, is contrary to the Statute and the very purpose of the optional clause system.[39] In the *Right of Passage case*, the subject of contestation was a reservation permitting the withholding of the jurisdicition conferred on the Court with immediate effect. However, in the *Fisheries Jurisdiction case,*[40] the reservation in question belonged to a different category; it was a valid reservation relating to conservation measures with respect to the sea,[41] and, there is no question that Canada was entitled to attach that reservation to its declaration of acceptance. In that case, one of the crucial issues was whether the Canadian measures against the Spanish vessel Estai, which implied – acccording to Spain – the use of force,

---

their nominal gold value. Between 1925 and 1955 there was diplomatic correspondence between France and Norway, since the French Government provided diplomatic protection to the French holders of the bonds involved, requesting the Court to adjudge that the above-mentioned loans stipulate in gold the amount of the borrower's obligation and the borrower was able to only discharge the substance of his debt by the payment of the gold value of the coupons and redeemed bonds.

[38] In 1957 Switzerland submitted an application to the Court against the United States of America relating to a dispute which had arisen with regard to the claim by Switzerland concerning the restitution by the United States of the assets of the Interhandel Company, vested in the United States during World War II. The application referred to the declarations in which both parties had accepted the compulsory jurisdiction of the Court.

[39] On the Connally reservation, see Chapter 8, Section I.

[40] In 1995, Spain filed an application instituting proceedings against Canada with respect to a dispute relating to the Canadian Coastal Fishing Protection Act, as amended on 12 May 1994, and the rules of application of that Act, and measures taken by the Canadian authorities on the basis of the above-mentioned Act, including the pursuit, boarding and seizure on the high seas of a Spanish fishing vessel – named Estai – flying the Spanish flag. The Applicant invoked as the basis of the Court's jurisdiction the declarations of acceptance of both States. It should be mentioned that two days prior to the above-mentioned measures against the Spanish ship, on 10 May 1994, Canada made a new declaration of acceptance and added a new reservation under subpara. 2(d) further excluding from the jurisdiction of the Court:

> disputes arising out of or concerning conservation and management measures taken by Canada with respect to vessels fishing in the NAFO Regulatory Area, as defined in the Convention on Future Multilateral Co-operation in the Northwest Atlantic Fisheries, 1978, and the enforcement of such measures.

[41] On the reservation, see Chapter 7, Section VI.

was within the sphere of the reservation attached to the declaration, or as Spain contended, 'Canada's reservation is invalid or inoperative by reason of incompatibility with the Court's Statute, the Charter of the United Nations and with international law.'

The Canadian reservation provoked a lively debate both in the literature of international law and in the Court, which was reflected in the opinions appended to the judgment.[42] Some of these opinions, especially those of Vice-President Weeramantry and Judge Bedjaoui suggest that there are certain inherent limits to the freedom of states to insert reservations in their declarations of acceptance.[43] With that connection, it's worth quoting a paragraph from Vice-President Weeramantry's dissenting opinion, who rightly stated that

> … any matter that arises for adjudication within optional clause territory would be governed strictly by the rules of the United Nations Charter and the Statute of the Court. One cannot contract out of them by reservations, however framed. The basic principles of international law hold sway within this haven of legality, and cannot be displaced at the wish of the consenting State.[44]

III SPECIFIC FEATURES OF RESERVATIONS TO DECLARATIONS OF ACCEPTANCE

The freedom to accept compulsory jurisdiction with reservations or limitations has been recognized not only in the literature of international law, but also by the two International Courts. Where a legal dispute involved limitations on, or reservations to, a declaration of acceptance, the majority of judges have accepted the limitation and not dealt with the question of admissibility. They have never contested the permissibility of reservations to declarations of acceptance and, as will be discussed later, confined themselves to inquiring into the compatibility of certain reservations with the Statute and the optional clause system.

---

42 President Schwebel, Judge Oda, Koroma and Kooijmans appended separate opinions to the Judgment, while Vice-President Weeramantry, Judges Bedjaoui, Ranjeva, Vereshchetin and Judge *ad hoc* Torres Bernárdez appended dissenting opinions to the Judgment of the Court.

43 See also Mariko Kawano, 'The Optional Clause and the Administration of Justice by the Court' in Ando-McWhinney-Wolfrum (2002) 425.

44 *Fisheries Jurisdiction case* (Spain v. Canada), (Jurisdiction of the Court), Judgment of 4 December 1998, Dissenting Opinion of Vice-President Weeramantry, *ICJ Reports 1998*, 501.

The position of the International Court of Justice on the admissibility of reservations or limitations is perhaps reflected most clearly in the Court's judgment in the *Case concerning Military and Paramilitary Activities in and against Nicaragua*, whereby the Court held that declarations accepting its compulsory jurisdiction

> are facultative, unilateral engagements, that States are absolutely free to make it or not to make. In making the declarations a State is equally free either to do so unconditionally and without limit of time for its duration, or to qualify it with conditions or reservations.[45]

The same principle was reaffirmed by the Court in the *Fisheries Jurisdiction case*, stating 'that States enjoy a wide liberty in formulating, limiting, modifying and terminating their declarations of acceptance of the compulsory jurisdiction of the Court under Article 36, paragraph 2, of the Statute.'[46]

Regarding the special features of reservations attached to declarations of acceptance, one should take into consideration the following:

(a) Reservations or limitations included in declarations of acceptance differ from reservations to treaties primarily because in the case of declarations of acceptance there is no treaty-like text which the contracting parties have agreed upon in the course of the elaboration of the instrument and which the state making a reservation wishes to depart from. So what is involved here is not the exclusion or amendment of a provision which was adopted by the contracting parties and furthermore departing from that provision would make it necessary to obtain the consent of other states parties to the treaty.[47] When making declarations of acceptance under the

---

[45] *Case concerning Military and Paramilitary Activities in and against Nicaragua* (Jurisdiction of the Court and Admissibility of the Application), Judgment of 26 November 1984, *ICJ Reports 1984*, 418.

[46] *Fisheries Jurisdiction case* (Spain v. Canada), (Jurisdiction of the Court), Judgment of 4 December 1998, *ICJ Reports 1998*, 452.

[47] In this context we have in mind acceptance of reservations and eventual objections to them. At first sight it might even be asked (chiefly when one is not fully conscious of the specific features of the optional clause system) whether Art. 36, paras. 2 and 3 of the Statute (notably the optional clause itself) may not be regarded as a kind of 'basic text' which states may exclude, amend, etc. by reservations to declarations of acceptance. Such an approach is mistaken by all means. Art. 36, paras. 2 and 3, of the Statute – as the text of a treaty adopted by the contracting parties, which a state may depart from by reservation – could

optional clause, states are completely free, as has been shown by more than nine decades of practice, to do so, in determining the obligations they assume in their declarations and the conditions they attach to them. This was expressed in the Court's finding in the *Fisheries Jurisdiction case*, in which the Court held that:

> Conditions or reservations thus do not by their terms derogate from a wider acceptance already given. Rather, they operate to define the parameters of the State's acceptance of the compulsory jurisdiction of the Court.[48]

(b) Owing to the principle of reciprocity, which can be considered to be a fundamental element of the optional clause system,[49] another feature of reservations to declarations of acceptance is that a reservation operates to modify the scope of the Court's compulsory jurisdiction not only for the declarant state, but, in principle, also for the other states parties to the optional clause system, whenever a state party to the system submits to the Court a dispute with a state, which made reservations or limitations to its declaration of acceptance. The principle of reciprocity means that the reservation or limitation made by the applicant state can be used against it by the respondent state and vice versa. All this carries an element of uncertainty, because a state party to the optional clause system is not in a position to know beforehand whether in a future dispute it might be more beneficial or unbeneficial having reservations or limitations included in its own declaration of acceptance or accepting reservations or limitations joined to the declaration of another state party to the system. This possibility is undoubtedly not foreign to treaty law either. Thus, the reservations or limitations included in declarations of acceptance, serve to secure a possibility to evade those certain unforeseen, or perhaps very much foreseen, issues in disputes which are submitted to the Court's decision.

One can state that it is not so far from the truth in supposing that another factor behind the rather rare practice of raising objections to reservations or limitations by states parties to the optional clause system, is perhaps

---

become of relevance, if the Statute provided for the compulsory jurisdiction of the Court, which states would be free to 'contract out' of.

[48] *Fisheries Jurisdiction case* (Jurisdiction of the Court), Judgment of 4 December 1998, *ICJ Reports 1998*, 453.

[49] On reciprocity see Chapter 6.

the fact that the exclusion of certain disputes from compulsory jurisdiction meets with approval by other states parties to the system. Of course, all this is very difficult to exemplify, but it can easily be supposed that, for instance, reservations excluding disputes connected with certain armed conflicts can be placed in this category and preventing the submission to the Court's decision of these disputes meets with the approval of other states involved in the particular armed conflict.

Numerous instances could be cited in respect of a reservation or limitation attached by a state to its declaration of acceptance being subsequently 'advantageous' or 'disadvantageous' to another state party to the optional clause system. In fact, the situation as to when the reservation or limitation inserted in a declaration will result in advantage or disadvantage to another party of the system is likely to vary from case to case. For an example of advantageous situation, one can refer to the case when the respondent state in its preliminary objection invokes a reservation attached to the declaration of acceptance of the applicant state and the objection is accepted by the Court. The best known case in point is the *Certain Norwegian Loans case*, in which Norway as the respondent invoked the limitation contained in the applicant state's (France) declaration of acceptance, modelled on the highly controversial subjective reservation to domestic jurisdiction, and the Court accepted the Norwegian objection and held that it – acting as the Court – was without jurisdiction.[50]

IV CLASSIFICATION OF RESERVATIONS ATTACHED TO DECLARATIONS OF ACCEPTANCE

Most authors in the literature on international law differentiate between three kinds of limitations joined to declarations of acceptance: specifically reservations *ratione personae, ratione materiae* and *ratione temporis* depending on whether the limitations cite personal, material or temporal factors in their exclusion from the scope of compulsory jurisdiction.[51]

---

[50] See the judgment of the Court on the preliminary objections. *Case of Certain Norwegian Loans,* Judgment of 6 July 1957, *ICJ Reports 1957*, 9–28.

[51] Cf. J.G. Merrills, 'The Optional Clause Revisited' (1993) 64, *BYIL*, 197–244. Renata Szafarz refers to other groups as well, thus to *ratio decidendi* and *ratione fori* reservations. Cf. Renata Szafarz, *The Compulsory Jurisdiction of the International Court of Justice.* Martinus (Nijhoff Publishers 1993) 55–6 and 57–8; Stanimir A. Alexandrov, *Reservations in Unilateral Declarations Accepting the Compulsory Jurisdiction of the International Court of Justice* (Martinus

The majority of reservations joined to the declarations of acceptances are *ratione materiae* limitations, excluding from the Court's compulsory jurisdiction special disputes or disputes relating to certain subject matters. There is a wide variety of these limitations and the main types are the following: reservations excluding those disputes which should be settled by other methods of peaceful settlement, reservations relating to hostilities and armed conflicts, reservations excluding disputes relating to territorial sovereignty, reservations on environmental disputes, limitations affecting constitutional questions, disputes relating to a specific treaty or specific treaties, reservations on foreign debts and liabilities, reservations on questions of domestic jurisdiction, etc.

Already between the two world wars reservations appeared excluding disputes between certain states, which are called *ratione personae* limitations. These limitations are referring either to a specially named state or states, or it could be that the reservation is formed in a rather general way, without mentioning by name any state or states, but referring to a special group of states. These limitations concern states having special relations with the declarant state which could be either very close contacts (e.g. belonging to the same association of sovereign nations like the Commonwealth of Nations – the best-known variant of this type of reservation is the so-called Commonwealth reservation) or states being on bad terms (unfriendly relations). As a consequence of these reservations, the compulsory jurisdiction of the Court could not be applied between two states although both are parties to the optional clause system. A special group of *ratione personae* reservations are those limitations which exclude disputes with non-sovereign states or territories. It is difficult to understand the ratio of these reservations since according to Article 34, paragraph 1, 'Only States may be parties in cases before the Court'.

The third class of reservations are limitations *ratione temporis*, which are based on Article 36, paragraph 3, of the Statute providing that the declarations may be made '… for a certain time'. On the basis that provision declaration of acceptance could be made either for a *fixed period or an indefinite duration.* The first group of declarations contain a clause fixing the period of validity. The declarations for an indefinite or unlimited duration are made either without reference to duration, or they provide for the duration, or the declaration declares that it remains in force until notice of termination or withdrawal. It should be mentioned

Nijhoff Publishers 1995); Kolb (2013), 464–71. The different class of reservations will be dealt in Chapters 7–8.

that states developed several variants of clauses concerning the duration of declarations of acceptance, and there are reservations combining fixed and indefinite duration. One could consider as a *ratione temporis* limitation those reservations which are excluding the retroactive effect of the instrument, or disputes arising at the time of war, as well as those seeking to prevent surprise applications.

In the case of some reservations their classification depends largely on the wording or formulation of the given reservation, for example in the case of limitations aiming to exclude from compulsory jurisdiction the events of war or hostilities. If the declaration is referring to disputes relating to events of war or hostilities then it could be considered as a reservation of *ratione materiae*; however, if the reservation provides for disputes arising *at the time* of war or even more precisely determines the dates of the events of war or hostilities, then it is a reservation *ratione temporis.*

One could use other classifications of reservations as well, for example Arangio-Ruiz differentiates between horizontal and vertical reservations.[52] The Italian professor calls 'horizontal' reservations the limitations *ratione materiae, ratione personae, ratione loci* and *ratione temporis*, because these clauses are concerned with distinctions between categories of state-to-state disputes, namely relating to disputes arising at the level of international relations. According to Arangio-Ruiz, belonging to this category are such old reservations regarding national honour, vital interest[53] etc. 'Vertical' reservations are those which are intended to exclude disputes pertaining to the jurisdiction or competence of national authorities, and include constitutional questions, questions of domestic legislation, issues reserved for national tribunals, disputes relating to the sovereignty or independence of the state. These reservations exclude from international consideration or decision matters, those disputes relating not to inter-state relations but to national law between private parties, or between state organs and private parties.[54]

---

52 Cf. Gaetano Arangio-Ruiz, 'The plea of domestic jurisdiction before the International Court of Justice: substance or procedure?' in Vaugham Lowe and Malgosia Fitzmaurice (eds), *Fifty years of the International Court of Justice*. Essays in honour of Sir Robert Jennings (Grotius Publications CUP 1996) 460.

53 Arbitration agreements concluded in the 19th century often included clauses to the effect that arbitral settlement was not to apply to questions affecting the 'vital interests', 'national honour', 'independence', etc. of states.

54 Arangio-Ruiz (1996) 460.

In the following chapters there will be a division between two categories of reservations, i.e. there are 'generally recognized' reservations, which could be considered as accepted by the international community of states, including reservations to declarations of acceptance which are recognized or approved by individual states. The other group of reservations consists of the so-called disputed reservations which undermine the optional clause system and make illusionary the acceptance of compulsory jurisdiction – these limitations will be called 'destructive reservations'.

5. The legal character of the optional clause system

The question concerning the legal character of the optional clause system deserves attention not only because it embodies a theoretical issue, but also because it is of great practical relevance, considering that the answers to be given to a number of important questions regarding declarations of acceptance – such as the rules governing the modification or withdrawal of declarations, the legal effects of reservations and the limitations attached to declarations, interpretation of declarations, etc. – depend on how one looks at the legal character of the optional clause system.

Considering the literature on international law, there are two basic ideas to be distinguished when discussing the legal character of the optional clause system. Both points of view start from the position that states recognize the Court's compulsory jurisdiction by unilateral declarations. However, a difference between the two approaches is revealed upon an appreciation of the system resulting from these declarations. One view emphasizes the unilateral nature of the optional clause system, while the other conceives the relations as being like those between states accepting the compulsory jurisdiction of the Court in a treaty-like relationship. As an extra third category of opinions, one could even highlight those authors who argue that the relation between states established by their declarations is a *sui generis* international engagement having bilateral and multilateral elements. Proponents of either the unilateral or the treaty-like nature views cite various decisions of the two International Courts, each of which undoubtedly contains a sentence, or half phrase, isolated from its context, that may appear to support one or the other point of view.

The problem of the legal character of the optional clause system is put by Anand in this way:

> The question is whether such an 'international engagement' is constitutionally to be regarded as founded upon a unilateral legislative act done *vis-à-vis* the Court, or as founded upon a bilateral, consensual transaction effected by the

> joining together of the declarations of any given pair of states through the Optional Clause.[1]

The uncertainty with respect to the relations established by declarations of acceptance is well reflected in the separate opinion of Judge Sir Robert Jennings submitted in the *Case concerning Military and Paramilitary Activities in and against Nicaragua,* stating that the declarations of acceptance establish some sort of relationship with other states that have made declarations; but it is not easy to say what kind of legal relationship it is.[2]

According to the British judge, that relationship is created by a great variety of unilateral declarations, all having the common element of being made within the framework of Article 36, paragraph 2, of the Court's Statute.

> The declarations are statements of intention; and statement of intention made in a quite formal way. Obviously, however, they do not amount to treaties or contracts; or at least, if one says they are treaties, or contracts, one immediately has to go on to say they are a special kind of treaty, or contract, partaking only of some of the rules normally applicable to such matters.[3]

Regarding the declarations of acceptance themselves, one can say that there is a common understanding that these are unilateral acts. Torres Bernárdez rightly pointed out that 'These declarations cannot be considered, either notionally or legally, as bilateral or multilateral instruments, not even with respect to the area of coincidence of the various consents.'[4] According to Robert Kolb an optional declaration is legally a hybrid.[5]

---

[1] R.P. Anand, *Compulsory Jurisdiction of the International Court of Justice.* (revised 2nd edn, Hope India Publications, Delhi, 2008) 143.

[2] *Case concerning Military and Paramilitary Activities in and against Nicaragua,* Jurisdiction of the Court and Admissibility of the Application, Judgment of 26 November 1984, Separate Opinion of Judge Sir Robert Jennings, *ICJ Reports* 1984, 547.

[3] *Id.*

[4] Santiago Torres Bernárdez, 'Reciprocity in the System of Compulsory Jurisdiction and in Other Modalities of Contentious Jurisdiction Exercised by the International Court of Justice' in Emmanuel G. Bello and Prince Bola A. Ajibola (eds) *Essays in Honour of Judge Taslim Olawale Elias* (Martinus Nijhoff Publishers 1992) vol. I, 291, 293.

[5] Kolb (2013) 454.

The Permanent Court in the *Phosphates in Morocco case*, held that

> The declaration, of which the ratification was deposited by the French Government on April 25th, 1931 is a unilateral act by which that Government accepted the Court's compulsory jurisdiction.[6]

In the *Anglo-Iranian Oil Co. case*, the International Court of Justice took a similarly clear stand, saying that

> … the text of the Iranian Declaration is not a treaty text resulting from negotiations between two or more States. It is the result of unilateral drafting by the Government of Iran, …[7]

In the *Norwegian Loans case* the International Court referred as well to the unilateral character of declarations of acceptance.[8] In the *Nicaragua case,* the Court came to address rather extensively the legal character of the declarations of acceptance and the admissibility of reservations to them, emphasizing:

> Declarations of acceptance of the compulsory jurisdiction of the Court are facultative, unilateral engagements, that States are absolutely free to make or not to make.[9]

After a few lines, the Court went on to pronounce that:

> In fact, the declarations, even though are unilateral acts, establish a series of bilateral engagements with other states accepting the same obligation of compulsory jurisdiction, in which the conditions, reservations and time-limit clauses are taken into consideration.[10]

The cited statements prove that the unilateral character of declarations of acceptance was affirmed by both International Courts.

---

[6] *Phosphates in Morocco* (Preliminary Objections), Judgment of 14 June 1938, *PCIJ Series*, A/B. No. 74, 23.

[7] *Anglo-Iranian Oil Co. case* (Preliminary Objection), Judgment of 22 July 1952, *IC.J Reports* 1952, 105.

[8] Cf. *Case of Certain Norwegian Loans,* Judgment of 6 July 1957, *ICJ Reports* 1957, 23.

[9] *Case concerning Military and Paramilitary Activities in and against Nicaragua* (Jurisdiction of the Court and Admissibility of the Application), Judgment of 26 November 1984, *ICJ Reports 1984*, 418.

[10] *Id.*

I THE CONTRACTUAL CHARACTER OF THE SYSTEM

The view that a multilateral treaty-like relationship is established between those states making declarations of acceptance is widely held in the literature of international law. It should be added that, in this case, the contractual relationship has been formulated by several related instruments rather than by a single one. There is no doubt about the well-known postulate of international treaty law that a treaty can be embodied not only in a single instrument, but in more related instruments as well.[11] Obviously, if the optional clause system is seen as a contractual regime, it is to be included in the latter category.

In the jurisprudence of the two International Courts, it is the *Electricity Company of Sofia and Bulgaria case* and the *Right of Passage case* that are usually relied upon for justifying the contractual character.

In the *Electricity Company of Sofia case*, the Permanent Court of International Justice referred to the date of the 'establishment of the juridical bond' between two states, Belgium and Bulgaria, under Article 36 of the Statute.[12]

The other case frequently mentioned in connection with contractual character, concerns the *Right of Passage case*. However, this case, which will be considered at a later stage, can be invoked to bear out the contractual character just as it can be cited in support of the unilateral character. In this case, the International Court of Justice certainly had in mind some sort of a contractual relationship between states parties to the optional clause system, declaring that:

> The contractual relations between the Parties and the compulsory jurisdiction of the Court resulting therefrom are established '*ipso facto* and without special agreement', by the fact of the making of the Declaration.[13]

Statements about the contractual character of the optional clause system, established by declarations of acceptance, are also to be found in the separate and dissenting opinions of the members of the two International Courts.

---

[11] Cf. Art. 2. of the Vienna Convention of 1969 on the Law of Treaties.

[12] *The Electricity Company of Sofia and Bulgaria case* (Preliminary Objection), Judgment of 4 April 1939, *PCIJ 1939 A/B*, No. 77, 81.

[13] *Case concerning Right of Passage over Indian Territory* (Preliminary Objection), Judgment of 26 November 1957, *ICJ Reports 1957*, 146.

At the time of the Permanent Court in his separate opinion submitted with respect to the *Electricity Company of Sofia and Bulgaria case*, Judge Anzilotti wrote:

> As a result of these Declarations, an agreement came into existence between the two States accepting the compulsory jurisdiction of the Court, in conformity with Article 36 of the Statute and subject to the limitations and conditions resulting from the declarations …[14]

More than ten years after the *Electricity Company of Sofia case,* in the *Anglo-Iranian Oil Co. case*, Judge Alvarez, when answering the question as to whether the Iranian declaration of acceptance (which he termed, not incidentally, a declaration of 'adherence') was unilateral or bilateral in character, wrote:

> … the Declaration is a multilateral act of a special character; it is the basis of a treaty made by Iran with the States, which had already adhered and with those which would subsequently adhere to the provisions of Art. 36, para. 2, of the Statute of the Court.[15]

Also, in his separate opinion given in the *Case of Certain Norwegian Loans*, Sir Hersh Lauterpacht touched briefly upon the legal character of the declarations of acceptance. That what was stated by the Court regarding the unilateral nature of the declarations of acceptance in the *Anglo-Iranian Oil Co. case*, was construed by Judge Lauterpacht to mean:

> … no more than that the declaration is the result not of negotiations but of unilateral drafting. Whether it is a treaty or a unilateral declaration, it is – if it is to be treated as a legal text providing a basis for the jurisdiction of the Court – a manifestation of intention to create reciprocal rights and obligations.[16]

Lauterpacht went on to compare the optional clause to a multilateral treaty concluded under the auspices of the United Nations General

---

[14] *The Electricity Company of Sofia and Bulgaria case* (Preliminary Objection), Judgment 4 April 1939 Separate Opinion by M. Anzilotti, *PCIJ*, 1939, A/B No. 77. 87.

[15] *Anglo-Iranian Oil Co. case* (Preliminary Objection), Judgment 22 July 1952, Dissenting Opinion of Judge Alvarez, *ICJ Reports 1952*, 125.

[16] *Case of certain Norwegian Loans,* Judgment of 6 July 1957, Separate Opinion of Judge Sir Hersch Lauterpacht, *ICJ Reports 1957*, 49.

Assembly, and he visualized the declarations of acceptance as an accession to a multilateral treaty elaborated by the General Assembly.[17]

In the *South West Africa case* Judges Sir Percy Spender and Sir Gerald Fitzmaurice in their joint dissenting opinion wrote that

> The quasi-treaty character which 'optional clause' declarations made under paragraph 2 of Article 36 of the Statute are sometimes said to possess, would arise solely from the multiplicity of these declarations and their interlocking character, which gives them a bilateral or multilateral aspect. A single such declaration, if it stood quite alone, could not be an international *agreement*.[18]

Then, the two judges stressed that declarations of acceptance can in no way be identified with 'treaties or conventions', referred to in Article 36, paragraph 1 of the Statute or there would have been no need for paragraph 2.[19]

Again, in a separate opinion given in the *Nicaragua case*, Judge Mosler adverted essentially to the contractual character when he said that the basis of operation for the optional clause is 'the consensual bond', and 'that comes into being at the time at which another state deposits its declaration'.[20]

Several prominent writers on international law refer to treaty-like relations between states that are parties to the optional clause system. Between the two world wars, Fachiri wrote that the declarations of acceptance are 'in form unilateral, the rights and obligations to which it gives rise are multilateral.'[21]

Hans Kelsen in his monumental work on the United Nations asserted that:

> The unilateral declaration of one state together with the unilateral declaration of another state constitute an agreement. This agreement, it is true, has not the character of a 'special agreement' within the meaning of the term used in Article 36, paragraph 1. But it is a general agreement insofar as the states by

---

[17] *Id.*

[18] *South West Africa case* (Preliminary Objections), Judgment of 21 December 1962, Joint Dissenting Opinion of Sir Percy Spender and Sir Gerald Fitzmaurice, *ICJ Reports 1962*, 476.

[19] *Id.*

[20] *Case concerning Military and Paramilitary Activities in and against Nicaragua* (Jurisdiction of the Court and Admissibility of the Application), Judgment of 26 November 1984, Separate Opinion of Judge Mosler, *ICJ Reports 1984*, 466.

[21] Alexander Pandelli Fachiri, 'Repudiation of the Optional Clause' (1939), 20, *BYIL*, 52, 56.

> making the declaration referred to in Article 36, paragraph 2, in relation to one another, agree to recognize the jurisdiction of the Court in all legal disputes, in case one party brings the dispute before the Court.[22]

Herbert Briggs similarly argued for the contractual character, and, in a lecture delivered at the Hague Academy of International Law, said that a declaration of acceptance:

> … is not a contractual engagement undertaken by the declarant State with the Court. It is in the nature of a general offer, made by declarant to all other States accepting the same obligation, to recognize as Respondent the jurisdiction of the Court, subject to the limitations specified in the offer.[23]

In the same lecture, Professor Briggs also spoke about a 'consensual bond accepting compulsory jurisdiction' existing between two declarant states.[24]

In connection with the views propounding the contractual character, Iglesias Buigues writes that, in the opinion of most authors, declarations are unilateral acts, which nevertheless have contractual effects (*effects contractuels*) in the sense that declarations contain sufficient elements for them to produce effects of a contractual character, albeit they remain unilateral in nature.[25] According to Iglesias Buigues, it is the parties' agreement on the Court's jurisdiction that forms the basis of the contractual relation. This is brought into being by the fact that the declarations are actually offers, made by the declaring states to each other, constituting a chain of offers and acceptances thereof, in the sense that when a state deposits its declaration with the Secretary-General it is both accepting the offers of those states – that are parties to the optional clause system – which have made declarations and submitting, on its part, an offer to any other state making a subsequent declaration.[26] According to the author, the real content of this agreement is determined

---

22 Kelsen (1951) 521–2.

23 H.W. Briggs, 'Reservations to the Acceptance of Compulsory Jurisdiction of the International Court of Justice' (1958), *RCADI*, vol. 093, 229, 245.

24 *Id.* 267.

25 Cf. J.L. Iglesias Buigues, 'Les déclarations d'acceptation de la juridiction obligatoire de la Cour internationale de Justice: Leur nature et leur interprétation.' (1972), 23, *ÖzöR*, 255–88, 259.

26 *Id.* 266–7.

when the declarations are applied in a concrete case, and the degree to which the declarations of two states overlap becomes apparent in that event.[27]

The view that accession to the optional clause system is an offer and an acceptance of the earlier offers, is not foreign to the members of the Court either. That idea was expressed by Vice-President Badawi in his dissenting opinion in the *Right of Passage case* in the 1950s, and was formulated again more than four decades later by Vice-President Weeramantry in the *Case concerning the Land and Maritime Boundary between Cameroon and Nigeria.*

According to Vice-President Badawi, Article 36 of the Statute with the words '*ipso facto* and without *special* agreement' 'stresses the conventional character of Declarations and it confirms that character by the expression "in relation to any other State accepting the same obligation".'[28] Some lines further he emphasizes the importance of the offers and the acceptances thereof with respect to the declarations made under the optional clause by saying 'But what creates the agreement here, as in every other meeting of wills, is always the basic idea of offer and acceptance'.[29] Vice-President Badawi stresses that the system of declarations of acceptance constitutes a contract by correspondence between the declarant state and the other states with the intermediary being the Secretary-General.[30]

In the *Case concerning the Land and Maritime Boundary between Cameroon and Nigeria*, Vice-President Weeramantry analysed the question of offers and acceptances and, comparing the national legislation of different states, came to the conclusion that the acceptance of an offer was necessary for a contract to come into being and a contract was made only if the offeror had been notified of the acceptance of his offer. In other words, in the case of mutual obligations created on the basis of Article 36, paragraph 2 the offeror must be informed as to whether or not his offer has been accepted and there can be no consensus in the absence of the communication of an acceptance.[31]

---

27 *Id.* 265.

28 *Case concerning Right of Passage over Indian Territory* (Preliminary Objections), Judgment of 26 November, 1957, Dissenting Opinion of Vice-President Badawi, *ICJ Reports 1954*, 154.

29 *Id.* 155.

30 *Id.* 155–6.

31 *Case concerning the Land and Maritime Boundary between Cameroon and Nigeria* (Preliminary Objections), Judgment of 11 June 1998, Dissenting Opinion of Vice-President Weeramentry, *ICJ Reports 1998*, 370–73.

The contractual character of the network of declarations of acceptance is emphasized by both Edith Brown Weiss[32] and Stanimir Alexandrov. In support of the contractual character, Alexandrov refers to the origin and treaty-like character of the optional clause, the Secretary-General's role in receiving and registering the notices of declarations made under the optional clause, and the practice of states in the making their declarations.[33]

After describing the contractual character of the optional clause system, Alexandrov refers to certain specific features of declarations of acceptance which include the following:

- the declarations are not treaty texts resulting from negotiations;
- unilateral declarations include an element of vulnerability and unpredictability;
- the mutual consent of parties under the optional clause is determined on the basis of reciprocity;
- obligations assumed by declarations of acceptance arise only when a special dispute is submitted to the Court.[34]

Alexandrov sees the elements of uncertainty due to the fact that, as they involve *erga omnes* obligations, the declarant state runs the risk, as the Court found in the *Right of Passage case*, of being immediately sued by a newly declarant state. The Bulgarian author exemplifies the elements of vulnerability and uncertainty by highlighting the *Nicaragua case*, claiming that in making its declaration accepting the Court's compulsory jurisdiction, the United States was not in a position to foresee that its relations with Nicaragua would worsen so much as to cause that state to submit an action against the Washington government before the International Court of Justice.[35]

One can argue that the said elements are in fact an attribute not only of the optional clause system. It may happen in the case of any treaty that relations between the contracting parties come to deteriorate markedly over time and that, in the space of perhaps a few years, let alone decades, the relationship of two states may undergo a change precluding the application of a treaty they concluded earlier. A long list of examples could be cited of interstate relations in order to illustrate other similar

---

32 Edith Brown Weiss, 'Reciprocity and the Optional Clause' in Damrosch (1987) 95–6.

33 Cf. Alexandrov (1995) 12–13.

34 Cf. *Id.* 13–16.

35 Cf. *Id.* 14.

situations. In practice, however, states take care to safeguard their interests in a considerable part of related treaties, and if relations between the contracting parties come to deteriorate to the extent that the parties do not find it desirable to apply a treaty *inter se*, they usually take steps to denounce, terminate or amend the treaty concerned.

With respect to declarations of acceptance, such 'cautious' steps are rather rare, and even when relations between two states tend to worsen, with the exception of a few cases, measures aren't taken to avoid the submission of a dispute to the Court under the optional clause. What is more frequent, however, is that only when a 'delicate' dispute is already before the Court do the states try to hamper the Court's decision-making process, among other things by raising preliminary objections[36] or by resorting to amend or terminate their declarations of acceptance.[37]

One should add also that the deterioration of interstate relations – as an unforeseeable element in connection with declarations of acceptance – is not so strange because these declarations relate to the acceptance of the compulsory jurisdiction of an international judicial forum, which is clearly tantamount to states reckoning with the emergence of disputes and having in mind a future resort to the judicial forum for the settlement of their disputes. Therefore, the element of uncertainty as a source of problems ensuing from the deterioration of relations should not be over-emphasized, since in the case of declarations of acceptance, states – by making such declarations – count a priori on the emergence of future disputes, which entails to some degree, as it were, the deterioration of relations between the parties. Of course, the picture varies from case to case with regard to the degree to which relations between the parties worsen, before they submit their disputes to the International Court.

Anyway, from the foregoing it becomes clear that the conception of the optional clause system as a contractual relation based on unilateral declarations is rather widespread both among the members of the Court and the writers of international law.

II THE INTERMEDIATE POSITION

As another apprehension of the legal character of the optional clause system, one should mention a so-called transitory view and according to Renata Szafarz:

---

[36] On the preliminary objections, see Chapter 10.

[37] On these questions, see Chapter 9.

> … it is a *sui generis* or quasi-treaty (which is the same thing) legal structure which consists of contractual and unilateral elements and which establishes a set of parallel bilateral relationships. Every relationship consists of contractual (both multilateral and bilateral) elements and a unilateral element. The provision contained in Article 36(2) of the ICJ Statute constitutes the multilateral element. Owing to the reciprocity principle reservations constitute the bilateral element. Non-symmetrical formal conditions contained in declarations constitute the unilateral element.[38]

Indisputably this approach reflects to some extent the reality; however, the inclusion of the Statute in the network of obligations is misleading, also giving a false picture regarding the legal character of the optional clause system. When making declarations of acceptance, the states are assuming obligations among themselves, and similarly when they are accepting a treaty containing a compromisory clause they are conferring jurisdiction on the Court – in both cases the Statute does not form a direct part of the network of obligations. It is true that the Statute provides the basis for declarations made under the optional clause, defining the basic elements of the system; however, the actual content of the obligations is determined by the declarant states themselves. The states in making their declarations of acceptance do not establish a contract with the Court, since the legal bound was already set up when they become a party to the Statute, but *they do establish a network of obligations in addition to that assumed upon signing and ratifying the Statute itself.*

Rosenne's approach can be classified as a transitory view as well, because the Israeli professor terms the optional clause system as *sui generis* international obligations. He wrote that these obligations were assumed under special rules of international law and although having some affinities with the types of obligations regulated by the law of international treaties, they are not on all fours with them.[39] He refers also to the fact that, in contrast to the process of treaty-making, no negotiations take place when declarations of acceptance are made and the terms on which a state accepts the Court's compulsory jurisdiction are not a matter of negotiations but follow from a unilateral act.[40]

---

38 Szafarz (1993) 81–2.
39 Rosenne (2006) vol. II. 792.
40 *Id.* 710.

III THE UNILATERAL CHARACTER OF THE OPTIONAL CLAUSE SYSTEM – THE REJECTION OF THE CONTRACTUAL RELATION

The partisans of the unilateral character of the optional clause system refer to the drafting history of the optional clause, and call attention to the 'misleading effect' if the rules of treaty law would be applied to the system of declarations made under the optional clause.[41]

The views emphasizing the unilateral character of the optional clause system likewise invoke various decisions of the two International Courts, such as those in the *Phosphates in Morocco case*, the *Anglo-Iranian Oil Co. case*, the *Norwegian Loans case,* the *Nuclear Tests cases,* the *Nicaragua case,* the *Case concerning the Land and Maritime Boundary between Cameroon and Nigeria* and the *Fisheries Jurisdiction case* between Spain and Canada, etc.

As mentioned earlier, the *Right of Passage case* can also be invoked to support the unilateral character of the optional clause system. There is no doubt that in the judgment on the preliminary objections in this case, one can find sentences, as quoted previously, suggesting the existence of a *contractual relation* (rapport contractuel) between states parties to the optional clause system. However, regarding the process in which such a relation is established, the Court leaned to the unilateral character of the system of declarations of acceptance in both rejecting India's second preliminary objection and pointing out that the only requirement for the validity of declarations of acceptance was that the parties should deposit them with the Secretary-General, there being no further obligation such as notification to the states parties to the Statute or lapse of a specified period of time after the deposition of the declaration.[42]

All this leads one to raise questions about whether the Court, in referring to contractual relations, really had in mind a genuine contractual relation between states parties to the optional clause system. If the Court had indeed conceived the optional clause system to be a contractual relation having some characteristics borrowed from the law of treaties, then in the *Right of Passage case* it would have accepted the

---

[41] Cf. Francisco Orrego Vicuña, 'The Legal Nature of the Optional Clause and the Right of a State to Withdraw a Declaration Accepting the Compulsory Jurisdiction of the International Court of Justice' in Ando-Whinney-Wolfrum (2002) 466.

[42] *Case concerning Right of Passage over Indian Territory* (Preliminary Objections), Judgment of 26 November, 1957, *ICJ Report, 1957*, 146–7.

argument of the Indian Government and some members of the Court[43] that a declaration of acceptance not only had to be deposited with the Secretary-General, but that the Secretary-General had to transmit copies thereof to the parties to the Statute and the declaration was not valid until the Secretary-General had fulfilled this obligation. This gives rise to the question of what the Court really meant by the terms 'contractual relation' (rapport contractuel) and 'consensual bond' (lien consensuel).

At the end of the 1990s the legal character of the optional clause system had been addressed in more depth by the Court in two cases, notably the *Case concerning the Land and Maritime Boundary between Cameroon and Nigeria* and the *Fisheries Jurisdiction case.* In both cases the problem of the legal character of the optional clause system arose as a result of the question as to whether the Vienna Convention on the Law of Treaties is applicable to declarations of acceptance.

In the *Land and Maritime Boundary case*, Nigeria as respondent submitted eight preliminary objections, with the first one relating to the legal nature of the system of declarations under the optional clause. Nigeria contended that its declaration of acceptance had been a matter of public record for some 30 years. However, Cameroon's declaration was undated and had been communicated to the Secretary-General on 3 March 1994 and the Office of the Secretary-General had transmitted copies of the Cameroonian declaration to Nigeria (and presumably to other parties to the Statute) nearly a year later. Nigeria maintained, accordingly, that when Cameroon filed the application on 29 March 1994, Nigeria did not know nor was not in a position to know that Cameroon had acceded to the optional clause system.[44]

In this case with regard to the optional clause system, the Court pointed out that:

> Any State party to the Statute, in adhering to the jurisdiction of the Court in accordance with Article 36, paragraph 2, accepts jurisdiction in its relations with States previously having adhered to that clause. At the same time, it makes a standing offer to the other States party to the Statute which have not yet deposited a declaration of acceptance. The day one of those States accepts

[43] Cf. *Id.* Dissenting opinions of Vice-President Badawi and Judge Chagla, 154–63, 166–80

[44] *Case concerning the Land and Maritime Boundary between Cameroon and Nigeria.* See Chapter I of the Preliminary Objections of the Federal Republic of Nigeria, *ICJ Pleadings*, vol I, 1.5. and 1.6.

> that offer by depositing in its turn its declaration of acceptance, *the consensual bond is established and no further condition needs to be fulfilled* (my emphasis – V.L.).[45]

Thereupon ensued the situation, which the Court described in 1957, whereby the declaring states '... may at any time find itself subjected to the obligations of the Optional Clause in relation to a new Signatory as the result of the deposit by that Signatory of a Declaration of Acceptance.'[46] This notwithstanding, in the *Land and Maritime Boundary case* the Court unequivocally ruled out the requirement to give any notice to the state making an offer. This was reflected in its finding that 'There is no specific obligation in international law for States to inform other States parties to the Statute that they intend to subscribe or have subscribed to the Optional Clause.'[47] Regarding the respective case, the Court went on by stating that: 'Consequently, Cameroon was not bound to inform Nigeria that it intended to subscribe or had subscribed to the Optional Clause.'[48]

The legal character of the optional clause system in the *Fisheries Jurisdiction case* involved a difference of views between Spain and Canada about the rules on the interpretation of reservations added to declarations of acceptance.[49]

According to Spain, the interpretation of reservations attached to declarations of acceptance was subject to the law of treaties, whereas Canada underlined the unilateral nature of declarations and reservations and further contended that the reservations should be interpreted in a natural way, with particular regard to the intention of the declaring state.

For its part, the Court came out once again emphasizing the unilateral nature of declarations when it explained that such an acceptance is a

---

[45] *Case concerning the Land and Maritime Boundary between Cameroon and Nigeria* (Preliminary Objections), Judgment of 11 June 1998, *ICJ Reports 1998*, 291.

[46] *Case concerning Right of Passage over Indian Territory* (Preliminary Objections), Judgment of 26 November 1957, *ICJ Reports 1957,* 146.

[47] *Case concerning the Land and Maritime Boundary between Cameroon and Nigeria* (Preliminary Objections), Judgment of 11 June 1998, *ICJ Reports 1998*, 297.

[48] *Id.*

[49] Canada, the respondent state, challenged the Court's jurisdiction on the basis of the terms of the reservation in para. 2 (d) of the Canadian declaration of 10 May 1994. Spain contended that the Canadian reservation was invalid or inoperative by reason of incompatibility with the Court's Statute, the Charter of the United Nations and international law.

unilateral act of state sovereignty regardless of whether or not special limitations are placed on an acceptance, and it subsequently reiterated its position in the *Case concerning the Land and Maritime Boundary between Cameroon and Nigeria* six months earlier. Regarding the interpretation of declarations of acceptance, the Court held that the rules on the interpretation of declarations are not identical to those established for the interpretation of treaties by the 1969 Vienna Convention on the Law of Treaties, and 'the provisions of that Convention may only apply analogously to the extent compatible with the *sui generis* character of the unilateral acceptance of the Court's jurisdiction.'[50]

The view of the Judges was divided in that case as well. It is worth mentioning the seperate opinion of Judge Oda, in connection with the unilateral character of declarations of acceptance, who wrote that the reservations attached to the declarations,

> … must, because of the declaration's unilateral character, be interpreted not only in a natural way and in context, *but also* with particular regard for the intention of the declarant State. Any interpretation of a *respondent* State's declaration against the intention of that State will contradict the very nature of the Court's jurisdiction, because the declaration is an instrument drafted unilaterally.[51]

The foregoing goes to show clearly that, also according to some recent decisions of the International Court of Justice, declarations of acceptance are not only unilateral acts, but the system constituted by them cannot be also regarded as relations of a contractual nature.

For the appreciation of the legal character of the system established by declarations of acceptance, it is necessary to take into consideration states' practice and especially their practice in making, terminating or withdrawing declarations of acceptance as well as the Court's position regarding the issue.[52]

Both the Statutes and the Rules of Procedure of the two International Courts are silent on the withdrawal of declarations of acceptance and how states parties to the optional clause system can get rid of their obligations concerning the Court's compulsory jurisdiction; it is entirely left to the decision of the declarant state how and under what conditions it breaks free from the 'bonds' of the clause. Several states have certainly included in their declarations various provisions on termination or

---

[50] *Fisheries Jurisdiction case* (Jurisdiction of the Court), Judgment of 4 December 1998, *ICJ Reports 1998*, 453.

[51] *Id.* Separate Opinion of Judge Oda, 479.

[52] On the termination of declarations of acceptance, see Chapter 9.

withdrawal, but not a single reference to them is to be found in a non-negligible part of any of the declarations of acceptance.

It should be noted that in a considerable part of declarations such provisions don't even imply any real restriction, for what the declarant states do is no more than reserve the right to denounce their declarations with immediate effect. States have in practice availed themselves of this possibility and have often modified or terminated their declarations of acceptance with the international community taking notice of such practice. In fact, the Court itself has never taken a definitive stand on the matter, and all it did in the *Nicaragua case* was confine itself to spelling out that 'the right to termination of declarations with indefinite duration is far from established.'[53]

True, there exist quite a few declarations which contain provisions on certain time-limits, period of notice, etc., concerning the termination or withdrawal of the instruments, but it should be stressed that it is left in every case to the declarant state to decide whether or not it includes such provisions in its declaration of acceptance. Should a state choose to terminate its declaration with respect to certain conditions, e.g. a period of notice, its act amounts to nothing more than a self-limitation of its own will.

This is well illustrated by the 1946 US declaration of acceptance, which contained the clause that to 'remain in force for a period of five years and thereafter until the expiration of six months after notice may be given to terminate this declaration.' In the *Nicaragua case* the Court held that:

> In making the declaration a State is equally free either to do so unconditionally and without limit of time for its duration, or to qualify it with conditions or reservations. In particular, it may limit its effect to disputes arising after a certain date; ... or what notice (if any) will be required to terminate it.[54]

By this ruling, the Court clearly confirmed the tenet that states are free to formulate the conditons of termination with respect to their commitments regarding the Court's compulsory jurisdiction.

In contrast to the foregoing, the entry into force of treaties, as well as the conditions for their withdrawal or termination, are subject to the agreement of the contracting states determined in the course of the

---

[53] *Case concerning Military and Paramilitary Activities in and against Nicaragua* (Jurisdiction of the Court and Admissibility of the Application), Judgment of 26 November 1984, *ICJ Reports 1984*, 420.

[54] *Id.* 418.

elaboration of the treaties, or, failing relevant provisions or agreement in the treaty itself, the general rules of international law apply.[55] In the case of declarations of acceptance, as is indicated by what has gone on before, all these matters are for the declarant state to decide; the decision not being able to be restricted in any way by the will of other states or any norm of international law.

For all these reasons it would be difficult to term this system of commitments – undertaken on the basis of the optional clause – as being of a contractual character. The declaring states themselves decide on what conditions, with what reservations, limitations, etc. they accept the compulsory jurisdiction of the Court, and, as Judge Oda pointed out in his separate opinion submitted in the *Nicaragua case*,

> For a treaty containing such a clause conferring a unilateral right entirely to alter or terminate terms of the treaty with immediate effect would surely be impossible: it would not be a treaty. Yet this is now almost normal practice in declarations of acceptance of the Optional Clause.[56]

No question there is a certain kind of judicial link between the states making declarations of acceptance; however, that relationship has no treaty-like character. The states parties to the optional clause system undertake, by accession to that system, a unilateral commitment regarding the Court's jurisdiction, which could create a bilateral legal relationship at a later stage. This is activated when concrete disputes are referred to the Court, and the content of such a legal relationship is clearly determined by the conditions, reservations and other limitations, which the parties may have formulated in their respective declarations of acceptance.

---

[55] Cf. especially Arts. 24, 54 and 56 of the 1969 Vienna Convention on the Law of Treaties.

[56] *Case concerning Military and Paramilitary Activities in and against Nicaragua* (Jurisdiction of the Court and Admissibility of the Application), Judgment of 26 November 1984, Separate Opinion of Judge Oda, *ICJ Reports 1984*, 510.

6. Reciprocity and the system of optional clause declarations

I THE STATUTE ON RECIPROCITY

International law is interwoven – perhaps more profoundly than any other branch of law – due to reciprocity in the sense that rights are being coupled with certain obligations in interstate relations and there must be some sort of correlation between the rights enjoyed and obligations assumed by states.[1] First of all, this is explained because in international law states are the law-makers who are equal and well aware that they should assume certain obligations in return for their rights, and vice versa. This thesis in international law holds true not only for law-making, but also for the application and enforcement of law. There is no doubt that the principle of reciprocity is most clearly manifested in the law of treaties; however, as will be seen in this chapter, it is also a basic element of the optional clause system under the Statutes of both Courts.[2]

Reciprocity is covered by Article 36, paragraphs 2 and 3 of the Statute of the International Court of Justice providing that:

> (2) 'The States to the present Statute may at any time declare that they recognize as compulsory *ipso facto* and without special agreement, in relation to any other State accepting the same obligation, the jurisdiction of the Court …' and
> (3) 'The declarations referred to above may be made unconditionally or on condition of reciprocity on the part of several or certain States, or for a certain time.[3]

---

[1] For more detail, see M. Virally, 'Le principe de réciprocité dans le droit international contemporaire' (1967), 122, *RCADI*, vol. III, 5–101.

[2] On the application of reciprocity to declarations of acceptance and to the reservations added to these declarations, see Alexandrov (1995) 26–39; Torres Bernárdez (1992) 295–309.

[3] The Statute of the Permanent Court contained in essence the same provisions by stating that

> The Members of the League of Nations and the States mentioned in the Annex to the Covenant may, either when signing or ratifying the Protocol to

At first sight, however clear these provisions appear to be, one can detect some confusion concerning the relationship between Article 36, paragraphs 2 and 3.[4] According to Kolb the relationship between these two provisions was neither very obvious nor much clarified when the Statute was elaborated.[5] This is likely due to the fact that while both paragraphs cover reciprocity, they refer to different aspects thereof.

Article 36, paragraph 2 is unambiguously clear about what the fundamental characteristic of the optional clause system is, namely that it is a *network of additional obligations and extra rights between a group of states parties to the Statute.* In the *Anglo-Iranian Oil Company case* Judge McNair described the optional clause as being representative of 'contracting-in', and not 'contracting-out'.[6] This regime operates only in the *inter se* relations of states that have made declarations of acceptance, and not in respect of all states party to the Statute. Professor Waldock, in his study on the optional clause, describes all this as a 'fundamental lack of reciprocity' between the position of states which either do or do not make declarations of acceptance.[7] The declaring states are continuously liable to be brought compulsory before the Court; however, states not making such declarations cannot be sued before the Court unless and until they choose to initiate proceedings before the Court as plaintiff and make a declaration under the optional clause.[8]

Article 36, paragraph 3 refers to reciprocity in connection with the content of declarations of acceptance, providing that reciprocity may be stipulated in the declarations. Thus 'Reciprocity governs not only the relationship *ratione personae* between the different states concerned

---

which the present Statute is adjoined, or at a later moment, declare that they recognize as compulsory *ipso facto* and without special agreement, in relation to any other Member or State accepting the same obligation, the jurisdiction of the Court … and

The declarations referred to above may be made unconditionally or on condition of reciprocity on the part of several or certain Members or States, or for a certain time.

4 In a similar sense, see H.W.A. Thirlway, 'The Reciprocity in the Jurisdiction of the International Court' (1984) 15, *NYIL*, 98; Rosenne (2006) vol. II. 731–2; I.F. Shihata, *The Power of the International Court to Determine its Own Jurisdiction* (Martinus Nijhoff, 1965) 147.

5 Kolb (2013) 474.

6 *Anglo-Iranian Oil Co. case* (Preliminary Objection), Judgment of 22 July 1952, Individual Opinion of President McNair, *ICJ Reports 1952*, 116.

7 Cf. Waldock (1955–6) 280.

8 *Id.*

('mutuality'), but determines also the scope *ratione materiae* of the jurisdiction of the Court'.[9]

The explanation for the Statute referring twice to reciprocity is offered by the documents which are connected to the drafting of the Statute, and the double reference can, in all likelihood, be attributed to the proposals of the Brazilian jurist, Fernandes, a member of the 1920 Advisory Committee of Jurists. Fernandes thought that states were free to accept the Court's jurisdiction conditionally or unconditionally. He saw one such condition as being reciprocity in respect of certain states or a certain number of states, including certain denominated states. The Brazilian expert argued that it is impossible for a state to accept the Court's compulsory jurisdiction without knowing the states with which it is to undertake such an obligation.

Regarding Fernandes's proposals, Thirlway comes to the conclusion that the Brazilian jurist's draft sought to allow states to pick and choose its partners in the compulsory jurisdiction relationship.[10] At any rate, it was under the influence of Fernandes's proposals that the section saying that 'the declarations referred to above may be made unconditionally or on condition of reciprocity on the part of several or certain Member States or for a certain time' was inserted in the Statute of the Permanent Court of International Justice. To our knowledge, the possibility for the 'choice of partners', which was the essence of Fernandes's motion, was only used by Brazil – which included in its 1920 declaration of acceptance a formula under which its declaration of acceptance was to be effective 'as soon as it has likewise been recognized as such by two at least of the Powers permanently represented on the Council of the League of Nations'.[11]

Waldock's interpretation that Article 36, paragraph 3, refers in fact not to reciprocity is essentially in harmony with Fernandes's concept. According to the British expert, what we have here is a provision authorizing states to accept compulsory jurisdiction for a definite period of time and on condition that the Court's compulsory jurisdiction is also accepted by a certain number of states or by particular named states. Thus, in the view of Waldock this is not a real 'condition of reciprocity', but one in which a declaration will not become effective until the Court's

---

9 Christian Tomouschat, 'Article 36' in Andreas Zimmermann, Christian Tomouschat, Karin Oellers-Frahm. (eds) *The Statute of the International Court of Justice.* A Commentary. (OUP 2006) 607.

10 Thirlway (1984 NYIL) 103–104.

11 According to Hudson, the condition included in the Brazilian declaration of acceptance was met on February 5, 1930. Cf. Hudson (1972) 684, footnote 8.

compulsory jurisdiction has been accepted by a certain number of states or by certain named states.[12]

As is provided by Article 36, paragraph 2 of both Statutes, a state recognizes the Court's compulsory jurisdiction in respect of states 'assuming the same obligation'. Here it is most likely that the drafters of the optional clause had in mind cases in which a state accepts the Court's jurisdiction in respect of only some of the four categories of disputes enumerated in paragraph 2.[13] However, what happened in practice instead, was that states, by attaching reservations to their declarations of acceptance, did not exclude categories (a), (b), (c) or (d) of the disputes enumerated in Article 36, paragraph 2 but, by naming them precisely or less precisely, formulated conditions or reservations as to time, persons or subject matters, etc. whereby they limited the scope of the obligations they undertook in respect of the Court's compulsory jurisdiction.

Emmanuel Decaux writes that the original idea was confined to the reciprocity of acceptance, namely with respect to states making declarations of acceptance, and did not imply any sort of full reciprocity comprising reservations and conditions.[14] According to the said author, at first sight Article 36, paragraph 2 allows for two extreme concepts: minimum reciprocity is satisfied by both parties adhering to the optional clause system, whereas maximum reciprocity requires the parties to make identical declarations of acceptance. The French author holds the view that if the making of reservations is not permitted, this distinction would be superfluous as states could make identical declarations only.[15] He concludes that in a concrete case an absolute identity is not required; it is sufficient if the two declarations are partially coinciding.[16]

Herbert Briggs stresses that 'Any assumption that the phrase "accepting the same obligation" requires identical Declarations or equivalent reservations would lead to the nullification of the system of compulsory jurisdiction' under Article 36, paragraph 2 of the Statute, because states have wide discretionary powers to unilaterally determine the conditions with regard to accepting the Court's compulsory jurisdiction.[17] One can fully agree with Professor Briggs that taking the passage 'accepting the

---

[12] Waldock (1955–6) 255.

[13] What was possible only at the time of the Permanent Court of International Justice.

[14] Cf. Emmanuel Decaux, *La réciprocité en droit international* (LGDJ 1980) 85.

[15] *Id.* 87.

[16] *Id.* 88.

[17] Briggs (1958) 242.

same obligation' literally implies that the system of compulsory jurisdiction would only operate between states having made completely identical declarations, and not in respect of other states.[18]

The passage 'accepting the same obligation', as Professor Waldock points out, does not mean that '*exactly or even broadly the same obligation of compulsory jurisdiction must have been accepted by each State*,' but, requires 'complete reciprocity in the operation of compulsory jurisdiction under the Optional Clause *as between two States which have accepted the obligation in different terms*.'[19]

In the literature of international law, several authors emphasize that the condition of reciprocity in the optional clause was designed to ensure jurisdictional equality of the parties before the Court.[20] This is especially so because, as Edit Brown Weiss goes on to say, the system of compulsory jurisdiction has evolved in such a way that there are potentially significant inequities among states who have accepted it.[21]

II THE REFERENCE TO RECIPROCITY IN DECLARATIONS OF ACCEPTANCE

A closer look at the declarations of acceptance made since the establishment of the Permanent Court reveals that references to reciprocity, in different formulations, can be found in most declarations of acceptance. There are declarations which allude to Article 36 of the Statute by using the phrases: 'on condition of reciprocity', 'subject to reciprocity', 'subject exclusively to reciprocity', or, 'on the basis of absolute reciprocity'. Also featuring has been the phrasing that the declaration creates an obligation in respect of 'States making identical declarations' or 'States accepting the same obligation', which is naturally equivalent to the aforesaid express stipulations of reciprocity. Several declarations contain the formula 'in relation to any other State accepting the same obligation that is to say on condition of reciprocity'; such a formula is termed by Briggs as the 'double formula of reciprocity'.[22] A rather specific formula regarding reciprocity was included in the 2003 declaration of acceptance of Peru saying that the 'declaration shall apply to countries that have entered reservations or set conditions with respect to it, with the same

---

18 *Id.* 242–3.
19 Cf. Waldock (1955–6) 257–8.
20 Cf. Alexandrov (1995) 39; Brown-Weiss (1987) 98.
21 Cf. Brown-Weiss (1987) 98–100.
22 Briggs (1958) 238.

restrictions as set by such countries in their respective declarations'. The Peruvian reservation practically explains the meaning of reciprocity, although in taking the literal sense of the reservation, the question could be raised, as to what happens with the declarations of those states which have neglected to incorporate reservations in their declarations of acceptance. On the other hand, some declarations of acceptance contain no reference to reciprocity, meaning that the declaring states recognize the Court's compulsory jurisdiction without providing for reciprocity.

Regarding the inclusion of reciprocity in declarations of acceptance, the question arises as to whether reciprocity applies to all declarations of acceptance and whether it even applies to those cases where states fail to make a reference to reciprocity or excluding reciprocity.[23] This question seems proper if only for the reason that, according to some authors, there is nothing to prohibit states from accepting the Court's compulsory jurisdiction without stipulating reciprocity. The view that a distinction can be made between declarations of acceptance unconditionally and on condition of reciprocity is associated – in the literature of international law – with Guiliano Enriques during the inter-war years and with Hambro among other authors in later times.[24]

According to Enriques, declarations of acceptance made with the reference to reciprocity imply acceptance of obligations of only those states having made identical declarations, whereas declarations made without referring to reciprocity apply, in the absence of a contrary provision, simply to obligations assumed in respect of states having ratified the Statute.[25] It calls for no further explanation than, based on this view, states having made declarations of the latter form would assume rather far-reaching obligations, for they would in fact accept the Court's compulsory jurisdiction in respect of all states party to the

---

23 Cf. *Id.* 238–9, Thirlway (1984 *NYIL*) 107.

24 Hambro writes

> The possibility of making declarations which are not based on reciprocity seems, further, to be supported by paragraph 3 of Article 36, which states unequivocally that declarations may be made 'unconditionally or on condition of reciprocity on the part of several or certain States. ... In view of these considerations it seems safe to assume that it is possible for a State to accept the jurisdiction of the Court without reciprocity, but that such unconditional acceptance cannot be presumed.

E. Hambro, 'The Jurisdiction of the International Court of Justice' (1950), 76, *RCADI*, vol. I, 125, 185.

25 Cf. G. Enriques, 'L'acceptation sans réciprocié de la jurisdiction obligatoire de la Cour Permamente de Justice' (1932) 59, *RDILC*, 834, 845.

Statute. In connection with such declarations, Bertrand Maus says that, in the absence of any will expressed to that effect, such declarations cannot be construed to imply an obligation wider than that expressed in the clause itself.[26]

Concerning Enriques's view, Thirlway points out that the author practically overlooks the reference to 'reciprocity', which is a kind of *communis error*, contained in a declaration referring to Article 36, paragraph 2 and that the possibility of excluding reciprocity is only given in respect of paragraph 3, which, however, covers a different sort of reciprocity.[27]

The concept that reciprocity is neither a discretionary condition nor a reservation – instead constituting the basis of the network of declarations made under Article 36 of the Statute – can be considered to be the view of the majority of writers. Reciprocity is a basic constitutional provision of the Statute applicable to all declarations of acceptance, including those of states having unconditionally accepted the Court's compulsory jurisdiction.[28] This is supported by the practice of the two Courts, which purports the statement that 'reciprocity' has always been interpreted as applying to all compulsory jurisdiction declarations. For that matter, practice over more than eight decades has shown that, as is asserted by Shabtai Rosenne, 'The real problem which the Court has faced was never whether or why reciprocity exists and within the framework of the compulsory jurisdiction, but how it affects the acceptance of the jurisdiction in the particular case.'[29]

III RECIPROCITY IN THE PRACTICE OF THE TWO COURTS

In the jurisprudence of the two International Courts, the question of reciprocity has emerged in a number of cases, with the parties, the Court and the writers not infrequently offering differing interpretations. The problem concerning the interpretation of reciprocity results from the fact that in 1920 the authors of the Statute did not contemplate how reciprocity would really operate with respect to reservations attached to declarations of acceptance, so the legislative intention provides no

26 Maus (1959) 100.

27 Thirlway (1984 *NYIL*) 107–108.

28 In a similar sense, see Waldock (1955–56) 255; Briggs (1958) 242; Anand (2008) 160.

29 Rosenne (2006) vol. II, 732.

guidance in this matter.[30] It is not accidental that Rosenne points to contradictions in the views of both the Permanent Court of International Justice and writers on reciprocity.[31]

In the jurisprudence of the Permanent Court of International Justice, the case of the *Phosphates in Morocco* was the first occasion that considered the question of reciprocity.[32] In that legal dispute, attention should be directed to, for the purpose of the present discussion, the French preliminary objection invoking the reservation to the French declaration of acceptance, which excluded the retroactive effect of the declaration.[33] According to the reservation, the Court's compulsory jurisdiction existed in respect of any dispute arising after the ratification of the declaration, i.e. after 25 April 1931, with regard to situations and facts subsequent to this ratification. On the basis of reciprocity, France claimed that the exclusion of the retroactive effect in relations between the two states – albeit the Italian declaration contained no reservation concerning earlier facts and situations – *was effective as from the date of ratification of the Italian declaration of acceptance.* Thus the Court's jurisdiction exists between the two states in respect of disputes arising on the basis of facts and situations subsequent to 7 September 1931. Decaux considers that the said objection of France not only involved reciprocity, but actually transplanted the French reservation into the Italian declaration[34] and that France invoked against Italy a pseudo-reservation embodied in the Italian declaration.[35]

For its part, the Court stated that:

> This (the Italian – V.L.) declaration does not contain the limitation that appears in the French declaration concerning the situations or facts with regard to which the dispute arose; nevertheless, as a consequence of the

---

30 Thirlway (1984 *NYIL*) 112.

31 Rosenne (2006) vol. II. 731–2.

32 In Morocco, a special régime was created by the General Act of Algeciras of 1906 and the Franco-German Convention of 1911, to which Italy had acceded. The legal dispute between Italy and France submitted to the Permanent Court by Italy was as a result of measures by Moroccan authorities described by the applicant as 'the monopolization of Moroccan phosphates … inconsistent with the international obligations of Morocco and France'. The application by the Italian Government invoked the compulsory jurisdiction conferred on the Court by declarations of acceptance made in 1929 by Italy and France under Art. 36, para. 2 of the Statute.

33 On these reservations, see Chapter 7, Section I.

34 Decaux (1980) 90.

35 *Id.*

> condition of reciprocity stipulated in paragraph 2 of Article 36 of the Statute of this Court, it is recognized that this limitation holds good as between the Parties.[36]

However, the Court did not consider the question as to whether the limitation excluding the retroactive effect should operate from the date of ratification of the Italian or the French declaration of acceptance, as the Court held that: 'The date preferred by one or other of the Governments would not in any way modify the conclusions which the Court has reached. It does not therefore feel called upon to express an opinion on that point.'[37]

Thus the Court recognized the application of reciprocity to reservations added to the declarations of acceptance made by the two states, but did not clarify the consequences ensuing therefrom. In that case, no problem was caused by this course of the Court, since there was an interval of a few months between the dates of the deposit of the two declarations of acceptance. However, one can easily imagine a case in which the date from which the reservation operated could have been of great importance.

Similarly, in the *Electricity Company of Sofia case* between Belgium and Bulgaria, the Court was confronted with a reservation excluding the retroactive effect of the declarations.[38] In that case, it was on the basis of reciprocity that the respondent state, Bulgaria – which in 1921 accepted the Court's jurisdiction only on the condition of reciprocity – invoked the reservation to the declaration of the applicant state, Belgium. The respective Belgian declaration, ratified on 10 March 1926, contained a reservation that the declaration applied to 'any disputes arising after the

---

36 *Phosphates in Morocco* (Preliminary Objections), Judgment of 14 June 1938, *PCIJ Series A/B No. 74*, 22.

37 *Id.* 25.

38 The dispute known as the *Electricity Company of Sofia and Bulgaria case* arose because a company registered under Belgian law, the Electricity Company of Sofia and Bulgaria, already since the beginning of the 20th century, held a concession from the Municipality of Sofia for electric lighting of the city of Sofia. In the 1930s, regarding the calculation of tariffs, a controversy arose between the Municipality and the company, which was dealt with by the Bulgarian courts and the Belgo-Bulgarian Mixed Arbitral Tribunal as well, however these fora dismissed the company's claim. Finally, in 1938, the Belgian Government instituted proceedings by filing an application with the Permanent Court. The Court's jurisdiction was based on the declarations of Belgium and Bulgaria recognizing the Court's compulsory jurisdiction and the Treaty of conciliation, arbitration and judicial settlement of 23 June 1931, which entered into force on 4 February 1933.

ratification of the present declaration with regard to situations or facts subsequent to this ratification'. The Permanent Court stressed that:

> Although this limitation does not appear in the Bulgarian Government's own declaration, it is common ground that, in consequence of the condition of reciprocity laid down in paragraph 2 of Article 36 of the Court's Statute and repeated in the Bulgarian declaration, it is applicable as between the Parties.[39]

Dealing with this decision, Alexandrov stresses that the Court expressly and irrevocably recognized that reciprocity applies to reservations *ratione temporis*.[40]

Despite their apparent similarity, the two above-mentioned cases are different. In the *Phosphates in Morocco case*, the respondent state invoked the reservation to its own declaration of acceptance as a bar to the Court's jurisdiction and the Court accepted that, referring to reciprocity. However, reciprocity came into question again when the respondent state wanted to have the date of exclusion of the retroactive effect counted from the date of deposit, not of its own declaration of acceptance, but that of its adversary, the applicant state, yet that matter was not decided by the Court. On the other hand, in the case of the *Electricity Company of Sofia*, a reservation excluding the retroactive effect was contained in the declaration of acceptance of the applicant state, and it was invoked by the respondent state on the basis of reciprocity.

The question of reciprocity has also been considered by the International Court of Justice in several cases.

Chronologically, mention should be made first of the *Anglo-Iranian Oil Company case*, which was submitted by the United Kingdom against Iran.[41] In that case, the respondent state invoked the reservation contained in its own declaration of acceptance excluding the retroactive effect of the declaration.[42] In its judgment on the preliminary objections, the Court emphasized that:

---

39 *The Electricity Company of Sofia and Bulgaria* (Preliminary Objection), Judgment of 4 April 1939, *PCIJ Series A/B*, 81.

40 Cf. Alexandrov (1995) 43.

41 In 1951 laws were passed in Iran on the nationalization of the oil industry, which affected, among others, the Anglo-Iranian Oil Co. The United Kingdom adopted the cause of the latter and in virtue of its right of diplomatic protection it instituted proceedings before the Court. The applicant based the Court's jurisdiction on its declaration of acceptance made in 1940 and that of the respondent dated 1930 and ratified in 1932.

42 By the terms of this reservation, the declaration did not apply to 'any disputes arising after the ratification of the present declaration with regard to

> By these Declarations jurisdiction is conferred on the Court only to the extent to which the two Declarations coincide in conferring it. As the Iranian Declaration is more limited in scope than the United Kingdom Declaration, it is the Iranian Declaration on which the Court must base itself. This is the common ground between the Parties.[43]

In connection with the *Anglo-Iranian Oil Company case*, Briggs notes that, since the respondent state was invoking the reservation to its own declaration as a bar to jurisdiction, there was no need for the reference to reciprocity, and it is likely that the Court and its President addressed that point 'as an elucidation provided by the Court on a question argued at some length by the Parties in the pleadings'.[44]

The above-cited statement regarding the 'coincidence' of declarations of acceptance has been repeatedly invoked by the Court; most recently in the case of *Land and Maritime Boundary* between Cameroon and Nigeria (preliminary objections)[45] and in the *Legality of the Use of Force cases* at the end of the 1990s.

Perhaps of greatest interest concerning the application of reciprocity with respect to declarations of acceptance is the *Certain Norwegian Loans case* instituted by France against Norway, which involved a subjective reservation of domestic jurisdiction.[46] The declaration of acceptance made by France contained a reservation under which the declaration did not apply to differences 'relating to matters, which are essentially within the national jurisdiction as understood by the Government of the French Republic'. In the Norwegian declaration of acceptance there was no such limitation, but, in its first preliminary objection, Norway contended that the International Court did not have jurisdiction in that case because by virtue of the declarations of acceptance, the Court had jurisdiction only with respect to legal disputes falling within one of

situations or facts relating directly or indirectly to the application of treaties or conventions accepted and ratified by Persia and subsequent to the ratification of this declaration …'. The dispute between the parties concerned the question as to whether the reservation was operative in respect of treaties and conventions accepted by Iran at any time or only regarding treaties and conventions accepted by Iran after the ratification of the declaration.

43 *Anglo-Iranian Oil. Co. case* (Preliminary Objections), Judgment of 22 July 1952, *ICJ Reports 1952*, 103.

44 Briggs (1958) 253.

45 *Case concerning the Land and Maritime Boundary between Cameroon and Nigeria* (Preliminary Objections), Judgment of 11 June 1998, *ICJ Reports 1998*, 298–9.

46 On these reservations, see Chapter 8, Section I.

the four categories enumerated in Article 36, paragraph 2, of the Statute and relating to international law. However, the subject matter of the dispute, as stated in the French application, related to the national law of Norway. In the second part of the objection, Norway relied on the principle of reciprocity in referring to the above-quoted reservation on national jurisdiction which was joined to the French declaration of acceptance.[47]

Concerning the above-mentioned issue relating to its own jurisdiction, the International Court of Justice stated that:

> … in the present case the jurisdiction of the Court depends upon the Declarations made by the Parties in accordance with Article 36, paragraph 2, of the Statute on condition of reciprocity; and that, since two unilateral declarations are involved, such jurisdiction is conferred upon the Court only to the extent to which the Declarations coincide in conferring it. A comparison between the two Declarations shows that the French Declaration accepts the Court's jurisdiction within narrower limits than the Norwegian Declaration; consequently, the common will of the Parties, which is the basis of the Court's jurisdiction, exists within these narrower limits indicated by the French reservation.[48]

Referring to the statements of its predecessor in the *Phosphates in Morocco case* and the *Electricity Company of Sofia case*, as well as its own findings in the *Anglo-Iranian Oil Co. case*, the International Court of Justice stressed that:

> In accordance with the condition of reciprocity to which acceptance of the compulsory jurisdiction is made subject in both Declarations and which is provided for in Article 36, paragraph 3, of the Statute, Norway, equally with France, is entitled to except from the compulsory jurisdiction of the Court disputes understood by Norway to be essentially within its national jurisdiction.[49]

In connection with the *Norwegian Loans case*, Decaux writes that it would have been possible to consider two concepts of reciprocity in this

---

[47] The second preliminary objection of Norway also referred to reciprocity *ratione temporis*, claiming that the Court was without jurisdiction because, under the French declaration of acceptance, the Court had jurisdiction in respect only of disputes relating to facts and situations subsequent to the ratification of the declaration. This question was not, however, considered by the Court. See *Case of Certain Norwegian Loans, ICJ Pleadings*, 132–6.

[48] *Case of Certain Norwegian Loans,* Judgment of 6 July 1957, *ICJ Reports 1957*, 23.

[49] *Id.* 24.

dispute; the first being an objective one, under which France has no discretionary power – by virtue of its reservation invoking national jurisdiction – but is bound by good faith. As the matters relating to loans do not belong to French national law, they thus cannot fall within Norwegian national law on the basis of reciprocity.[50] By contrast, under the subjective concept, the position of France is less important; the law operating between the two parties is constituted not by the content of the French reservation, but by the Norwegian Government's interpretation thereof whereby it is as if the reservation had been made by Norway. However, the French author claims that this was not expressed by Norway, but by the Court's judgment in its stead.[51] Rather than consider the positions of France and Norway on international bonds, the Court based itself on the assumption that the determination of matters falling within national jurisdiction was subjective and the parties' declarations were sufficient, falling outside the consideration by the Court.[52]

Thirlway likewise holds that, with respect to the scope of reciprocity, the Court went rather far in the *Norwegian Loans case* as it had not simply 'written' into the Norwegian declaration a reservation of the French declaration of acceptance, but it had also adapted the declaration to its new environment in the sense that it had turned matters understood by the French Government to be within national jurisdiction into ones understood by the Norwegian Government to fall within Norwegian national jurisdiction.[53]

Regarding the above-cited passage of the judgment in the *Norwegian Loans case*, Briggs raises the question as to why, in relation to the condition of reciprocity contained in the declarations, the Court referred to paragraph 3, and not paragraph 2, of Article 36 although the issue occasionally emerged that reciprocity was not an absolute condition of Article 36 of the Statute, because paragraph 3 thereof permits unconditional declarations as well as those subject to reciprocity.[54] Regarding that matter, in its earlier judgments, the Court argued for the statutory condition of reciprocity contained in Article 36, paragraph 2, as it also appeared in the Court's opinion in the *Norwegian Loans case*. Therefore, Briggs is of the view that the reference to paragraph 3 instead of paragraph 2 is thus probably an error.[55]

---

50 Decaux (1984) 97.
51 *Id.*
52 *Id.* 98.
53 Cf. Thirlway (1984 *NYIL*) 115.
54 Briggs (1958) 255.
55 *Id.* 256.

On the other hand, Renata Szafarz's conclusion is that the reference in this case to paragraph 3 instead of paragraph 2 is to a certain degree inconsistent with the Court's earlier decisions, but may also justify the inclusion of the condition of reciprocity in declarations, regardless of the fact that reciprocity is covered by Article 36, paragraph 2 of the Statute.[56] The Polish professor emphasizes that the reservation in this case underwent a significant transformation, as the principle of reciprocity enabled Norway to invoke the relevant reservation not in its original form, notably in its applicability to France, but in a modified form to allow its content to be applied to Norway. She adds that the effects of reservations in declarations of acceptance differ essentially in this respect from reservations attached to treaties and the effects of the principle of reciprocity have much more far-reaching implications for reservations attached to declarations of acceptance.[57]

Alexandrov takes a more understanding attitude towards the Court and writes that:

> The only way to apply reciprocity was to allow Norway to exclude the same category of disputes *as regards Norway.* … since the class of matters which could be determined by France to be within its domestic jurisdiction would not necessarily coincide with the class of matters which another State could determine to be within its own domestic jurisdiction.[58]

It should be mentioned that the Court has faced strong criticism for its decision in the *Norwegian Loans case*; however, one should acknowledge that the Court did not have much choice in terms of ways to pronounce itself, for if it had decided that the French reservation 'relating to matters, which are essentially within the national jurisdiction as understood by the Government of the French Republic' was either admissible or inconsistent with the Statute, its decision would have most likely produced harmful effects on the system of the Court's compulsory jurisdiction. To avoid such pernicious consequences, the Court came to a decision by widening the scope of the principle of reciprocity to an undoubtedly significant level, thus also creating a good opportunity to demonstrate the backlash effect of the French reservation.

Shortly after the judgment rendered in the *Norwegian Loans case*, the Court had to decide again on the question of reciprocity in two other cases.

---

56 Szafarz (1993) 45.

57 *Id.* 45.

58 Alexandrov (1995) 82.

The first was the *Interhandel case* between Switzerland and the United States regarding the restitution by the United States of the assets of the Société internationale pour participants industrielles et commerciales S.A. (Interhandel). Within the time-limit fixed for the filing of the Counter-Memorial, the United States filed four preliminary objections.[59] Of interest to our subject is the second objection, in which the United States contested the Court's jurisdiction by contending that the dispute had arisen before the Swiss declaration of acceptance became binding, i.e. on 28 July, 1948. Referring to what had been stated by the Court in the *Anglo-Iranian Oil Company case*, namely that declarations should coincide with respect to conferring jurisdiction, the Washington Administration argued that since the United States' declaration of acceptance contained a clause limiting the Court's jurisdiction to disputes 'hereafter arising', given the Swiss declaration contained no such clause, according to the principle of reciprocity, between the United States and Switzerland, the Court's jurisdiction should be limited to disputes arising after 28 July 1948 – the date the Swiss declaration came into force. The Court rejected the objection and pointed out the following:

> Reciprocity in the case of Declarations accepting the compulsory jurisdiction of the Court enables a Party to invoke a reservation to that acceptance which it has not expressed in its own declaration but which the other Party has expressed in its own Declaration. … Reciprocity enables the State which has made the wider acceptance of the jurisdiction of the Court to rely upon the reservations to the acceptance laid down by the other Party. There the effect of reciprocity ends. It cannot justify a State, in this instance, the United States, in relying upon a restriction which the other Party, Switzerland, has not included in its own declaration'.[60]

Thus, in the *Interhandel case*, the United States sought a double application of reciprocity. Decaux wrote: 'the double application of reciprocity, which, contrary to its single application securing the equality of the parties, is creating inequality, and Washington wanted the application of a Swiss (non-existent) reservation, excluding the retroactive effect and conferring advantage to the United States only'.[61]

However, by rejecting the American stand, the Court created a clear situation, defining the limits of reciprocity and blocking the way to the potential abuse of double reciprocity.[62]

When considering the issue of limitations to declarations of acceptance, the Court, in dealing with the *Interhandel case*, faced a similar

---

[59] See *Interhandel case, ICJ Pleadings*, 301–27.

[60] *Interhandel case* (Preliminary Objections), Judgment of 21 March 1959, *ICJ Reports 1959*, 23.

[61] Decaux (1980) 104.

[62] Cf. *Id.* 106.

situation to that in the *Phosphates in Morocco case*. Unlike its predecessor, however, the Court examined the question thoroughly, clearly determining the aforementioned limitations with respect to the application of reciprocity.

The question of reciprocity was considered by the International Court of Justice in the greatest detail in the *Case concerning Right of Passage over Indian Territory*. As has already been mentioned, a specific feature of this case was that Portugal submitted an application against India three days after the deposit of its declaration of acceptance.[63] In response, India filed six preliminary objections, some of which related also to the question of reciprocity.[64]

In that case the subject of debate was, among other topics, a limitation included in the Portuguese declaration of acceptance (the third condition of the declaration of Portugal) providing that:

> 3) The Portuguese Government reserves the right to exclude from the scope of the present declaration, at any time during its validity, any given category or categories of disputes, by notifying the Secretary-General of the United Nations and with effect from the moment of such notification.

India contended that the cited condition was incompatible with the object and purpose of the optional clause, and was invalid among other reasons because it stood against the basic principle of reciprocity underlying the optional clause, as it gave a right to Portugal, which was denied to the other declaring states that accepted the Court's compulsory jurisdiction without such a condition.[65] India maintained also that Portugal had violated the principle of 'equality, mutuality and reciprocity' when it filed its application before the Secretary-General had time to transmit copies of the Portuguese declaration of acceptance, to the other parties to the Statute, including India.[66]

---

[63] The Portuguese declaration was dated 19 December 1955, and Portugal submitted its application on 22 December 1955.

[64] See *Case concerning Right of Passage over Indian Territory,* Preliminary Objection of the Government of India, *ICJ Pleadings*, vol. I, 97–188.

[65] See the first objection.

[66] See the second objection. The fourth preliminary objection was closely related to the second one. In the objection, India argued that, since it had no knowledge of the Portuguese declaration before Portugal filed its application, it was debarred from invoking – on the basis of reciprocity – the third Portuguese condition and the dispute which was the subject matter of the Portuguese application was excluded from the jurisdiction of the Court.

The Court rejected the Indian objections and held that the third condition caused no uncertainty and did not contradict the basic principle of reciprocity underlying the optional clause, since any such reservation, by virtue precisely of the principle of reciprocity, must become automatically operative against the declaring state in relation to other signatories of the optional clause.[67]

The Court likened reservations about the right to modify declarations with immediate effect to clauses covering the right of denunciation by simple notification with immediate effect, stating that there is no essential difference between the situations created by these clauses, with regard to the degree of certainty, and the third condition of the Portuguese declaration which leaves open the possibility of a partial denunciation.[68] In connection with the modification of declarations of acceptance, the Court pointed out that 'when a case is submitted to the Court, it is always possible to ascertain what are, at that moment, the reciprocal obligations of the Parties in accordance with their respective Declarations'.[69] It stressed that the manner of filing the Portuguese application did not, in respect of the third Portuguese condition, violate the rights under Article 36 of the Statute concerning reciprocity in such a way as to constitute an abuse of the optional clause.[70] The Court concluded that the manner of filing the Portuguese application was neither contrary to Article 36, nor in violation of any right of India under either the Statute or its declaration of acceptance.[71]

Dealing with the position of the Court in the *Right of Passage case*, Decaux states that, in effect, it would have been possible to interpret reciprocity in either a wider or narrower sense. According to the wider interpretation, maintained by India, reciprocity generally applies to all obligations and rights deriving from declarations made under the optional clause. On the other hand, according to the narrower interpretation appearing in the Court's decision, the determinant factor concerning the reciprocal rights and obligations of the parties is the time that the proceedings are instituted.[72]

---

[67] *Case concerning Right of Passage over Indian Territory* (Preliminary Objections), Judgment of November 26 1957, *ICJ Reports 1957*, 144.

[68] *Id.* 143–4.

[69] *Id.* 143.

[70] *Id.* 147–8.

[71] *Id.* 147.

[72] Cf. Decaux (1980) 102.

During the 1980s, new problems emerged regarding the application of reciprocity in the *Case concerning Military and Paramilitary Actions in and against Nicaragua.*

In the legal dispute submitted by Nicaragua against the United States, one of the most important points of controversy between the parties arose out of the fact that three days before Nicaragua filed its application the United States, by a note to the International Court, had modified its 1946 declaration of acceptance to exclude from the Court's jurisdiction certain disputes relating to Central America and Central American States.[73] The United States declaration of acceptance originally fixed six months' notice for the termination of the declaration; Nicaragua's declaration contained no such restriction. The United States claimed that it had modified its declaration of 1946 by its notification dated 6 April 1984, thus the Court was without jurisdiction on 9 April 1984, the date on which Nicaragua filed its application. The Washington Administration invoked reciprocity in an effort to render its 1984 notification immediately effective. That argument sought to ensure that since the Nicaraguan declaration, being indefinite in duration, was subject to a right of immediate termination, without previous notice by Nicaragua, the United States' declaration thus could also be terminated with immediate effect by virtue of the principle of reciprocity regardless of the six months' notice proviso in the United States declaration. The Court refused to accept the American argument and emphasized that:

> The maintenance in force of the United States Declaration for six months after notice of termination is a positive undertaking, flowing from the time-limit clause, but the Nicaraguan Declaration contains no express restriction at all. It is therefore clear that the United States is not in a position to invoke reciprocity as basis for its action in making the 1984 notification which purported to modify the content of the 1946 Declaration.[74]

In that case the Court made a very important statement regarding reciprocity by stating that:

---

[73] Under the terms of the United States notification of 6 April 1984, the 1946 American declaration of acceptance 'shall not apply to disputes with any Central American State or arising out of or related events in Central America … Notwithstanding the terms of the aforesaid declaration (i.e. the declaration of acceptance of 1946), this proviso shall take effect immediately and shall remain in force for two years …'.

[74] *Case concerning Military and Paramilitary Activities in and against Nicaragua* (Jurisdiction of the Court and Admissibility of the Application), Judgment of 26 November 1984, *ICJ Report 1984*, 419.

> The notion of reciprocity is concerned with the scope and substance of the commitments entered into, including reservations, and not with the formal conditions of their creation, duration or extinction. It appears clearly that reciprocity cannot be invoked in order to excuse departure from the terms of a State's own declaration, whatever its scope, limitations or conditions.[75]

In other words, the Court held that the six months' notice formed an integral part of the American declaration of acceptance and constituted a condition which must be taken into account, regardless of whether it related to the termination or modification of the declaration.

The *Nicaragua case* provoked, if for no other reason than its political relevance, a great deal of discussion in the literature of international law. The Court's findings regarding reciprocity and the limits thereof were consistent with the view, as expounded in the majority of writings published before the *Nicaragua case,* that reciprocity cannot be applied to the formal conditions, duration, or extinction of the declarations of acceptance.

In connection with the *Nicaragua case,* mention should be made of Spain's declaration of acceptance of 1990, which extended the principle of reciprocity to the conditions for the termination of the declaration. Spain, most certainly guided by an endeavour to avoid a situation similar to that in which the United States found itself in the *Nicaragua case*, fixed not only six months' notification for the withdrawal of the declaration, but added another paragraph as well stating that '… in respect of States which have established a period of less than six months between notification of the withdrawal of their Declaration and its becoming effective, the withdrawal of the Spanish Declaration shall become effective after such that shorter period.'[76]

Thus, Spain intended to apply reciprocity to the withdrawal of the declaration. Up to now, that condition as laid down by the Spanish declaration has not yet been referred to in a case, but, at any rate, it would be of interest to know the position of the Court regarding that condition, especially because it contradicts what was stated in the

---

75 *Id.*

76 According to Pastor Ridruejo, that reservation was not included in the draft of the declaration elaborated by a group of experts but was suggested by the Consejo de Estado, who wondered that in view of the principle of reciprocity 'when would the withdrawal of the Spanish declaration take effect compared to a State that set a shorter notification period or one that set no period at all'. Cf. José Antonio Pastor Ridruejo, 'The Spanish Declaration of Acceptance of the Compulsory Jurisdiction of the International Court of Justice' (1991), 1. *Span Yrb. Int'l L* (Brill, 1991), 19–34, 29.

Nicaragua case, seeing that it applies reciprocity to the procedural aspects of the declaration.

It is another question as to how reciprocity could function in those cases submitted under the optional clause where there are more than two parties involved in the litigation. As Rosenne points out, one could expect that in those cases the application of the principle of reciprocity would be applied *mutatis mutandis* as in the cases with two parties.[77]

IV CONSEQUENCES OF RECIPROCITY

One can say that the principle of reciprocity forms part of the optional clause system by virtue of the express terms of Article 36 of the Statute; however, this entails several consequences, of which only a few can be highlighted now.

As noted earlier, the reference to reciprocity in Article 36, paragraph 3, was incorporated in the Statute on the basis of the proposal by Fernandes. At the time, through the inclusion of reciprocity, Fernandes sought to ensure that states knew exactly the other states, in respect of which, they had assumed obligations concerning the compulsory judicial settlement of disputes. By doing so, the Brazilian jurist thus wanted to eliminate an element of uncertainty. At that time, however, no one thought that there was another implication of reciprocity which, according to Rosenne, '... operates to crystallize and determine the scope of the jurisdiction in the concrete case'.[78] All this means that so long as a concrete legal dispute is not submitted to the Court, there is some uncertainty accompanying the obligations of states under the optional clause and *it is only in principle that the Court's jurisdiction exists in respect of disputes covered by declarations of acceptance.* No state is in a position to know in advance which dispute will in practice be actually subject to the Court's jurisdiction and no state can be absolutely certain that the Court's jurisdiction will really extend to a particular dispute covered by its declaration of acceptance, for, in the last analysis, the Court's jurisdiction always depends also on whether the particular dispute is covered by the opponent state's declaration of acceptance. It could occur that a state has recognized the compulsory jurisdiction of the Court in respect of a rather wide range of disputes, but this notwithstanding the Court may in practice deal with a much narrower range of legal disputes by reason of

---

[77] Cf. Rosenne (2006) vol. II, 737.
[78] *Id.* 736.

the fact that the opponent parties have accepted the compulsory jurisdiction of the Court in respect of a much more limited scope of disputes.

This was reflected in the Court's judgment in the *Nicaragua case* by saying:

> The coincidence or interrelation of those obligations thus remain in a state of flux until the moment of the filing of an application instituting proceedings. The Court has then to ascertain whether, at that moment, the two States accepted 'the same obligation' in relation to the subject-matter of the proceedings.[79]

In order to ensure the equality of the parties to the fullest extent, reciprocity has also been applied to reservations attached to declarations of acceptance. This has gone the length of entitling the states, which have recognized the Court's jurisdiction unconditionally, to avail themselves of the benefits of reservations to declarations of acceptance provided by the opponent party. And as Briggs points out: 'The result is that application of the condition of reciprocity tends to equalize Declarations made with or without reservations.'[80]

In other words, a state making its declaration of acceptance without reservations or with some specific reservations recognizes the Court's compulsory jurisdiction in all other matters not affected by the reservations. This means also that it has made an offer to the other states party to the optional clause system to the effect that it can be sued before the Court in any other matter. If a dispute is brought before the Court, and the declaration of acceptance of the applicant state contains reservations, the possibility exists for the respondent state to avail itself of the benefits of reciprocity and to invoke, if it so wishes, the reservations contained in the applicant state's declaration of acceptance. It is precisely the principle of equality of the parties that limits the reference to the reservations contained in the declaration of an opponent party on the basis of reciprocity, and, as is also exemplified by the *Interhandel case*, the application of double reciprocity was rejected by the Court relying on the principle of equality.

Considering that a state may, by virtue of reciprocity, invoke the reservation to a declaration of an opponent party, reservations tend, in practice, to make their effect felt more often than not, precisely against

---

[79] *Case concerning Military and Paramilitary Activities in and against Nicaragua* (Jurisdiction of the Court and Admissibility of the Application), Judgment of 26 November 1984, *ICJ Report 1984*, 420–21.

[80] Briggs (1958) 245.

the state making a reservation, which is to say that this is a double-edged weapon.[81] Such has been the case whenever the Court established the lack of its jurisdiction on the basis of a reservation contained in the declaration of an applicant state, and the respondent state, relying on reciprocity, succeeded the rejection of the application.[82]

81 Cf. Decaux (1980) 88.
82 This is what happened, e.g. in *Certain Norwegian Loans case*.

7. Generally accepted reservations to declarations of acceptance

As has already been mentioned, in the last more than ninety years, states had elaborated a great variety of different reservations and limitations to their declarations of acceptance and thus narrowing its obligations under the optional clause.[1] Most of these reservations and limitations gain currency in the international community; however, they are also reservations which are unquestionably destructive to the whole optional clause system. For this reason in this present work, the classification of different reservations attached to declarations of acceptance will be made according to both their acceptance by the international community of states and their influence on the optional clause system. In this chapter those reservations will be discussed which are considered to be limitations generally accepted by the international community of states.

I RESERVATIONS EXCLUDING THE RETROACTIVE EFFECT OF DECLARATIONS OF ACCEPTANCE

Within national laws and international law it is a well-established principle that – with the exception of some very special cases – the commencement of obligations do not have retroactive effects.

In the case of declarations accepting the compulsory jurisdiction of the International Court of Justice and its predecessor (the Permanent Court of International Justice) the situation is just the opposite. The retroactive effects of declarations of acceptance are the general rule and, in order to exclude the retroactive effect, the declaring state should expressly stipulate this in its declaration of acceptance.

This is the reason why among the reservations added to declarations of acceptance one frequently meets with limitations whereby states try to prevent the submission of disputes which have emerged before the

[1] On these reservations see also Harold J. Owen, 'Compulsory Jurisidiction of the International Court of Justice: A Study of its acceptance by Nations' (1968–69) 3, *Ga. L. Rev.*, 704, 713–26.

making of declarations under Article 36, paragraph 2 of the Statute or arisen in times previous to certain dates (the so-called exclusion date or critical date), or dated back in origin to such periods. In connection with such limitations, the Permanent Court of International Justice pointed out in the *Phosphates in Morocco case* that the limitation was intended:

> … a revival of old disputes, and to preclude the possibility of the submission to the Court by means of an application of situations or facts dating from a period when the State whose action was impugned was not in a position to foresee the legal proceedings to which these facts and situations might give rise.[2]

The limitations excluding any retroactive effect of declarations of acceptance are typical *ratione temporis* reservations. However, depending on whether the reservation concerns disputes or a state itself one can speak of two kinds of reservations excluding a retroactive effect. One is *material* in nature and can be linked to a dispute or the emergence of facts and situations giving rise to disputes. The other is *personal* due to its characteristics and related to the international legal status of a state in the sense that a declaration applies or does not apply to disputes reaching back to the time of the earlier international legal status of the declaring state, or those conflicts dating back to another political system of that state.

Shabtai Rosenne, too, distinguishes retroactivity *ratione personae* and retroactivity *ratione materiae*. The eminent Israeli professor, however, makes this distinction according to a different approach than that stated above, emphasising a clear distinction must be maintained between retroactivity *ratione personae* and retroactivity *ratione materiae*. He differentiates 'between retroactivity as regards the period of time during which the obligation as such to accept the jurisdiction of the Court is in existence and retroactivity as regards the period of time comprised within the scope of that obligation.'[3]

(a) Excluding Retroactivity *Ratione Materiae*

Taking into consideration more than ninety years of states' practice one can see that the reservations excluding retroactive effect are encountered

---

2 *Phosphates in Morocco* (Preliminary Objections), Judgment of 14 June 1938, *PCIJ Series A/B*, No. 74, 24.

3 Shabtai Rosenne, *The Time Factor in the Jurisdiction of the International Court of Justice* (Leyden, A.W. Sijthoff 1960) 53–4.

with various wordings. The most frequent version is that where the declaration applies only to 'future disputes' or ones arising after the declaration is made or 'in the future',[4] or those legal disputes arising out of facts and situations subsequent to or continuing to exist after the entry into force of the declaration.[5] Under another formula the declaration does not apply to disputes occurring prior to the date the declaration was made, 'including any dispute the foundations, reasons, facts, causes, origins, definitions, allegations or bases of which existed prior this date, even if they are submitted or brought to the knowledge of the Court hereafter'.[6] Also known are declarations which specify that the Court has no jurisdiction over disputes *prior* to the exclusion date, nor disputes that have arisen out of facts or situations prior to the exclusion date.[7] Similarly, there are declarations which apply to disputes, situations, etc. *subsequent* to or after the exclusion date.[8] In some declarations the critical date is defined by days, months and years, whilst in others the critical date is the date of the signature, ratifications, deposition, etc. of the declaration of acceptance. Very often the critical date is an important event in the history of the declaring state.[9] One can find a rather interesting formula in the 1987 declaration of acceptance of Suriname saying that it recognises the jurisdiction of the court 'in all disputes, which have arisen prior to this Declaration and may arise after this Declaration'; thus, it creates a clear situation that Suriname recognizes the retroactive effect of its declaration of acceptance. A special variant of the reservation was included in the 2005 declaration of acceptance of

---

[4] See, e.g. the declarations of Barbados (1980), Gambia (1966), Liberia (1952), Paraguay (1996), the Philippines (1972) and Senegal (1958).

[5] See, e.g. the declarations of Bulgaria (1992), Canada (1994), Germany (2008), Hungary (1992), Lithuania (2012), Luxembourg (1930), Malawi (1966) and Slovakia (2004).

[6] See, e.g. the declaration of India (1974).

[7] On this point, see the declaration of Poland (1996).

[8] See the declarations of Columbia (1937), Guinea (1998), Japan (2007), Kenya (1965), the Netherlands (1956), Pakistan (1948), Sudan (1958), Sweden (1957) and the United Kingdom (2004). In the declarations of Japan, Pakistan and Sweden, the dates referred to in the declarations of acceptance were the dates when their first or previous declarations of acceptance were made. The Governments of the Netherlands and Columbia even referred to the dates that they accepted the compulsory jurisdiction of the Permanent Court of International Justice, being 5 August 1921 and 6 January 1932 respectively.

[9] See, e.g. the declarations of Guinea and Sudan where the critical dates were the day of independence (Sudan) or a date very close to the day when the independence was declared (Guinea).

Portugal excluding those disputes which refer 'to territorial titles or rights or to sovereign rights or jurisdiction, arising before 26 April 1974 or concerning situations or facts prior to that date'.[10]

The reservations precluding the retroactive effect of declarations are one of the most frequent limitations in declarations of acceptance, and such reservations are included in about 40 per cent of the declarations currently in force.

The reservations excluding retroactivity *ratione materiae* can be consigned, on the authority of Rosenne, to three types, notably:

(a) limitation of the acceptance of compulsory jurisdiction to future disputes (simple formula of exclusion);
(b) limitation of acceptance of compulsory jurisdiction to disputes arising out of future facts and situations;
(c) a more sophisticated formula of the limitation under b) limiting the acceptance of compulsory jurisdiction to disputes occurring in the future and arising out of future facts and situations.[11]

Rosenne refers to the reservations under paragraphs b) and c) as the 'double exclusion formula'.[12]

Regarding these reservations, Alexandrov rightly points out that while it may present a practical problem in establishing the exclusion date, it is far more complicated to establish the date when a specific dispute has arisen.[13] According to Anand, the reservation has led to considerable indefiniteness.[14] Within the literature of international law, authors have been raising several questions regarding reservations, for example, 'Does the verb refer to the time at which the injurious event occurs? Or to the time when the claim is first put forward through appropriate channels? Or when the claim has been rejected and the parties have finally disagreed?' What does the situation prior to ratification mean?[15] How can the relations between situations or facts and the dispute be determined? How

---

10 The date of the bloodless military coup, known as the Carnation Revolution, opened the way to the restoration of democracy in Portugal.

11 The 1925 Belgian declaration of acceptance was the first one having the formula'in any disputes arising after the ratification of the present declaration with regard to situations or facts subsequent to this ratfication.'

12 Cf. Rosenne (1960) 36.

13 Alexandrov (1995) 44.

14 Cf. Anand (2008) 228.

15 *Id.* 230.

can the relations between situations and facts and the critical date be determined?[16]

The answers to some of these questions were given by the two International Courts.

From the jurisprudence of the two International Courts in connection with the exclusion of retroactive effect of declarations of acceptance, one should allude first of all to the *Mavrommatis Palestine Concession case,*[17] despite the fact that in the dispute the Permanent Court's jurisdiction was founded, not on declarations of acceptance, but on a treaty provision. In its judgment, the Court held that:

> in case of doubt, jurisdiction based on an international agreement embraces all disputes referred to it after its establishment. ... The reservation made in many arbitration treaties regarding disputers arising out of events previous to the conclusion of the treaty seems to prove the necessity for an explicit limitation of jurisdiction (in order that it may not apply to all disputes – V.L.).[18]

In that decision the Permanent Court has in fact decided that, with respect to declarations of acceptance, '*retroactivity is a rule*'. Thus in the absence of express provisions excluding previous situations, facts or disputes, the Court's jurisdiction is not limited to the disputes arising after the establishment of the Court or after the date of the adoption of the instrument conferring jurisdiction.[19]

After that judgment, the states formulated their declarations of acceptance even more carefully in order to make their undertakings regarding the Court's compulsory jurisdiction abundantly clear. One could say that, although there are some obscure and vague reservations added to the declarations of acceptance, states are trying to include reservations referring to the time-framing of the declarations which are as clear as possible.

In the *Phosphates in Morocco case* the Permanent Court of International Justice interpreted a reservation on excluding the retroactive effect of a declaration of acceptance.

---

16 Cf. Maus (1959), 136–8.

17 The dispute was submitted by Greece against Great Britain, alleging the refusal of the Palestine Government and consequently the refusal of the British Government to recognize the rights of a Greek national (Mr Mavrommatis) regarding the concessions for public works in Palestine.

18 *The Mavrommatis Palestine Concession* (Objection to the jurisdiction of the Court), Judgment of 30 August 1924, *PCI.J Series A*, No. 2, 35.

19 Cf. Rosenne (1960) 54–5.

In that dispute the Court's jurisdiction was based, among other things, on the parties' declarations of acceptance; however, the French declaration contained the reservation that its declaration was to apply 'for all disputes arising after ratification with regard to situations or facts subsequent to ratification', i.e. after 25 April 1925. In its preliminary objection the French Government acknowledged that the dispute had indeed arisen after the said date, but asserted that the situations and facts giving rise to the dispute had preceded that date.

In its judgment on the preliminary objections, the Court found that, as the dispute did not arise with regard to situations or facts subsequent to the ratification of the French declaration of acceptance, it therefore had no jurisdiction to adjudicate the dispute.[20] The Court interpreted the reservation attached to the French declaration of acceptance as excluding the retroactive effect and held that:

> … the only situations or facts falling under the compulsory jurisdiction are those which are subsequent to the ratification and with regard to which the dispute arose, that is to say, those which must be considered as being the source of the dispute.[21]

The Court went on and stated that in regard to each concrete case it is necessary to decide separately whether a particular situation or fact is prior or subsequent to a certain date. In answering these questions, however, one should always keep in mind the will of the state; it having accepted compulsory jurisdiction subject to certain limits, and hence only recognizing this compulsory jurisdiction in respect of disputes which have arisen out of situations and facts subsequent to its declaration.[22]

The *Electricity Company of Sofia and Bulgaria case* involved similar issues, and the Permanent Court recalled what was said in the *Phosphates in Morocco case*, emphasizing that only those situations or facts must be taken into account which are considered to be the source of the dispute.[23] In connection with facts and situations giving rise to disputes the Court held:

---

[20] *Phosphates in Morocco* (Preliminary Objections), Judgment of 14 1938, *PCIJ Series A/B*, No. 74, 29.

[21] *Id.* 23.

[22] Cf. *Id.* 24.

[23] *Electricity Company of Sofia and Bulgaria* (Preliminary Objection), Judgment of 4 April 1939, *PCIJ Series A/B*, No. 77, 82.

Appealing to the principle of reciprocity inserted in the Belgian declaration of acceptance of 25 September 1925, Bulgaria claimed that the Court lacked

> It is true that a dispute may presuppose the existence of some prior situation or fact, but it does not flow that the dispute arises in regard to that situation or fact. A situation or fact in regard to which a dispute is said to have arisen must be the real cause of the dispute.[24]

Subsequently, the International Court of Justice has likewise dealt with similar issues in several other cases.

In one of its preliminary objections filed in the *Right of Passage case*, the Indian Government as the respondent claimed that its declaration of acceptance made on 28 February 1940, applied to disputes arising out of situations or facts subsequent to 5 February 1930,[25] but the dispute referred to the Court by the Portuguese application concerned situations and facts prior to the aforementioned date.[26]

In its judgment on the merits, the Court in answering that objection emphasized that:

> The dispute before the Court, … could not arise until all its constituent elements had come into existence. Among these are the obstacles which India is alleged to have placed in the way of exercise of passage by Portugal in 1954. The dispute therefore as submitted to the Court could not have originated until 1954.[27]

The Court also examined India's preliminary objection from the angle that the dispute was one with regard to facts and situations prior to 5 February 1930 – referring to the judgment of the Permanent Court in the *Electricity Company of Sofia and Bulgaria case* – and made a clear distinction, 'between the situations or facts which constitute the source of the rights claimed by one of the Parties and the situations or facts which are the source of the dispute.'[28] The Court in its judgment of the *Right of Passage case* pointed out that these two elements were constituted by both the existence of the right of passage between the enclaves and – concerning the part of India – the obstacles raised to the exercise of that right; the dispute submitted to the Court arose from all of the said

---

jurisdiction in the case because the dispute had arisen out of a situation occurring previous to the entry into force of the Belgian declaration.

24 *Id.*

25 That was the date when India made its previous declaration of acceptence, which was renewed in 1940.

26 *Case concerning Right of Passage over Indian Territory,* Preliminary Objections of the Government of India, *ICJ Pleadings*, 185.

27 *Case concerning Right of Passage over Indian Territory* (Merits), Judgment of 12 April 1960, *ICJ Reports 1960*, 34.

28 *Id.* 35.

elements and, although some of its parts originated in earlier times, this whole came into existence only after 5 February 1930.[29]

The *Interhandel case* similarly concerned reservations excluding the retroactive effect of declarations of acceptance. In its first preliminary objection the United States contended that the International Court of Justice had no jurisdiction to hear and determine the matters raised by the Swiss application because the dispute between the parties arose before the entry into force of the United States' declaration of acceptance on 26 August 1946.[30]

After a thorough examination of the antecedents of the case, the Court concluded that the dispute had arisen after the entry into force of the US declaration of acceptance and rejected the preliminary objection by stressing that 'the facts and situations which have led to a dispute must not be confused with the dispute itself'.[31]

In the *Anglo-Iranian Oil Co. case* there emerged problems as to whether the Court's jurisdiction only covered disputes with regard to situations or facts relating directly or indirectly to the application of treaties concluded by Iran arising after the ratification of the declaration of acceptance, or whether it extended, as was argued by the United Kingdom, to all disputes connected to the application of all treaties concluded by Iran at any time. In point of fact, the phrase 'and subsequent to the ratification of the present declaration' – included in the Persian declaration of 1930 – may refer alike to 'the treaties and conventions accepted by Persia' and to the words 'regarding situations and facts'.[32] The Court considered the declaration of acceptance according to the rules of grammatical interpretation and, further considering the intent of the Iranian Government expressed at the time of accepting the Court's compulsory jurisdiction, it came to the conclusion that the Persian declaration of acceptance was limited to disputes relating to the application of treaties and conventions concluded by Iran after ratification of the declaration of acceptance.[33]

---

29 *Id.*

30 Cf. *Interhandel case,* Preliminary Objections Submitted by the United States of America, *ICJ Pleadings*, 310–15.

31 *Id.* 22. The Court reached the same conclusion concerning the second preliminary objection, in which the Court's jurisdiction was contested on the basis that the dispute had arisen before the Swiss declaration of acceptance had entered into force, i.e. before 28 July 1948.

32 *Anglo-Iranian Oil Co. case* (Preliminary Objection), Judgment of 22 July 1952, *ICJ Reports 1952*, 104.

33 *Id.* 107.

The application of reservations excluding the retroactive effect of declarations of acceptance has likewise emerged in the cases concerning *Legality of Use of Force* between the former Yugoslavia (later Serbia and Montenegro) and ten NATO states. Immediately after the filing of applications against ten NATO states, Yugoslavia requested for an indication of provisional measures, but the Court in its Orders of 2 June 1999 rejected the request in all the ten cases.[34]

Of special interest to our subject are five cases – namely those which Yugoslavia instituted against Belgium, Canada, the Netherlands, Portugal and the United Kingdom – as in those cases the respondent states relied on reciprocity for invoking the *ratione temporis* reservation to the applicant state's declaration of acceptance excluding the retroactive effect of the declaration.[35] The Court accepted the arguments of the respondent states and held that it had no *prima facie* jurisdiction to entertain the applications submitted by the Belgrade Government, since the NATO air strikes giving rise to the disputes started on 24 March 1999, whereas the Yugoslav declaration of acceptance containing the reservation excluding the retroactive effect of the instrument was dated on 25 April 1999.

(b) Excluding Retroactivity *Ratione Personae*

As mentioned earlier, the other limitation excluding the retroactive effect of declarations of acceptance is connected to the international status of the declaring state and it refers to disputes originating at the time of the earlier international status of the declaring state – thus the reservation relates to either retroactivity before the date on which the state commenced its existence as an independent international personality, or a former political regime of the given state.

According to Rosenne, the practice of the states that had emerged in the wake of World War I differed in this respect from that of the states that were created after World War II.[36] Since several new states – having emerged in the wake of World War I – did not limit the scope of their

---

[34] See, e.g. the case concerning *Legality of Use of Force* (Yugoslavia v. Belgium) (Request for Indication of Provisional Measures), Orders of 2 June 1999, *ICJ Reports 1999*, 124–41.

[35] As a matter of fact, Yugoslavia's declaration of acceptance of 25 April 1999 contained the reservation that the FRY recognized the Court's compulsory jurisdiction 'in all disputes arising or which may arise after the signature of the present Declaration, with regard to the situations or facts subsequent to this signature'.

[36] Cf. Rosenne (1960) 57.

declarations of acceptance only to disputes arising subsequent to their independence, these declarations of acceptance thus did not contain any exclusion clauses excluding the retroactive effect of the declaration. By contrast, the majority of new states that came into being shortly after World War II excluded disputes arising before, or relating to events occurring before their independence, by precisely referring to the date of independence.[37]

Interestingly, this tendency ceased to be typical of declarations occurring at a later date, with the declarations of acceptance made by some former colonial territories not containing exclusion stipulations regarding disputes originating in their pre-independence period.[38] However, one is able to find instances of an opposite practice as well, for example, Nigeria added to its 1998 declaration of acceptance an exclusion clause stating that the declaration did not apply to 'disputes in relation to matters which arose prior to the date of Nigeria's independence period, including any dispute the causes, origins or bases of which arose prior to that date'.[39]

At first sight, the practice of several former colonial states, being not to preclude from the Court's compulsory jurisdiction any disputes reaching back to colonial times, contradicts the endeavour of these states – which was revealed, for instance, during the negotiations concerning both the 1978 Vienna Convention on the Succession of States in Respect of Treaties, as well as the 1983 Vienna Convention on Succession of States in Respect of State Property, Archives and Debts – to pursue the 'clean slate' rule to liberate themselves from their obligations originating in colonial times. Acceptance of the Court's jurisdiction over eventual disputes reaching back to colonial times can in all certainty be traced back to the fact that these states have had many more 'accounts to settle' with the old colonial powers than the latter have had with them and the

---

[37] *Id.* 58. See, e.g. the declaration of acceptance of Israel (1950, 1956), Pakistan (1949, 1957) and Sudan (1958).

[38] This can be exemplified by the declarations of Guinea-Bissau (1989), Cameroon (1994), the Democratic Republic of the Congo (1989), the Ivory Coast (2001), Lesotho (2000), Marshall Islands (2013), Mauritius (1968), Somalia (1963), Swaziland (1969), Togo (1979) and Uganda (1963).

[39] This declaration of Nigeria, laced with quite a few reservations, replaced one of 1965 which contained but one reservation concerning reciprocity. Perhaps we are not far from the truth in supposing that the making of the Nigerian declaration of 1998 is associated with the Court's Judgment regarding the preliminary objections in the *Case concerning the Land and Maritime Boundary* between Cameroon and Nigeria and in formulating its new declaration of acceptance the Nigerian Government responded to the 'lessons' of this case.

International Court of Justice appeared to be a suitable forum for settling various disputes stretching back even to the colonial period.[40]

The question regarding the retroactive effect of declarations of acceptance is of special interest in respect of those states that have experienced a change of political system in the 1990s or a revolution.

In this context, it is worthwhile taking into account the practice of the former socialist states, of which several have made a declaration accepting the compulsory jurisdiction of the International Court of Justice after 1990. A reservation excluding the retroactive effect of a declaration of acceptance can be found in those of Poland (1990, 1996), Bulgaria (1992), Hungary (1992), Yugoslavia/Serbia and Montenegro (1999), Slovakia (2004) and Lithuania (2012). It is interesting to note that no such limitation is contained in the declarations of acceptance of two former members of the former Soviet Union: Estonia (1991) and Georgia (1995). The declarations of these states consequently apply to disputes which have arisen during the period of pre-independence and include those disputes which extend back into Soviet times. In the case of Estonia, this can to some extent be explained by the fact that the 1991 declaration of acceptance of Estonia is almost identical to the Estonian declaration made in 1923.

The Hungarian, Polish, Slovak and Yugoslav declarations of acceptance contain the 'double exclusion formula', as these states have sought to ensure the applicability of their declarations only to disputes relating to future facts and situations.

One could believe that – considering the 20th-century history of Central and Eastern European states, fraught as it has been with trials and afflictions – it stands to reason that the declarations of acceptance by these states have sought to exclude disputes relating to past facts and situations.

In summing up the reservations that exclude retroactive effect, it can be stated that the practice of the two International Courts goes to show that in the absence of an express reservation excluding retroactive effect, declarations also cover either disputes arising before the making of a declaration or those disputes relating to facts and situations occurring before the state became party to the optional clause system.

---

[40] For the relations between the developing countries and the International Court of Justice, see Cesare P.R. Romano, 'International Justice and Developing Countries: A Quantitative Analysis' (2002) 1, *Law & Prac Int'l Courts & Trib*, 367–99.

II RESERVATIONS PREVENTING SURPRISE APPLICATIONS

It was after the judgment of the International Court of Justice regarding the preliminary objections in the legal dispute between Portugal and India concerning *Right of Passage over Indian Territory* in 1957 that reservations appeared which were aimed at preventing unexpected or surprise applications. As mentioned previously, Portugal submitted an application against India three days after the deposit of its respective declaration of acceptance, and the Court recognized that step as a lawful one, stating that:

> A State accepting the jurisdiction of the Court must expect that an Application may be filed against it before the Court by a new declarant State on the same day on which that State deposits with the Secretary-General its Declaration of Acceptance.[41]

With a view of preventing the occurrence of such cases, a new type of reservation appeared in the model of the reservation included in the United Kingdom's 1957 declaration of acceptance. The reservation to the British declaration excludes from the Court's compulsory jurisdiction any disputes with states that have adhered to the optional clause system only for the purpose of bringing a given dispute before the Court, or where the declaration of acceptance was deposited or ratified less than 12 months prior to the filing of the application.[42] Accordingly the aim of the reservation was to prevent a 'surprise application' and to hamper a newly declarant state from filing an application against a state – already party to the optional clause system – right after, or within a short time of, the deposit of its declaration of acceptance, perhaps even before the respondent state concerned would be able to learn that the newly declarant state had adhered to the optional clause system.[43]

---

[41] *Case concerning Right of Passage over Indian Territory* (Preliminary Objections), Judgment of 26 November 1957, *ICJ Reports 1957*, 146.

[42] This reservation was further complicated by Israel. On this point, see Israel's declaration of acceptance of 1956 as modified in 1984. The wording of the modification differs from the British formula or the one contained in other declarations of acceptance as Israel fixed the 12 months' time limit not only for acceptance of the Court's compulsory jurisdiction, but also for an amendment of a declaration.

[43] For an analysis of the problems connected with this, see Waldock (1955–56) 280–83.

Over the course of time, reservations preventing surprise applications have become widespread and more than a quarter of the declarations in force contain such a stipulation, which has come to be known in two variants.

One type includes those reservations preventing surprise applications which, like the formula used in the United Kingdom's declaration of acceptance of 1957, actually consist of two parts.[44] According to the first part, the Court's compulsory jurisdiction does not cover disputes whereby any other party to the dispute has accepted the compulsory jurisdiction of the Court 'only in relation to or for the purpose of such dispute', while the second part provides for the Court lacking jurisdiction in cases where any other party to the dispute deposited or ratified its declaration of acceptance less than twelve or six months prior to the filing of the application bringing the dispute before the Court.[45]

The other variant of reservations preventing surprise applications contains only the second part of the reservation mentioned above; namely it only excludes disputes in respect of those where one of the parties accepted the Court's compulsory jurisdiction less than six or twelve months prior to the filing of the application.

The two variants of reservations preventing surprise applications produce rather different legal effects. The six or twelve months' limitation entails a suspension for six or twelve months of the Court's compulsory jurisdiction between a state that has added such a reservation to its declaration of acceptance and a newly declarant state, since the two states cannot institute proceedings against each other under the optional clause during the above-mentioned periods. After the lapse of the six- or twelve-month period, however, this limitation terminates, meaning that reservations preventing surprise applications cease to be an obstacle in submitting a dispute to the Court's decision.

The reservations preventing surprise application imply, furthermore, that there is the possibility for a state unwilling to see a dispute with a newly declarant state brought before the Court to withdraw its declaration

---

[44] Among the declarations of acceptance falling within this class are those of Australia (2002), Bulgaria (1992), Cyprus (2002), Germany (2008), Hungary (1992), India (1974), Japan (2007), Lithuania (2012), Malta (1966), Mauritius (1968), New Zealand (1977), Nigeria (1998), the Philippines (1972), Poland (1996), Portugal (2005), Slovakia (2004), Somalia (1963), Spain (1990) and the United Kingdom (2004).

[45] Such a reservation was included in the 1988 declaration of Cyprus, which stipulated a period of six months. The 2002 declaration of Cyprus, like all the other declarations nowadays in force, provides for a 12-month period.

of acceptance within a period of twelve or six months, if faced with an application that it considers lacking bona fides,[46] thus barring a particular dispute from being nonetheless brought before the Court even after the lapse of the said periods. Of course, the 'success' of such acts also depends on the provisions relating to the amendment or termination of the given state's declaration of acceptance, for if the declaration has fixed a period of six or twelve months for amendment or termination as well, the need is certainly pressing to amend or terminate the declaration lest the deadline be missed.

The situation is more complicated with regard to the other group of reservations preventing surprise applications, where the limitation is intended to prevent the Court from deciding on the dispute of a state which has made a declaration of acceptance precisely for the purpose of submitting the given dispute to the Court.[47] Here, in fact, there arise two questions; first, whether the reservation makes it impossible for a given dispute to ever be brought before the Court, and second, whether it can be proved that a state has accepted compulsory jurisdiction under the optional clause only in relation to or for the purpose of the dispute to be submitted to the Court.

The problem of reservations preventing surprise applications has emerged in two of the cases concerning the *Legality of Use of Force*; notably in the dispute between Yugoslavia and Spain, and between Yugoslavia and the United Kingdom, since reservations with 12 month exclusion clauses were contained in the declarations of acceptance of both Spain and the United Kingdom.[48]

The 12-month requirement preventing surprise applications was considered in connection with the preliminary objections in the *Legality of Use of Force case* between Yugoslavia and the United Kingdom, as the Yugoslavian Memorial acknowledged that the application against the

---

[46] Judge Oda referred to this in his individual opinion appended to the orders on provisional measures in the *Case concerning Legality of Use of Force*. See *Case concerning Legality of Use of Force* (Yugoslavia v. Belgium), Request for the Indication of Provisional Measures, Order of 2 June 1999, Separate Opinion of Judge Oda, *ICJ Reports 1999*, 150.

[47] See the declaration of acceptance of the Marshall Islands (2013).

[48] In both cases these reservations came into question in connection with the fact that Yugoslavia made a declaration of acceptance on 26 April 1999 and filed an application with the Court against ten NATO states three days later, i.e. on 29 April 1999.

It should be mentioned that the respondent states invoked the reservation preventing surprise applications already in connection with the Yugoslavian request for the indication of provisional measures.

United Kingdom failed to meet the 12-month requirement of the British declaration of acceptance; however the Belgrade Government further argued that the requirement would be satisfied if the oral hearings on the merits started after 25 April 2000.[49]

According to Belgrade, the 12-month reservation in respect of a newly declarant state was to pass until the commencement of the oral proceedings rather than the filing of the application. That argument evidently ignores that – under the well-established practice of the Court – the date of filing an application is the critical date, or the threshold of the case at which the Court's jurisdiction must be established. So, as a consequence of the 12-month requirement of the British declaration of acceptance, the Court would have jurisdiction between Yugoslavia/Serbia and Montenegro and the United Kingdom only in respect of disputes submitted after 25 April 2000.

The reservation to prevent surprise applications raises the question of its time limits, namely of how long one can refer to that part of the reservation excluding disputes with states which have accepted the compulsory jurisdiction of the Court for the purpose of submitting a particular dispute or disputes to the Court. It would obviously be odd to refer to this reservation months or perhaps years after the making of a declaration containing the above-mentioned limitation, although there is the possibility that the declarant state acted 'with foresight' and indeed made a declaration of acceptance in view of a conflict evolving. At the same time, however, any state that, shortly after depositing its declaration of acceptance, proceeds to file an application with the Court against any other state party to the optional clause system would be easy to charge with having made a declaration of acceptance only for the purpose of bringing a particular dispute before the Court. States having made declarations of acceptance with the purpose of bringing particular disputes before the Court have generally been charged with bad faith.[50] One can challenge this argument by saying that the Court's mission is to help states in their settlement of disputes by peaceful means and for this very reason, it appears to be stretching things to term a state as acting in bad faith or abusing rights by making use of a possibility of resolving a conflict by peaceful means and in accordance with international law.

---

[49] See *Case concerning Legality of Use of Force,* Preliminary Objections of the United Kingdom, Oral Proceedings, public sitting held on 19 April 2004. http://www.icj-cij.org/docket/files/113/4453.pdf (accessed 23 October 2013).

[50] This charge was laid against Yugoslavia by the United Kingdom in the cases concerning the *Legality of Use of Force*.

In the literature of international law there are views questioning the issue as to whether reservations preventing surprise applications do actually protect effectively against abuse.[51] Since states are free to formulate their declarations of acceptance, they may tailor a declaration in such a way as to conceal their intention with regard to accepting the Court's compulsory jurisdiction – which may only be for the purpose of bringing a particular dispute before the Court – while the 12-month exclusion clause as fixed in the British, Indian and other declarations of acceptance could be evaded by playing for time, because after the lapse of the prescribed six or twelve months a newly declarant state may resort to the Court even against a state whose declaration of acceptance contains a reservation preventing surprise applications.

Reservations preventing surprise applications have come to be fully accepted in present days, as is perhaps best evidenced by the fact that in the *Case concerning the Land and Maritime Boundary* between Cameroon and Nigeria the Court, in its judgment on preliminary objections, pointed out that: 'In order to protect itself against the filing of surprise applications, in 1965, Nigeria could have inserted in its Declaration an analogous reservation to that which the United Kingdom added to its own Declaration in 1958.'

One can consider as a special variant of the reservations preventing surprise applications the limitation found in the French declaration of acceptance of 1959, which excludes from the scope of compulsory jurisdiction:

> Disputes with any State which, at the date of occurrence of the facts or situations giving rise to the dispute, has not accepted the compulsory jurisdiction of the International Court of Justice for a period at least equal to that specified in this declaration'(i.e. the French declaration of acceptance of 1959 – V.L.)

This respective French reservation is a special combination of limitations serving to prevent surprise applications and exclude retroactive effects. The first part of the reservation protects France against such actions as Portugal followed in the *Right of Passage case*, because the declaration must have already been submitted to the UN Secretary-General at the time of either the occurrence of the disputed events or the situation

---

[51] Cf. Samuel A. Bleicher, 'ICJ Jurisdiction: Some New Considerations and a Proposed American Declaration' (1967) 6 *e, Colum. J.f Transnat'l L.* 61, 80–81.

giving rise to legal dispute.[52] There is a difference between that part of the French reservation and the other limitations preventing surprise actions, as the French reservation totally excludes the submission of a dispute to the Court, if the adverse party was not a party to the optional clause system at the date of occurrence of the facts or the time of the situation giving rise to the dispute; however, as has already been discussed, the reservations preventing surprise applications do not exclude the possibility of submitting a given dispute to the Court, they only require the lapse of a period fixed in the reservations themselves. The second part of the French reservation refers to the time limitation of the adverse party's declaration of acceptance, requiring the state to have recognized the Court's compulsory jurisdiction for at least as long a period as France has, which means three years under the terms of the first paragraph of the 1959 French declaration of acceptance.[53]

Thus, the reservation contained in the 1959 French declaration of acceptance is essentially a refined version of those reservations that were made to prevent surprise applications, to the degree that it makes it insufficient for a certain period to lapse between the date of accession by the adverse party – which is having a dispute with France – to the optional clause system and the date of filing an application; furthermore it is also necessary that such a state should be a party to the Court with respect to the optional clause system at the time of the emergence of facts and situations giving rise to the legal dispute. The latter phrase actually makes the reservation similar to limitations excluding retroactive effect. Precisely for this reason, one of the problems related to the said reservation is the serious difficulty in ascertaining the date of the emergence of facts and situations serving as a basis for the dispute. The fact that such a reservation is nowadays contained in no single declaration of acceptance is in all probability accounted for by the complexity thereof and the difficulties in its eventual application. In the mid-1960s France, too, withdrew its declaration containing the reservation and omitted that limitation from its 1966 declaration of acceptance.

---

52 *Id.* 82–3.

53 The 1959 French declaration was for a term of three years and thereafter was to remain in force until notification of termination.

III RESERVATIONS REFERRING TO SPECIAL RELATIONS WITH GIVEN STATES

(a) The Commonwealth Reservation

Limitations seeking to exclude from the scope of compulsory jurisdiction any dispute with either states having especially close relations to declaring states, or those states having no diplomatic relations with a declarant state or not being recognized by that state, can all be mentioned as typical examples of *ratione personae reservations.*

The so-called Commonwealth reservation represents the best-known variant of reservations of this class. As early as the inter-war period, the member states of the British Commonwealth of Nations, except Ireland, joined to their declarations of acceptance, on the basis of the '*inter se*' doctrine, a limitation to the effect that the declaration does not apply to 'disputes with the Government of any other Member of the League which is a member of the British Commonwealth of Nations, all of which disputes shall be settled in such manner as the parties have agreed or shall agree'.[54] That limitation refers to the special relations between the member states of the British Commonwealth, and, as was stressed by Sir Austen Chamberlain in his often-quoted address to the British Parliament, the related disputes are 'such as should be solved by ourselves'.[55]

Today, with the disintegration of the British Empire, it may appear anachronistic for declarations of acceptance to include the 'Commonwealth reservation', yet such reservations are still in force and, as was shown by the *Case concerning the Aerial Incident of 10th August 1999*, they continue to be applied.[56] In the proceedings instituted by Pakistan

---

[54] Lauterpacht calls these limitations as 'reservations as to inter-imperial disputes'. Cf. Lauterpacht (1930) 147. On this score see the declarations of acceptance by Australia, Canada, India, New Zealand, the Union of South Africa and the United Kingdom in 1929. The Commonwealth reservation can be found in several declarations of acceptance even today, thus in those of Barbados (1980), Canada (1994), Gambia (1966), India (1974), Kenya (1965), Malta (1983), Mauritius (1968) and the United Kingdom (2004).

[55] *The Times*, 28 January 1930, quoted by Robert Y. Jennings 'The Commonwealth and International Law' (1953) 30, *BYIL*, 320, 326.

[56] The aerial incident took place along the Pakistani–Indian border, a region forming the object of the dispute, where the Indian air-defence, using an air-to-air missile, shot down a Pakistani aircraft which was doing regular training flights. The contentions of the two states were in contradiction as to whether the aircraft was downed in the Indian or the Pakistani airspace. At any rate, the crew of 16 lost their lives. Pakistan founded the Court's jurisdiction on, inter alia, its

against India, the Delhi Government in its preliminary objection requested the rejection of the application on the grounds, inter alia, that one of the reservations in the 1974 Indian declaration of acceptance excludes all disputes involving India from the jurisdiction of the Court in respect of any state which 'is or has been a Member of the Commonwealth of Nations'.[57] Pakistan contended that the Commonwealth reservation was in breach of good faith as well as various provisions of the Charter and the Statute of the Court – being *ultra vires* of Article 36, paragraph 3 – and as such had no legal effect. It was furthermore an extra-statutory reservation which had lost its *raison d'être*, making it obsolete.[58]

In its interpretation of the Indian declaration of acceptance the Court stated that since 1947 all of India's declarations of acceptance had contained the Commonwealth reservation and that at the time it made its declaration of 1974 India had even modified that reservation to the effect that the limitation applied not only to disputes with the present members of the British Commonwealth of Nations, but also to disputes with the government of any state which 'has been a Member of the Commonwealth'.[59] The Court stated that:

> While the historical reasons for the original appearance of the Commonwealth reservation in the declarations of certain States under the optional clause may have changed or disappeared, such considerations cannot, however, prevail over the intention of a declarant State, as expressed in the actual text of its declaration.[60]

---

own declaration of acceptance dated 13 September 1960 and that of India dated 15 September 1974.

[57] Cf. *Case concerning the Aerial Incident of 10th August 1999*, Preliminary Objections to the Jurisdiction of the Court. Counter Memorial of the Government of India, 10 August, 1999. http/icjwww/idcoket/ipi/ipi-pleadings (accessed 17 July 2013).

[58] Cf. *Case concerning the Aerial Incident of 10th August 1999.* Memorial of the Government of Pakistan on Jurisdiction. 10 January 2000. http/icjwww/idcoket/ipi/ipi-pleadings (accessed 17 July 2013).

As regards the claim that the reservation was obsolete, Pakistan stated that as of today the members of the Commonwealth of Nations were no longer united by a common allegiance to the Crown, and the modes of dispute settlement originally contemplated had never been established.

[59] This formula was incorporated in the declaration of the United Kingdom in 2004.

[60] *Case concerning the Aerial Incident of 10th August 1999* (Jurisdiction of the Court), Judgment of 21 June 2000, *ICJ Reports 2000*, 31.

Thus the Court reaffirmed its position, asserted several times, that the determinant factor in the interpretation of declarations of acceptance was the will of the declaring state and that even if a declaration contained a reservation which might at first sight appear to be anachronistic, the Court must observe and apply it.

(b) Reservation Excluding Specially-mentioned States

A reservation similar to the Commonwealth one can be found in Iraq's 1938 declaration of acceptance. That limitation excluded from the Permanent Court's jurisdiction 'Disputes with the Government of any Arab State, all of which disputes shall be settled in such a manner as the Parties have agreed or shall agree.' Interestingly, a similar reservation did not appear in the declaration of acceptance made by any other Arab state.

In all likelihood, the Commonwealth reservation inspired the Government of Ireland to include in its 2011 declaration of acceptance a reservation excluding 'any legal dispute with the United Kingdom of Great Britain and Northern Ireland in regard to Northern Ireland'. The peculiarity of that reservation is that in respect of another state it excludes only a special category of disputes, i.e. those which relate to Northern Ireland.

(c) Reservations Referring to Recognition or Diplomatic Relations

The limitations concerning states which the declaring state has not recognized or with which there are no diplomatic relations are in essence the opposite of the reservations referring to close relations between certain declaring states. These reservations similarly originated in the inter-war period. According to available data, the 1930 declarations of acceptance of Yugoslavia and Romania included such limitations. The Romanian declaration specifically stated that 'it accedes to the Optional Clause … in respect of the Governments recognized by Romania'. There is a high probability that in formulating that reservation the Romanian Government primarily had in mind the Soviet Union. Even nowadays there are declarations of acceptance containing such a reservation.[61]

A limitation substantially akin to the above-mentioned reservation appeared in Poland's declaration of 1931, with the difference, however, that in that case the declaring state shifted upon any opponent state a decision on the existence of diplomatic relations inasmuch as the

---

61 See the declaration of acceptance of India (1974), Nigeria (1998) and Djibouti (2005).

declaration excluded disputes 'arising between Poland and States which refuse to establish or maintain normal diplomatic relations with Poland'.

A limitation identical with the Polish reservation was included in Israel's 1950 declaration of acceptance.[62] In connection with such reservations, Alexandrov writes that the term 'normal relations' is so broad in meaning that it allows removal from the Court's jurisdiction disputes practically with any state.[63] In 1956, Israel replaced the said declaration with a new one modifying and clarifying the cited limitation in the sense that the new declaration was not to apply to:

> any dispute between the State of Israel and any other State whether or not a member of the United Nations which does not recognize Israel or which refuses to establish or to maintain normal diplomatic relations with Israel and the absence or breach of normal relations precedes the dispute and exists independently of that dispute;

A reservation relating to non-recognition by the declarant state can be found in India's declaration of acceptance of 1974, which excludes from the scope of compulsory jurisdiction 'disputes with the Government of any State with which, on the date of an application to bring a dispute before the Court, the Government of India has no diplomatic relations or which has not been recognized by the Government of India.'

The reservations referring to the absence of diplomatic relations or to non-recognition are by all means indicative of bad relations between states, and it is therefore a welcomed development that such a reservation is now only contained, using identical wording, in the declarations of acceptance of India and Djibouti.

(d) Reservations Excluding Non-sovereign States or Territories

Only two declarations of acceptance in force provide for the exclusion of non-sovereign states or territories; these are the declarations of acceptance of India (1974) and Djibouti (2005). With these reservations the declaring states didn't want to exclude disputes with colonial territories – nowadays being an anachronism – but to exclude disputes with states having the status of nasciturus.

---

[62] The limitation applies to states that refuse to 'establish or maintain normal diplomatic relations' with Israel.

[63] Cf. Alexandrov (1995) 121.

IV RESERVATIONS CONCERNING OTHER METHODS OR MEANS OF PEACEFUL SETTLEMENT OF DISPUTES

(a) Different Variants of the Reservation

Soon after the Permanent Court of International Justice was established, the very first declarations of acceptance contained reservations limiting the Court's jurisdiction to disputes where 'the parties have not agreed to have recourse to another method of dispute settlement'.[64] In later times, these reservations appeared having a broader meaning that applied not only to agreements already in existence, but also to future ones stipulating the use of other methods of peaceful settlement. The reservations concerning other methods of peaceful settlement have become one of the limitations that is most frequently resorted to and found in a large part of the declarations made in both the inter-war and post-World War II period.

The drafters of the United Nations Charter were also mindful of the possibility of conflicting treaty clauses on jurisdiction, as is reflected in Article 95 of the Charter, which runs as follows: 'Nothing in the present Charter shall prevent Members of the United Nations from entrusting the solution of their differences to other tribunals by virtue of agreements already in existence or which may be concluded in the future.'

On this provision, Kelsen writes that it allows member states 'to submit their disputes in accordance with pre-existing or newly concluded treaties to *ad hoc* tribunals of arbitration or to establish – for instance by regional agreements – another permanent court of justice'.[65] They can even submit their disputes to special courts having compulsory jurisdiction, thereby excluding the jurisdiction of any other court even that of the International Court of Justice.[66]

By including in their declarations of acceptance reservations regarding other methods of peaceful settlement, states are trying to avoid possible collisions between different methods of dispute settlement in respect of a particular dispute, in such a way that they accord precedence to other methods of peaceful settlement over proceedings before the International Court under the optional clause.

---

[64] This type of limitation first appeared in the Netherlands' declaration of acceptance of 1921, which excluded disputes 'in regard to which the parties have not agreed to have recourse to some other means of friendly settlement'.

[65] Kelsen (1951) 477.

[66] *Id.*

In practice, states have devised a number of variations of reservations concerning other methods of peaceful settlement and such reservations can be consigned to the following groups.[67]

(i) The first group includes clauses of a general nature, with limitations covering other methods of peaceful settlement in general terms[68] and relating to any other methods like negotiation, conciliation, mediation, arbitration, etc., also known as declarations which enumerate other methods of dispute settlement.
(ii) The second group of reservations relates to a more restricted set of means by referring not to all 'other methods of peaceful settlement', but only to disputes entrusted to other tribunals by the parties by virtue of an agreement already in existence or which may be concluded in the future.[69]
(iii) As a third group, one can mention a rather special type of reservation which excludes from the Court's compulsory jurisdiction disputes which are ruled out in advance from judicial settlement or arbitration by a treaty, convention, agreement, etc. Thus, in that case, the reservation relates not to another court or tribunal but

---

[67] On the variations of the reservation, see. J.G. Merrills (1993) 225.

[68] See, e.g. the declarations of acceptance of Australia (2002), Austria (1971), Barbados (1980), Belgium (1958), Botswana (1970), Cambodia (1957), Canada (1994), Djibouti (2005), Gambia (1966), Germany (2008), Guinea (1998), Honduras (1960, 1986), Hungary (1992), India (1974), the Ivory Coast (2001), Kenya (1965), Lesotho (2000), Lithuania (2012), Luxembourg (1930), Madagascar (1992), Malawi (1966), Marshall Islands (2013), the Netherlands (1956), New Zealand (1977), Nigeria (1998), Peru (2003), the Philippines (1972), Poland (1996), Portugal (2005), Senegal (1985), Slovakia (2004), Spain (1990), Sudan (1958), Suriname (1987), Swaziland (1969) and the United Kingdom (2004).

[69] Such a reservation is contained in the declarations of e.g., Estonia (1991), Japan (2007), Liberia (1952), Pakistan (1960), the United States (1946), the wordings of the declarations of Estonia, Pakistan and the United States are almost identical. The declaration of Japan differs from the others in the respect that it provides not only to tribunals but to arbitration as well. It should be mentioned that there could be other formulas as well, e.g. the 1996 declaration of Norway referring, with rather complicated wording, to all disputes concerning the law of the sea in respect of the United Nations Convention on the Law of the Sea and the Agreement of 4 December 1995 for the Implementation of the Provisions of the United Nations Convention on the Law of the Sea of 10 December 1982 relating to the Conservation and Management of Straddling Fish Stocks and Highly Migratory Fish Stocks.

to those matters which under a treaty in force could not be settled by a judicial fora.[70]

The reservations concerning other methods of peaceful settlement are not to be confused with those limitations preventing the parties from instituting proceedings before the Court unless they have previously conducted negotiations or resorted to conciliation. Such clauses resemble reservations relating to other methods of peaceful settlement in that they also provide for recourse to other means when settling disputes; however, in such a case the clause entails a requirement for the parties to first resort to that method of dispute settlement, the Court being open to them only in case of exhausting those means of settling their dispute. By contrast, the reservations concerning other methods or means of peaceful settlement involve the obligation for the parties to use other methods or means to resolve their dispute and not submit the dispute to the Court under the optional clause. So, in one case the proviso practically delays the submission of the dispute to the Court, with negotiations, conciliation, etc. to be first resorted to before instituting proceedings before the Court, whereas in the other case the reservation is intended to exclude the submission of a particular dispute or disputes to the Court under the optional clause.

With their reservations concerning other methods or means of peaceful settlement, the parties may stipulate to resolve their disputes not only by negotiation, conciliation and the like, but also by ad hoc arbitration or by another tribunal instead of the International Court of Justice.[71] One may count on a growing number of such clauses in the future, if not only for the reason of the fact that there exist today several international fora to settle interstates disputes.

Among the currently functioning international tribunals specific mention is deserved for three institutions, notably the Permanent Court of Arbitration, the International Tribunal for the Law of the Sea in Hamburg and the mechanisms of conciliation and arbitration established within the framework of the Organization of Security and Cooperation in Europe (OSCE).

There is no doubt that the Permanent Court of Arbitration established by the Convention for the Pacific Settlement of International Disputes of 1899 may in principle be 'competitive' with the International Court of

---

[70] See the declarations of Cambodia (1957), Malta (1966) and Mauritius (1968).

[71] On these questions, see Yuval Shany, *The Competing Jurisdictions of International Court and Tribunals* (OUP 2004).

Justice, but that forum, during its existence of more than a century, had never been a rival of the Permanent Court of International Justice and has not been a competitor to its successor, the International Court of Justice, although there is a revival of the Permanent Court of Arbitration which provides services for the resolution of disputes involving various combinations of states, state entities, intergovernmental organizations, and private parties.

The OSCE Dispute Settlement System, the pan-European mechanism for conciliation and arbitration as established within the framework of OSCE in the mid-1990s, is applicable to a rather wide range of international disputes.[72] A specific feature of this mechanism is that it is only residual according to Article 19 of the Convention on Conciliation and Arbitration within the OSCE. As has been pointed out in the literature, that subsidiary serves to confine the application of the OSCE convention on dispute settlement to a rather narrow field,[73] and hence there is little likelihood of it coming into conflict with the compulsory jurisdiction of the International Court of Justice.

With regard to the clause concerning other tribunals, it is worthwhile taking into account the International Tribunal for the Law of the Sea, chiefly because the competence of that court covers general and traditional maritime disputes – which are also in the competence of the International Court – and it has repeatedly dealt with such cases.[74]

The establishment of the International Tribunal for the Law of the Sea was supported first of all by the developing countries during the negotiations concerning the United Nations Convention on the Law of the Sea.[75] At that time, which were under the influence of the International Court's decisions in the cases concerning South-West Africa and Northern Cameroon, the creation of a new tribunal on the law of the sea

---

[72] The Convention on Conciliation and Arbitration within the OSCE was adopted by the Council of the Organization of Security and Cooperation in Europe (OSCE) at its Stockholm meeting of 14–15 December 1992 and entered into force on 5 December 1994.
See Karin Oellers-Frahm, 'The Mandatory Component in the OSCE Dispute Settlement System' in Janis (1992) 195–211.

[73] The reason for this lies in the fact that the Convention was acceptable to states with such a provision only. Cf. Laurence Cuny, *L'OSCE et le réglement pacifique de différends: La Cour de conciliation et d'arbitrage* (Publications de l'Institut Universitaire de Hautes Etudes Internationales 1997) 73 et seq.

[74] Cf. Elihu Lauterpach,: *Aspects of the Administration of International Justice* (Grotius Publications Limited 1991) 20.

[75] The proposal for the establishment of a tribunal of the law of the sea was originally made by the United States.

was called for in which they were to have more seats than in the International Court of Justice.[76]

The Convention on the Law of the Sea as in the case of other conventions provides for the settlement by peaceful means of a dispute between contracting parties concerning the interpretation and the application of the Convention.[77] Regarding the means of peaceful settlement, the Convention is rather wide-ranging, embracing all methods from negotiations to judicial settlement. At the same time, however, the Convention leaves a wide scope open for the International Court of Justice to decide on disputes regarding the law of the sea, a fact proved in practice as well, for there have been several such disputes referred to the International Court of Justice since the establishment of the International Tribunal for the Law of the Sea.

If states choose not to turn to the International Court of Justice, but instead seek any other tribunal, such a choice can be seen as a typical clause within the ambit of reservations on other means of peaceful settlement. The same is the case with disputes in which the International Tribunal for the Law of the Sea exercises exclusive jurisdiction.[78]

The possible tension between declarations of acceptances – excluding other means or methods of peaceful settlement, the Convention on the Law of the Sea and the 1993 Convention for the Conservation of Southern Bluefin Tuna – emerged in the *Southern Bluefin Tuna case* (Australia and New Zealand v. Japan),[79] especially because the applicant states, Australia and New Zealand, could unilaterally refer the dispute to the International Court of Justice; however, they preferred to submit the dispute to an arbitral tribunal constituted under Annex VII, Article 287 of the United Nations Convention on the Law of the Sea.[80]

---

[76] Cf. Gilbert Guillaume,'La Cour Internationale de Justice. Quelques propositions concrètes à l'occassion du Cinquantenaire' (1996) 100, *RGDIP*, 323, 329–30.

[77] Cf. UN Convention on the Law of the Sea, Arts. 279 and 283.

[78] Such disputes are, e.g., those relating to the immediate release of vessels and their crews and therefore not amenable to a decision by the International Court of Justice. Furthermore, the disputes mentioned in Arts. 187 and 292 of the Convention on the Law of the Sea cannot be brought before the International Court of Justice because they are disputes between private people, who may not have recourse to the International Court of Justice.

[79] Cf. Bernard H. Oxman 'Complementary Agreements and Compulsory jurisdiction' (2001) 95, *AJIL*, 277, 298.

[80] Cf. Shany (2004) 30.

(b) The Reservation in Practice

There are several questions raised by reservations concerning other methods of peaceful settlement of disputes. First of all, does the reservation exclude once and for all the proceedings before the Court in the disputes involved?

In his study analysing the 1929 British declaration of acceptance[81] Lauterpacht put forward questions as to whether the effect of the reservation is 'merely suspensive or does it altogether exclude recourse to arbitration', what happens in case of a failure of the conciliation procedure and what occurs when the parties are unwilling to accept it. 'Does the signature of the Optional Clause become operative, or is the abortive procedure of conciliation tantamount to a final fulfilment of the duty of peaceful settlement?'[82] Although, to the best of our knowledge, this issue has not yet arisen in the jurisprudence of the two International Courts, the eminent British expert being right in pointing out that 'The wording of the reservation does not warrant a confident answer to these questions.'[83]

The reservations relating to other methods of peaceful settlement exclude the possibility for disputes affected by them to be submitted to the two Courts only under the optional clause. However, the reservations raise no obstacle to the situation in which the parties bring the dispute before the Court in some other way, for example, by compromise or by an agreement to be concluded in the future. Such an alternative could easily be envisaged if the parties were unable to resolve their dispute by using other methods or means of peaceful settlement as originally envisaged, in the case, for instance, mediation or conciliation were failing. Since the reservation relating to other methods of peaceful settlement is contained in the parties' declaration of acceptance, the foregoing makes it clear that the dispute affected by the reservation cannot be brought before the Court *under the optional clause.* At the same time, however, nothing forbids the parties from referring the dispute to the Court via a compromise.

In connection with reservations on other means of peaceful settlement, Anand deals with another question, notably that of what will happen in

---

81 The 1929 British declaration of acceptance excluded among other things from the scope of the declaration 'Disputes in regard to which the parties to the dispute have agreed or shall agree to have recourse to some other method of peaceful settlement.'

82 Lauterpacht (1930) 147.

83 *Id.*

case of a conflict between the Court's compulsory jurisdiction and a clause relating to other methods of peaceful settlement. On this point he distinguishes two cases depending on whether special treaties concerning pacific settlement of disputes were concluded by the states before or after having accepted the compulsory jurisdiction of the International Court.[84] With regard to treaties concluded after the acceptance of the Court's compulsory jurisdiction, Anand concurs with Hambro's view, that in such cases a situation may arise where one of the parties would like to bring the matter before the Court under the optional clause, whereas the other state would prefer to use any other method or means of peaceful settlement, as provided for by the treaty concluded later. The author holds that such cases are governed by the general rules on conflicts between treaties, namely 'that the later treaty abrogated the earlier, or special treaty abrogated the general one.'[85] Referring to Hambro's statements, Anand notes that one may even argue that, since the Statute forms an integral part of the Charter, a declaration of acceptance is to be virtually regarded as an obligation under the United Nations Charter and that obligation, according to Article 103 of the Charter, precedes other obligations.[86]

The effects of future treaties concerning other methods or means of peaceful settlement on jurisdiction under the optional clause are dealt with by Merrills as well. The British professor maintains that if the reservation on other methods or means of peaceful settlement covers treaties to be concluded in the future – providing for other methods or means of settlement – it allows the parties to agree on an alternative procedure even after a dispute has been referred to the Court under the optional clause.[87] In that event, however, according to Merrills, the parties need not invoke the reservation relating to other methods of peaceful settlement, because during the course of proceedings they may at any time agree to discontinue the proceedings in order to resolve their dispute by another means. Thus in these situations it is not necessary for a state to refer to the reservation and as a result it is likely to be rather rare in practice for the reservation to be relied upon.[88]

Despite their rather high incidence, the reservations concerning other methods or means of peaceful settlement have received little attention before the two International Courts.

---

84 Anand (2008) 233.
85 *Id.* 234.
86 *Id.*
87 Merrills (1993) 225.
88 *Id.*

There is but one example, the *Electricity Company of Sofia and Bulgaria case*, which can be mentioned since the commencement of the Permanent Court of International Justice. In that legal dispute the applicant state, Belgium, referred the Court's jurisdiction to the optional clause declarations of the two states and the Treaty of conciliation, arbitration and judicial settlement of 23 June 1931 which entered into force on 4 February 1933. The Belgian declaration of acceptance of the optional clause contained a reservation relating to other methods of peaceful settlement, whereas the Belgian-Bulgarian Treaty of 1931 included the following provision:

> All disputes with regard to which the Parties are in conflict as to their respective rights shall be submitted for decision to the Permanent Court of International Justice, unless the Parties agree, in the manner hereinafter provided, to have resort to an arbitral tribunal.

Since in its preliminary objection Bulgaria contested the Court's jurisdiction, the aforementioned case gave rise to the questions of how the declarations of acceptance and the Treaty of 1931 were interrelated from the point of view of the jurisdiction of the Permanent Court of International Justice[89] and to what extent the 1931 Treaty, while in force, had influenced the Court's jurisdiction under the optional clause.[90] The Permanent Court provided no answers to these questions. The Court seems to have borne in mind only that its jurisdiction was based on the optional clause and Article 4 of the Treaty of 1931, paying no attention to the reservation of the Belgian declaration concerning other methods or means of peaceful settlement on the one hand and, on the other, giving no consideration to the sentence in Article 4 of the Treaty of 1931 to the effect that the Permanent Court of International Justice as a forum of dispute settlement was open to the parties only if they failed to agree on arbitral settlement. In his dissenting opinion, Judge van Eysinga pointed out that the Belgian declaration of acceptance was in fact subsidiary and

---

[89] The Belgian-Bulgarian Treaty of 1931 remained in force until 3 February 1938. Bulgaria's declaration of acceptance was dated 12 August 1921 and Belgium's declaration of acceptance was dated 10 March 1926.

[90] It should be noted that this did not become so clearly apparent from what the parties themselves had stated. In his dissenting opinion, Judge van Eysinga rightly observed that in their arguments the parties did not state clearly the problem of concurrent sources of jurisdiction. Cf. The *Electricity Company of Sofia and Bulgaria* (Preliminary Objection), Judgment of 4 April 1939, Dissenting Opinion by Jonkheer van Eysinga, *PCIJ Series A./B.* Fascicule No. 77, 111.

it was not to apply to cases for which the parties had provided some other method of peaceful settlement.[91] A similar conclusion was reached by Judge Hudson, who in his dissenting opinion explained that since the two systems, namely the jurisdiction based on the optional clause and the Treaty of 1931, were different, and furthermore the parties had agreed to pursuing recourse with respect to other means of peaceful settlement, for precisely that reason the Court's jurisdiction in that case may be based only on the Treaty of 1931.[92]

From the jurisprudence of the International Court of Justice one should refer to two cases in which the Court was confronted with the questions concerning reservations relating to other methods or means of peaceful settlement; however, as we will see the substance of the problems connected with these reservations was not dealt with in these cases.

The first one was the *Case concerning Certain Phosphate Lands in Nauru*. In 1989, Nauru – known to be one of the world's smallest states, situated in the archipelago of Micronesia – filed an application against Australia on the basis of the optional clause in respect of a 'dispute … over the rehabilitation certain phosphate lands (in Nauru) worked out before Nauruan independence'.[93] In its preliminary objection Australia invoked the reservation to its own declaration of acceptance concerning other means of peaceful settlement as well as the fact that the matter of rehabilitation had been repeatedly raised at different fora of the United Nations before Nauru finally waived, as was alleged at least by Australia, its claims to rehabilitation of the phosphate lands in an agreement between the Nauru Local Government Council on the one side and Australia, New Zealand and the United Kingdom on the other side on 14 November 1967. In view of all this, Australia claimed that with regard to the matters raised in Nauru's application, Nauru and Australia had agreed

---

91 *Id.*

92 Cf. *Id.* Dissenting Opinion of Judge Hudson, 124.

93 The application founded the Court's jurisdiction on the declarations of acceptance of the two states which were submitted by Australia on 17 March 1975 and Nauru on 29 January 1988. For the application, see http.//www.icj-cij.org/icj www/icases/iNAUSpleadings/inaus-application (accessed 17 July 2013). According to Professor Tomuschat, Nauru made an optional clause declaration only with the purpose of being able to file an application against Australia, and after doing so did not see any advantage in maintaining its submission to the compulsory jurisdiction of the Court and did not renew its declaration made for a fixed period. Cf. Tomuschat, in Zimmermann-Tomuschat-Oellers-Frahm (2006) 634.

'to have recourse to some other method of peaceful settlement' within the meaning of the reservation, and therefore, on the strength of the reservation attached to the Australian declaration of acceptance, the Court had no jurisdiction to decide on the dispute.[94] The Court did not find it necessary to examine what Australia had stated concerning other methods of peaceful settlement, because declarations made under Article 36, paragraph 2 of the Statute relate only to disputes between states and Nauru had not yet been an independent state at the time the 1967 agreement was concluded.[95]

The other case is the *Arbitral Award of 31 July 1989* (Guinea-Bissau v. Senegal). The dispute which concerned the maritime boundary between the two African states was considered at the end of the 1980s by an Arbitration Tribunal consisting of three arbitrators. More specifically, Guinea-Bissau, which challenged the existence and validity of the arbitral award of 31 July 1989, instituted proceedings against Senegal on 23 August 1989 on the basis of the declarations of acceptance of the two states.[96] No reservation was attached to Guinea-Bissau's declaration of acceptance; however, Senegal's declaration contained reservations including one that: 'Senegal may reject the Court's competence in respect of: Disputes in regard to which the parties have agreed to have recourse to some other method of settlement; …' and specified that the declaration was applicable solely to 'all legal disputes arising after the present declaration …'.

On that basis, Senegal argued that if Guinea-Bissau were to challenge the arbitral decision on the merits, it would be raising a question excluded from the Court's compulsory jurisdiction by way of Senegal's

---

94 For the Australian preliminary objection, see http://www.icj-cij.org/icjwww/icases/iNAUSpleadings/Pobjaustralia (accessed 17 July 2013).

95 For all these reasons the Court held that there was but one question to be answered regarding the matter, namely that as to whether after 31 January 1968 – when Nauru acceded to independence – Australia and Nauru had concluded an agreement whereby they undertook to settle the dispute relating to rehabilitation of the phosphate lands by resorting to an agreed procedure other than recourse to the Court. There being no such agreement, the Court rejected the objection raised by Australia and, as was already mentioned, didn't deal with the reservation on other methods of peaceful settlement. Cf. *Case concerning Certain Phosphate Lands in Nauru* (Preliminary Objections), Judgment of 26 June 1992, *ICJ Reports 1992*, 246–7.

96 Senegal's declaration of acceptance regarding compulsory jurisdiction was dated 2 December 1985 and that of Guinea-Bissau was dated 7 August 1989. For the application, see http://www.icj-cij.org/icj www/icases/idm/idmiorders/idm.iapplication (accessed 23 October 2013).

declaration of acceptance, as the parties had, in the Arbitration Agreement of 12 March 1985, made a provision that disputes concerning the maritime delimitation were to be subject to the Arbitration Agreement. Consequently the dispute submitted to the Court fell into the category of disputes excluded by the reservation on 'other means of settlement' that was included in Senegal's declaration of acceptance.

Again, in that case the Court did not dwell on the reservation concerning other means of peaceful settlement, because it held that the reservation in question did not affect its jurisdiction as the parties had agreed, during the proceedings, to draw a distinction between the substantive dispute relating to maritime delimitation, and the dispute relating to the Award rendered by the Arbitration Tribunal. The subject of the proceedings before the Court included only the latter dispute; arising after the Senegalese declaration of acceptance, and not able to be deemed an appeal against or revision of the Award. It was the dispute over the maritime boundary between the two states that was referred to the Arbitration Tribunal, whereas proceedings before the Court concerned the existence and the validity of the Arbitral Award and did not involve the merits of the delimitation dispute.[97]

V RESERVATIONS RELATING TO HOSTILITIES AND ARMED CONFLICTS

(a) Different Variants of the Reservation

The limitations concerning disputes that arise out of different hostilities and armed conflicts may appear as either *ratione materiae* or *ratione temporis* reservations and date as far back to the period between the two world wars. In the 1920s, in most declarations of acceptance, the exclusion of disputes relating to different hostilities or armed conflicts was not directly referred to in the scope of compulsory jurisdiction, because these disputes were already covered by those time limitations stipulating that the Court's jurisdiction was to apply to future disputes only. Such exclusion clauses, as Rosenne points out, were designed to prevent retroactive application of the declarations of acceptance.[98] In doing so, states were seeking to prevent disputes – connected with World War I – from being submitted to the Permanent Court of International

97 Cf. *Case concerning the Arbitral Award of 31 July 1989,* Judgment of 12 November 1991, *ICJ Reports 1991*, 61–2

98 Rosenne (2006) vol. II 773.

Justice. According to Rosenne, that matter was of particular significance and importance especially in view of the measures of economic warfare and warfare at sea adopted by both sides – the legality of which was being seriously contested by each other and by neutrals.[99] The author holds the view that the initial hesitation of the United Kingdom and other great powers in accepting the compulsory jurisdiction of the Permanent Court, 'was due to their concern regarding the consequences of the compulsory jurisdiction on their exercise of belligerent rights, especially in economic warfare'.[100]

A limitation relating to wartime events was first formulated in Poland's declaration of acceptance of 1931 to the effect that the declaration was not to apply to disputes 'connected directly or indirectly with the world war or with the Polish–Soviet war'.[101]

After the outbreak of World War II, from September 1939, a number of states like France, the United Kingdom and several members of the British Commonwealth of Nations (Australia, Canada, India, New Zealand, South Africa) first announced by Notes that their declarations of acceptance were not to apply to disputes connected with the current hostilities, and then they made new declarations of acceptance excluding from the operation of their declarations 'disputes arising out of events occurring during the present war' or 'disputes arising out of events occurring at a time when His Majesty's Government in the United Kingdom were involved in hostilities'.[102] The core and substance of their argument was that the system of collective security established by the Covenant of the League of Nations for the preservation of peace, of which the Permanent Court of International Justice had also been a part, had collapsed and they could not maintain their obligations after the change in circumstances.[103]

After 1945, limitations and reservations concerning hostilities and armed conflicts grew in frequency and, over time, even became more

---

[99] *Id.*

[100] *Id.* 774

[101] That declaration never entered into force.

[102] See the declarations of Australia (1940), India (1940), New Zealand (1940), the Union of South Africa (1940) and the United Kingdom (1940).

[103] As has already been mentioned objections against these reservations were presented by Belgium, Brasil, Denmark, Estonia, Haiti, the Netherlands, Norway, Peru, Sweden, Switzerland and Thailand.

On the objections, see, *Sixteenth Report of the Permanent Court of International Justice,* (June 1.5th, 1939–December 31st, 1945) *PCIJ Series* E. No. 16, 333.

extensive and more complicated, bringing within the scope of reservations a widening range of disputes, as the later reservations came to exclude from the compulsory jurisdiction of the Court not only disputes relating to wartime events, disputes connected with hostilities or conflicts with the involvement of declaring state in war, but also those hostilities relating to individual and collective self-defence, action against aggression and participation in peace-keeping missions, etc.[104]

With regard to reservations on disputes connected with armed conflicts, hostilities, etc., Maus writes that the declarations generally used two criteria, a temporal and a causal, for the definition of disputes covered by these reservations.[105] He mentions for example, the Canadian declaration of acceptance as modified in 1939 and the British declaration of 1957, in which the reservations relate to disputes arising out of events that occurred during World War II, regardless of whether or not they were connected with the hostilities. The said declarations accordingly refer to certain events that occurred at a specified time, defined so minutely as to fix the period using the exact dates of 3 September 1939 to 2 September 1945 in the UK declaration. This example was followed by Israel, whose declaration of acceptance of 17 October 1956 excluded from the Court's compulsory jurisdiction, 'Disputes arising out of events occurring between 15 May 1948 and 20 July 1949'.

A wider range of disputes is covered by those reservations which refer, not to disputes that arose at the time of a specific armed conflict, but generally to disputes that arose out of events occurring at a time when the declaring state 'was or is involved in hostilities'.[106] As can be seen, the said limitations apply not only to armed conflicts during World War II, but to all kinds of conflicts, including domestic ones. With regard to the application in concrete cases of reservations concerning hostilities and armed conflicts, Maus emphasizes that in such cases special attention should be given to whether or not the particular state was involved in the hostilities at the time of the events that gave rise to the dispute and

---

[104] Among the declarations currently in force, reservations concerning hostilities, armed conflicts, etc. can be found in the declarations of Djibouti (2005), Germany (2008), Honduras (1986), Hungary (1992), India (1947), Kenya (1965), Malawi (1966), Malta (1983), Mauritius (1968), Nigeria (1998), Sudan (1958). A reservation relating exclusively to defensive military action taken as a result of national defence is contained in the declaration of Greece (1994).

[105] Maus (1959) 144.

[106] See e.g. the declarations of Australia (1954), New Zealand (1940) and the Union of South Africa (1955).

whether there is a causal link, direct or indirect, between the said events and the dispute.[107]

One of the most complicated types of reservations relating to hostilities and armed conflicts can be found in Israel's declaration of acceptance of 17 October 1956,[108] which contains, along with the reservation excluding the events between 15 May 1948 and 20 July 1949, a rather wide limitation, practically embracing all armed conflicts taking place with Israeli involvement.[109] That reservation reads as follows:

> disputes arising out of, or having reference to, any hostilities, war, state of war, breach of peace, breach of armistice agreement or belligerent or military occupation (whether such war shall have been declared or not, and whether any state of belligerency shall have been recognized or not) in which the Government of Israel are or have been or may be involved at any time.

Again, in this respect, a similar reservation, rather complicated and comprising a wide range of armed conflicts, was attached to the 1992 declaration of acceptance of the Republic of Hungary, with the reservation applying to all disputes other than:

> (c) disputes relating to, or connected with, facts or situations of hostilities, war, armed conflicts, individual or collective actions taken in self-defence or the discharge of any functions pursuant to any resolution or recommendation of the United Nations, and other similar or related acts, measures or situations in which the Republic of Hungary is, has been or may in the future be involved.

By making that reservation Hungary was seeking to exclude from the Court's compulsory jurisdiction any dispute connected with any armed action, irrespective of how the Republic of Hungary might be involved in a particular action. The inclusion of this limitation in the Hungarian declaration of acceptance can be explained – in addition to the general arguments in favour of such reservations – by the fact that at the time the declaration was made the war in the Balkans was raging a few kilometres from the Hungarian border and Hungary, while striving to stay clear of

---

107 Maus (1959) 144–5.

108 That declaration of acceptance replaced another one dated 4 September 1950, which was expressed to be for a period of five years.

109 Israel terminated this declaration on 21 November 1985 and has not since made a new declaration of acceptance. Not long before the termination, Isreal amended its 1956 declaration of acceptance by a declaration on 28 February 1984.

that conflict, wanted to avoid in any way becoming a party to any dispute before the Court in connection with the Balkan war.

A rather new version of the reservation can be found in the declaration of acceptance of Germany (2008) explicitly excluding from the scope of the declaration of acceptance not only any dispute relating to, arising from, or connected with the deployment of armed forces abroad, or disputes relating to the involvement in such deployments or decisions thereon, but also those disputes relating to, arising from or connected 'with the use for military purposes of the territory of the Federal Republic of Germany, including its airspace, as well as maritime areas subject to German sovereign rights and jurisdiction'.

(b) The Court's Jurisprudence Regarding the Reservation

The reservations relating to armed conflicts have received scant attention before the two Courts.

In the *Case concerning Border and Transborder Armed Actions*, instituted by Nicaragua against Honduras in the 1980s, the respondent state, Honduras referred to the reservation contained in its declaration of acceptance that was associated with armed conflicts, but the Court, in its judgment on jurisdiction and the admissibility of the application, did not deal with that reservation.[110]

It should be added that a reservation concerning armed conflicts appeared in Honduras's 1986 declaration of acceptance, which replaced the one made on 20 February 1960.[111] According to Professor Merrills, Honduras modified its declaration of acceptance because it sought to

---

[110] In the *Case concerning Border and Transborder Armed Actions* (Nicaragua *v.* Honduras), the International Court of Justice in the end did not base its jurisdiction on the parties' declarations of acceptance, because it concluded that Art. XXXI of the Pact of Bogotá provided a basis for its jurisdiction and deemed it unnecessary to deal with the question as to whether the 1986 Honduran declaration of acceptance was opposable to Nicaragua in this case. Cf. *Case concerning Border and Transborder Armed Actions* (Nicaragua *v.* Honduras) (Jurisdiction of the Court and Admissibility of the Application), Judgment of 20 December 1988, *ICJ Reports 1988*, 76–88.

[111] According to the Honduran reservation, the Court's jurisdiction is not to apply among others to:

> '(c) disputes relating to facts or situations originating in armed conflicts or acts of a similar nature which may affect the territory of the Republic of Honduras, and in which it may find itself involved directly or indirectly.'

exclude the Court's jurisdiction in respect of disputes involving allegations of armed incursions into Nicaraguan territory from Honduras.[112] This seems to be supported, furthermore, by the fact that the Honduran declaration of acceptance was modified on 22 May 1986 and Nicaragua filed an application with the International Court of Justice against Honduras on 28 July 1986.

In connection with the *Case concerning Legality of Use of Force* (Serbia and Montenegro v. United Kingdom) one could raise the question as to whether in that dispute the British Government could have invoked the reservation relating to armed conflicts as contained in its 1963 declaration of acceptance if that declaration had still been in force at the time of the cases concerning the NATO air strikes.[113]

Nowadays, when armed forces of different nations act on behalf of the international community of states and take part in different actions of humanitarian intervention including peace creating, peacekeeping, peace enforcement, etc. actions, reservations relating to hostilities and armed conflicts seem to be concurrently included in more and more declarations of acceptance and an increasing frequency of references to such reservations cannot be ruled out either.

VI RESERVATIONS EXCLUDING DISPUTES RELATING TO TERRITORIAL SOVEREIGNTY

The reservations excluding territorial disputes represent, according to the traditional classification of reservations, a typical limitation of *ratione materiae*. The concept of territorial sovereignty is to be broadly interpreted in respect of these reservations and if there is a general reference to territorial sovereignty then it covers the land territory, maritime zones and airspace of the declaring state.

Such a reservation can be said to have first appeared in the Greek declaration of acceptance of 1929, in which the Hellenic Government excluded from its acceptance of compulsory jurisdiction any 'disputes relating to the territorial status of Greece, including disputes relating to its rights of sovereignty over its ports and lines of communication'. A similar limitation was included in the declarations of acceptance of Iran

---

112 Cf. Merrills (1993) 233.

113 That reservation was under para. V of the 1963 British declaration of acceptance which excluded 'disputes arising out of, or having reference to, any hostilities, war, state of war, or belligerent or military occupation in which the United Kingdom Government is or has been involved'.

in 1930 and Iraq in 1938, with the difference that the Persian declaration referred to rights of sovereignty over 'its islands and ports' instead of 'ports and lines of communication', while the Iraqi declaration mentioned sovereign rights over 'its waters and communications'. The limitation in the Romanian declaration of 1930 was broader inasmuch as it excluded from compulsory jurisdiction 'any question of substance or of procedure which might directly or indirectly cause the existing territorial integrity of Romania and her sovereign rights, including her rights over her ports and communications, to be brought into question.'

It is not accidental that between the two world wars, reservations excluding territorial disputes were to be found in the declarations of acceptance precisely by the aforementioned states. From the beginning of the 20th century Iran had territorial disputes with Great Britain over the Bahrain islands in the Persian Gulf,[114] whereas Greece and Romania acquired considerable territories in the wake of World War I. It appears, therefore, that the beneficiaries of territorial changes after World War I were seeking to avoid submission to the Permanent Court with regard to disputes relating to territorial questions. In the case of Romania, the inclusion of clauses concerning communications and ports was also motivated by the fact that Romania was struggling for jurisdiction and control of the upriver stretch of the Danube between Galatz and Braila against the European Commission of the Danube and the Permanent Court in its advisory opinion on the *Jurisdiction of the European Commission of the Danube*, held that under the law in force the European Commission possessed the same powers regarding the maritime sector of the Danube from Galatz to Braila as the sector below Galatz.[115] In all likelihood that decision in Bucharest was considered as an offence to the sovereignty of Romania and the Romanian Government was trying to prevent, by means of a reservation, any related dispute being referred to the Permanent Court of International Justice.

After World War II, the practice continued of including in the declarations of acceptance reservations excluding territorial disputes, and over the course of time, more and more complicated variants of the reservation were formulated.[116] These reservations expressly stated that

---

[114] Cf. Ali Naghi Farmanfarma, 'The Declarations of Members Accepting the Compulsory Jurisdiction of the International Court of Justice' (Imprimerie Gaugin & Laubscher S.A., 1952), 72.

[115] See *Jurisdiction of the European Commission of the Danube*, Advisory Opinon of 8 December 1927, *PCIJ Series B*, No. 14.

[116] The reservations referring simply to 'disputes with respect to or in relation with the borders of the Republic of Suriname' (Suriname, 1987) or

limitations apply – in addition to territorial and border disputes, and delimitation and demarcation of frontiers – to disputes concerning maritime zones and airspace. Moreover, certain declarations refer not only in general terms to maritime zones, but specify those distinct areas affected by the reservation, namely excluding from the scope of compulsory jurisdiction disputes relating to bays, islands, territorial sea, contiguous zones, the exclusive economic zone, the continental shelf,[117] as well as matters concerning the superjacent airspace of territorial waters.[118]

The growing number of reservations excluding disputes relating to the law of the sea is in all certainty due to the recodification, in the 1970–80s, of the law of the sea on the one hand and, in the case of the latest declarations, due to the fact that the International Tribunal for the Law of the Sea was established in 1996.

The inclusion in declarations of acceptance of reservations concerning territorial sovereignty was related in some cases to concrete legal disputes, as is exemplified by Nigeria, which in 1999 modified its declaration of 1965 by adding additional reservations, one of them being a rather comprehensive limitation affecting territorial disputes that applied to land and maritime zones as well as its airspace.[119] We are not far from the truth in supposing the inclusion of that limitation in Nigeria's declaration of acceptance to have been related to the fact that regarding the land and maritime boundaries between Cameroon and Nigeria, the former had instituted proceedings against the latter under the optional clause in 1994 and in its judgment of 1998 the Court rejected Nigeria's preliminary objections, while ruling that it had jurisdiction.[120]

---

excluding 'disputes with regard to the territory or State boundaries' (Poland, 1996) are rather scarce.

[117] Rather complicated reservations concerning maritime disputes and disputes over different marine zones can be found in the declarations of Australia (2002), Honduras (1986), India (1974), Malta (1983), Nigeria (1998) and the Philippines (1971).

[118] On this score, see the declarations of Honduras (1986), India (1974) and Nigeria (1998).

[119] Para. VIII of the 1998 Nigerian declaration of acceptance reads as follows: 'disputes concerning the allocation, delimitation or demarcation of territory (whether land, maritime, lacustrine or superjacent airspace) unless the Government of Nigeria specially agrees to such jurisdiction and within the limits of any such special agreement;'

[120] See the *Case concerning the Land and Maritime Boundary between Cameroon and Nigeria* (Preliminary Objections), Judgment of 11 June 1998, *ICJ Reports 1998*, 275–327.

One of the most peculiar reservations concerning territorial disputes can be found in the declaration of acceptance of Djibouti (2005) covering any dispute with the Republic of Djibouti relating to its territorial status, frontiers, etc, as well as its maritime zones, islands, bays, gulf, airspace etc.[121]

Despite the fact that a large part of legal disputes submitted to the two International Courts concerned territorial disputes existing before the Courts, few references were made to reservations relating to territorial sovereignty or territorial disputes. This may suggest, among other things, that the said reservations contain fairly clear and unambiguous limitations in general on the one hand and, on the other hand, the disputes relating to territorial sovereignty belong to the class of interstate disputes which the International Court of Justice is the most generally accepted and most suitable forum to decide.

From the rare instances referring to those kinds of reservations one could mention the dispute of *Whaling in the Antarctic* between Australia and Japan.[122] In that case the respondent state, Japan, on the basis of reciprocity, tried to contest the Court's jurisdiction over the dispute, arguing that it fell within one of the reservations of Australia's declaration excluding from the Court's jurisdiction 'any dispute concerning or

---

[121] The declaration of acceptance provides that:

this declaration shall not apply to: …

7. Disputes with the Republic of Djibouti concerning or relating to:
(a) The status of its territory or the modification or delimitation of its frontiers or any other matter concerning boundaries;
(b) The territorial sea, the continental shelf and the margins, the exclusive fishery zone, the exclusive economic zone and other zones of national maritime jurisdiction including for the regulation and control of marine pollution and the conduct of scientific research by foreign vessels;
(c) The condition and status of its islands, bays and gulfs;
(d) The airspace superjacent to its land and maritime territory; and
(e) The determination and delimitation of its maritime boundaries.

[122] On 31 May 2010, Australia submitted an application against Japan regarding Japan's continued pursuit of a large-scale programme of whaling under the Second Phase of its Japanese Whale Research Program under Special Permit in the Antarctic ('JARPA II'), in breach of obligations assumed by Japan under the International Convention for the Regulation of Whaling ('ICRW') 1, as well as its other international obligations for the preservation of marine mammals and the marine environment. The applicant based the Court's jurisdiction on its own and Japan's declaration of acceptance. On 20 November 2012, New Zealand filed in the Registry of the Court a Declaration of Intervention, which was decided admissible by the Court.

relating to the delimitation of maritime zones, including the territorial sea, the exclusive economic zone and the continental shelf, or arising out of, concerning, or relating to the exploitation of any disputed area of or adjacent to any such maritime zone pending its delimitation'.[123]

The judgment of the International Court of Justice in the *Aegean Sea Continental Shelf case* provides guidance in the interpretation of reservations concerning territorial sovereignty, albeit the Court's jurisdiction was not based on optional clause declarations, but instead on the 1928 General Act for the Pacific Settlement of International Disputes read with Article 36, paragraph 1, and Article 37 of the Statute.[124]

In 1976, Greece instituted proceedings against Turkey in respect of a dispute concerning the delimitation of the continental shelf pertaining to each of the two states in the Aegean Sea and their rights thereover. Both the Greek and Turkish instruments of accession to the 1928 General Act were accompanied by declarations with reservations, and one of the reservations included in the Greek instrument of accession excluded:

> (b) disputes concerning questions which by international law are solely within the domestic jurisdiction of States, and in particular disputes relating to the territorial status of Greece, including disputes relating to its rights of sovereignty over its ports and lines of communication.

The Turkish Government took the position that, whether or not the General Act is assumed to be still in force, reservation (b) of the Greek instrument of accession would exclude the Court's competence with respect to the dispute submitted by Greece. Thus, in that case the Court had to determine whether questions connected with continental shelf boundaries in the Aegean Sea should be covered by the above-cited reservation and what was to be understood by the phrase 'disputes relating to the territorial status of Greece'.[125]

---

[123] See *Whaling in the Antarctic* (Australia v. Japan: New Zealand intervening) Japan's Counter Memorial of 9 March 2012.

[124] In its application, Greece relied on, first, Art. 17 of the 1928 General Act for the Pacific Settlement of International Disputes, and Art. 36, para. 1 and Art. 37 of the Statute of the International Court of Justice, and second, the Greek-Turkish joint communiqué issued at Brussels on 31 May 1975. The Greek Government contended that the Act must be presumed to be in force between Greece and Turkey. According to Greece, Art. 17 of the General Act contained a jurisdictional clause which, read in combination with Art. 37, and Art. 36, para. 1 of the Statute, sufficed to establish the Court's jurisdiction.

[125] Cf. *Aegean Sea Continental Shelf.* Observations of the Government of Turkey on the Request by the Government of Greece for Provisional Measures of

The Greek Government argued that a restrictive view of the meaning should be taken, where the territorial status was not to be conceived of *in abstracto*, as it was bound up with the territorial settlements established after World War I.[126]

In interpreting the cited reservation of the Greek instrument of accession to the General Act, the Court considered the Greek declaration of acceptance made in 1929 as well, only two years before Greece's accession to the General Act, because the 1929 declaration of acceptance contained the reservation of 'disputes relating to the territorial status of Greece'. The Court examined that reservation in the context of the Greek reservation to the General Act and reasoned that it was hardly conceivable that at the time of acceding to the General Act, Greece, in its instrument of accession to the General Act, should have intended to give to its reservation of 'disputes relating to the territorial status of Greece' a scope which differed fundamentally from that given to it in its declaration of acceptance made some two years earlier.

The Court even dismissed the Greek argument which claimed that the concept of the continental shelf was completely unknown in 1928 – which was when the General Act was adopted – and 1931 – which was when Greece became a party to the General Act – and regarding the concept of territorial status the Court provided that:

> Once it is established that the expression 'the territorial status of Greece' was used in Greece's instrument of accession as a generic term denoting any matters comprised within the concept of territorial status under general international law, the presumption necessarily arises that its meaning was intended to follow the evolution of the law and to correspond with the meaning attached to the expression by the law in force at any given time.[127]

In its findings, the Court consequently held that the phrase 'disputes relating to the territorial status of Greece' must be interpreted in accordance with the rules of international law existing today – not those existing in 1931.[128] The judgment given by the International Court of Justice in the *Aegean Sea Continental Shelf case* points to a broad interpretation of the concept of territorial disputes. It suggests the conclusion that if in a particular case reference is made to an earlier

---

Protection. *ICJ. Pleadings*, 73, and Memorial of Greece (Questions of Jurisdiction) *Id.* 239–45.

[126] *Id.* 248–51.

[127] *Aegean Sea Continental Shelf case* (Jurisdiction of the Court), Judgment of 19 December 1978, *ICJ Reports 1978*, 32.

[128] *Id.* 33–4.

reservation of a general nature concerning matters of the law of the sea, the evolution of the law of the sea and the evolution of the coastal state's rights of exploration and exploitation over different maritime zones should all be taken into account.

VII RESERVATIONS RELATING TO ENVIRONMENTAL DISPUTES

From the 1970s onwards, several states have inserted in their declarations of acceptance limitations relating to environmental disputes. One can distinguish between two classes of these reservations. One group contains limitations that apply in general to all disputes over environmental issues. The other group consists of reservations that refer to a special group of environmental disputes which in most cases include disputes relating to certain maritime zones.

One of the first reservations of a general nature virtually encompassing all environmental disputes was to be found in Poland's declaration of acceptance of 1990, which excluded from the Court's compulsory jurisdiction 'disputes with regard to pollution of the environment, not connected with the treaty obligations of Poland'. This reservation concerning environmental issues was reiterated by Poland in its new declaration of acceptance of 1996, with the difference being that the new declaration refers to disputes relating to 'environmental protection' on the one hand and omits the phrase 'not connected with treaty obligations' on the other. This in turn – as is also recognized by Renata Szafarz – results in the formula of the declaration of 1996 being broader in scope than the formula of the declaration of 1990,[129] and thus it applies to a wider range of environmental disputes. Another Polish expert, Wojciech Góralczyk, considers the reservation excluding environmental disputes in the Polish declaration of acceptance of 1990 to be the most controversial part of the declaration[130] and the reason behind the exclusion of disputes connected with the pollution of the environment lies in the fact that customary environmental law had not yet sufficiently crystallized and Poland might

---

129 Cf. Renata Szafarz, 'The Modification of the Scope of I.C.J. Jurisdiction in Respect of Poland' in Ando-McWinney-Wofrum (2002) vol. I, 546.

130 Wojciech Góralczyk, 'Changing Attitudes of Central and Eastern European States towards the Judicial Settlement of International Disputes' in Daniel Bardonnet (ed.) *Le réglement des différends internationaux en Europe: Prospectives d'avenir* (Colloque à La Haye, 6–8 septembre 1990) (Martinus Nijhoff, 1991) 494.

be feared to be declared liable for unpredictable environmental damages.[131] This reasoning is hard to accept, and it is a pity that rather than abandoning its reservation excluding issues of environmental pollution, Poland widened the scope of the reservation in its 1996 declaration of acceptance.

Among the new declarations under the optional clause it is Slovakia's 2004 declaration of acceptance that also contains a comprehensive reservation concerning environmental issues.

As mentioned earlier, the other group of reservations concerning environmental disputes excludes from compulsory jurisdiction only environmental issues affecting certain specific areas. A typical example of such a limitation is to be found in Canada's 1970 declaration of acceptance providing that the declaration does not apply to:

> disputes arising out of or concerning jurisdiction or rights claimed or exercised by Canada in respect of the conservation, management or exploitation of the living resources of the sea, or in respect of the prevention or control of pollution or contamination of the marine environment in marine areas adjacent to the coast of Canada.

Subsequently, similar reservations appeared in the declarations of Barbados (1980)[132] and Malta (1966, amended 1983).[133]

In the 1994 Canadian declaration of acceptance, a new reservation was introduced that further excluded from the jurisdiction of the Court:

> (d) disputes arising out of or concerning conservation and management measures taken by Canada with respect to vessels fishing in the NAFO Regulatory Area, as defined in the Convention on Future Multilateral Co-operation in the Northwest Atlantic Fisheries 1978, and the enforcement of such measures.[134]

---

[131] *Id.*

[132] The reservation added to Barbados's declaration of acceptance is identical word for word with the Canadian reservation.

[133] The new reservation attached to the 1966 declaration of acceptance of Malta reads as follows:

> 'the acceptance of the Government of Malta of the jurisdiction of the Court shall be limited to all disputes with Malta other than … (d) the prevention or control of pollution or contamination of the marine environment in marine areas adjacent to the coast of Malta.'

[134] On 10 May 1994, the same day as the deposition of its declaration of acceptance, the Canadian Government submitted to the Parliament Bill C–29 amending the Coastal Fisheries Protection Act by extending its area of application to include the Regulatory Area of the Northwest Atlantic Fisheries

The reservation of the 1994 Canadian declaration was lengthily discussed in the *Fisheries Jurisdiction case*, as the Court had to establish whether that reservation applied to the dispute submitted by Spain. Thus, one of the crucial questions was whether the measures taken by Canada, including the enforcement measures and use of force, could constitute 'conservation and enforcement measures' under the reservation.

The incompatibility of paragraph 2 *(d)* of Canadian declaration with the Statute or the Charter was not raised. However, according to Judge *ad hoc* Torres Bernárdez, the interpretation of the reservation was in a manner contrary to the Statute, the United Nations Charter and international law.[135]

The Court interpreted the reservation 'in a natural and reasonable way, having due regard to the intention of (Canada) at the time when it accepted the compulsory jurisdiction of the Court', and it found that the dispute submitted by Spain:

> constitutes a dispute 'arising out of' and 'concerning' 'conservation and management measures taken by Canada with respect to vessels fishing in the NAFO Regulatory Area' and 'the enforcement measures'. It follows that this dispute comes within the terms of the reservation contained in paragraph 2 *(d)* of the Canadian declaration of 10 May 1994. The Court consequently has no jurisdiction to adjudicate upon the present dispute.[136]

Returning to the limitations inserted in declarations of acceptance, it is regrettable that as mankind has become increasingly aware of preservation of the environment, there are some states which have included in their declarations of acceptance reservations on environmental matters.[137]

Organization (NAFO). Bill C–29 was adopted by Parliament, and received Royal Assent on 12 May 1994. The Coastal Fisheries Protection Regulations were also amended, on 25 May 1994 and again on 3 March 1995.

135 Cf. *Fisheries Jurisdiction case* (Spain v. Canada), Jurisdiction of the Court, Judgment of 4 December 1998, Dissenting Opinion of Judge ad hoc Torres Bernárdez, *ICJ Reports 1998*, 636.

136 *Fisheries Jurisdiction case* (Spain v. Canada), Jurisdiction of the Court, Judgment 4 December 1998, *ICJ Reports 1998*, 467.

137 It should be mentioned that in 1993 the Court established a special Chamber for Environmental Matters composed of seven members for environmental cases under Art. 26, para. 1 of the Statute. The chamber was periodically reconstituted until 2006; however, no single case was referred to the chamber and in 2006 the Court decided not to hold elections for the bench of that chamber.

VIII RESERVATIONS CONCERNING DISPUTES UNDER CONSIDERATION BY THE COUNCIL OF THE LEAGUE OF NATIONS OR THE SECURITY COUNCIL

It is the French declaration of acceptance of 1924 that contained the limitation stipulating that if one of the parties summoned the other party before the Council of the League of Nations under Article 15 of the Covenant, then during the attempt to settle the dispute by conciliation, neither party was entitled to have recourse to the Court.[138] It was in essence this reservation that inspired those reservations referring to the proceedings before the Council of the League of Nations – exemplified initially in the 1929 declaration of the United Kingdom and then subsequently in those declarations of other states such as Iran (1930), France (1929) and the Member states of the British Commonwealth of Nations.[139] With these reservations the declaring states reserve themselves the right to request suspension of the proceedings before the Permanent Court of International Justice in respect of disputes which have been submitted to the Council of the League of Nations or are under the consideration thereof. The reservations in declarations made by the Member states of the Commonwealth of Nations differed from the reservation joined to the 1924 French declaration mainly in that they

---

[138] According to the 1924 French declaration of acceptance, it has adhered to the optional clause of Art. 36, para. 2 of the Statute of the Court, 'subject to the observations made in the First Committee of the Fifth Assembly to the effect that "one of the Parties to a dispute may summon the other before the Council of the League of Nations, with a view to an attempt to effect a pacific settlement as provided in paragraph 3 of Article 15 of the Covenant and, during this attempt to settle the dispute by conciliation, neither Party may summon the other before the Court of Justice".' That declaration was never ratified by France, so it never entered into force, and in 1929 France made a new declaration of acceptance.

[139] See the declarations of Australia (1929, 1940), Canada (1929), India (1929, 1940), New Zealand (1929, 1940), South Africa (1929, 1940) and the United Kingdom (1940).

Several writers believe that the British reservation was inspired by the discussions held in a committee of the Fifth Assembly of the League of Nations, as in recognizing the Court's compulsory jurisdiction a state may 'reserve the right of laying disputes before the Council of the League of Nations with a view to conciliation in accordance with paragraphs 1–3 of Article 15 of the Covenant, with the proviso that neither party might, during the proceedings before the Council, take proceedings against the other in the Court.' Cf. Anand (2008) 235 and Hudson (1972) 470.

reserved the right to suspend proceedings with certain time limitations. According to these reservations, the request for suspension was to be made within ten days of notification of the initiation of proceedings before the Court and the duration of suspension was not to be longer than 12 months except when the parties had so agreed or all members of the Council of the League not involved in the dispute had so decided.

The greatest danger in connection with the said reservations is their implication of the possibility of removing a case from the Court, particularly if one considers that the parties may agree on a suspension longer than 12 months as stated in the reservations. The double-edged nature of playing for time is referred to by Lauterpacht, too, who writes that the state including such a reservation in its declaration may happen to be an applicant, and 'see the justice of her claims delayed as the result of the very same reservation which she formulated in order to strengthen her position as defendant'.[140]

With regard to the reservation in question, Anand refers to the Memorandum accompanying the 1929 British declaration of acceptance and states, inter alia, that there are certain disputes 'which are really political in character though juridical in appearance'. According to the Memorandum, disputes of this kind could be dealt with more satisfactorily by the Council and the aforementioned reservation was inspired by that very reason.[141] Anand asserts, moreover, that since the reservation provides no definition as to the disputes to be referred to the Court, states are in fact completely free to decide what they consider to be 'really political in character'.[142]

Furthermore, reservations affecting the Council of the League of Nations produced another variant appearing in Italy's 1929 declaration of acceptance; the limitation therein expressing that the Court's jurisdiction is only to be accepted in disputes that have proved impossible to solve through diplomatic channels or as a result of the action of the Council of the League of Nations. Reservations of the same meaning were contained in the declarations of Czechoslovakia (1929), Peru (1929) and Romania (1930, 1936), the respective reservations expressing that the declaring state reserved itself the right to submit the dispute to the Council of the League of Nations before having recourse to the Court.

Since the effect of the declarations of acceptance providing for the compulsory jurisdiction of the Permanent Court should be regarded as

---

140 Lauterpacht (1930) 159.
141 Anand (2008) 236.
142 *Id.* 236.

conferring jurisdiction to the International Court of Justice under Art. 36, para. 5 of the Statute, in connection with reservations referring to the procedure before the Council of the League of Nations the question has arisen whether the Security Council can be regarded as replacing the Council of the League of Nations.[143] In any case, this question is no longer of relevance because not a single declaration containing a reservation on the procedure before the Council of the League of Nations is in force today.

After the establishment of the International Court of Justice, similar reservations to the aforementioned limitations were formulated and in these reservations the Security Council figured instead of the League's Council.[144]

It is clear that the purpose of the reservation was to avoid the same dispute being considered by the Court and the Security Council simultaneously and in this respect the reservation gives certain liberty to the parties. It should be mentioned that in the *Case concerning Military and Paramilitary Activities in and against Nicaragua*, the Court dealt with situations where the same dispute was considered simultaneously by both the Court and the Security Council; however, the reservation in question was not brought up in those cases, since the declarations of acceptance of the parties did not contain such a limitation.[145]

Again, there is a further problem connected with this reservation. The limitation regarding the suspension of proceedings differs from the other reservations attached to declarations of acceptance which are reservations on substantive law. Such a reservation is a procedural clause by which the declaring state reserves itself the right to request suspension of proceedings before the Court in certain situations. This is worthy of attention chiefly because suspension of proceedings is neither provided for by the Statute nor the Rules of Court. There is no doubt that in certain cases proceedings before the Court often happen to be 'dormant' because at the request of the parties the Court sets rather long time limits or intensive negotiations progress between the parties with the prospect of reaching a settlement out of court. At any rate, suspension of proceedings as an institution of procedural law is unknown in proceedings before the

---

143 Kelsen affirms that the wording of Art. 36, para. 5 of the Statute does not admit an interpretation that the Council of the League of Nations can be replaced by the Security Council in respect of the limitation in question. Cf. Kelsen (1951) 528.

144 See, e.g. Australia's declaration of 1954.

145 On this score, see Alexandrov (1995) 106–12.

International Court,[146] which is a reason why the question of compatibility with the Rules of Court arises in connection with reservations providing for suspension of proceedings before the Court in cases where the same dispute is under consideration by the Security Council.

IX OBJECTIVE RESERVATION OF DOMESTIC JURISDICTION

Reservations excluding questions of domestic jurisdiction have become one of the limitations most frequently resorted to in our days. A distinction can be drawn between two types of such reservations. One category includes what may be called 'objective' criterion, meaning that in most of these declarations states are referring to international law as a comparatively objective 'criterion' for defining the disputes which are excluded from the Court's compulsory jurisdiction; in the literature of international law such limitations are termed 'objective reservations of domestic jurisdiction'. The other category consists of reservations by which the declaring states explicitly reserve themselves the right to determine matters of domestic jurisdiction, a reason why such reservations are commonly referred to as 'subjective reservations of domestic jurisdiction'.[147] Reservations of the latter category have only appeared after World War II.

(a) Variants of the Reservation

Under the terms of objective reservations of domestic jurisdiction, questions relating to domestic jurisdiction, according to international law, are excluded from the scope of the Court's compulsory jurisdiction.

Limitations of this type appeared in declarations of acceptance of the Permanent Court in the late 1920s for the first time and in 1929; this is exemplified by the actions of Australia, Canada, India, New Zealand, the Union of South Africa and the United Kingdom, which after mutual consultations attached to their respective declarations of acceptance a uniform reservation to the effect that the compulsory jurisdiction of the

---

[146] On this score, see Gerhard Wegen, 'Discontinuance and Withdrawal' in Zimmermann-Tomuschat-Oellers-Frahm (2006) 1258–60.

[147] Cf. Henryk de Fumel, *Les réserves dans les déclarations d'acceptation de la jurisdiction obligatoire de la Cour Internationale de Justice*. Université de Nancy, Publications de Centre Européen Universitaire, Nancy, 1962, 14; and Rosenne (2006) vol. I, 393–5.

Court did not apply to 'disputes with regard to questions which by international law fall exclusively within the jurisdiction of' the United Kingdom, South Africa, etc. Other states were soon to follow the example of the United Kingdom and the members of the British Commonwealth of Nations with such a limitation being attached to their declarations of acceptance.[148]

A considerable part of the declarations of acceptance made after World War II contain objective reservations of domestic jurisdiction.[149] Today the objective reservations of domestic jurisdiction are worded in various ways. One of the variants follows the formula of matters or questions falling 'exclusively' within the domestic jurisdiction of the declarant state by international law,[150] which originated, as Merrills points out, of Article 15, paragraph 8 of the Covenant.[151] Another group of states reproduces the terminology of Article 2, paragraph 7 of the Charter, referring to matters falling 'essentially' within domestic jurisdiction.[152] The third group simply refers to disputes with regard to matters falling or subject to domestic jurisdiction, either mentioning 'under international law' or making no reference to international law.[153] Merrills is of the view that the variance of the wording makes no substantial difference, and these types of reservations are otherwise superfluous because under Article 36, paragraph 2 of the Statute the Court's competence is confined to matters of international law.[154]

---

[148] On this score, see the declarations of Albania, Persia, Romania and Yugoslavia of 1930 as well as those of Poland (1931), (another declaration of) Albania (1935), Argentina, Romania (1936), Brazil (1937), Iraq (1938), Egypt (1939), and Australia, Great Britain, India, New Zealand and South Africa of 1940. Cf. Alexandrow (1995) 148.

[149] Among the declarations currently in force, such a reservation can be found in the declarations of Barbados (1980), Botswana (1970), Canada (1994), Gambia (1966), Guinea (1998), Honduras (1986), Hungary (1992), India (1974), the Ivory Coast (2001), Kenya (1965), Madagascar (1992), Malta (1966), Mauritius (1968), Nigeria (1998), Pakistan (1960), Poland (1996), Senegal (1985), Slovakia (2004) and Swaziland (1969).

[150] See the declarations of Barbados (1980), Canada (1994), the Ivory Coast (2001), Djibouti (2005), Gambia (1966), Guinea (1998), Hungary (1992), Kenya (1965), Madagascar (1992), Malta (1966, 1983), Mauritius (1968), Pakistan (1960), Poland (1996), Senegal (1985) and Slovakia (2004).

[151] Merrills (1993), 239.

[152] See the declarations of Botswana (1970), India (1974), Nigeria (1998), Swaziland (1969).

[153] There is no reference to international law in the declaration of Cyprus (2002).

[154] Merrills (1993) 239.

In the case of these declarations and others as well the question emerges as to what should be covered by the term 'domestic jurisdiction', especially because in several cases international law provides no clear guidance as to what falls within the domestic jurisdiction of states.[155] Among the reservations of domestic jurisdiction, however, the real problem is posed not by objective reservations of domestic jurisdiction, but by the 'refined' versions thereof, i.e. the subjective reservations of domestic jurisdiction.[156]

(b) The Jurisprudence of the Two Courts Regarding the Reservation

The question of domestic jurisdiction was considered by the Permanent Court of International Justice for the first time – although not in connection with optional clause declarations – in an advisory opinion on the *Nationality Decrees Issued in Tunis and Morocco (French Zone)*.[157] The question before the Court for an advisory opinion was that of whether the dispute between France and Great Britain regarding the national decrees issued in Tunis and Morocco (French Zone) on 8 November 1921 and their application to British subjects, is or is not, by international law, a matter of domestic jurisdiction under Article 15, paragraph 8 of the Covenant.

In its advisory opinion the Court made two important statements. In connection with the scope of domestic jurisdiction the Court held that 'whether a certain matter is or is not solely within the jurisdiction of a

---

155 The Institut de droit international dealt with that question and according to its resolution adopted at the Session of Aix-en-Provence in 1954, reserved domains are those state activities where the state's competence is not bound by international law, and the extent of that depends on international law and it changes with the development of that. Institut de droit international, Session d'Aix-en-Provence – 1954, resolution La détermination du domaine réservé et ses effets' (Art. 1. paras. 1 and 2).

156 These reservations will be discussed in Chapter 8.

157 The request for an advisory opinion was referred to the Court by the Council of the League of Nations and concerned the Decrees of 8 November 1921 issued by the Bay of Tunis and the President of the French Republic on the one hand, and by the Sheriff of Morocco and the President of the French Republic, on the other, concerning the nationality of certain persons born in Tunis and Morocco. Since early 1922 the British Government protested against the French Government regarding the above-mentioned decrees and their application to British nationals. The case was placed on the agenda of the Council which decided to request an advisory opinion from the Court.

State is an essentially relative question, it depends upon the development of international relations'.[158]

Regarding Article 15, paragraph 8 of the Covenant, it emphasized that: 'The words "solely within the domestic jurisdiction" seem rather to contemplate certain matters which, though they may very closely concern the interests of more than one State, are not, in principle, regulated by international law.'[159]

Two contentious cases before the Permanent Court of International Justice, notably the *Losinger and Co. case* and the *Electricity Company of Sofia and Bulgaria case*, similarly involved the question of domestic jurisdiction.

In 1935 Switzerland filed an application against Yugoslavia in the *Losinger and Co. case* under the optional clause in connection with the contract for the construction of certain railways in the District of Pozarevac in Yugoslavia.[160]

The Yugoslavian declaration of acceptance of 1930 contained a limitation excluding 'disputes with regard to questions which, by international law, fall exclusively within the jurisdiction of the Kingdom of Yugoslavia'.

Yugoslavia raised a preliminary objection, asking the Court to declare that it had no jurisdiction, claiming that the dispute did not affect questions of international law. Incidentally, the Yugoslavian argument was not based so much on the reservation of domestic jurisdiction in its declaration of acceptance, as rather Article 36, paragraph 2, subparagraphs (b) and (c) of the Statute of the Permanent Court, under which the Court's compulsory jurisdiction covers only questions of international law. The Court did not decide on the problem raised by Yugoslavia, because the proceedings had been interrupted at the request of the parties.[161] This case is nevertheless of interest because it was the first in which the Court's jurisdiction was based on a declaration of acceptance containing a reservation of domestic jurisdiction, although the Court

---

158 *Nationality Decrees Issued in Tunis and Morocco (French Zone) on 8 November 1921*, Advisory Opinion 7 February 1923, *PCIJ Series B.* Advisory Opinion No.4. 24.

159 *Id.* 23–4.

160 Switzerland's declaration of acceptance was registered in 1921 and on 1 March 1926 the Swiss Government renewed it for an additional ten years. The Yugoslavian declaration was dated 16 May 1930.

161 See the *Losinger & Co. case*, Order (Preliminary Objection), 27 June 1936; Order (Discontinuance), December 14, 1936. *PCIJ Series A/B.* No. 67. 15–25 and No. 69, 99–102.

declined to regard the reservation as one depriving it of its jurisdiction *in limine litis*.[162]

In *The Electricity Company of Sofia and Bulgaria case*, reference was likewise made to the issue of domestic jurisdiction, although the reservation of domestic jurisdiction was not included in the declarations of acceptance of the parties. In the proceedings instituted by Belgium against Bulgaria the latter submitted a preliminary objection declaring that the object of the dispute was a matter within its domestic jurisdiction as it did not fall within any of the categories of Article 36 of the Statute, which is a general provision enumerating legal disputes for which the Court has jurisdiction. In other words, Bulgaria referred to the article of the Statute as one preventing the Court from dealing with matters of domestic jurisdiction. The Court found that the Bulgarian objection was related to the merits of the case, for the argument that the dispute contained no international elements was so fundamental that this plea couldn't be regarded as possessing the character of a preliminary objection.[163]

On the basis of the foregoing it can be stated that while the problem of domestic jurisdiction was touched upon before the Permanent Court of International Justice, little mention was made regarding objective reservations of domestic jurisdiction. The cases mentioned above hold some interest solely for taking an approach with respect to the concept of domestic jurisdiction, and both the Permanent Court and the parties were chiefly concerned with the relationship between domestic jurisdiction and Article 36 of the Statute.

In the jurisprudence of the International Court of Justice, reference to an objective reservation of domestic jurisdiction was made in the *Anglo-Iranian Oil Co. Case.* Both the declarations of acceptance of the United Kingdom and Iran contained the objective reservation of domestic jurisdiction, and the 1930 Persian declaration of acceptance excluded from the Court's compulsory jurisdiction '(c) disputes with regard to questions which, by international law, fall exclusively within the jurisdiction of Persia'.

In that legal dispute Iran put forward that the Persian declaration had been made at the time of the League of Nations and it applied only to disputes within exclusive domestic jurisdiction under international law. However, since the 1930s, international law has undergone changes, this

---

162 Cf. Briggs (1958) 316.

163 *The Electricity Company of Sofia and Bulgaria* (Preliminary Objection), Judgment April 4, 1939, *PCIJ Series A/B*. No. 77, 83.

reservation is considered as 'having regard to the substitution of Article 2, paragraph 7 of the Charter of the United Nations for Article 15, paragraph 8 of the Covenant of the League of Nations, must be understood as extending to questions which are essentially within the domestic jurisdiction of States'. Thus, the Iranian declaration of 1930 should be seen as if it used the wording of Article 2, paragraph 7 of the Charter.[164]

The International Court of Justice, for its part, did not pronounce on the question raised by Iran concerning Article 2, paragraph 7 of the Charter, since it accepted Iran's preliminary objection referring to a reservation excluding the retroactive effect of the Persian declaration of acceptance.[165]

In the *Anglo-Iranian Oil Company case* the question of domestic jurisdiction emerged in another context as well. In its first preliminary objection submitted to the Court, Iran contended that under Article 2, paragraph 7 of the Charter, the Court should declare that it lacks jurisdiction *ex officio*, because the matters dealt with by the Iranian nationalization laws of 1951, challenged by the United Kingdom in that case, were essentially within the domestic jurisdiction of states, and no organ of the United Nations had power to interfere with them. The Tehrani Government maintained that, the Statute of the International Court of Justice formed an integral part of the Charter, and as the International Court of Justice was the principal judicial organ of the United Nations, Article 2, paragraph 7 of the Charter applied to the Court as well and clearly restricted the Court's jurisdiction in matters at issue.[166]

In connection with the jurisprudence of the International Court of Justice, mention should also be made of the *Right of Passage case*, in which reference was likewise made to the domestic jurisdiction of states. In the fifth preliminary objection India relied on the reservation of its

---

[164] Cf. *Anglo-Iranian Oil Co. case. ICJ Pleadings*, 291–2, 470–71, 501–2. As could be seen in that case, the Persian Government did not claim a unilateral right to decide whether or not the Court lacked jurisdiction in the case. According to Rajan, this is to the credit of the Belgian jurist Henri Rolin's wisdom, who acted in the case as Iran's Advocate and also participated in the negotiations of the San Francisco Conference dealing with Art. 2, para. 7 of the Charter. Cf. M.S. Rajan, *United Nations and Domestic Jurisdiction* (Orient Longmans, 1958) 450.

[165] *Anglo-Iranian Oil Co. case, ICJ Pleadings*, 295–6.

[166] *Anglo-Iranian Oil Co. case, ICJ Pleadings*, 292–3.

declaration of 1940 in which it expressly excluded from India's acceptance of compulsory jurisdiction all 'disputes with regard to questions which by international law fall exclusively within the jurisdiction of India', and argued that the dispute which was the subject matter of the Portuguese Application fell within the terms of this exception.[167]

This argument was not accepted by the Court and its judgment on the merits found that the matter could not be deemed to come within the domestic jurisdiction of India by virtue of international law, for in that case reference was made to a Treaty of 1779, the practice of states, international customs and the principles of international law as it interprets them. The Court held that the parties had placed themselves on the plane of international law.[168] It did not fall exclusively within the jurisdiction of India to decide upon either the existence of a right of passage of Portugal as against India, or such an obligation of India towards Portugal, or the alleged failure to fulfil that obligation.[169]

(c) The Reservation of Domestic Jurisdiction and the Covenant

At the time of the Permanent Court, reservations of domestic jurisdiction were based in some measure on Article 15, paragraph 8 of the Covenant, which ran as follows:

> If the dispute between the parties is claimed by one of them, and is found by the Council to arise out of a matter which by international law is solely within the domestic jurisdiction of that party, the Council shall so report, and shall make no recommendation as to its settlement.

In connection with that paragraph, Professor Waldock writes that this provision of the Covenant determined the content of the reserved domain by reference to international law and departed from the completely subjective phrases of old formula.[170] Thus it can be seen as a novelty that

---

[167] Cf. *Case concerning Right of Passage over Indian Territory, ICJ Pleadings*, vol. I, 122.

[168] The Court was of the view that the questions raised in the fifth preliminary objections of India could not be decided on without prejudicing the merits of the dispute and decided to join that objection to the merits of the case.

[169] *Case concerning Right of Passage over Indian Territory* (Merits), Judgment of 12 April 1960, *ICJ Reports 1960*, 33.

[170] Cf. C.H.M Waldock, 'The Plea of Domestic Jurisdiction before International Legal Tribunals' (1954), 21, *BYIL*, 96, 104.

efforts were made to rely on international law with respect to defining the matters of domestic jurisdiction, since as Lawrence Preuss rightly points out:

> Recourse to international law as a criterion for the determination of matters of domestic jurisdiction constituted an innovation in international organization, for practice prior to the League had established no standard other than that of the political judgment of the interested state. The substitution of an objective legal standard must, therefore, be regarded as making an immense progress through the elimination of that element of arbitrariness which had therefore made the entire process of peaceful settlement of disputes dependent upon the transient interests, necessity or goodwill of every party to a dispute.[171]

Moreover, the relevant wording of the Covenant not only left it to the subjective appreciation of the parties to the dispute to decide on whether the reservation applied to the particular case, but expressly referred to the decision of the Council or the Assembly.[172] The quoted paragraph of the Covenant undoubtedly applied only to conciliation by the Council and the Assembly, whilst not affecting other methods of dispute settlement, including international adjudication. Still, it had an influence on the judicial settlement of disputes too, inasmuch as states inserted into their arbitration agreements and declarations of acceptance such reservations that copied the phrases used by the Covenant rather than the old formulas referring to 'vital interests, independence and the honour' found in general treaties of arbitration in the pre-League period.[173]

As regards the objective reservations of domestic jurisdiction, the United Kingdom declared at the time that 'this is merely an explicit recognition of a limitation on the jurisdiction of the Permanent Court which results from international law itself'.[174] As early as the inter-war period the literature of international law contained different views regarding the reservations of domestic jurisdiction, and one particular author argued that the reservation included in the 1929 British declaration of acceptance had a rather adverse effect on the system of the optional clause declarations. In his famous and often-quoted study, published soon

---

171 Laurence Preuss, 'Article 2, paragraph 7, of the Charter of the United Nations and Matters of Domestic Jurisdiction' (1949) 74, *RCADI*, vol. I, 574, 562–3.

172 Waldock (1954) 104.

173 *Id.* 105.

174 *Memorandum on the Signature … of the Optional Clause …* Great Britain, Parliamentary Papers, Misc., No. 12, (1929) Cmd. 3452, p. 12, quoted by Briggs (1958) 310.

after the making of the British declaration of acceptance, Hersch Lauterpacht was sharply critical of the reservation of domestic jurisdiction, stating that such reservations created great uncertainty mainly in respect of who was competent in deciding whether a question fell within the domestic jurisdiction of the United Kingdom.[175] On the object of the reservation, the eminent British expert, later a member of the International Court of Justice, took a risk in making the observation that 'unless it was meant to have the effect of preventing the Court from deciding on the question of its jurisdiction in these matters, it is difficult to see what is the object of the reservation'.[176]

It should be noted that at the time Lauterpacht stood quite alone with this opinion. The contemporary thinking on reservations of domestic jurisdiction is better reflected by Hudson's contention, who, in his monograph published between the two world wars, wrote this:

> It is difficult to see what is accomplished by this exclusion; if a dispute relates to questions which fall within exclusively national jurisdiction, it does not fall within one of the classes enumerated in paragraph 2 of Article 36.[177]

From this it follows that if the Court should find that the object of the dispute before it falls within the domestic jurisdiction of one of the parties, then by virtue of international law, it must *ex officio* reject the application.

(d) The Reservation of Domestic Jurisdiction and Article 2, Paragraph 7 of the Charter

The provision of the Charter on domestic jurisdiction (Art. 2, para. 7) is held by many authors to be one of the most controversial provisions of the entire instrument and one of the most frequently quoted at different fora of the United Nations.[178]

The difficulties connected with the said paragraph originate mainly from the fact that while Article 15, paragraph 8 of the League Covenant attributed the decision as to whether a matter regarding the domestic jurisdiction of states fell to the League's Council, the proposal submitted to the San Francisco Conference did not address the question and thus

---

175 Cf. Lauterpacht (1930) 148.
176 *Id.* 149.
177 Hudson (1972) 471.
178 Cf. M.S. Rajan (1958), 63.

paved the way for a vivid discussion.[179] Efforts were made on several occasions to fill this gap by way of interpretation, which resulted in further confusion. Watson maintains that it was an intentional omission by the founders that Article 2, paragraph 7 contains no language relating to the power of authoritative interpretation of that provision,[180] as at the San Francisco Conference the representatives of several states proposed a precise provision entrusting the International Court of Justice with the duty of deciding on the matters falling within the domestic jurisdiction of states, but that proposal was rejected.[181]

Against this background it is understandable that opinions in the literature on international law are deeply divided on who is authorized to decide on matters falling within the domestic jurisdiction of states on the one hand and, on the other hand, the extent to which the International Court of Justice is affected by Article 2, paragraph 7 of the Charter. Particularly questionable is the relationship between this provision of the Charter and that in Article 36, paragraph 6 of the Statute, which lays down the well-established rule that: 'In the event of a dispute as to whether the Court has jurisdiction, the matter shall be settled by the decision of the Court.'

The uncertainty surrounding Article 2, paragraph 7 of the Charter is clearly illustrated by the fact that according to Kelsen, both interpretations are possible when considering whether the Court is bound by the statement of a state accepting the Court's compulsory jurisdiction and claiming that a given dispute has arisen out of matters which are essentially within the Court's jurisdiction or the Court has the power to decide this question independently of the party.[182] Others believe that Article 2, paragraph 7 of the Charter does not affect Article 36, paragraph 6 of the Statute, which practically makes an exception of the general rule laid down by Article 2, paragraph 7.[183]

A considerable proportion of the authors in the literature of international law take the view that it is for the states to determine what

---

179 Bruno Simma, Hermann Mosler, Albrecht Randelzhofer, Christian Tomuschat, Rüdiger Wolfrum, Andreas Paulus, Eleni Chaitidou (eds), *The Charter of the United Nations. A Commentary.* (2nd edn, OUP 2002), vol. I, 170.

180 Cf. J.S. Watson, 'Autointerpretation, Competence and the Continuing Validity of Art. 2, (7) of the UN Charter' (1977) 71, *AJIL*, 60, 67.

181 *Id.* 62.

182 Cf. Kelsen (1951) 784.

183 Cf. Vulcan (1947–48) 50.

belongs to their domestic jurisdiction, also emphasizing that the deliberations at the San Francisco Conference on Article 2, paragraph 7 go to show that states sought to widen the scope of domestic jurisdiction.[184]

Watson founds this view on the fact that at the San Francisco Conference, 'at a time when most nations of the world were at a high water mark of cooperation, they balked at the idea of surrendering their power of autointerpretation.'[185]

The inclusion of Article 2, paragraph 7 in the Charter was with the intention of limiting the competence of political organs of the United Nations – these competences had greatly increased in comparison to those of the League of Nations. International law as a criterion was left out of the new formulation and the word 'exclusive' was replaced with 'essentially' in order to enlarge the sphere of domestic jurisdiction.

After the *Anglo-Iranian Oil Company case* the literature on international law experienced a surge of debate on the relationship between Article 2, paragraph 7 of the Charter and the Statute of the International Court of Justice.

In one of his studies Waldock writes that Iran's argument in the *Anglo-Iranian Oil Co. case* does not hold water because the different provisions of the Charter show that, although the Statute is an integral part of the Charter, 'the internal evidence of the Charter and the Statute suggest that in either instrument the word "Charter" is used to denote only the articles of the Charter itself'.[186] Waldock goes on to argue that if one interprets Article 2, paragraph 7 of the Charter in the way propounded by Iran, it does not follow at all that the effect of this provision of the Charter is to apply to a reservation dealing with 'matters essentially within domestic jurisdiction' when considering the Court's jurisdiction in contentious cases. There is in the wording of Article 2, paragraph 7 nothing to prevent the Court or any other organ of the United Nations from intervening in matters which are essentially within the domestic jurisdiction of any state, given that the states concerned have authorized it to do so in an instrument dehors of the Charter.[187] Article 2, paragraph 7 of the Charter has no relevance for matters in dispute before

---

[184] Cf. Preuss (1949) 570–604; Rudolf L. Bindschindler; 'La délimitation des compétences des Nations Unies' (1963) 108, *RCADI* , vol. I, 307, 392–3; Alfred Verdross; 'The Plea of Domestic Jurisdiction before an International Tribunal and a Political Organ of the United Nations,' (1968) 28, *ZaöRV*, 33, 34; Watson (1977) 61–6.

[185] Watson (1977) 62.

[186] Cf. Waldock (1954) 122.

[187] *Id.* 123.

the Court, since neither the Charter nor the Statute confer any authority to the Court to decide on or entertain any contentious matter without the consent of the parties. The situation would be different, however, if the Charter provided for obligatory jurisdiction.[188] In other words, Waldock holds that Article 2, paragraph 7 of the Charter in no way affects the Court's jurisdiction in that case.

Waldock's view is shared by Shihata, who believes that Article 2, paragraph 7 of the Charter does not seem to be relevant to the work of the Court, for if the Court once does find that the parties have accepted its jurisdiction to adjudicate on a case, it will not be precluded from exercising its jurisdiction in view of Article 2, paragraph 7.[189] If, however, the Court concludes that the parties have not accepted its jurisdiction, it need not resort to Article 2, paragraph 7 of the Charter in order to justify its lack of jurisdiction.[190] According to the author, this provision of the Charter cannot serve but as a subsidiary argument in favour of renouncing jurisdiction in cases where the parties' consent is not beyond doubt and the matter is not clearly of an international character. In such cases the Court may declare that as an organ of the United Nations it is not authorized to deal with issues within the domestic jurisdiction of states which have not been clearly submitted to it.[191]

A position contrary to the preceding ones was taken by Henri Rolin, who represented Iran in the *Anglo-Iranian Oil Co. case.* The eminent Belgian expert of international law argued that under Article 92 of the Charter the Statute forms an integral part of the Charter and the two instruments are essentially deemed to be one treaty. The phrase 'the present Charter' in Article 2, paragraph 7 should also be understood to mean the Statute annexed thereto. Consequently, Article 2, paragraph 7 which forbids the United Nations from intervening in matters which are within the domestic jurisdiction of states, accordingly applies to the International Court of Justice as well, which is the principal judicial organ of the United Nations.[192]

The same view is held by Dubisson, who interestingly bases his position on the advisory opinion in the *Interpretation of Peace Treaties with Bulgaria, Hungary and Romania* and concludes by adducing

---

188 *Id.*

189 Ibrahim I. Shihata, *The Power of the International Court to Determine its own Jurisdiction* (Martinus Nijhoff 1965) 232.

190 *Id.*

191 *Id.*

192 *Anglo-Iranian Oil Co. case, ICJ Pleadings*, 466–8.

arguments *a contrario* that the Court feels itself bound by Article 2, paragraph 7, of the Charter.[193]

Arangio-Ruiz takes an approach to reservations of domestic jurisdiction different from that of the above-cited authors and, drawing upon the jurisprudence of the two International Courts with regard to the plea of domestic jurisdiction, is of the opinion that neither Court really applies the 'international law as a criterion', for the only way to apply that criterion would be to examine the merits of the given cases in order to decide whether the objecting state was or was not bound by the international obligation in question.[194]

As regards the relationship between objective reservations of domestic jurisdiction and Article 2, paragraph 7 of the Charter, one could say that the authors who emphasize the existence of a close relationship between the two instruments are justified in doing so. There is no doubt that during the inter-war period the Covenant and the Statute of the Permanent Court of International Justice were two separate instruments, but the situation has been different since the entry into force of the Charter, as it appears from the report on the Statute of the International Court of Justice adopted at the San Francisco Conference, which was also referred to in the Dumbarton Oaks Proposals, that stated precisely that the Court would be the principal judicial organ of the United Nations and its Statute, to be annexed to the Charter, would be an integral part thereof and all members of the International Organization should become *ipso facto* parties to the Statute of the Court.[195] It seems, however, that when the decision was made to interlink the two instruments, the amendments ensuing from the linkage were not reflected in the texts of the instruments. This accounts for the fact that wherever the words 'Charter' or 'Statute' are used, they are always understood to mean one of the two instruments only.

Returning to the objective reservations of domestic jurisdiction, it could be maintained that, since states are free to submit their disputes to international adjudication, and contemporary international law does not provide for compulsory settlement of international disputes by the International Court, the determinant factor is above all the position taken by the parties. At the same time, however, if in a concrete dispute a state claims that the particular matter is within its domestic jurisdiction by virtue of international law, the Court must have the right and duty to

---

193 Michel Dubisson, *La Cour International de Justice* (*LGDJ*, 1964) 87.

194 Arangio-Ruiz (1996) 455.

195 *UNCIO Documents*, vol. XIV, 649.

decide on that question. Considering that today international law is more developed and governs a much wider range of questions than it did 60 or 70 years ago, the related matters are much easier to decide upon at present. Whenever the Court finds that a particular matter in dispute belongs to the ambit of international law under treaty and customary law, it will continue the proceedings, but in the case where a dispute brought before the Court affects the question of domestic law, the Court naturally must renounce the case and rule that it lacks jurisdiction.

X LIMITATIONS AFFECTING CONSTITUTIONAL QUESTIONS

The declarations of acceptance by certain Latin-American states during the inter-war period referred to constitutional questions as a limitation to the Permanent Court's compulsory jurisdiction. Such a restriction appeared first in Salvador's instrument of ratification of the Protocol of Signature of the Statute of the Permanent Court,[196] and the reservation in question reads as follows: 'The provisions of this law do not apply to any disputes or differences concerning points or questions which cannot be submitted to arbitration in accordance with the political constitution of this Republic.'[197]

Hudson believes that the origins of this reservation can be traced to the Arbitration Agreement of 1899 between Argentina and Uruguay, which excluded from arbitration any dispute affecting the 'constitutional principles of the State'.[198] A reservation likewise relating to constitutional questions is to be found in the declarations of Brazil (renewed 1937) and Argentina (1935), with the difference that, under the terms of these declarations, the Court's compulsory jurisdiction does not apply to disputes which by 'international law fall within the local jurisdiction', the court's jurisdiction or relate to the constitutional regime of each state.

The first questions to arise in connection with these reservations include those of who, in a concrete legal dispute, will be competent to decide that a given matter cannot be submitted to an arbitral tribunal

---

[196] The declaration of acceptance of Salvador was included in the instrument of ratification of the Protocol of Signature of the Statute, and deposited on 29 August 1930. The Protocol of Signature of the Statute was subject to reservations formulated in the decision of the Executive Power of El Salvador of 1930.

[197] The reservation referred to Salvador's Constitution of 1886. For that matter, the declaration was in effect until 1973.

[198] Hudson (1972) 471.

under the constitution of a particular state, and what is to be regarded as a question relating to the constitutional régime.[199] If such a decision lies with the Court, which is in conformity with the provisions of Article 36, paragraph 6 of the Statute, the result would be an interpretation by the Court of the constitutions of the parties. If, however, the parties insist on interpreting their own constitutions, as follows from the principle of state sovereignty, the Court would be deprived from deciding on its own jurisdiction, which contradicts Article 36, paragraph 6 of the Statute.

Incidentally, no plea of constitutional question has ever been invoked in the disputes submitted to the two International Courts, so the two Courts have evaded ever having to pronounce on such a rather problematical reservation. A similar limitation is contained in no other declaration of acceptance that is presently in force.

XI RESERVATIONS LINKING THE DECLARATION OF ACCEPTANCE TO THOSE OF OTHER STATES

In its declaration of acceptance of 1921, Brazil tied the recognition of the Court's compulsory jurisdiction to the condition that compulsory jurisdiction was accepted by at least two of the powers permanently represented on the Council of the League of Nations, specifically providing that:

> we declare recognize as compulsory, in accordance with the said resolution of the National Legislature, the jurisdiction of the said Court for the period of five years, on condition of reciprocity and as soon as it has likewise been recognized as such by two at least of the Powers permanently represented on the Council of the League of Nations.

As mentioned already, this passage of the Brazilian declaration is ascribable to the proposal of the Brazilian jurist, Fernandes, who, in the course of negotiations on the Permanent Court's Statute presented the draft article on the Court's compulsory jurisdiction which provided that states were free to accede to the optional clause unconditionally or under certain conditions, and one of the conditions could be the acceptance of compulsory jurisdiction by a certain number of states or specifically named states. This version of the clause was rejected, but, obviously

[199] The situation might be even more complicated if the respondent state invokes, on the basis of reciprocity, the reservation contained in the declaration of acceptance of the applicant state that relates to constitutional questions, saying that the legal dispute submitted to the Court affects matters that cannot be submitted to an arbitral tribunal by virtue of its own political constitution.

owing to Fernandes, it was nonetheless incorporated into Brazil's declaration of acceptance. Because of that limitation, the 1921 Brazilian declaration of acceptance entered into force rather late, for, among the permanent members of the Council of the League, Germany and the United Kingdom were the first to ratify their declarations of acceptance in 1928 and 1930, respectively.[200]

XII RESERVATIONS ON DISPUTES RELATING TO A SPECIFIC TREATY OR TREATIES

Some of the declarations accepting the compulsory jurisdiction of the Permanent Court contained limitations excluding from the Court's jurisdiction any dispute relating to a specific treaty. Of particular interest in this context is the Polish declaration of 1931, which, obviously owing to Poland's political situation after World War I, excluded disputes resulting directly or indirectly from provisions of the Treaty of Peace between Poland and Bolshevik Russia and Soviet Ukraine, signed at Riga on 18 March 1921.[201]

To some extent also falling under this category is the limitation included in India's 1974 declaration of acceptance which relates to disputes where the Court's jurisdiction 'is or may be founded on the basis of a treaty concluded under the auspices of the League of Nations, unless the Government of India specially agrees to the Court's jurisdiction in each case.' Due to that reservation, the Indian Government actually suspended the application of the compromisory clause of quite a few treaties concluded between the two world wars, only allowing the application thereof on condition of India's special consent to the proceedings in such cases.

Egypt's declaration of acceptance of 22 July 1957 similarly contains a stipulation concerning a specific treaty, providing that:

> the Government of the Republic of Egypt accept as compulsory *ipso facto*, on condition of reciprocity and without special agreement, the jurisdiction of the International Court of Justice in all legal disputes that may arise under the said paragraph 9 (b) of the above Declaration (on the Suez Canal and the

---

200 For all these reasons, the Brazilian declaration did not enter into force until 5 February 1930.

201 The Treaty of Riga ended the Polish–Soviet War and established the Soviet–Polish border which remained in force until World War II.

arrangements for its operation. – V.L.) dated 24 April 1957, with effect as from that date.

As a result of the 1957 Declaration referred to in Egypt's declaration of acceptance, occurring shortly after the Suez crisis, Egypt unilaterally recognized the validity of the Constantinople Convention of 1888 – which concerned the legal status of the Suez Canal – and the provisions of the Security Council's Resolution of 13 October 1956. Thus, the 1957 Egyptian declaration of acceptance conferred jurisdiction on the Court over disputes relating to the application of only a single treaty. From this point of view, the declaration is more like a compromisory clause of a treaty, with the difference being, however, that on the one hand, it formally appears in a declaration of acceptance and, on the other hand, the Court's compulsory jurisdiction connected with the treaty relates not only to the contracting parties of the particular treaty, but also to states party to the optional clause system.

The making of the Egyptian declaration of acceptance was by all means of great political significance,[202] since until the conclusion of the peace treaty with Israel, dated 26 March 1979, Egypt had relied precisely on the Constantinople Convention for obstructing free navigation of merchant vessels to or from Israel, claiming that doing so in time of war was admissible under that Convention.

One can say that the 1957 Egyptian declaration of acceptance contradicts the provisions of Article 36 of the Statute. On the one hand, as was noted earlier, states are required by the new Statute to accept the Court's compulsory jurisdiction in respect of all disputes enumerated in subparagraphs (a) to (d) of paragraph 2, whereas it was only during the existence of the Permanent Court of International Justice that states were allowed to limit the scope of their declaration of acceptance to some classes of disputes mentioned in paragraph 2. On the other hand, Article 36, paragraph 3 permits the inclusion of certain limitations or reservations to the declarations of acceptance. The Egyptian declaration, however, contains no reservation or limitation derogating from an obligation of a broader scope, but instead one which recognizes the Court's compulsory jurisdiction only in relation to a single treaty.

These questions involved in respect of the Egyptian declaration of acceptance were not raised at the time the declaration was deposited, in

---

[202] All the more so since at that time Israel was also a party to the optional clause system.

all probability because, among other things, that declaration of acceptance provided a certain kind of added guarantee that Egypt would assure free navigation in the Suez Canal.

XIII RESERVATIONS RELATING TO FOREIGN DEBTS AND LIABILITIES

The 1980 declaration of acceptance by Poland included a rather peculiar reservation to the effect that disputes relating to 'foreign liabilities or debts' were not regarded as falling within the jurisdiction of the Court.

Prior to the Polish declaration of acceptance a reservation relating to debts was contained in only one document, namely that of Salvador's instrument of ratification of the Protocol on the Signature of the Statute of the Permanent Court, which excluded disputes 'to pecuniary claims made against the Nation'.

For that matter, the reservation relating to foreign debts did not figure in the draft declaration of acceptance elaborated by the Section of the International Law of the Legislative Council.[203] The said limitation was in all likelihood 'devised' by the political decision makers concerned with the declaration, bearing in mind the foreign debts of Poland in formulating the reservation.

The reservation relating to foreign debts is also to be found in Poland's 1996 declaration of acceptance.

[203] Szafarz (1993) 88.

8. Destructive reservations

I SUBJECTIVE RESERVATION OF DOMESTIC JURISDICTION (CONNALLY RESERVATION)

(a) Appearance of the Reservation and its Variants

Among the reservations to declarations of acceptance, the most disputable are subjective reservations of domestic jurisdiction. This type of reservation is otherwise termed as 'self-judging reservation', 'automatic reservation', or 'Connally reservation'.

The term 'automatic reservation' – as applied in reference to subjective reservations of domestic jurisdiction – owes its wide acceptance to Sir Hersch Lauterpacht's separate opinion appended to the judgment on the preliminary objections in the *Norwegian Loans case*. According to Judge Lauterpacht, the term 'automatic reservation' is a good indication of the 'automatic' operation of the reservation in the sense that the Court's function concerning such reservations is confined to registering the decision of the defendant state, which is not subject to review by the Court.[1]

The origin of these reservations goes back to 1945, when the Senate of the United States discussed the US declaration of acceptance.[2] Senator Morse, who introduced the relevant bill, had prepared the draft of the American declaration in cooperation with Manley D. Hudson, who was one of the most prominent experts on the Permanent Court of International Justice. In its original version the draft declaration contained an objective reservation of domestic jurisdiction.

---

1 Cf. *Case of Certain Norwegian Loans*, Judgment of 6 July 1957, Separate Opinion of Judge Sir Hersch Lauterpacht, *ICJ Reports 1957* 34. The detailed analysis of Judge Lauterpacht's opinion will be dealt with later in this chapter.

2 On this score, see Decisions No. 160 and No. 196 of the Senate, United States of America, Congressional Records. The question of the American declaration of acceptance was addressed by a subcommittee of the Senate's Foreign Affairs Committee, hearing several prominent jurists and representatives of various organizations.

The debate in the Senate over the draft focussed attention on the question of who was to decide on matters falling within the domestic jurisdiction of the United States. According to Lawrence Preuss, the debate in the Senate revealed that little was known about domestic jurisdiction 'except its extreme sanctity'.[3] Several members of the Senate voiced concern over extending the Court's compulsory jurisdiction to matters relating to immigration, the tariff, etc, and the like. It was on this point that Senator Connally of Texas came forward with the proposal that the phrase 'as determined by the United States of America' should be added at the end of the reservation of domestic jurisdiction.[4] Connally argued that under the UN Charter the United Nations could not intervene in matters within the domestic jurisdiction of states, whereas the provisions of the Charter would allow the Court to hold that such sensitive subjects like immigration, tariffs, or the Panama Canal be deemed as international ones.[5] Senator Connally's amendment was subject to a fair share of sharp criticism from several members of the Senate, which nevertheless adopted the Connally amendment, on 2 August 1946.[6] Shortly afterwards, on 26 August 1946, the United States made a declaration accepting the compulsory jurisdiction of the International Court of Justice. The document:

> Provided that this declaration shall not apply to
>
> (a) Disputes the solution of which the parties shall entrust to other tribunals by virtue of agreements already in existence or which may be concluded in the future; or
>
> (b) Disputes with regard to matters which are essentially within the domestic jurisdiction of the United States of America as determined by the United States of America; or …

The reservation with the Connally amendment became 'popular' immediately. The example of the United States was followed by a number of states, with comparable or even word for word limitations being included specifically in the declarations of acceptance by France (1947), Mexico (1947), Liberia (1952), the Union of South Africa (1955), the Philippines (1971), Pakistan (1948, 1957), Sudan (1957), Malawi (1966) and the

---

3 Cf. Lawrence Preuss, 'The International Court of Justice, the Senate and Matters of Domestic Jurisdiction' (1946) 40, *AJIL*, 720, 725.

4 US 92. Congressional Record, 10, 624.

5 *Id.*

6 By a vote of 51 to 12, with 33 abstentions. *Id.*, 10, 697.

United Kingdom (1957), whose declaration can practically be consigned to this category and about which we will have more to say later.

The declarations of acceptance containing similar reservations to the US declaration are generally classified in three groups:[7]

(i) The first group consists of declarations which confer to the declaring state the decision to 'determine' the matters which are essentially in domestic jurisdiction. Such are the declarations of the United States (1946), South Africa (1955), Malawi (1966), Pakistan (1957) and Sudan (1958), which accordingly follow the 'original' American formula.

(ii) The second group includes declarations referring to domestic jurisdiction with phrases like 'understood' or 'considered' by the declaring state or in the 'opinion' of the declaring state. Such a formula first appeared in the 1947 French declaration of acceptance and was included in the declarations of Liberia (1952), Mexico (1947) and the Philippines (1972). Accordingly these limitations can in point of fact be termed as reservations under the 'French formula'.[8]

(iii) The third group is characterized by the British declaration of April 1957 excluding from the Court's compulsory jurisdiction all disputes 'relating to any question which, in the opinion of the Government of the United Kingdom, affects the national security of

---

7 Cf. Crawford (1979) 67–8, fn.

8 In the case of France one may speak of three declarations of acceptance, which actually served to vary the reservations concerning domestic jurisdiction.

The compulsory jurisdiction of the International Court of Justice was recognized by France for the first time in 1947, with its declaration containing, among other things, the reservation that the declaration was not to apply 'to disputes relating to matters which are essentially within the national jurisdiction as understood by the Government of the French Republic'. Instead, the 1959 French declaration of acceptance included the limitation that the declaration was not to affect 'disputes relating to questions which by international law fall exclusively within domestic jurisdiction'. Thus the declaration of 1959 contained an objective domestic jurisdiction reservation. This reservation was included in the 1966 declaration, but 'the disputes concerning activities connected with national defence' were also added to the state of war reservation as contained in the declaration of 1959.

The French Government finally withdrew its declaration of acceptance in 1974. For the French declaration of acceptance, see Simone Dreyfus, 'Les déclarations souscrites par la France aux termes de l'article 36 du Statut de la Cour internationale de la Haye', (1959) 5, *AFDI*, 258–72.

the United Kingdom or of any of its dependent territories'.[9] This limitation can be referred to as the 'British formula'.[10]

(b) First Appraisals of the Reservation

Almost from the first moment the United States declaration of acceptance and the Connally amendment thereto aroused the interest of, and even came under attack from, international law writers.[11] Preuss wrote that 'The effect of the Connally Amendment is to give to the United States a veto upon the jurisdiction of the Court after a dispute has been referred to it by an applicant state.'[12] Edvard Hambro puts it in a more diplomatic way when he points out that such reservation may obviously become a source of great danger.[13]

Soon after the Senate's debate on the Connally amendment an American author wrote that,

> It might be optimistic to assert that United States would never abuse its privilege and never attempt to evade an obligation to adjudicate before the International Court on colorable grounds. It is to be hoped that it will never declare that an issue which another party seeks to adjudicate before the Court concerns a matter which is essentially within the domestic jurisdiction, unless evidence of the law of nations as revealed in the acquiescence of States generally sustains its decision.[14]

Even Hudson, one of the most authoritative American experts in international adjudication, disagreed with the reservation added to the United States declaration of acceptance. In one of his articles he notes that the

---

[9] Para.V. of the declaration made on 18 April 1957.

[10] The British declaration containing this reservation was in force for about one and a half years, and in November 1958 the United Kingdom made a new declaration omitting the said limitation.

[11] Preuss holds that the reservation is formulated in too general and inaccurate terms and the criteria used in the text are political rather than legal, a reason why it is not desirable for such a limitation to be included in a declaration accepting the compulsory jurisdiction of a judicial forum which is to act on the basis of international law. Cf. Preuss (1946) 725.

[12] *Id.* 729.

[13] Hambro (1948) 149.

[14] Cf. Charles Cheney Hyde, 'The United States Accepts the Optional Clause' (1946) 40, *AJIL*, 778, 780.

introduction by other states of a reservation similar to the American one in their declarations of acceptance will constitute a distinctly backward step.[15]

For all this, the American declaration of acceptance containing the Connally reservation remained in force for almost 40 years, albeit at the end of the 1950s there was a campaign to withdraw the said reservation.[16] Those advocating repeal of the limitation substantiated their arguments by appealing to the interests of the United States, claiming, inter alia, that the United States, being one of the countries with the highest record of investments abroad, might much more frequently need to protect its claims in a world court. In such cases, however, the adverse party may simply rely on reciprocity for invoking the Connally reservation of the United States declaration of acceptance, thereby removing the case from the Court's compulsory jurisdiction.[17] Another argument was that since the judgments of the International Court of Justice could not be enforced except through the Security Council, whenever the Court would be seized of a matter within domestic jurisdiction, rendering a judgment thereon, the United States as a permanent member of the Security Council could veto any recommendation for action by the rest of the Security Council, thus preventing any effect being given to the judgment.[18] Nevertheless, these arguments failed to convince the Washington Government and the declaration containing the said reservation remained in force until 1986.[19]

---

[15] Manley O. Hudson, 'The Twenty-Fifth Year of the World Court' (1947) 41, *AJIL*, 1 12.

[16] The United States declaration of acceptance was also addressed by the Foreign Affairs Committee of the Senate on several occasions. The experts heard were trying to convince the members of the Committee that withdrawal of the Connally reservation would not cause the United States to lose control over matters like immigration, regulation of tariffs and duties, navigation of the Panama Canal, etc. All these efforts were of little avail, and the Committee finally adopted no resolution to withdraw the reservation. For that matter, withdrawal was advocated by such political figures as Attorney General William P. Rogers and Senator Hubert Humphrey, who served as Vice-President of the United States between 1965 and 1969.

[17] Cf. John Dixon Jr, 'The Connally Amendment – the Conflict between Nationalism and an Effective World Court' (1964) 53, *Ky L. J.*, 164, 169.

[18] Cambrell: The United Nations, the World Court and the Connally Reservation. 47, *A.B.A. Journal*, 57. (1961), quoted by Dixon (1964) 169–70.

[19] By its Note of 5 October 1986, the United States terminated its declaration of acceptance of 1946 containing the subjective reservation of domestic jurisdiction, with effect of six months from the date of the notification.

(c) The Reservation in the Jurisprudence of the Court

In the jurisprudence of the International Court of Justice the dispute between France and the United States concerning the *Rights of Nationals of the United States of America in Morocco* was the first case in which the Court's jurisdiction was founded on the declarations of acceptance containing subjective reservations of domestic jurisdiction of both parties. Interestingly, however, neither party advanced any argument in connection with that reservation.[20] During the proceedings the only reference made to the said reservation was in the memorandum of the United States stating that although it did not concur with the allegations concerning the compulsory jurisdiction of the Court that were presented by the French Government, 'its abstaining from raising the issue does not affect its legal right to rely in any future case on its reservations contained in its acceptance of the compulsory jurisdiction of the Court'.[21]

The United States declaration of 1946 is usually referred to as the paradigm of declarations of acceptance containing subjective reservations of domestic jurisdiction, yet the first and thorough consideration of such reservations before the Court took place in relation not to the United States declaration, but to the French declaration of acceptance of 1947, notably in the *Case of Certain Norwegian Loans.*

As has already been mentioned, in 1955, France filed an application against Norway with the International Court of Justice in the interest of French nationals, regarding the case of certain Norwegian loans issued on the French market and other foreign markets by Norwegian banks. The application based the Court's jurisdiction on Article 36, paragraph 2 of the Statute of the Court and the declarations of acceptance made by France and Norway. The French declaration contained a reservation providing that, 'This declaration does not apply to differences relating to matters which are essentially within the national jurisdiction as understood by the Government of the French Republic', whilst in the Norwegian declaration of acceptance there was no such limitation. Norway

[20] Although in that case the United States filed a preliminary objection, in that objection it made no mention of the subjective reservation of domestic jurisdiction included in the American declaration of acceptance. For that matter, the preliminary objection was later withdrawn by the Washington Government. On this score, see the Court's Order of 31 October 1951. *Case concerning Rights of Nationals of the United States of America in Morocco,* Order of 31 October 1951, *ICJ Reports 1951*, 109–11.

[21] *Case concerning Rights of Nationals of the United States of America in Morocco*, *ICJ Pleadings*, vol. I, 262.

submitted preliminary objections, and in the first objection it referred to the principle of reciprocity in order to rely upon the restriction placed by France on her own undertakings, i.e. the subjective reservation of domestic jurisdiction added to the French declaration acceptance.[22] The Court accepted the Norwegian argument and, basing itself on the limitation of the French declaration of acceptance, found that it was without jurisdiction. In its judgment, the Court stressed that, 'In accordance with the condition of reciprocity to which acceptance of the compulsory jurisdiction is made subject in both Declarations ... Norway, equally with France, is entitled to except from the compulsory jurisdiction of the Court disputes understood by Norway to be essentially within its national jurisdiction'.[23]

A few months after the Court's judgment in the *Case of Certain Norwegian Loans* the World Court came to be seized by a legal dispute in which the Connally reservation was invoked by the very United States which had 'invented' the subjective reservation of domestic jurisdiction.

The respective case was the *Interhandel case*, brought before the Court by Switzerland against the United States of America in 1957. The applicant requested the Court to declare that the United States was under an obligation to restore to the Swiss company, named Interhandel, its assets vested in the United States during World War II.[24]

The question of the subjective reservation of domestic jurisdiction in the *Interhandel case* was first raised in connection with the Swiss request for indication of interim measures of protection, arguing that as long as the case was pending the United States should not part with the disputed assets and not sell them. The United States challenged the Court's jurisdiction, on the one hand, arguing that the sale or disposition of the vested stock of the company at issue were matters exclusively within the domestic jurisdiction of the United States[25] and, on the other hand,

---

22 Norway argued that the International Court of Justice lacked jurisdiction over the matter since the Court's jurisdiction, within the meaning of the declarations of acceptance, applies only to legal disputes falling within one of the four categories of disputes enumerated in Art. 36, para. 2 of the Statute and relating to international law. In the view of the Norwegian Government, the loan contracts were governed by municipal law and not by international law and on the basis of reciprocity Norway had the right to rely upon the restrictions placed by France in her own undertakings. Cf. *Case of Certain Norwegian Loans, ICJ Pleadings*, vol. I, 121–32.

23 *Case of Certain Norwegian Loans*, Judgment of 6 July 1957, *ICJ Reports 1957*, 24.

24 For the Swiss application, see *Interhandel case, ICJ Pleadings*, 8–15.

25 See the Fourth Preliminary Objection. *Id.* 320–21.

the seizure and retention of stock in an American corporation, done in the exercise of the war powers, were not matters of international law but rather were recognized by international law to be within the domestic jurisdiction of the United States.[26]

The Swiss reply to the American preliminary objections and during the course of the oral proceedings Professor Guggenheim dealt at length with the admissibility and validity of subjective reservations of domestic jurisdiction.[27] But the Court did not, even in connection with the preliminary objections, consider the subjective reservation of domestic jurisdiction, for it upheld the third preliminary objection for the reason that Interhandel had failed to exhaust the local remedies available in the United States.[28]

The subjective reservations of domestic jurisdiction were touched upon in connection with one of the cases regarding the aerial incident of 27 July 1955. With respect to the tragedy of the Israeli aircraft of 27 July 1955 on Bulgarian territory, proceedings against Bulgaria were instituted before the Court not only by Israel,[29] but also by the United States of America and Great Britain, because the casualties included American and British nationals.[30] For the purpose of the present discussion, this dispute

---

[26] In its Order of 24 October 1957 the Court rejected Switzerland's request for indicating interim measures of protection, because, on the basis of the available information, it found that there was no danger of a sale of the shares. Cf. *Interhandel case* (Request for the Indication of Interim Measures of Protection), Order of 24 October 1957, *ICJ Reports 1957*, 105–12.

[27] Cf. *Interhandel case, ICJ Pleadings*, 407–09 and 574–80.

[28] Cf. *Interhandel case* (Preliminary Objections), Judgment of 21 March 1959, *ICJ Reports 1959*, 26–9.

[29] See *Case concerning the Aerial incident of 27 July 1955* (Israel v. Bulgaria).

[30] The United States application against Bulgaria founded the Court's jurisdiction on the basis that Bulgaria had accepted the compulsory jurisdiction of the Permanent Court in 1921 – this acceptance was unconditional and the acceptance was transferred to the new Court by virtue of Art. 36, para. 5 of the Statute upon the date of admission of Bulgaria into the United Nations – on the one hand and, on the other, the Court's jurisdiction was not based on its own declaration of acceptance, but rather its submission to the Court's jurisdiction regarding the case at hand. (For the American application, see *Aerial Incident of 27 July 1955* (United States of America v. Bulgaria), *ICJ Pleadings*, 22–4. Bulgaria protested against the proceedings and, on the basis of reciprocity, invoked, inter alia, the subjective reservation of domestic jurisdiction added to the United States declaration of acceptance. (See Preliminary Objections of the Government of the People's Republic of Bulgaria, *Aerial Incident of 27 July 1955* (United States of America v. Bulgaria), *ICJ Pleadings*, 271–3.)

is of interest in so far as the Government of the United States of America, in its observations and submissions on the preliminary objections of Bulgaria, maintained, in contrast to its position stated in the *Interhandel case*, 'that the reservation in question does not permit the Government of the United States, or any other government seeking to rely on this reservation reciprocally, arbitrarily to characterize the subject matter of a suit as 'essentially within the domestic jurisdiction', even though the subject matter is quite evidently one of international concern and has been treated so by the parties to the case.[31]

Mention of subjective reservations of domestic jurisdiction before the International Court of Justice has been made in yet another dispute, notably the *Case concerning Military and Paramilitary Activities in and against Nicaragua*. However, the reservation was not relied upon by either party in that dispute. On the other hand, in its Counter-memorial of 17 August 1984 presented to the Court, the Washington Government made essentially the same statement it had made over 30 years earlier in the *Case concerning Rights of Nationals of the United States of America in Morocco*, notably to the effect that in the present case the United States does not invoke paragraph (b) of its declaration of acceptance of 1946 (the so-called Connally Reservation). 'This determination is without prejudice to the rights of the United States under that proviso in relation to any subsequent pleadings, proceedings or cases before this Court.'[32]

It should be added that the Court's decision in the *Nicaragua case* revived the discussion not only on the Connally reservation and but on the necessity of the optional clause system as well.[33]

Thus, among the aforementioned cases, it was only in the *Norwegian Loans case* and the *Interhandel case* that the subjective reservation of domestic jurisdiction was considered. It should be added, however, that the Court had in fact sidestepped the question of how far subjective reservations of domestic jurisdiction were admissible and valid, but some judges did make a detailed study of the matter in their separate and dissenting opinions. Especially oft-quoted is the British Judge Sir Hersch

---

The Court delivered no judgment in that case, since the United States had requested the discontinuance of the proceedings and removal of the case from the Court's list.

[31] See *Aerial Incident of 27 July 1955* (United States of America v. Bulgaria), *ICJ Pleadings*, 305.

[32] *Case concerning Military and Paramilitary Activities in and against Nicaragua*, USA Counter–memorial, *ICJ Pleadings*, vol. II, 8, note 1.

[33] See Gary L. Scott and Craig L. Carr, 'The ICJ and Compulsory Jurisdiction: The Case for Clausing the Clause'(1987) 81, *AJIL*, 57–76.

Lauterpacht's separate opinion appended to the judgment in the *Case of Certain Norwegian Loans*, which took a most definite stand against the Connally reservation.

The attitude of the International Court of Justice was particularly disputable in the *Case of Certain Norwegian Loans*, since in that legal dispute the Court recognized, without stating the reasons, as a priori valid a reservation on whose lawfulness and admissibility there were set forth strongly divided views in the literature on international law. In that case as Sir Robert Jennings, who later became a member and even President of the Court, points out, the question of the validity of a subjective reservation of domestic jurisdiction was not directly raised by the parties in their submissions, but was raised indirectly by Norway in relying upon the incriminated reservation.[34] However, the Court took the position that, since the validity of the reservation had not been questioned by the parties,

> the Court has before it a provision which both Parties to the dispute regard as constituting an expression of their common will relating to the competence of the Court. The Court does not therefore consider that it is called upon to enter into an examination of the reservation in the light of considerations which are not presented by the issues in the proceedings. The Court, without prejudging the question, gives effect to the reservation as it stands and as the Parties recognize it.[35]

Judge Sir Hersch Lauterpacht sharply criticized that attitude of the Court stating that 'the fact that she (Norway – V.L.) did not raise the particular issue of the validity of the French Acceptance as a whole cannot endow with validity an instrument otherwise invalid. ... The defendant State cannot, by refraining from raising objections, grant dispensation from invalidity. No one could do it – including, perhaps, the Court itself.'[36]

According to Briggs, the most satisfactory aspect of the *Norwegian Loans case* was that 'the peremptory reservation worked to the detriment

---

[34] Cf. R(obert) Y. Jennings, 'Recent Cases on "Automatic" Reservations to the Optional Clause' (1958) 7, *ICLQ*, 349, 360.

[35] *Case of Certain Norwegian Loans, ICJ Reports 1957*, 27.

[36] *Id.* Separate Opinion of Judge Sir Hersch Lauterpacht. 61. For the criticisms, see also E.K. Nantwi, *The Enforcement of International Judicial Decisions and Arbitral Awards in Public International Law* (A.W. Sijthoff, 1966) 47; Judge Guerrero's dissenting opinion, *Case of Certain Norwegian Loans*, Judgment of 6 July 1957. Dissenting Opinion of Judge Guerrero, *ICJ Reports 1957*, 68, and J.H.W. Verzijl: Cour Internationale de Justice – Affaire relative à Certains Emprunts Norvegiens (1957) 4, *NTIR*, 373, 398–9.

of the State which had introduced it into its Declaration'.[37] The *Norwegian Loans case* had one more 'happy consequence', namely the fact that the Court's decision prompted France to make a new declaration of acceptance in 1959, omitting the subjective reservation of domestic jurisdiction and replacing it with an objective reservation of domestic jurisdiction.

(d) The Reservation as an Escape Clause

Regarding subjective reservations of domestic jurisdiction the literature on international law reflects a unanimity of views that states should act in good faith when declaring – by referring to this reservation – that a matter falls within domestic jurisdiction. As noted above, it was practically this same point which the United States stressed in the case instituted against Bulgaria regarding the aerial incident of 27 July 1955 saying that reservation (b) of the United States declaration of acceptance 'does not permit the United States or any other State to make an arbitrary determination (i.e. on matters of domestic jurisdiction – V.L.), in bad faith'.[38]

But what is the situation where a state invokes in bad faith the subjective reservation of domestic jurisdiction? Can the Court examine whether a state acted in good faith or not? Many authors answer this question in the affirmative, believing that a key to solving the problems of subjective reservations of domestic jurisdiction lies in conferring on the Court the right to review whether a state has invoked such a reservation in good faith.[39]

Maus writes that the American declaration of acceptance did not expressly accord this right to the Court. He maintains, however, that the Court may decide whether a state has acted in good faith. If a state invokes the reservation in bad faith, it virtually steps beyond the boundaries of its right to determine the Court's jurisdiction and in that event the general rule laid down in Article 36, paragraph 6 of the Statute comes into operation.[40] That is to say that, 'In the event of a dispute as to whether the Court has jurisdiction, the matter shall be settled by the decision of the Court'. The author holds that refusal to confer on the

---

[37] Briggs (1958) 344.

[38] *Aerial Incident of 27 July 1955* (United States v. Bulgaria), *ICJ Pleadings*, 308.

[39] Cf. John H. Crabb, 'On Judging the Connally Amendment (1962)', 50, *Geo. L. J.*, 529, 536–9.

[40] Maus (1959) 159.

Court the right to impartially examine whether states have acted in good faith actually amounts to recognizing the right of states to misuse the reservation. Regarding this point he refers to the finding of the Court in the *Corfu Channel case* that the Court is not bound by the decision of a state which has declared in bad faith that a matter is essentially within its domestic jurisdiction.[41]

Maus, too, seems to feel the weakness of his view, as seen from the angle of practice and then goes on to dwell on the question of whether matters exist which can be said to have been declared – to be within domestic jurisdiction – in bad faith by a state. On this score he points out the following: the right of the Court to decide whether a state has invoked its domestic jurisdiction in bad faith is difficult to apply in practice. Referring to Lauterpacht's separate opinion added to the Court's judgment in the *Case of Certain Norwegian Loans*, Maus asserts that subjective reservations of domestic jurisdiction are worded in such broad terms as to practically cover any dispute which the state concerned wishes to declare to be within its domestic jurisdiction.[42]

In the view of another author, Crabb, the borderline for the Court's decision would no longer be whether the dispute was domestic as a matter of law, 'but whether it had been determined to be so reasonably and in good faith by the defendant State'.[43] He believes that since in such cases the function of the Court 'would be determining in a substantial way the question of its own jurisdiction, and not merely registering a veto', Article 36, paragraph 6 of the Statute is not violated either.[44]

According to Shihata 'The question of domestic jurisdiction is elastic enough to allow a wide use of the reservation, which is not necessarily an abuse of it'. Anyhow, he concludes that the Court will have to decide, at least on a prima facie basis, whether the reservation was properly invoked.[45]

A position diametrically opposed to these views is taken by Sir Hersch Lauterpacht, who, in his separate opinion, delivered in the *Case of Certain Norwegian Loans*, firmly opposed having the Court vested with the right to examine whether a state claimed bona or mala fide that the particular matter was within its domestic jurisdiction. In taking this position Judge Lauterpacht based himself, on the one hand, on the intent of states making such reservation and, on the other hand, starting from

41 *Id.*
42 *Id.* 159–60.
43 Crabb (1961) 539.
44 *Id.* 538.
45 Cf. Shihata (1965) 297.

practical considerations, on the difficulty in separating 'domestic' from 'international' matters. On this score he writes that 'it is possible for a State to maintain, without necessarily laying itself open to an irresistible charge of bad faith, that practically every dispute concerns a matter essentially within its domestic jurisdiction'.[46] A few lines below he goes on to assert that: 'The Court has no power to give a decision on the question whether a State has acted in good faith in claiming that a dispute covers a matter which is essentially within its domestic jurisdiction'.[47]

In point of fact, Sir Hersch Lauterpacht repeated the same position in his dissenting opinion in the *Interhandel case*, adding that the Court must exercise the greatest caution in attributing to a sovereign state bad faith, an abuse of right, or unreasonableness in the fulfilment of its obligations.[48]

Sir Percy Spender, in his separate opinion appended to the judgment in the *Interhandel case*, came to a similar conclusion, arguing that the Court would, by examining whether a state invoked in good faith the subjective reservation of domestic jurisdiction to the American declaration, virtually modify that reservation in such a way that the declaration would be read as containing the words '"provided it is so determined by the United States of America in good faith". There is no room of redrafting the reservation and giving it a different meaning to what its words bear and which they clearly enough were intended to bear.'[49]

It is abundantly clear that where an international obligation is involved the Court has the right and duty to consider the regularity of the argument advanced. In other cases the situation is much more difficult to handle, because lack of good faith is hard to prove, and, as is referred to the arbitral award in the *Lac Lenoux case* by Jean-Pierre Cot, it is a well-crystallized legal principle that bad faith cannot be presumed.[50] One could say that the examination of bona or mala fide pleas of the subjective reservation of domestic jurisdiction is a rather heavy responsibility, complex and delicate.[51] So it appears that Anzilotti was justified

---

46 *Case concerning Certain Norwegian Loans,* Judgment of July 6, 1957, Separate Opinion of Judge Sir Hersch Lauterpacht, *ICJ Reports 1957*, 52.

47 *Id.*

48 *Interhandel case* (Preliminary Objections), Judgment of 21 March 1959, Dissenting Opinion of Sir Hersch Lauterpacht, *ICJ Reports 1959*, 111.

49 Cf. *Id.* Separate Opinion of Sir Percy Spender, 59.

50 Cf. Jean-Pierre Cot, 'La bonne foi et la conclusion des traités' (1968) 3, *RBD*, *I* 140, 141.

51 Cf. Shihata (1965) 291.

in writing, in connection with the *Electricity Company of Sofia and Bulgaria case*, that the theory of abuse of rights is an extremely delicate question, and a judge should hesitate in applying it to such a question as the compulsory jurisdiction of the Court.[52]

In addition, the question arises as to what the Court would achieve by finding that the subjective reservation of domestic jurisdiction was invoked in bad faith by a state.

If the Court should find a state to have acted in bad faith by alleging a dispute before the Court to be within its domestic jurisdiction, such a decision would doubtlessly be hotly debated in view of the authority of the International Court of Justice; it being doubtful whether it would serve to promote the peaceful settlement of the particular dispute. A decision of the Court establishing a bad faith plea of domestic jurisdiction would, in a considerable number of cases, result in the Court declaring that it had jurisdiction over the dispute. It is nonetheless questionable whether that decision would be accepted by the state concerned.

So, if one is to take a realistic approach to subjective reservations of domestic jurisdiction, two factors must be kept in mind. First, both the states and the International Court of Justice have, in the last analysis, recognized as valid the reservations in question and, second, these reservations open up the possibility for abuse and evading the obligations undertaken in respect of the Court's compulsory jurisdiction. It was not by chance that in his Report of 1956–57 the Secretary-General of the United Nations stated that the subjective reservations of domestic jurisdiction 'render the whole system of compulsory jurisdiction illusory'.

(e) The Reservation and the Statute

The objection most frequently raised is that subjective reservations of domestic jurisdiction are inconsistent with Article 36, paragraph 6 of the Statute, which provides that: 'In the event of a dispute as to whether the Court has jurisdiction, the matter shall be settled by the decision of the Court'.

The best-known proponent of this view is Sir Hersch Lauterpacht, who, in his separate opinion written in the *Norwegian Loans case*, explains that the automatic reservation to the French declaration of acceptance is in conflict with Article 36, paragraph 6 of the Statute,

---

[52] *Electricity Company of Sofia and Bulgaria* (Preliminary Objection), Judgment of 4 April 1939. Separate Opinion by M. Anzilotti. *PCIJ Series A/B*, 77, 98.

because the French declaration leaves it to the Government of the French Republic to determine which matters fall within national jurisdiction in a concrete dispute, and more notably which matters are excluded from the Court's compulsory jurisdiction. Judge Sir Hersch Lauterpacht says that:

> The French reservation is thus not only contrary to one of the most fundamental principles of international – and national – jurisprudence according to which it is within the inherent power of a tribunal to interpret the text establishing its jurisdiction. It is also contrary to a clear specific provision of the Statute of the Court as well as to the general Articles 1 and 92 of the Statute and of the Charter, respectively, which require the Court to function in accordance with its Statute.[53]

Sir Hersch Lauterpacht holds that automatic reservations actually deprive the Court of its power to determine its jurisdiction, since in the case of declarations containing such a reservation the Court's jurisdiction is decided by the state invoking the reservation, and the Court, by taking notice of the reservation, does not but practically 'register' the position of the state concerning the Court's jurisdiction.

The eminent authority on international law emphasizes that:

> Governments are under no compulsion, legal or moral, to accept the duties of obligatory judicial settlement. When accepting them, they can limit them to the barest minimum. But the existence of that minimum, if it is to be a legal obligation, must be subject to determination by the Court itself and not by the Government accepting it.[54]

He argues these reservations operate to debar the Court from deciding on its jurisdiction, because the question of jurisdiction is settled once a state has invoked its domestic jurisdiction. If the state appealing to the reservation has decided that the Court lacks jurisdiction under the reservation, the question of jurisdiction cannot be contested any more. In other words, Article 36, paragraph 6 of the Statute no longer has any relevance, and the application of this paragraph is confined to registration of the fact that the defending state has taken a decision on the Court's jurisdiction.[55]

In like manner, Judge Guerrero in his dissenting opinion added to the judgment in the *Norwegian Loans case* by stating that 'The great defect

---

[53] *Case of Certain Norwegian Loans,* Judgment of 6 July 1957, Separate Opinion of Judge Sir Hersch Lauterpacht, *ICJ Reports 1957*, 44.

[54] *Id.* 65.

[55] *Id.* 47–8.

of this reservation is that it does not conform either to the spirit of the Statute of the Court or to the provisions of paragraphs 2 and 6 of Article 36'.[56] He pointed out that the principle embodied in Article 36, paragraph 6 of the Statute is common to all international arbitral and judicial tribunals and the International Court of Justice would perhaps be the only tribunal that would be compelled to prevent itself from dealing with a dispute submitted to it once the subjective reservation of domestic jurisdiction had been invoked by one of the parties.[57]

Sir Percy Spender comes to the same conclusion in the *Interhandel case*.[58] President Klaestad and Judge Armand-Upon likewise underlined that the reservation was in conflict with the Statute.[59]

Views similar to those of the Judges are also met within publications appearing after the Court's decisions, with several authors contending that subjective reservations of domestic jurisdiction are contrary to the Statute.[60] Waldock is of the view that: 'By looking only at the form and not the substance of the United States reservation, it may perhaps be possible to reconcile it with the letter, although not the spirit, of Article 36 (6) of the Statute'.[61]

Other authors claim that these reservations do not deprive the Court of its right to ultimately decide on the question of jurisdiction.[62] As Crawford writes: 'No doubt the making of such a reservation demonstrates little faith in the Court, but enough, one would have thought, to leave to the Court the competence to determine whether an automatic reservation had in fact been invoked'.[63]

One should agree with that view, since the reservation does not formally deprive the Court of its competence to decide on jurisdiction. If in a concrete case one of the parties invokes the reservation and the opponent party contests it, the Court remains competent to 'decide' on

---

56 Cf. *Id.* Dissenting Opinion of Judge Guerrero, 68.

57 Cf. *Id.* 69.

58 *Interhandel case* (Preliminary Objections), Judgment of 21 March 1959, Separate Opinion of Sir Percy Spender, *ICJ Reports 1959*, 56–7.

59 Cf. *Id.* Dissenting Opinion of President Klaestad and Dissenting Opinion of Judge Armand-Ugon, 77–8 and 92.

60 On this score, see Rajan (1958) 122.

61 Waldock treated this question in both of his studies published in the mid-1950s in the British Year-Book of International Law. Waldock (1955–6) 272.

62 Cf. Crawford (1979) 73, Shihata (1965), 297; and Maus (1959) 156. For that matter, Maus asserts that the subjective reservations of domestic jurisdiction are contrary to Art. 36, para. 2 of the Statute only, but not to Art. 36, para. 6. Maus (1959) 156.

63 Crawford (1979) 73.

the dispute, albeit in that event it should decide in favour of the state referring to the subjective reservation of domestic jurisdiction. Thus, although the Court doesn't have much choice in legal disputes when one of the parties refers to a subjective reservation of domestic jurisdiction as being a bar to the Court's jurisdiction, even in those cases the Court nevertheless retains, one should stress, a rather small measure of discretion as to a decision – since it is for the Court to decide on the justification for the invocation, the existence of the reservation, etc.

II MULTILATERAL TREATY RESERVATION (VANDENBERG RESERVATION)

(a) Appearance of the Reservation

The appearance of a multilateral treaty reservation – otherwise known as the Vandenberg reservation – is connected with the 1946 US declaration of acceptance, and the history of its elaboration resembles that of the Connally reservation.

The origin of this limitation can be traced back to the Memorandum which John Foster Dulles – head of the United States' delegation to the United Nations General Assembly and later Foreign Secretary of State – sent to a subcommittee of the Foreign Affairs Committee of the Senate on 10 July 1946. In his Memorandum, Dulles explained that in the case of disputes under multilateral treaties a matter at issue might arise in relations not only between two states – party to the given multilateral treaty – which are parties before the Court, but also between the other contracting parties to that treaty. In view of such matters it would be necessary to make it clear that it was not compulsory to submit to the Court a dispute arising under that multilateral treaty solely on the grounds that certain states party to the treaty were required to do so under the optional clause, the reason being that the other states party to the treaty had not undertaken to resort to the Court and thereby become parties, so they were not bound by Article 94 of the Charter providing that each Member of the United Nations 'undertakes to comply with the decision of the International Court of Justice in any case to which it is a party'.[64] It was on the basis of the Dulles Memorandum that – on the proposal of Senator Vandenberg – the Senate decided to also include in

[64] On the Dulles Memorandum, compare and see Anand (2008) 220–21; and Briggs (1958) 306–07. According to Briggs, Hudson called the Dulles Memorandum, 'a jumble of ideas'.

the United States' declaration of acceptance a limitation providing that the declaration shall not apply to 'disputes arising under a multilateral treaty, unless (1) all parties to the treaty affected by the decision are also parties to the case before the Court, or (2) the United States of America specially agrees to jurisdiction'.

It was characteristic of the Senators that, as is pointed out by Briggs, they had adopted the reservation without clarifying debate and without understanding its meaning and implications.[65]

According to Judge Ruda, the Washington Government intended, by making that reservation, to avoid a situation in which it would be obliged to apply a multilateral treaty in a certain way in line with the Court's judgment, while the other states party to the treaty and not participating in the proceedings remained free to apply the treaty in different ways from that determined by the judgment of the Court, since according to Article 59 of the Statute the decision of the Court had no binding force except between the parties and in respect of the particular case.[66]

Relying on the related Senate documents, Maus writes that the Senators were not aware at the time of the reservation modifying the jurisdiction already conferred to the Court and believed that by making that reservation they actually settled an issue.[67] However, the solution to the problem is unresolved, for the reservation is vague and, as will be seen later, lends itself to various interpretations.

For that matter, Kelsen asserts that the wording of the reservation was modelled on Article 62, paragraph 1 of the Statute, which refers to 'an interest of a legal nature which may be affected by the decision in the case', having the meaning that all parties to the multilateral treaty which may be affected by the decision of the Court are also parties to the case before the Court.[68]

The example of the Vanderberg reservation was followed once again by other states, with certain variations of the reservation found in several declarations of acceptance made under the optional clause.[69]

---

65 Briggs (1958) 307.

66 Cf. *Case concerning Military and Paramilitary Activities in and against Nicaragua* (Jurisdiction of the Court and Admissibility of the Application), Judgment of 26 November 1984, Separate Opinion of Judge Ruda, *ICJ Reports 1984*, 456.

67 Maus (1959) 165.

68 Cf. Kelsen (1951) 530.

69 On this score, see the declarations of acceptance by Djibouti (2005), El Salvador (1973), India (1956), Malawi (1966), Malta (1966), Pakistan (1948) and the Philippines (1972).

(b) The Notion of 'Being Affected'

The multilateral treaty reservation, given its uncertainty and vagueness, was criticized by numerous authors in the literature on international law. What was most frequently written in criticism was that the reservation withdrew, at the will of the declaring state, a large fraction of legal disputes arising under multilateral treaties covered by the optional clause.[70]

The vagueness of the reservation is manifested chiefly in the first part of the limitation and linked to the phrase 'all parties to the treaty affected by the decision are also parties to the case before the Court'. This passage raises the question of who or what should be understood by the word 'affected'; all the parties to the treaty or the multilateral treaty itself?[71] If the reference is to the parties, then an answer should be given to the question of when a party to the treaty is to be deemed 'affected'.[72] If, on the other hand, it is the treaty that is to be considered 'affected', then 'affected' are, under the reservation, all parties to the treaty and hence they all should participate in the proceedings before the Court. In other words, it is not clear whether the authors of the multilateral treaty reservation had in mind the participation in proceedings, over a dispute arising under a multilateral treaty, *of all parties to that treaty or only the parties affected by the dispute*. This possibility of two different interpretations allows for a restrictive and broader conception of the reservation, depending on whether the reference is to all parties to a multilateral treaty or only the states affected by the dispute.

If the authors of the reservation wanted to secure participation in the proceedings of all parties to a multilateral treaty, attainment of that aim is next to impossible in practice, since, in some cases, it would call for ensuring the presence of as many as fifty or a hundred states before the Court, the examination of their written submissions, etc. This in turn would present a task almost impossible to perform, not to mention that there would also be the uncertainty surrounding the intention of all states party to the treaty to become parties to the case before the Court, for it may well be imagined that several contracting parties have no interest whatever in having the given dispute decided by the Court.

Later on the multilateral treaty reservations came to be formulated in clearer terms. Thus, for instance, the declarations of Djibouti (2005), India (1974) and the Philippines (1972) contain the literally uniform text

---

70 Cf. Waldock (1955–6) 275.

71 Cf. Kelsen (1951) 530.

72 Anand (2008) 222.

that 'all parties to the treaty are also parties to the case before the Court'. In this way, the said reservations make it unambiguously clear that all states party to the multilateral treaty are to participate in the proceedings before the Court, which is to say that the states mentioned above included in their respective declarations the broader meaning of the reservation. In connection with these reservations a statement by Judge Sette-Camara in the *Nicaragua case* should be referred to; he observed that the broader meaning of the reservation might have rather far-reaching consequences and such reservations would require the appearance before the Court of all member states of the United Nations and the Organization of American States, for example, in the *Nicaragua case*, together with the original parties in the case.[73]

Judge Sir Robert Jennings, in his separate opinion delivered on the preliminary objections in that same case termed as bizarre the idea that as many as twenty to thirty states participate in the proceedings, but for all that, he considered that the declaring state was entitled to make such a reservation, the practical result being that the Court had no jurisdiction in the absence of special agreement.[74] In his dissenting opinion appended to the judgment on the merits of the case he emphasized that, in spite of the difficulties connected with the reservation, the Court had to respect and apply it.[75]

In the jurisprudence of the International Court of Justice, multilateral treaty reservations were considered for the first time in the *Case concerning Military and Paramilitary Activities in and against Nicaragua.*

In its Memorandum presented in response to Nicaragua's application and during the course of the oral proceedings the United States advanced the point that Nicaragua had invoked in its application, four multilateral treaties, the United Nations Charter, the Charter of the Organization of American States, the 1933 Montevideo Convention on Rights and Duties of States and the Havana Convention on the Rights and Duties of States

---

[73] Cf. *Case concerning Military and Paramilitary Activities in and against Nicaragua* (Merits), Judgment of 27 June 1986, Separate Opinion of Judge Sette-Camara, *ICJ Reports 1986*, 192.

[74] Cf. *Case concerning Military and Paramilitary Activities in and against Nicaragua* (Jurisdiction of the Court and Admissibility of the Application), Judgment of 26 November 1984 Separate Opinion of Judge Sir Robert Jennings, *ICJ Reports 1984*, 554.

[75] *Case concerning Military and Paramilitary Activities in and against Nicaragua* (Merits), Judgment of 27 June 1986, Dissenting Opinion of Judge Sir Robert Jennings, *ICJ Reports 1986*, 529.

in the Event of Civil Strife. The Washington Government argued that since the dispute submitted to the Court 'had arisen' under the treaties listed, the Court, according to the multilateral treaty reservation contained in the United States declaration of acceptance, could only exercise jurisdiction if all parties to the treaty affected by the decision of the Court were also parties to the case. For its part, the Washington Government did name the said states (Costa Rica, El Salvador and Honduras) and maintained that if only one of them was found by the Court to be 'affected', the United States reservation would take full effect.[76]

In the judgment on preliminary objections the Court acknowledged that the multilateral treaty reservation included in the United States declaration of acceptance was vague and lent itself to two different interpretations; it pointed out that it was not clear as to what was 'affected', according to the terms of the proviso, the treaties themselves or the parties to them.[77] So, in fact, the Court did nothing else than repeat the question formulated in the literature of international law with respect to the reservation. The matter was not, however, resolved by the Court, for two reasons. First, because, according to the judgment, the reservation had been interpreted by the United States itself as applying only to states affected by the decision (i.e. Washington sought to apply the restrictive concept of the reservation), and the three neighbouring states that might be affected had also been indicated by Washington.[78] Second, the Court found that the multilateral treaty reservation did not affect its jurisdiction in that case, as Nicaragua invoked a number of principles of customary and general international law, which had been enshrined in conventions relied upon by Nicaragua. The Court emphasized: 'The fact that the above-mentioned principles, recognized as such, have been codified or embodied in multilateral conventions does not mean that they cease to exist and to apply as principles of customary law, even as regards countries that are party to such conventions.'[79]

---

[76] *Case concerning Military and Paramilitary Activities in and against Nicaragua. ICJ Pleadings*, vol. II. Cf. USA Counter-Memorial, Part III, 86–91.

[77] *Case concerning Military and Paramilitary Activities in and against Nicaragua* (Jurisdiction of the Court and Admissibility of the Application), Judgment of 26 November 1984. *ICJ Reports 1984,* 424.

[78] For that matter, the United States did not but merely mention the other possible construction of the reservation, namely that requiring participation in the proceedings of all states party to the multilateral treaties in question.

[79] *Case concerning Military and Paramilitary Activities in and against Nicaragua* (Jurisdiction of the Court and Admissibility of the Application), Judgment of 26 November 1984, *ICJ Reports 1984*, 424.

By taking this view the Court practically avoided the application in the concrete case of the multilateral treaty reservation.

Over and above these points, the Court's judgment covered the question as to who was to decide whether a state was or was not 'affected' by a future decision of the Court. The Court held that should a state consider itself affected by the decision, it would either file an application itself or submit a request for intervention. The Court could identify the states 'affected' only when the general outline of judgment to be given became clear.[80] 'Certainly the determination of the states "affected" could not be left to the parties but must be made by the Court'.[81] This line of the Court's reasoning is similar to that of Kelsen, who, shortly after the multilateral treaty reservation had appeared in the United States' declaration of acceptance, wrote that the question as to which states were affected by a decision of the Court can be decided 'only after the Court had assumed and exercised jurisdiction in the dispute concerned'.[82]

The question of 'affected' states was likewise considered by the Court in dealing with the merits of the case. The Court for convenience first dealt with the case of El Salvador, as there were certain special features regarding the position of this state.[83] The United States did not participate in that phase of the proceedings, but the Court considered at length the United States' contention based on the multilateral treaty reservation. In connection with the reservation, the Court stated that 'the reservation does not require, as a condition for the exclusion of a dispute from the jurisdiction of the Court, that a State party to the relevant treaty be "adversely" or "prejudicially" affected by the decision, even though this is clearly the case primary at view.'[84]

In other words, application of the reservation does not require determining whether the state is adversely or otherwise 'affected'; 'the condition of the reservation is met if the state will necessarily be

---

[80] *Id*. 425.

[81] *Id.*

[82] Kelsen (1951) 530.

[83] According to the United States, it was primarily for the benefit of El Salvador and to help it respond to an alleged armed attack by Nicaragua that it provided assistance. Under Art. 51 of the Charter, El Salvador had an inherent right of self-defence and a right to request that the United States provided economic and military assistance to El Salvador. Cf. *Case concerning Military and Paramilitary Activities in and against Nicaragua, ICJ Pleadings*, vol. II, 89.

[84] Cf. *Case concerning Military and Paramilitary Activities in and against Nicaragua* (Merits), Judgment of 27 June 1986, *I.C.J. Reports 1986*, 37.

"affected", in one way or the other.'[85] The Court held that in the concrete case the multilateral treaty reservation operated as a bar to certain documents being invoked as multilateral treaties, but it did not in any way affect the consideration of Nicaragua's claims based on customary international law.[86] That is to say according to the Court, it had jurisdiction under Article 36, paragraph 2 of the Statute to consider the claims of Nicaragua based on customary international law, but it had to exclude from its jurisdiction the consideration of the claims upon the Charter of the United Nations and the Charter of the Organization of American States. As for this finding, Judge Oda, in his dissenting opinion, expressed the view that the Court should have proved, not that it could apply customary and general international law independently, that Nicaragua's claims had *not* arisen under the above-mentioned two multilateral treaties.[87]

At any rate, the Court's decision on the merits of the *Nicaragua case* similarly failed to answer several important questions relating to multilateral treaty reservations, and, as is pointed out by Briggs, the Court disregarded the fact that a reservation stipulating that 'all States party to a multilateral treaty and affected by the decision shall also participate in the proceedings' has a destructive effect on international adjudication and is inconsistent with the Statute of the Court. Instead, the Court stuck to the term 'affected state' without thoroughly examining whether El Salvador's rights were affected by the case at all or what was meant by that term in the context of Article 59 of the Statute, which provided that the decision of the Court was binding only on the parties to the case.[88] According to the well-known American professor, the Court satisfied itself that El Salvador was 'affected', but it did not make such a finding regarding Honduras, albeit that country was the base of operations against Nicaragua.[89]

In recent years, in the *Case concerning the Aerial Incident of 10 August 1999*, the multilateral treaty reservation was touched upon. In response to Pakistan's application, India filed preliminary objections invoking, inter alia, the fact that both its declaration of acceptance of 1974 and Pakistan's declaration contained a multilateral treaty reservation, which barred Pakistan from invoking the Court's jurisdiction against

---

85 *Id.*

86 Cf. *Id.* 92–7.

87 *Id.* Dissenting Opinion of Judge Oda, 219.

88 Herbert W. Briggs, 'The International Court of Justice Lives up to its Name' (1987) 81, *AJIL*, 78, 81.

89 *Id.*

India.[90] India contended that the United Nations Charter, on which Pakistan founded its claims, belonged exactly to the category of multilateral treaties to which the reservation applied.

The multilateral treaty reservation was not considered in that case since, as mentioned earlier, the Court found that the Commonwealth reservation included in the Indian declaration of acceptance was validly invoked in that legal dispute and it had no jurisdiction to entertain the application filed by the Islamic Republic of Pakistan.[91]

(c) Problems Regarding the Participation of Third States in the Proceedings

Those who defend the multilateral treaty reservation usually argue that this limitation serves to protect the interests of third states party to a given multilateral treaty. Such reasoning is not convincing because Articles 62 and 63 of the Statute expressly provide for safeguarding the interests of third states by entitling those states to intervene in the proceedings before the Court.[92] Therefore, as is rightly stated by Professor Joe Verhoeven, the reservation defends the interests of only one state, that which has written the reservation into its declaration of acceptance.[93]

A closer look at multilateral treaty reservations leads us to make the point that in certain cases protecting of the interests of third states may prove all too strong an asset, since a state or states party to a multilateral treaty may happen to have no interest whatsoever in having a dispute regarding, for example, the interpretation or application of the treaty decided by the Court. On a broader meaning of the multilateral treaty reservation, the consent even of these states is required in respect of

---

[90] Cf. *Case concerning Aerial Incident of 10 August 1999,* Preliminary Objections to the Jurisdiction of the Court. Counter Memorial of the Government of India, 82, para icjwww/idocket/ipi/ipi_pleadings (accessed 17 July 2013).

Para. 7 of the Indian declaration of acceptance excluded from the Court's compulsory jurisdiction 'any dispute arising from the interpretation or application of a multilateral treaty, unless at the same time *all the parties to the treaties* are also joined to the case before the Court'.

[91] *Case concerning Aerial Incident of 10 August 1999* (Jurisdiction of the Court), Judgment of 21 June 2000, *ICJ Reports 2000*, 32.

[92] Regarding intervention, see Christine Chinkin, 'Article 63, Article 64' in Zimmermann-Tomuschat-Oellers-Frahm (2006) 1331–92; Geneviève Guyomar, *Commentaire du Réglement de la Cour Internationale de Justice* (A. Pedone 1983) 542–56; and J.M. Ruda, 'Intervention before the International Court of Justice' in Lowe- Fitzmaurice (1996) 487–502.

[93] Cf. Verhoeven (1987) 1177.

proceedings before the Court, yet, under the reservation, these states are not obliged to participate in the proceedings, that is to say they may refuse their participation. By so doing they undoubtedly protect their own interests, but, at the same time, they jeopardize the interests of those states party to the treaty which, on the other hand, seek to have the dispute decided by the Court. At any rate, the reservation gives states a measure of manoeuvre to decide, despite their commitment undertaken with respect to the compulsory jurisdiction of the Court, and actually on a case-by-case basis, whether a particular legal dispute may be dealt with by the Court.

In exploring a solution to these problems arising out of the multilateral treaty reservation Louis Sohn suggested that the reservation should be reworded to exclude from compulsory jurisdiction 'disputes relating to a multilateral treaty, unless all the parties to that treaty have agreed that any decision rendered in any such dispute between two or more of them will be binding upon all of them …'.[94] Professor Lori Damrosch is critical of Sohn's suggestion, which she believes to have more disadvantages than advantages and she raises the question of its compatibility with Article 94 of the United Nations Charter and Article 59 of the Court's Statute. She is of the view that Professor Sohn's proposal purports to derogate from the binding character of the Court's decisions in contentious cases, because the unanimous consent as mentioned in the proposal can hardly be expected to be given by states with no interest in a particular matter.[95]

It should be mentioned that according to the Statute and the Rules of Court, intervention is the procedural device by which the interests of a third state, not party to the proceedings before the Court, are protected. Without dwelling on questions of intervention one can state that there exists in fact two methods of intervention, depending on whether intervention is based on Article 62 or Article 63 of the Statute.

---

[94] After the withdrawal in 1986 of the United States 1946 declaration of acceptance, experts of international law have written widely on what the new United States' declaration of acceptance should contain, among other things a draft of a new declaration of acceptance was by elaborated Professor Louis Sohn.

On Sohn's draft, see Louis B. Sohn, 'Compulsory Jurisdiction of the World Court and the United States Position: The Need to Improve the United States Declaration' in Anthony Clark Arend (ed.) *The United States and the Compulsory Jurisdiction of the International Court of Justice* (University Press of America 1986) 3–28.

[95] Cf. Lori Fisler Damrosch, 'Multilateral Disputes' in Damrosch (1987) 398.

Under Article 62 states are empowered to intervene in a case if they consider that a legal interest of theirs may be affected; in such case the state can request that the Court be permitted to intervene. The permission may be granted or refused, upon the decision of the Court, considering whether or not the intervening state's legal interests are affected by the proceedings instituted.

On the other hand, Article 63 covers precisely those cases, which involve the interpretation of a multilateral treaty before the Court, and in which, other states party to the treaty are permitted to intervene, along with the parties involved in the case.[96] Intervention under Article 63 thus accords to the states party to the multilateral treaty a right to intervene.

Participation by third states in proceedings before the Court under a multilateral treaty reservation has some similarities with intervention under Article 63; nevertheless, there are significant differences between the two cases.

(i) According to the multilateral treaty reservation, proceedings before the Court cannot take place unless the other states party to a multilateral treaty also participate therein – whether only the states affected by the Court's decision or all states party to the multilateral treaty should participate has no relevance here – with the reservation practically exercising some sort of pressure on these states to get involved and participate in the proceedings, since the Court cannot decide on the legal dispute without their presence. By contrast, in the case of intervention under Article 63 it is exclusively for the interested state to decide whether or not to make use of its right to intervene.

(ii) Under the general rule governing intervention, it is for the Court to decide on intervention, even in the case of intervention under Article 63. Whereas in the case of a multilateral treaty reservation the Court is actually left without discretion to decide on the participation in the proceedings of states other than the original parties to the case, because the reservation makes it to some extent

---

96 Art. 63 reads as follows:

1. Whenever the construction of a convention to which States other than those concerned in the case are parties is in question, the Registrar shall notify all such States forthwith.
2. Every State so notified has the right to intervene in the proceedings; but if it uses this right, the construction given by the judgment will be equally binding upon it.

an obligation of the states affected to participate in the proceedings or else the proceedings before the Court cannot take place at all.

In connection with the multilateral treaty reservation, the question also arises as to what will be the position in the proceedings of the other states party to the multilateral treaty. This is an open question, all the more so since the position in the proceedings of the intervening state is similarly awaiting full clarification.

It was in 1992, for the first time since the establishment of the International Court of Justice, that the Court permitted a third state to intervene in the *Case concerning the Land, Island and Maritime Frontier Dispute*. Until this case the literature on international law was also rather uncertain about the position in the proceedings of the intervening state.[97] Precisely for that reason the ad hoc Chamber, composed of members of the Court, when permitting Nicaragua's intervention in the legal dispute between El Salvador and Honduras,[98] found it appropriate to give some indication of the extent of the procedural rights acquired by Nicaragua as a result of that permission.[99] The Chamber held that the intervening state does not become a party to the proceedings, and does not acquire the rights, or become subject to the obligations (which attach to the status of a party, under the Statute), the Rules of Court and the general principles of procedural law. At the same time, however, the intervening state is also vested with certain rights, such as the right to be heard, but this does not carry through with regard to the obligations of being bound by the decision.[100]

With respect to multilateral treaty reservations this means that, on a broader meaning of the reservation, for instance, all states party to a multilateral treaty (which may number 20 or 30 or even more) should participate in proceedings over a particular case, all having the right to be heard by the Court! It needs no further explanation that this would not be a viable path in practice.

If, on the other hand, the intervening state is a non-party in the case, the Court's decision is not binding on it. In the *Case concerning the*

---

[97] Cf. Angelo Davi', *L'intervento davanti alla Corte Internazionale di Giustizia* (Jovene, 1984) 209–15.

[98] For that matter, the case involved intervention under Art. 62 of the Statute.

[99] Cf. *Case concerning the Land, Island and Maritime Frontier Dispute* (Application by Nicaragua for Permission to Intervene), Judgment of 13 September 1990, *ICJ Reports 1990*, 135.

[100] *Id.* 135–6.

Land, Island and Maritime Frontier Dispute this reasoning was also practically upheld by the Chamber, which concluded that in the circumstances of the present case the Chamber's judgment was not *res judicata* for Nicaragua.[101] In dealing with this matter Rosenne points out – similar to the declaration made by Judge Oda in that case[102] – that, since the case concerned a territorial dispute, the Chamber's judgment was binding not only on the parties; it was valid *erga omnes.* Precisely for this reason, Professor Rosenne stated that it was difficult to understand why the Chamber did not somehow refer in the judgment to Nicaragua's declaration – which was made at the time it submitted its request for intervention – stating that 'Nicaragua intends to subject itself to the binding effect of the decision to be given'.[103]

In respect of the multilateral treaty reservation all this leads to the conclusion that if the Court should be seized of a dispute under a declaration of acceptance containing a multilateral treaty reservation and the states party to the treaty in question also wish to participate in the proceedings before the Court under the terms of the multilateral treaty reservation, it can be taken as very likely that, having regard to the judgment in the *Case concerning the Land, Island and Maritime Frontier Dispute*, these states would be considered by the Court as non-parties in the proceedings and not bound by the judgment of the Court. It is not sure, of course, that in a dispute regarding a multilateral treaty the Court would by analogy apply its jurisprudence regarding intervention and it is also unlikely that under the multilateral treaty reservation the Court would recognize for third states participating in a case more rights than it had conceded to the intervening state in the *Case concerning the Land, Island and Maritime Frontier Dispute*.

(d) The Consent to the Proceedings

The second part of the multilateral treaty reservation as contained in the United States declaration of acceptance and stipulating in fact an alternative condition, provides that in a dispute arising under a multilateral treaty the Court may not have jurisdiction unless 'the United States of America specially agrees to jurisdiction'. This practically means nothing else than disputes as to multilateral treaties cannot be brought

---

[101] Cf. *Case concerning the Land, Island and Maritime Frontier Dispute,* Judgment of 11 September 1992, *ICJ Reports 1992*, 610.

[102] Cf. *Id.* Declaration of Judge Oda, 619–20.

[103] Shabtai Rosenne, *Intervention in the International Court of Justice* (Martinus Nijhoff Publishers, 1993) 155.

before the Court solely under the optional clause and the consent of the state having the multilateral treaty reservation in its declaration of acceptance – and, on the basis of reciprocity, the consent of even the opponent party – is required in such proceedings.

Hudson asserts that this clause of the reservation shows a confusion of thought, for if the United States agrees to jurisdiction, it is virtually that consent which, functioning, as it were, as a special agreement, constitutes the basis for the Court's jurisdiction, and there would be no question of applying the declaration of acceptance.[104] One can say that in respect of the reservation it is unclear whether the special consent of the United States practically replaces the declaration of acceptance and that lack of its consent deprives the Court of its compulsory jurisdiction in disputes arising under multilateral treaties. Waldock, referring to Lauterpacht's view, writes that if his view is correct, the reservation practically operates to preclude the United States from being brought before the Court in a dispute regarding a multilateral treaty unless the United States specifically consents to jurisdiction after the case has arisen.[105]

In respect of multilateral treaty reservations the question also arises as to how reciprocity affects this limitation, especially that part of it which requires even a separate consent from the declaring state regarding the Court's jurisdiction, since according to the principle of reciprocity a reservation may be invoked by the opponent party as well.

(e) Compatibility of the Reservation with the Statute

Also, the question of compatibility with respect to obligations under the Statute and the optional clause arises in connection with multilateral treaty reservations, both with the first part of the reservation on account of its vagueness, as has been discussed already, and the second part thereof, which requires the declaring state's special consent regarding the jurisdiction of the Court. This part of the reservation is clearly contrary to the obligation undertaken under Article 36, paragraph 2 of the Statute and even the spirit of the optional clause, which provides that states 'declare that they recognize as compulsory *ipso facto* and without special agreement' the jurisdiction of the Court. Owing to the second part of multilateral treaty reservation the parties' declarations of acceptance become useless, since the Court's compulsory jurisdiction cannot come into play in disputes arising under multilateral treaties and such disputes

---

[104] Manley Hudson 'World Court – America's Declaration Accepting Jurisdiction'. 32, *A.B.A. Journal* (1946), 836, quoted by Anand (2008) 221.

[105] Waldock (1955–6) 274.

cannot be decided by the Court unless the state having that reservation in its declaration – and, the opponent party, on the basis of reciprocity – specially agrees to submit the legal dispute to the Court.

One can say that with this part of multilateral treaty reservations, the declaring state nullifies the obligations undertaken in respect of the Court's compulsory jurisdiction, by its accession to the optional clause system. As mentioned earlier, this is practically the case with subjective reservations of domestic jurisdiction as well. However, one could think that this is perhaps even more readily perceptible with multilateral treaty reservations than subjective reservations of domestic jurisdiction.

From the foregoing it becomes clear that multilateral treaty reservations have a destructive effect on the compulsory jurisdiction system as the subjective reservations of domestic jurisdiction have, chiefly because the broad concept of interpretation of the 'affected' states, barred proceedings before the Court over disputes arising under multilateral treaties. As for the other part of these reservations, by the said stipulation, declaring states unquestionably take back the compulsory jurisdiction which they conferred on the Court. All this is detrimental to the judicial settlement of international disputes, all the more so since multilateral treaty reservations expressly concern disputes concerning the interpretation or application of treaties and a considerable part of the cases brought before the Court involve precisely such disputes.

As has already been said, the Court while applying a subjective reservation of domestic jurisdiction retains a certain measure of discretion to decide on its own jurisdiction and – in the context thereof – its competence under Article 36, paragraph 6 of the Statute. If in a legal dispute submitted to the Court a state decides not to invoke the subjective reservation of domestic jurisdiction, the Court may go on with the proceedings, as the application of the reservation is not automatic and parties should refer to it before the Court. In the case of multilateral treaty reservations, especially with regard to the second part of such reservations, the parties have no such 'discretion' and, if one clings strictly to the wording of these reservations, the Court may not, in matters covered by the reservations, assume jurisdiction unless the parties specially agree thereto. Of course, it may also happen that multilateral treaty reservations are not invoked, but in that event the Court's jurisdiction is practically founded not on declarations of acceptance, since under these the Court could not deal with a particular matter in any way, instead the Court would deal with it on the *forum prorogatum*, i.e. on the parties' consent to jurisdiction in a given dispute.[106]

---

[106] Cf. Waldock (1954) 133–4.

III THE COURT'S POSITION TOWARDS DESTRUCTIVE RESERVATIONS

One can see that destructive reservations added to declarations of acceptances raise a number of important questions. It would be primarily for the Court to decide on questions concerning limitations especially with disputable clauses because these limitations are contrary to the spirit and the letters of the optional clause. This relates to subjective reservations of domestic jurisdiction and multilateral treaty reservations as well. However, in dealing with a variety of matters the Court has in fact avoided giving clear answers to these questions. Nevertheless, several members of the Court have argued that the Court had to examine *ex officio* the validity of the disputed reservations.

In his separate opinion submitted in the *Norwegian Loans case*, Sir Hersch Lauterpacht emphasized that the Court would have had to examine *ex officio* the validity of the French reservation, since the Court's jurisdiction cannot be founded on anything but valid documents. For this very reason he claims, the fact that the defendant state did not raise 'the particular issue of the validity of the French Acceptance as a whole cannot endow with validity an instrument otherwise invalid.'[107] In the *Interhandel case*, Judge Sir Hersch Lauterpacht was even more determined not to have the Court postpone the decision on the validity of the automatic reservation and the manner of its exercise, because of the applicant state raising these questions in that legal dispute.[108]

In the *Norwegian Loans case* Judge Guerrero, too, expressed the view that the Court would have to take a position on whether the French reservation was compatible with the Statute.[109] He stressed that the consensus of the parties was not sufficient for establishing the Court's jurisdiction and that it was also necessary to ascertain 'whether that *consensus* is (was) compatible with the provisions of the Statute and whether it can be applied without the Court's being obliged to depart

---

[107] Cf. *Case of Certain Norwegian Loans,* Judgment of 6 July 1957, Separate Opinion of Sir Hersch Lauterpacht, *ICJ Reports 1957*, 61.

[108] *Interhandel case* (Preliminary Objections), Judgment of 21 March 1959, Dissenting Opinion of Sir Hersch Lauterpacht, *ICJ Reports l959*, 102.

[109] It will be noted merely as a point of interest that Judge Guerrero voted against the operative part of the Judgment, whilst Judge Sir Hersch Lauterpacht agreed with that part of the Judgment, although he made a vigorous attack on the majority position of the Court.

from those provisions'.[110] Judge Guerrero referred to the fact that in an analogous situation, notably the case of the *Free zones of Upper Savoya and the district of Gex*, the Permanent Court of International Justice decided *ex officio* on the incompatibility of the Franco-Swiss Agreement with respect to the provisions of the Statute and did not wait for the parties to raise that question.[111]

It would have been another problem if an eventual decision of the Court held that a declaration of acceptance containing the subjective reservation of domestic jurisdiction also had an effect on the declarations of a number of states which have had no opportunity to express their view on the matter. According to Judge Lauterpacht, under Article 63 of the Statute, as was already mentioned, it would have been preferable to give to the states having the subjective reservation of domestic jurisdiction in their declarations of acceptance the opportunity to intervene in the case before the Court. Since it failed to do so, the states concerned could take the position that by virtue of Article 59 of the Statute the authority of the Court's decision was limited to the case at hand and 'they are at liberty to assert their attitude on the matter on another occasion'.[112]

The problem of the invalidity of multilateral treaty reservations was referred to by Judge Mosler in the Nicaragua case.[113] Judge Mosler pointed out that the Court never had the opportunity to decide whether a whole declaration under the optional clause may be invalid because an ineffective reservation had to be considered an essential part of it.[114]

Those who challenge the International Court of Justice for having failed to take a different stand on the question of the validity of those reservations which contain rather disputable contents are undoubtedly right at first glance, but if one examines this problem more carefully and probes into it, in light of the Court's possible findings on the matter, one must admit that the International Court of Justice was right to refrain from taking a definitive stance on these delicate issues.

---

[110] Cf. *Case of Certain Norwegian Loans,* Judgment of 6 July 1957, Dissenting Opinion of Judge Guerrero, *ICJ Reports 1957*, 68.

[111] *Id.* 68.

[112] Cf. *Case of Certain Norwegian Loans,* Judgment of 6 July 1957, Separate Opinion of Sir Hersch Lauterpacht, *ICJ Reports 1957*, 63–4.

[113] *Case concerning Military and Paramilitary Activities in and against Nicaragua* (Jurisdiction of the Court and Admissibility of the Application), Judgment of 26 November 1984, Separate Opinion of Judge Mosler, *ICJ Reports 1984*, 468–9.

[114] *Id.* 469.

Had the Court decided on the validity of destructive reservations, it could have concluded either the validity or invalidity of the reservations. If the Court had decided on the invalidity of such reservations then it would have had to decide also on the severability of these invalid reservations from the declarations themselves.

Had the Court decided that multilateral treaty reservations, subjective reservations of domestic jurisdiction or the declarations containing such limitations were valid, it would have obviously exposed itself to sharp criticism on the one hand and undermined its own prestige and authority on the other, since in connection with these reservations it would have explicitly acknowledged that its competence to decide on the question of its own jurisdiction had shrunk to a rather narrow scope. In addition, a definitive stance of the Court on clearly accepting as valid the contested reservations and the declarations of acceptance containing such reservations would by all means have afforded for states a kind of 'encouragement' to attach such limitations to their declarations of acceptance.

The other avenue open to the Court would have been a pronouncement on the invalidity of destructive reservations. Here, as was already mentioned, other questions arise:

(i) whether there exists the possibility of severing the invalid reservation from the declaration of acceptance,
(ii) whether the invalidity of a reservation affects the whole declaration of acceptance.

Both the views of the judges of the International Court of Justice and the position of writers on international law are divided as to the extent to which an invalid reservation affects the declaration of acceptance itself. According to one view, invalidity bears upon the declaration of acceptance as a whole, whereas the other view argues that invalidity has no effect on the declaration itself. In the case of subjective reservations of domestic jurisdiction a distinction may be drawn even within the second view according to the few words 'as determined by the United States of America' – as invalidity is regarded as going to the 'automatic clause' only – or the reservation as a whole.

In the *Case of Certain Norwegian Loans*, Sir Hersch Lauterpacht comes to the conclusion that an invalid condition cannot be severed from the declaration as a whole, because that possibility can only be entertained in the case of provisions or conditions which are not essential elements of the undertaking. According to Lauterpacht the declaring state considers the subjective reservation of domestic jurisdiction as being an essential limitation on obligations and should the Court find the declaration to be valid without the reservation, it would be ignoring an essential and deliberate condition of the declaration.[115]

In the *Interhandel case* Judge Lauterpacht restated his arguments concerning the invalidity of automatic reservations,[116] and a similar position was adopted by Judge Sir Percy Spender.[117] It can be observed that Lauterpacht's reasoning did not run along quite the same lines in the two cases. In the *Case of Certain Norwegian Loans* he asserted that the invalidity of the automatic reservation to the French declaration had rendered the French declaration of acceptance invalid *ab initio*, whereas in the *Interhandel case* he expressed the opinion that so long as the reservation of the United States declaration of acceptance was not declared invalid by the Court in appropriate proceedings, the limitation had to be deemed to exclude the Court's jurisdiction on the merits. All this led Briggs to conclude that in the *Case of Certain Norwegian Loans* the Court could not, according to Lauterpacht, have jurisdiction because the reservation was invalid, although in the *Interhandel case*, the Court lacked jurisdiction because the invocation of the reservation had to be treated as valid.[118]

In the literature of international law a similar view to Lauterpacht's opinion in the *Norwegian Loans case* was taken by Waldock[119] and Dubisson, the latter author maintaining that subjective reservations of domestic jurisdiction are null and void and that if the reservation in question constitutes a substantial element of the declaration of acceptance, the very declaration is equally null and void.[120]

Maus considers that a declaration containing the Connally reservation is to be deemed null as it runs counter to the object of the optional clause.[121] The same point is stressed by Robert Jennings, who argues that 'Once it is decided that the reservation is void there would seem to be no choice but to regard the Acceptance as void'. The British professor goes on by saying that should only the reservation, and not the declaration, be found invalid by the Court, such a finding would result in precisely the

---

115 *Case of Certain Norwegian Loans,* Judgment of 6 July 1957, *ICJ Reports 1957*, 57–8.

116 Cf. *Interhandel case* (Preliminary Objections), Judgment of 21 March 1959, Dissenting Opinion of Sir Hersch Lauterpacht, *ICJ Reports 1959*, 101–02.

117 Cf. *Id.* Separate Opinion of Sir Percy Spender, 59.

118 Briggs (1958) 353.

119 See Waldock (1954) 133.

120 Cf. Dubisson (1964) 189.

121 Cf. Maus (1959) 160.

opposite of that which had been intended by the declaring state, for the Court would establish its jurisdiction in matters which the state concerned had clearly indicated its unwillingness to submit to the Court.[122]

Again, the problem of invalidity and the question of severability of an invalid clause from the rest of the declaration arise in connection with multilateral treaty reservations, but this set of problems has received much less attention than have the subjective reservations of domestic jurisdiction. In the *Nicaragua case* Judge Mosler asks whether the declaration of acceptance as a whole is affected by the invalidity of the multilateral treaty reservation.[123] He, too, leaves this question unanswered, however, confining himself to stating that if the answer is yes, then its effect would be worse than applying the reservation and maintaining the rest of the declaration.[124]

The views that an invalid reservation is severable from the declaration and apart from the invalid part, the rest of the declaration of acceptance remains in force, disregard a very important aspect of the problem. If a reservation or a clause appended to a declaration of acceptance is deemed non-existent, whilst the rest of the declaration is considered valid, the obligations of the declaring state are extended without the consent thereof – this is not in line with the jurisprudence of the two International Courts; that subscribes to jurisdiction only existing with respect to the *questions consented by the parties*! This was expressed in the judgment of the Permanent Court in the *Chorzów Factory case* and reiterated by both Courts in several other cases, stating that 'the Court's jurisdiction is always a limited one, existing only in so far as States have accepted it'.[125]

The issue of the severability of a reservation from the declaration of acceptance also emerged in the *Fisheries Jurisdiction case*. According to President Schwebel, if the declaring state treats a reservation as an essential element without which the declaration would not have been

---

122 Cf. Jennings (1958) 362.

123 Cf. *Case concerning Military and Paramilitary Activities in and against Nicaragua* (Jurisdiction of the Court and Admissibility of the Application), Judgment of 26 November 1984, Separate Opinion of Judge Mosler, *ICJ Reports 1984*, 468.

124 Cf. *Id.* 469.

125 *Case concerning the Factory at Chorzów* (Jurisdiction) Judgment of 26 July 1927, *PCIJ Series A*. Judgment No. 8, 32.

made, the Court is not free to hold the reservation invalid or ineffective while treating the remainder of the declaration to be in force.[126]

As mentioned already, the International Court of Justice did not decide upon the validity of either the subjective reservations of domestic jurisdiction or the multilateral treaty reservations.

To declare null and void optional clause declarations containing subjective reservations of domestic jurisdiction or multilateral treaty reservations would have resulted in depriving such declarations of acceptance even of the limited legal effect they have retained despite these limitations with respect to the compulsory jurisdiction of the International Court of Justice.

The reason being that if, in the *Norwegian Loans case* and the *Interhandel case*, the Court had found that the French and American declarations of acceptance were invalid as a whole on the grounds of subjective reservations of domestic jurisdiction, a decision to that effect would have affected a number declarations of acceptance in force containing the subjective reservation of domestic jurisdiction. As Sir Hersch Lauterpacht himself suggested, the form in which the invalidity of those declarations would have been spelled out would have been a different matter, of course.[127] However, the Court's pronunciation that a declaration of acceptance is to be invalid on the grounds of a subjective reservation of domestic jurisdiction in the cases before it would have affected, directly or indirectly, the declarations of some seven other states.[128] Thus, in the last analysis, all these points would have combined to increase the adverse effects of subjective reservations of domestic jurisdiction on the optional clause system. Pronouncing the invalidity of declarations containing such reservations would have operated to rule out even the theoretical possibility of the Court's compulsory jurisdiction coming into play over matters which were not affected by the reservations or, situations whereby the parties still had not invoked the said reservation in a concrete case, as happened in the *Rights of Nationals of the United States of America in Morocco case*.

---

[126] *Fisheries Jurisdiction case* (Spain v. Canada) (Jurisdiction of the Court) Judgment 4 December 1998. Separate Opinion of President Schwebel. *ICJ Reports 1998*, 473.

[127] As mentioned previously, Judge Sir Hersch Lauterpacht suggested that all states whose declarations of acceptance contained the incriminated reservation should be permitted to intervene in the cases concerned with the reservation.

[128] At the time of the proceedings the subjective domestic jurisdiction reservation was included in the declarations of acceptance of India, Liberia, Mexico, Pakistan, South Africa and the United States of America.

Therefore, in the light of the considerations discussed above, it could be maintained that the Court was wise to hand down no decision on the validity of the disputed reservations.

The only solution to the problems connected with destructive reservations could be achieved by states abandoning the practice of including such limitations in their declarations of acceptance.[129] It should be noted that some progress has been made in this field in so far as the declarations of acceptance containing such reservations have decreased in number, and several states – France in 1974, Pakistan in 1960, the Republic of South Africa in 1967 and the United States in 1986 – have withdrawn their respective declarations of acceptance containing subjective reservations of domestic jurisdiction. The only flaw in the withdrawal of declarations containing such reservations is that in the majority of cases the said states brought themselves to take that step by reason either of proceedings formally started (see e.g., the withdrawal of the United States declaration in connection with the *Nicaragua case*)[130] or the Court's decision going against the declaring state. At any rate, subjective reservations of domestic jurisdiction are to be found at present in the declarations of only Liberia (1952), Malawi (1966), Mexico (1947), the Philippines (1972) and Sudan (1958).

The decrease of subjective reservations of domestic jurisdiction is likewise indicated by the fact that since the 1970s no single state has made a declaration under the optional clause containing such a limitation. The number of multilateral treaty reservations has also decreased and in the last twenty years there was only one state, Djibouti (2005), who added that limitation to its declaration of acceptance.

---

[129] In point of fact this was also suggested by the *Institute of International Law* when in the resolution – adopted at its Session of 1959 at Neuchâtel and having regard to the position taken by the International Court of Justice in the *Norwegian Loans case* and the *Interhandel case* – it urged states to withdraw their subjective reservations of domestic jurisdiction and called their attention to the danger that such reservations might also be invoked against them by the opponent party. Cf. Résolution sur 'Compétence obligatoire des instances judiciaires et arbitrales internationales' *Annuaire de l'Institut de Droit International*. Session de Neuchâtel, 1959, tome II.

[130] The Washington Government in no way concealed the fact that it had ultimately withdrawn its declaration of acceptance by reason of the proceedings instituted by Nicaragua against it. Cf. *U.S. Dep't St. Bull.*, January 1986, 68.

9. Termination and amendment of declarations of acceptance

I THE SILENCE OF THE TWO STATUTES ON TERMINATION AND AMENDMENT

Notwithstanding that neither the Statute of the Permanent Court, nor the present Court's Statute contain provisions on the termination and amendment of declarations of acceptance, the states have made great use of the possibility for terminating, withdrawing, denouncing, modifying, or amending their declarations of acceptance.[1] They have not only inserted provisions on termination, amendment, etc., in their declarations of acceptance, but also taken the opportunity to terminate or amend their declarations.

Before going on further it should be mentioned that the terminology used by states regarding the termination of their declarations of acceptance is far from uniform and the terms 'termination', 'denunciation' and 'withdrawal' are used alternately by states intending to end their declaration of acceptance.

In the law of treaties one can find similar terms, but there is a sharp distinction made between the termination and denunciation of a treaty. 'Termination' is the broader term, meaning the ending of a treaty – by whatever method that may involve – either by the act of one or all of the contracting parties or the operation of the relevant treaty provision or law in certain events, such as state succession or war.[2] There are several circumstances in which treaties come to an end, these include: execution,

[1] In view of the absence from the Statute of any provision on termination, withdrawal, denunciation and amendment of declarations of acceptance, under the established practice, the procedure of termination, withdrawal, denunciation and amendment follows the same procedure encountered when making the declarations of acceptance; namely the notification on termination, modification etc. of declarations of acceptance must be transmitted to the Secretary-General of the United Nations, who is to forward them to the states party to the Statute and to the Registrar of the Court.

[2] Cf. Lord McNair (1961) 491.

breach of the treaty, conclusion of a new treaty, fundamental change in circumstances, supervening impossibility of performance, expiry of the period fixed for the duration of the treaty, occurrence of a particular event as provided for in the treaty itself – denunciation being but one of these expedients. 'Denunciation' is a unilateral act by one of the contracting parties which is aimed at terminating the treaty, in relation to itself, in accordance with the intent of the contracting parties either expressed or understood by interpretation. In the case of a bilateral treaty, lawful denunciation terminates the treaty itself.[3] Denunciation is also resorted to in respect of multilateral treaties, although withdrawal would be the correct term in this case. At any rate, denunciation of a multilateral treaty by one of the contracting parties does not generally mean termination of the treaty itself.[4]

If one is to be precise, the terms termination, denunciation and withdrawal could also be distinguished in the case of declarations of acceptance. Here too, termination is the broader term, meaning that, on the one hand, a declaration loses effect on expiry of the specific period therein and, on the other hand, the declaring state, by denouncing or withdrawing its declaration of acceptance is getting rid of its obligations undertaken in respect of the compulsory jurisdiction of the Court. However, the distinction between denunciation and withdrawal is of no relevance to declarations of acceptance, because a particular declaration ceases to be in effect in both cases owing to the act of the declaring state. There are no other grounds for termination in the case of declarations of acceptance, if only the International Court decides to affirm a declaration null and void. Although denunciation and withdrawal, as previously stated, have the same meaning in respect of declarations of acceptance, here-in-after, in concrete cases, the same terms applied by a given state for the termination of its declaration of acceptance will be used.

II DECLARATIONS OF ACCEPTANCE ON TERMINATION AND AMENDMENT

Regarding the duration of declarations of acceptance, one can find in the Statute of the of two Courts one single provision in Article 36, paragraph

---

3 Aust (2002) 224.

4 Cf. *Id.*

3 reading: 'The declarations referred to above may be made unconditionally or on condition of reciprocity on the part of several or certain states, or for a certain time'.

This paragraph admits of two specific instances regarding the duration of declarations: a declaration of acceptance is made either for a fixed period or for indefinite duration. In practice, however, the situation is more complicated than that, as states have developed several variants of clauses concerning the duration of declarations of acceptance.[5]

The divergence of declarations of acceptances in that respect was recognized by the International Court when it held that: 'Nor is there any obligation, notwithstanding paragraphs 2 and 3 of Article 36, to mention such matters as periods of duration, conditions or reservations, and there are acceptances which have in one or more, or even in all, of these respects maintained silence.'[6]

The declarations of acceptance made after the establishment of the Permanent Court of International Justice were either made for a fixed period of years (initially five and later fifteen or even twenty years) or an indefinite period, and some declarations did not specify any period at all for the duration of the instrument. A great part of these declarations were silent about termination, withdrawal, denunciation and amendment. The 1929 British declaration of acceptance, being the first valid declaration of acceptance, contained a formula that was to remain in force for ten years and 'thereafter until such time as notice may be given to terminate the acceptance'. This formula came to be included in the declarations of acceptance of several members of the British Commonwealth and later in the declarations of acceptance of other states as well.

It should be noted that in his oft-cited study published in 1930, Hersch Lauterpacht, referring to the above-quoted formula of the 1929 British declaration of acceptance, raised the following questions:

> Will Great Britain then be at liberty to terminate it (the declaration of acceptance – V.L.) at any moment which may suit her convenience, for instance, to avoid an impending action before the Court? And, in view of the operation of the rule of material reciprocity, will other States be in a position to adopt a similar course as against Great Britain?[7]

---

[5] On the time-limitations of declarations of acceptance, see Shigeru Oda, 'Reservations in the Declarations of Acceptance of the Optional Clause and the Period of Validity of Those Declarations: the Effect of the Shultz Letter' (1988) 59, *BYIL*, 1–29; and Alexandrov (1995) Annex III, 154–9.

[6] *Case concerning the Temple of Preah Vihear* (Preliminary Objections), Judgment of 26 May 1961, *ICJ Reports 1961*, 32.

[7] Lauterpacht (1930) 144.

As has already been mentioned, states have developed different variants of the provisions on the duration and termination, withdrawal or denunciation of their declarations of acceptance. Thus there are declarations which are made for an indefinite duration or fixed period, but are silent on termination, others provide for termination with immediate effect, or termination occurring on the day of publication of the related note or upon receipt of notification thereof by the Secretary-General of the United Nations; finally, a great number of declarations stipulate that termination does not become effective except after a lapse of a specified period or at the expiration of a certain period of notice.

The provisions of the declarations of acceptance regarding the amendment of the instruments are more or less in line with those on termination. Thus, one can find declarations which are silent regarding amendment, and others either containing a six-month notice, or stipulating the right to amend the instrument with immediate effect or taking effect on the date of the receipt of the note on amendment by the Secretary-General.[8] In most instances the conditions for the amendment of declarations are the same as those relating to termination, for example, states which fix a six months' notice for termination are also stipulating a six months' notice for the entry into force of the amendment.[9] However, there are also declarations where the stipulations relating to termination or amendment of declarations differ, thus for example, the 1946 US declaration of acceptance provided for termination but there was no provision on the amendment of the instrument.

III STATES' PRACTICE AND MOTIVATIONS

Since the establishment of the Permanent Court the majority of states amended, terminated, withdrew etc. their declarations of acceptance and some of them more than once.[10] Several declarations of acceptance have been terminated either due to expiration of the instruments or as a consequence of the withdrawal or denunciation of the declarations by the

---

[8] See, e.g. the declarations of acceptance of Canada (1994), Ireland (2011), the Ivory Coast (2001), Lithuania (2012), Madagascar (1992), Malta (1966), Mauritius (1968), Nigeria (1998), Peru (2003), Slovakia (2004), Somalia (1963), Togo (1979) and the United Kingdom (2004).

[9] See, e.g. the declarations of Bulgaria (1992), Hungary (1992) and Poland (1996).

[10] See Appendix.

declaring states. After the termination of their declarations, states frequently made new ones either changing the conditions for the acceptance of compulsory jurisdiction or amending the reservations attached to their declarations. It should be added that sometimes amendments of declarations of acceptance, or the substitution of existing declarations by new ones may also have the merit that the wording of the instruments become clearer and, as has also happened, certain complicated and practically inapplicable limitations are omitted from the instruments.

Although states have often amended their declarations of acceptance, or replaced by a new one, there are few cases of leaving the optional clause system. Since the establishment of the International Court of Justice until January 2014, 83 states recognized the compulsory jurisdiction of the Court by declarations of acceptance, while during that period 15 states left the optional clause system.[11]

Regarding the causes of termination or amendment of declarations of acceptance, in some instances the intention of the states was clear and evident, in others one could only guess the intent of the states in question. In several cases states terminated or amended their declarations of acceptance in order to prevent proceedings being instituted against them in respect of a dispute. In other cases it is quite obvious that either the submission of a given dispute to Court, or the decision of the Court in a dispute affected the declaring state, thus prompting it to terminate or amend its declaration of acceptance.

While discussing the cases of termination of declarations of acceptances and the motivations behind them it is worth differentiating between instances when a state is withdrawing its declaration of acceptance and making a new one, amending the instrument anticipating a dispute to be submitted to the Court's decision, or intending to completely withdraw from participation in the optional clause system.

At the beginning of World War II in 1939–40, several states such as France, the United Kingdom and some members of the British Commonwealth of Nations (Australia, Canada, India, New Zealand and South Africa) notified the Secretary-General of the League of Nations that, in view of the changes in circumstances, they would not be regarding their acceptance of the optional clause as covering disputes arising out of events occurring during hostilities under way,[12] and in a few months most

[11] These were Bolivia, Brasil, China, Colombia, El Salvador, France, Guatemala, Iran, Israel, Nauru, Serbia, South Africa, Thailand, Turkey and the United States of America.

[12] See *PCIJ Series* E., No. 16. Sixteenth Annual Report of the Permanent Court of International Justice (15 June 1939–31 December 1945) 332–44.

of them made new declarations of acceptance containing reservations relating to hostilities and armed conflicts, or amended their declarations. At the time some states expressed their reservations with regard to these actions.[13] Norway and Sweden proposed that the Permanent Court pronounce on the legal effects of these denunciations,[14] but obviously enough, the Court could not do so as it had no power to determine similar matters except in concrete cases.[15] Although the instances mentioned above are usually examined together, it is necessary to make some distinction between the actions of the members of the British Commonwealth compared with the actions of France.[16]

The difference lies in the fact that the declarations of the members of the Commonwealth were made in 1929–30 for a ten-year period and it was exactly at the expiry of that period that they withdrew their declarations, making new declarations with reservations relating to hostilities and war events. A different situation obtained for France, since the French declaration of acceptance was set to expire in 1941; however, the notification of the French Government relating to hostilities and the amendment of its declaration of acceptance was dated 11 September 1939. Thus, France in contrast to the members of the British Commonwealth – which withdrew their declarations practically on the expiry of their terms – amended its declaration made for a fixed period before the expiry of that period.

The characteristic of the above-mentioned instances were that the members of the British Commonwealth and France were not compelled by a concrete dispute to withdraw or amend their declarations. In addition, they terminated or amended declarations made for fixed periods and did not turn their backs on the optional clause system, remaining parties thereto but excluding from the scope of compulsory jurisdiction such disputes as might be related to war events under way.

To illustrate the termination of declarations of acceptance as a preventive measure from states' practice after World War II, one could mention that in 1954 the Australian Government withdrew its declaration of 1940,[17] in the face of the danger of Japan instituting proceedings before

---

[13] Cf. the declarations and letters of Belgian, Brazilian, Danish, Dutch, Estonian, Haitian, Norwegian, Peruvian, Siamese, Swedish and Swiss Governments. *Id.* 333, 335, 337.

[14] Cf. *Id.* 333.

[15] Cf. Alexandrov (1995) 61.

[16] Cf. Rosenne (1960) 24–5.

[17] The Australian declaration of 1940 had originally been made for a period of five years and thereafter was to remain valid until notice of termination, that is

the International Court regarding pearl fisheries. The 1940 declaration was replaced by a new one excluding 'disputes arising out or concerning jurisdiction or rights claimed or exercised by Australia – (a) in respect of the continental shelf of Australia and the territories under the authority of Australia, as that continental shelf is described or delimited in the Australian Proclamations of 10 September 1953 or under the Australian Pearl Fisheries Acts'. According to Judge Oda, Australia took that step a few months after the two countries had agreed to jointly submit to the International Court of Justice their dispute on Japanese pearl-fishing on Australia's continental shelf subject to successful negotiations on a *modus vivendi*.[18] Thus, in all probability, Australia terminated its declaration of acceptance and made a new one in an effort to prevent proceedings from being eventually instituted by unilateral application while the negotiations were in progress.

It was for similar reasons in respect of preventing the submission of a dispute to the Court's decision that in 1955 the United Kingdom terminated its declaration, which was made a little short of five months before, subsequently substituting it with another one containing a new reservation excluding 'disputes in respect of which arbitral or judicial proceedings are taking, or have taken place with a state which, at the date of the commencement of the proceedings, had not itself accepted the compulsory jurisdiction of the International Court of Justice'. According to writers of international law, the text of that reservation suggests that the United Kingdom suddenly amended its declaration of acceptance in order to prevent the submission to the Court of its dispute with Saudi Arabia over the Buraimi Oasis after a breakdown in attempted arbitration.[19]

Mention may also be made of Canada, which in 1970 amended its declaration of acceptance to insert a new reservation with a view of avoiding disputes that seemed likely to question the lawfulness of Canada's 1970 legislation establishing an anti-pollution zone with respect to claimed Canadian jurisdiction extending 100 miles off its northern coast into Arctic waters. Again, in 1994, Canada terminated its 1985

---

to say that Australia terminated a declaration which, after the lapse of the five-year period had become one for an indefinite duration.

[18] Cf. Oda (1988) 8.

[19] Cf. Waldock (1955–6) 268, and see Separate Opinion of Sir Robert Jennings in the *Case concerning Military and Paramilitary Activities in and against Nicaragua* (Jurisdiction of the Court and Admissibility of the Application), Judgment 26 November 1984, Separate Opinion of Sir Robert Jennings, *ICJ Reports 1984*, 551.

declaration and made a new one which included a new reservation by reason of the Canadian Coastal Fisheries Protection Act. It was precisely that step which was contested by Spain in the *Fisheries Jurisdiction case* between Spain and Canada.

Malta, in the 1980s, amended its declaration of acceptance twice in two years. The 1966 Maltese declaration contained no reservation concerning territorial disputes. However, in 1981, shortly before it attempted to intervene in the dispute between Tunisia and Libya in the *Continental Shelf case*, Malta had amended its declaration to make it clear that the declaration also applied to disputes over the continental shelf.[20] The Court nevertheless dismissed Malta's request for permission to intervene in the legal dispute between Tunisia and Libya.[21] Again, in 1983, Malta amended its 1966 declaration to insert rather detailed reservations relating to its territory, including the territorial sea, and the status thereof, the continental shelf or any other zone of maritime jurisdiction, and the resources thereof, etc. Professor Merrills asserts that this modification by the Maltese Government served to prevent Italy from instituting any action against Malta, since the Italian request for permission to intervene in the *Continental Shelf case* (Libya/Malta), was dismissed by the Court.[22]

One could also refer to the amendment of the 1929 Nicaraguan declaration of acceptance which involved adding a reservation in 2001, thus excluding 'any matter or claim based on interpretations of treaties or arbitral awards that were signed and ratified or made, respectively, prior to 31 December 1901'. Costa Rica objected formally to the reservation formulated by Nicaragua and stated, among other points, that the above-mentioned reservation intended to avoid the submission of a claim by Costa Rica against Nicaragua before the Court for its failure to abide according to the provisions agreed upon by both countries in the Cailas-Jerez Treaty of 1858 and the Cleveland Award of 1888.[23]

Thus one of the characteristics of the above-mentioned cases was that although the states had tried to tailor their declarations of acceptance by amendment or replacing by a new declaration in order to avoid the submission of a dispute to the Court's decision, nevertheless they

---

20 See the Maltese declaration of 23 January 1981.

21 See *Continental Shelf* (Tunisia/ Libyan Arab Jamahiriya) (Application to Intervene), Judgment of 14 April 1981, *ICJ Reports 1981*, 3.

22 Merrills (1993) 236.

23 For the objection of Costa Rica, see *Multilateral Treaties Deposited with the Secretary General*. Status as at 1 April 2009, vol. I, XI–XIV.

remained a party to the optional clause system via their amended declaration of acceptance or new declaration of acceptance.

As was already mentioned, some states withdraw their declarations of acceptance without making new ones, thus the termination of declarations of acceptance results in a complete withdrawal of these states from the optional clause system. Although these cases have not been numerous, some of them have had a considerable impact on the optional clause system.

In most cases here again the motivation of the states' actions was the anticipation of proceedings before the Court, or a decision given by the Court; however, the states' reaction in these cases was to leave the system of the Court's compulsory jurisdiction.

At the time of the Permanent Court among the well-known cases of a termination of a declaration of acceptance one could refer to Paraguay, which in 1938 withdrew with immediate effect its declaration of acceptance made without reference to duration and being silent about withdrawal. According to contemporary news, Paraguay withdrew its declaration which was made in 1933, because it had anticipated that Bolivia would institute proceedings against it before the Permanent Court in connection with the Gran Chaco border dispute. Incidentally, Paraguay justified the termination of its declaration of acceptance by, inter alia, its withdrawal from the League of Nations.[24] The above-mentioned action of Paraguay was criticized at the time by several states, not only Bolivia, which was directly affected by the withdrawal.[25] The Permanent Court of International Justice never took a position on Paraguay's withdrawal of its declaration and Paraguay continued to be listed, even after World War II, among the states recognizing the compulsory jurisdiction of the Court.[26]

As an example when the termination of a declaration of acceptance had the effect of a complete withdrawal of a state from the optional clause system, it is worth mentioning the case where the South African Government terminated its 1955 declaration of acceptance by a note of

---

24 Paraguay left the League of Nations in 1935.

25 Cf. Hudson (1972) 476.

26 The Paraguayan declaration of acceptance was retained in the list of declarations recognizing as compulsory the jurisdiction of the Court in the Court's Yearbook until the year 1959–60, though with an explanatory footnote mentioning the withdrawal and the observations there on. It was in 1996, more than half a century after the withdrawal of its declaration, that Paraguay deposited again a declaration of acceptance.

12 April 1967.[27] There is every likelihood that this action may have been related to the fact that in the years of 1950 and 1960 the International Court of Justice had dealt with the problems connected with the former Mandate of South West Africa (Namibia) in contentious cases and in advisory opinions as well. True, the Court in its decision of 1966 rejected the application filed by Liberia and Ethiopia, two former member states of the League of Nations, against South Africa, yet the government of South Africa, evidently wanting no new proceedings regarding the former mandate before the Court, chose to terminate its declaration of acceptance. South Africa has not since that time made a declaration of acceptance.

Also, in 1974, France terminated its 1966 declaration of acceptance while it was a respondent before the Court in the *Nuclear Tests* cases instituted by Australia and New Zealand separately in 1973. In both cases France failed to appear before the Court and did not put forward its argument,[28] and on 2 January 1974 it terminated its declaration of acceptance.[29] Since 1974, France is not a party to the optional clause system.

After 1984 a great deal of discussion was provoked by the United States firstly amending and then terminating its 1946 declaration of acceptance while the *Case concerning Military and Paramilitary Activities in and against Nicaragua* was under consideration by the Court. As mentioned earlier, the United States by its notification of 6 April 1984, which was signed by the United States Secretary of State, George Shultz (the so-called Shultz Letter), amended its 1946 declaration of acceptance, stating that 'the declaration shall not apply to any dispute with any Central American State or arising out of or related to events in Central America, the modification shall take effect immediately and shall remain in force for two years.' Subsequently, in a notification received by the Secretary-General on 7 October 1985, the government of the United States of America gave notice of the termination of its declaration of 26 August 1946. That step had a big echo not only from a legal point of view, but because this time, again, a great power withdrew its consent to the Court's compulsory jurisdiction. The possibility of accepting the Court's compulsory jurisdiction by a new declaration of acceptance by

---

[27] The 1955 declaration was without time limitation and being in force 'until such time as notice may be given to terminate'.

[28] On the problems of non-appearance, see Chapter 10.

[29] The French 1966 declaration of acceptance, which provided that it was to remain in force 'until such time as notice may be given of the termination of this acceptance'.

the United States has been dealt with by several committees, experts etc.; however, until 2014 the United States hadn't returned to the optional clause system.[30]

One could also suppose that the termination by Colombia of its 1932 declaration of acceptance by a note registered on 5 December 2001, had some connection with its dispute against Nicaragua regarding the sovereignty of certain islands and their surroundings (*Territorial and Maritime Dispute* (Nicaragua v. Colombia)), which was submitted to the Court's decision by Nicaragua one day after the termination of the Columbian declaration of acceptance, on 6 December 2001. This situation reminds us of what happened in the *Nicaragua case*, that the United States of America via the Shultz Letter amended its declaration of acceptance three days prior to the submission of the Nicaraguan application. However, in the *Territorial and Maritime Dispute*, in contrast to the *Nicaragua* case, the Court found no purpose in examining whether the parties' declarations of acceptance could have provided a basis for its jurisdiction since it first examined the preliminary objection raised by Colombia to the Court's jurisdiction under the Pact of Bogotá and concluded that it had jurisdiction on the basis of Article XXXI of the Pact.[31]

IV PERMISSIBILITY TO TERMINATE OR AMEND DECLARATIONS OF ACCEPTANCE

The problem of termination of declarations of acceptance was treated in the literature of international law already before World War II, and that time in connection with the withdrawal of Paraguay's declaration of

---

[30] On the evaluation of the United States' declaration of acceptance and alternatives to the 1946 declarations, see among others Anthony Clark Arend (ed.), *The United States and the Compulsory Jurisdiction of the International Court of Justice.* Papers and Proceedings of a Workshop sponsored by The Center for Law and National Security at Charlottesville, Virginia on 16 and 17 August 1985. (Center for Law and National Security, University Press of America 1986); Louis B. Sohn, 'Suggestions for the Limited Acceptance of Compulsory Jurisdiction of the International Court of Justice by the United States' (1988). Scholarly Works. Paper 206. http://digitalcommons.law.uga.edu/fac_artchop/206 (accessed 13 October 2013).

[31] See *Territorial and Maritime Dispute* (Nicaragua v. Colombia) (Preliminary Objections), Judgment of 13 December 2007, *ICJ Reports 2007*, 832.

acceptance in 1938.[32] Opposed to the step of Paraguay, Fachiri argues that the object of the optional clause is to be an efficient system of compulsory jurisdiction and that this object 'would be entirely defeated if it were open to accepting States to withdraw at will, since withdrawal at will means that the submission of any given dispute to the Court can always be prevented.'[33] The author holds that declarations of acceptance made for an indefinite period cannot be withdrawn except when the other states party to the optional clause system consent thereto.[34] Other authors assert that the states party to the optional clause system enter into a contractual arrangement and that denunciation of declarations of acceptance must, by analogy, be under the control of the rules governing the termination of treaties.[35] According to Waldock 'there is no right of unilateral termination of a declaration under the Optional Clause unless the right has been expressly reserved in the declaration';[36] this also holds for variation or modification of a declaration previously made which is still in force.[37]

Later on the view on the permissibility of unilateral termination of declarations with indefinite duration becomes generally accepted, and not the permissibility, but the conditions of termination of declarations were the subject of the dispute. Especially, whether is it permitted to terminate a declaration of acceptance with immediate effect or is it necessary to insert a reasonable period of notice.

In connection with the permissibility of terminating, withdrawing, denouncing declarations of acceptance made for an unlimited period and being silent about the right to terminate one must not overlook the fact that the optional clause was adopted in place of a general treaty regarding compulsory international adjudication. At that time it was believed that the optional clause system was an important step in the way of introducing compulsory international adjudication in interstate relations. What happened instead was that only a limited number of states made declarations of acceptance, with many of them recognizing the compulsory jurisdiction of the Permanent Court of International Justice but for a fixed period, and making declarations of acceptance with growing

---

32 The 1933 Paraguay declaration of acceptance contained no time limitation and there was no reference to termination.

33 Fachiri, 56.

34 *Id.* 59.

35 Cf. Hambro (1948) 142.

36 Cf. Waldock (1955–56) 265.

37 *Id.*

numbers of more and more complicated limitations and reservations. The states recognizing the Permanent Court's or the International Court's compulsory jurisdiction without limitations provided faith that compulsory international adjudication would become general, and, adhering to the optional clause system, they believed that other members of the international community would follow suit. If it wasn't allowed or the states which had made declarations of acceptance unconditionally were restricted to terminate declarations, they would be placed at a disadvantage in comparison with those states that were much more distrustful or reluctant of compulsory adjudication. Therefore, not to permit the termination of declarations of acceptance or to restrict the termination of those declarations which were made without time limitations and unconditionally would be a punishment inflicted on the states which have tried to promote the judicial settlement of international disputes and the establishment of a universal system of international adjudication under the optional clause.

It should be added that although the amendment of a declaration of acceptance has a different effect than the termination of the instrument, especially in those cases where the termination of a declaration of acceptance has had the result of the complete withdrawal of the state's consent from the Court's compulsory jurisdiction, nevertheless, both in the literature of international law and the Court's practice, the issues of termination or amendment of declarations were treated together.

That was clearly reflected in the Court's jurisprudence when in the *Right of Passage case* it considered the reservation included in the 1955 Portuguese declaration of acceptance by which the Portuguese Government reserved itself the right to exclude from the scope of the declaration of acceptance, at any time during its validity, any given category or categories of disputes. According to the Court the uncertainty resulting from the right of Portugal to avail itself at any time to amend the conditions of its declaration of acceptance, was substantially the same as that created by the right claimed by many states, to terminate their declarations of acceptance by simple notification without notice.[38] In the

---

[38] The Court recalled that in the course of that proceeding India had done so when it denounced its 1940 declaration of acceptance (relied upon by Portugal in its application), which it simultaneously substituted by a new declaration incorporating reservations which were absent from the 1940 declaration; according to the Court with that 'India achieved, in substance, the object of Portugal's Third Condition.'

Case concerning Right of Passage over Indian Territory (Preliminary Objections), Judgment 26 November 1957, *ICJ Reports 1957*, 143.

view of the Court, there was no essential difference regarding the degree of uncertainty between a situation resulting from the right of total denunciation and that resulting from a condition in a declaration of acceptance leaving open the possibility of a partial denunciation.[39]

The same view was expressed by the Court in the *Nicaragua case* when it stated on the Shultz Letter which was presented by the United States as an amendment to its 1946 declaration of acceptance. In its judgment on jurisdiction and admissibility of the Nicaraguan application, regarding the Shultz Letter the Court's view was that there is no difference whether the note of 6 April was seen as a modification or termination of the 1946 US declaration of acceptance.[40]

V IMMEDIATE EFFECT V. PERIOD OF NOTICE

In the International Court's practice, the problem of a notification with immediate effect emerged in the *Right of Passage case* when India in its first preliminary objection contended that the reservation included in the Portuguese declaration of acceptance – in which Portugal reserved itself the right to exclude from the scope of its declaration any given category or categories of disputes, at any time during its validity, by notifying the Secretary-General, with such exclusion becoming effective from the moment of such notification – was incompatible with the object and purpose of the optional clause, with the result that the declaration of acceptance was invalid.[41] In the *Right of Passage case* the Court didn't investigate all aspects of the question raised by India and confined itself to stating that the words used in the condition of the Portuguese declaration of acceptance, construed in their ordinary sense, meant simply that a notification under that condition applied only to disputes brought before the Court *after* the date of the notification, and no retroactive effect could thus be imputed to such a notification.[42]

---

39 *Id.* 144.

40 Cf. *Case concerning Military and Paramilitary Activities in and against Nicaragua* (Jurisdiction of the Court and Admissibility of the Application), Judgment 26 November 1984, *ICJ Reports 1984*, 417–18.

41 Cf. First preliminary objection of the government of India, see *Case concerning Right of Passage over Indian Territory*, *ICJ Pleadings*, vol. I, 108–12.

42 *Case concerning Right of Passage over Indian Territory* (Preliminary Objections), Judgment 26 November 1957, *ICJ Reports 1957*, 142.

In the *Case concerning Military and Paramilitary Activities in and against Nicaragua* the question of the period of notice and the problem of termination or amendment of a declaration with immediate effect was addressed in detail. Before the *Nicaragua case*, as was indicated by Judge Mosler,[43] the Court formerly had not considered this issue but pronounced on the reverse situation, notably in the *Right of Passage case*, when it dealt with the question whether Portugal had the right to institute proceedings against India a few days after the submission of the Portuguese declaration of acceptance.

In the *Nicaragua case* one of the most important questions about the 1984 notification was whether the United States was free to disregard the clause of its declaration of acceptance providing that 'the present Declaration shall remain in force for a term of five years and shall thereafter continue in force for six months from notification of its denunciation'. On that point the Court stated:

> Although the United States retained the right to modify the contents of the 1946 Declaration or to terminate it, a power which is inherent in any unilateral act of a State, it has, nevertheless assumed an inescapable obligation towards other States accepting the Optional Clause, by stating formally and solemnly that any such change should take effect only after six months have elapsed as from the date of notice.[44]

Thus the Court in the *Nicaragua case* clearly expressed that the period of notice for the termination, withdrawal etc. of declarations of acceptance was subject primarily to the particular declaration itself, that is, the termination, withdrawal or amendment of a declaration of acceptance could not become effective except upon expiry of the period stated in the declaration itself, and a state could not, even by invoking reciprocity, depart from the period of notice as stipulated in its own declaration of acceptance.[45]

---

43 *Case concerning Military and Paramilitary Activities in and against Nicaragua* (Jurisdiction of the Court and Admissibility of the Application), Judgment 26 November 1984, Separate Opinion of Judge Mosler, *ICJ Reports 1984*, 467.

44 *Id.* 419.

45 The Court also rejected the US Government's argument adduced by reliance on reciprocity in an effort to disregard the six-month period of notice and ensure the immediate effect of its 1984 notification. As has been mentioned in connection with the principle of reciprocity, the Court firmly stated that reciprocity did not apply to the formal conditions of the creation, duration, extinction of declarations of acceptance.

Regarding the possibility of terminating a declaration of acceptance with immediate effect the Court held that:

> But the right of immediate termination of declarations with indefinite duration is far from established. It appears from the requirements of good faith that they should be treated, by analogy, according to the law of treaties, which requires a reasonable time for withdrawal from or termination of treaties that contain no provision regarding the duration of their validity.[46]

In his individual opinion appended to the judgment, Judge Mosler added to the Court's decision that from the 'nature' of declarations of acceptance made 'unconditionally' it does not follow that they may be terminated at any time and with immediate effect.[47] Referring by analogy to Article 56 of the 1969 Vienna Convention on the Law of Treaties, Judge Mosler pointed out that the termination of an obligation must be governed by the principle of good faith and the withdrawal without any period of notice does not correspond with this principle if a particular declaration was made unconditionally.[48]

It appears that the Court's finding quoted above served to evade even the appearance of accepting the permissibility of terminating declarations with immediate effect and the Court in endeavouring to block avenues of abuse opened by immediate termination of declarations of acceptance was referring to the law of treaties with this end.

The Court's statement rejecting the immediate termination of declarations of acceptance was the subject of sharp criticism both by several members of the Court and authors of international law.

Some members of the Court, thus Judges Oda, Sir Robert Jennings and Schwebel, disagreed with the Court's findings not only regarding the termination or amendment of declarations of acceptance, but on the period of notice as well. Judge Oda, making a detailed analysis of the declarations of acceptance that have been deposited since the foundation of the Permanent Court, concluded that in 1956 Portugal established the precedent of reserving the right to exclude with immediate effect any category of disputes from the scope of a declaration of acceptance and that example has been followed by a number of states, so much so that at the time of the *Nicaragua case* that right had been

---

46 *Case concerning Military and Paramilitary Activities in and against Nicaragua* (Jurisdiction of the Court and Admissibility of the Application), Judgment 26 November 1984, *ICJ Reports 1984*, 420.

47 *Id.* Separate Opinion of Judge Mosler, 467.

48 *Id.*

reserved by 15 states.[49] Taking into consideration states' practice Judge Sir Robert Jennings pointed out that:

> States now – though the position was probably different during the earlier, more promising period of the Optional Clause jurisdiction – have the right, before seisin of the Court, to withdraw or alter their declaration of acceptance, with immediate effect, and, moreover, even in anticipation of a particular case or class of cases.[50]

Judge Schwebel reached the same conclusion and tried to demonstrate that even, assuming that Nicaragua's declaration of acceptance was binding, Nicaragua could terminate it at any time with immediate effect and by operation of the rule of reciprocity the United States likewise could terminate its adherence to the Court's compulsory jurisdiction, vis-à-vis Nicaragua, with immediate effect.[51]

Referring to what was said by the Court, at first sight, the reasoning relying on the law of treaties seems to be a good analogy regarding the period of notice. However, it is a different matter whether the aforesaid reference proves substantiated enough upon close examination, especially if one considers that not even the Vienna Convention on the Law of Treaties failed to provide an absolute rule on the question of unilateral denunciation of treaties; and the Convention, according to a commentator, 'provided a rule of uncertain content and ambit and may have clouded the issue for ever'.[52]

In the *Nicaragua case* the International Court of Justice referred to those rules on the termination of treaties which stipulate for a certain 'reasonable period of notice' in respect of terminating treaties concluded for an unlimited period. The question is therefore one that is concerned with whether the rules on a reasonable period of notice are applicable to declarations of acceptance.

With regard to the period of notice it is worthwhile considering in the first place the relevant provisions of the 1969 Vienna Convention on the Law of Treaties. Art. 56, para. 2 of the Convention provides a 12-month period of notice for treaties containing no provision on termination, denunciation and withdrawal, but the right of denunciation or withdrawal may be implied by the nature of the treaty. This 12 months' notice cannot, however, be considered prevalent, as is expressed first of all in

---

49 *Id.* Separate Opinion of Judge Oda, 508–09.

50 *Id.* Separate Opinion of Judge Sir Robert Jennings, 553.

51 *Id.* Dissenting Opinion of Judge Schwebel, 616–27.

52 Cf. Kelvin Widdows, 'The Unilateral Denunciation of Treaties Containing No Denunciation Clause' (1982) 53, *BYIL*, 83.

the comments of the International Law Commission on the final draft of the Vienna Convention, where the Commission stated: 'Where the treaty is to continue indefinitely subject to a right of denunciation, the period of notice is more usually twelve months, though admittedly in some cases no period of notice is required.'[53] However, this document makes no reference to specific cases in which the period of notice can be disregarded.

The period of notice in the law of treaties serves to ensure, inter alia, that a contracting party or parties does or does not enter upon or make preparations in the performance of a treaty, especially in cases where one of the other parties is considering the denunciation of the given treaty. In other words, the bona fide contracting party should have time to prepare itself for the termination of the treaty in the foreseeable future or withdrawal of certain contracting parties therefrom.

In the case of declarations of acceptance this appears to be otherwise, compared with the case of treaties. The essence of the obligations assumed in declarations of acceptance is that disputes with other parties to the optional clause system and covered by the scope of the declarations, could be referred by unilateral application to the Court's decision. Thus, in the case of declarations of acceptance a state meets its duties deriving from its declaration by subjecting itself to the Court's jurisdiction. To meet this obligation does not call for 'preparations' of the kind referred to in respect of treaties. Of course, it is important for states party to the optional clause system to be aware of two things: which states are party to the system and how long the bond between them exists, in other words, how long they can count on submitting to the Court's decision their dispute with another state party to the system. Thus, one could conclude that the aforementioned justifications for a period of notice to the performance of treaties do not up hold well in respect of unilateral declarations of acceptance.

One could say that regarding the immediate termination of declarations of acceptance the Court was in a difficult situation, states' practice on the provisions for terminating declarations of acceptance was divided. The declarations of acceptance of a group of states reflected a certain kind of established practice; however, another tendency had been emerging with the endeavour that the declarations of acceptance might be terminable with immediate effect. The Court being aware of the influence of the immediate termination of declarations of acceptance on the optional

[53] Cf. Rauschning (ed.) (1978) 394.

clause system decided on the maintenance of the solution which would be less harmful to the Court's compulsory jurisdiction.[54]

The *Nicaragua case* had not only a big echo, but influenced states' practice when composing their declarations of acceptance. Regarding that connection one could refer to the fact that since 1990, 28 declarations of acceptance were submitted and in the overwhelming majority of the declarations, thus in 20 declarations, the declaring states reserved the right to terminate the instrument at any time and with immediate effect.[55] Thus states' practice contradicts what was said by the Court regarding the immediate termination of declarations of acceptance. One could say that the majority of declaring states not only wanted to create a clear situation and secure themselves the liberty in the termination of their declarations of acceptance, but they also tried to show their disagreement with what was said by the Court.

---

[54] It should be mentioned that well before the *Nicaragua case* both the Institute of International Law and the International Law Association dealt with the termination of declarations of acceptance and the problem of the period of notice. The resolution on 'Compulsory Jurisdiction of International Courts and Tribunals' of the Institute adopted at its session of Neuchâtel in 1959 suggested a period of notice not less than 12 months.

The other proposal was made at the 1964 Tokyo Conference of the International Law Association, where members of the Japanese Branch suggested amending Art. 36, para. 3 of the Statute to the effect that 'The denunciation of any declaration shall only be effective at least twelve months (alternatively, six months) after its notification to the Secretary-General of the United Nations.' Both proposals can be said to be reasonable and to result, if accepted, in more clearly-worded rules governing the time limitation and termination of declarations of acceptance.

[55] See the declarations of acceptance of Australia (2002), Bulgaria (1992), Cameroon (1994), Canada (1994), the Ivory Coast (2001), Cyprus (2002), Djibouti (2005), the Commonwealth of Dominica (2006), Estonia (1991), Germany (2008), the Republic of Guinea (1998), Hungary (1992), Ireland (2011), Japan (2007), Lesotho (2000), Lithuania (2012), Madagascar (1992), the Marshall Islands (2013), Nigeria (1998), Norway (1996), Paraguay (1996), Portugal (2005), Slovakia (2004), Spain (1990), Timor-Leste (2012) and the United Kingdon (2004).

VI AMENDMENT OR TERMINATION OF DECLARATIONS OF ACCEPTANCE WHILE A PROCEEDING IS UNDER WAY

From states' practice one can also find several instances where the declaring state amended or terminated its declaration of acceptance after it had been made respondent in proceedings before the Court and the amendment or the termination of the declaration was the consequence of the proceedings in question.

As an example of such instances one could refer to Iran which, after the Court had indicated provisional measures in the *Anglo-Iranian Oil Company case*, in 1951, terminated its 1930 declaration of acceptance which provided that it was to remain in force for a term of six years and thereafter 'it shall continue to bear its full effects until notification is given of its abrogation'. A similar situation obtained in connection with the *Case concerning Right of Passage over Indian Territory*, where shortly after the filing of the Portuguese application India withdrew its declaration of 1940, which was without time limitation and replaced it with a new one of 7 January 1956, containing reservations absent from its previous declaration.[56]

These actions raised the question of the consequence of terminating or amending declarations of acceptance in respect of the proceedings under way.

In the *Right of Passage case* with regard to such situations the Court held that:

> It is a rule of law generally accepted, as well as one acted upon in the past by the Court, that once the Court has been validly seised of a dispute, unilateral action by the respondent State in terminating its Declaration, in whole or in part, cannot divest the Court of jurisdiction.'[57]

The International Court made it clear that such a notification could not have retroactive effect and it applies only to disputes brought before the Court after the date of the notification, thus it could not cover cases

[56] Portugal instituted proceedings against India on 22 December 1955. The Indian Government's note on withdrawal and its new declaration of acceptance of compulsory jurisdiction was dated 7 January 1956.

[57] *Case concerning Right of Passage over Indian Territory* (Preliminary Objections), Judgment 26 November 1957, *ICJ Reports 1957*, 142.

already pending;[58] the Court added that this principle applies both to total denunciation, and partial denunciation.[59]

That decision was in line with the Court's statement in the *Nottebohm case* instituted by Lichtenstein against Guatemala a few years before the *Right of Passage* case.[60] In the proceedings, since the Guatemalan declaration of acceptance expired a few weeks after the filing of the application by Liechtenstein, Guatemala as a result contested the Court's jurisdiction.[61] In its judgment delivered on the preliminary objections the Court stated:

> Once the Court has been regularly seised, the Court must exercise its powers, as these are defined in the Statute. After that, the expiry of the period fixed for one of the Declarations on which the Application was founded is an event which is unrelated to the exercise of the powers conferred on the Court by the Statute, …
>
> An extrinsic fact such as the subsequent lapse of the Declaration, by reason of the expiry of the period or by denunciation, cannot deprive the Court of the jurisdiction already established.[62]

This same rule applies to the amendment of declarations of acceptance. Proceedings are also not affected by one of the parties amending its

---

[58] *Id.*

[59] Cf. *Id.*

[60] The *Nottebohn case* was a legal dispute between Lichtenstein and Guatemala. In December 1951, Lichtenstein had filed an application instituting proceedings against Guatemala, claiming that the government of Guatemala had acted contrary to international law and incurred international responsibility by the unjustified detention, internment and expulsion of Friedrich Nottebohm, a Lichenstein national and as a result of the sequestration and confiscation of his property. Lichtenstein demanded restitution and compensation from Guatemala for the various measures against Mr Nottebohm and his property. The application referred to the declarations by which both parties had accepted the compulsory jurisdiction of the Court.

[61] The preliminary objection filed by Guatemala was to the effect that the declaration by which Guatemala had accepted the compulsory jurisdiction of the Court had been made on 27 January 1947 for five years and had therefore expired on 26 January 1952, about five and a half weeks after Liechtenstein had submitted its application on 17 December 1951. Guatemala contended that the Court had undoubtedly jurisdiction at the time the application was filed, but the Court lacked jurisdiction to deal with the case after the expiration of the Guatemalan declaration of acceptance. Cf. *Nottebohm case, ICJ Pleadings*, vol. I, 162–9.

[62] *Nottebohm case* (Preliminary Objection), Judgment 18 November 1953, *ICJ Reports 1953*, 122–3.

declaration of acceptance and excluding from the scope of the Court's compulsory jurisdiction a certain dispute or disputes through the insertion of a new reservation in the declaration of acceptance. The Court's jurisdiction should be established at the time of the seising of the Court; if at that time the Court has jurisdiction to deal with a dispute, the termination or modification of a declaration of acceptance has no influence on the case under consideration by the Court.

A special problem is posed by a situation when after the termination or amendment of a declaration of acceptance one of the parties subsequently modifies its claims in a case already under consideration by the Court, requesting the Court's decision on matters not covered by the original application.

From the jurisprudence of the International Court of Justice as an example one can cite the *Anglo-Iranian Oil Company case*, in which Iran claimed that one of the British memorandums submitted to the Court after the denunciation of the Persian declaration of acceptance covered such issues which were not mentioned in the original application of the British Government and, therefore, the Court was without jurisdiction to decide on them because they had been submitted after the termination of the Persian declaration of acceptance.[63] The Court didn't consider that particular question raised by Iran as it found that it lacked jurisdiction.[64] On the basis of the foregoing it can be stated that after the termination or amendment of a declaration of acceptance the Court can deal only with the submissions of the original application and it has no jurisdiction to decide on matters subsequently raised by one of the parties.

63 Cf. *Anglo-Iranian Oil Co. case, ICJ Pleadings*, 603–05.

64 Cf. *Anglo-Iranian Oil Co. case* (Preliminary Objection), Judgment 22 July 1952, *ICJ Report 1952*, 99.

10. Objecting to the Court's jurisdiction

I PROCEDURAL MEANS TO CHALLENGE THE COURT'S JURISDICTION

Since in most cases the seising of the Court under declarations of acceptance happens years after the acceptance of the Court's compulsory jurisdiction by the parties to a dispute, thus states very often find themselves faced with proceedings instituted before the Court in legal disputes which they may never have thought to be ever submitted to the Court's decision. In such cases one should not be suprised that the respondent states are challenging the Court's jurisdiction in the form of preliminary objections, which is a procedural institution covered by the Rules of the Court. It should be noted that this action is typical not only for disputes submitted on the basis of declarations of acceptance, but also for cases where the title of the Court's jurisdiction is a treaty provision.

The raising of a matter of jurisdiction by a preliminary objection is a legal right of states which forms part of their litigation strategy and as Rosenne points out 'no valid reason, legal or political, can exist to require a state to refrain from exercising its right if it is so minded'.[1]

The procedure to be followed when the respondent is exercising that right is regulated in a rather detailed manner by the Rules of the Court. Under Article 79 of the Rules one could differentiate between either objection to the jurisdiction of the Court or admissibility of the application.[2] Thus, preliminary objections could relate either that the Court having no jurisdiction to consider the dispute or they could be concerned with the application not corresponding to the requirements.[3] Both in the practice of the Permanent Court and the International Court in several

---

1 Rosenne (2006) vol. III, 826–7.

2 On that, see Tomuschat (2006) 646–9.

3 The consequence of the raising of preliminary objections is that according to Art. 79, para. 5 of the Rules of the Court, the proceedings on the merits shall be suspended and a time limit should be fixed by the Court or the President, if the Court is not sitting, within which the other party may present a written statement of its observations and submission. The Court's decision on the

cases, the respondents had based their preliminary objections on the reservations joined to their own or, by reference to reciprocity, the adverse party's declaration of acceptance.

At the time of the Permanent Court, declarations of acceptance have been relied upon as founding the jurisdicition of the Court in 11 cases.[4] From these 11 cases only in five instances – the *Losinger case*, the *Phosphates in Morocco case*, the *Panevezys-Saldutiskis Railway case,* the *Electricity Company of Sofia and Bulgaria case* and the *Pajzs, Csáky, Esterházy case* – did the respondent state raise preliminary objections.[5] However, it was only in the *Losinger case* that the Court rejected the preliminary objection, in the other cases it upheld the objections,[6] which proves that at the time of the Permanent Court the preliminary objections were well founded.

After World War II, the raising of preliminary objections became a wide-spread practice and according to Dame Rosalyn Higgins, former President of the Court, in the first 62 years of its existence nearly half of the disputes submitted to the Court required separate hearings on jurisdictional issues.[7] It should be added that the overwhelming majority of these cases were disputes submitted under declarations of acceptance.[8]

No question that the raising of preliminary objections delays the Court's decision on the merits of the dispute, but since the Court has no

---

preliminary objections appears in the form of a judgment. On this, see Guyomar (1983) 498–518.

[4] These were the following: *Denunciation of the Belgian–Chinese Treaty; Legal Status of Eastern Greenland case; the two South Eastern Greenland cases; Losinger case; Pajzs, Csáky, Esterházy case; Diversion of Water from the Meuse; Phosphates in Morocco; Panevezys–Saldutiskis Railway; Electricity Company of Sofia and Bulgaria; Gerliczy cases.*

[5] As a sixth case, one could mention the *Gerliczy case* in which the Hungarian Government notified the Permanent Court that it intended to raise preliminary objections; however, although the time limits were extended in view of the war events, the Hungarian preliminary objections were not presented.

[6] The Court upheld the objection in the *Phosphates in Morocco*, the *Panevezys–Saldutiskis Railway*, and in part the *Electricity Company of Sofia and Bulgaria cases*; however, in the *Pajzs, Csáky, Esterházy case* the objections were joined to the merits.

[7] Cf. Speech H.E. Judge Rosalyn Higgins, President of the International Court of Justice, to the Sixth Committee of the General Assembly on 31 October 2008. http://www.icj-cij.presscom/files/1/14841pdf (accessed 13 September 2013).

[8] One could also mention cases in which the respondent disputed the Court's jurisdiction but not in the form of preliminary objection, see e.g. *Questions relating to the Obligation to Prosecute or Extradite* (Belgium v. Senegal).

general compulsory jurisdiction, its jurisdiction is based on the consent of the parties and no state is compelled to submit its dispute to the Court's decision. Thus, if a state is of the opinion that the Court has no jurisdiction it is quite normal that it refers to that fact and tries to challenge the Court's jurisdiction.

It should be emphasized that presenting preliminary objections to the jurisdiction of the Court could not be considered as any kind of mistrust in the World Court. It is quite normal that a litigant is trying to defend its case and there could be situations when the best means seems to be challenging the Court's jurisdiction.[9]

Although the Court having well-established procedural rules and long-standing jurisprudence on the cases of preliminary objections, their growing number have caused scepticisms regarding the optional clause system.

II THE NON-APPEARANCE

The other practice which was used on several occasions by states to demonstrate the lack of the Court's jurisdiction to entertain a case has been the refusal to appear before the Court.[10] According to Elkind: 'Failure to appear and failure to accept the compulsory jurisdiction of the Court are both aspects of the same problem, a refusal to accept the principle of third-party settlement of disputes.'[11]

In most cases of failure to appear before the Court there were some, at least apparent, grounds for the jurisdiction of the Court, nevertheless, one of the parties didn't take part in the proceedings before the Court. Thus in those cases the parties in one way or another had already accepted the Court's jurisdiction and still failed to appear before the Court. Practically

---

[9] As an exemple one could refer to the *Ahmadou Sadio Diallo case* (Republic of Guinea v. Democratic Republic of the Congo) in which the Democratic Republic of the Congo acknowledged that the parties' declarations of acceptance were sufficient to found the jurisdiction of the Court in that case; nevertheless, it challenged the admissibility of Guinea's Application and raised two preliminary objections.

[10] In the literature of international law, authors draw a distinction between *non-appearance* and *default*. Cf. Elkind (1984) 79–82; and Pierre Michel Eisemann, 'Les effets de la non-comparution devant la Cour internationale de Justice' (1973) 19, *AFDI*, 351, 355–6.

[11] Jerome B. Elkind, *Non-appearance before the International Court of Justice*. Functional and Comparative Analysis (Martinus Nijhoff Publishers, 1984) 187.

this is when one can speak of non-appearance, and the provisions of Article 53 of the Statute apply to such cases.

In respect of the failure of a party to appear in the proceedings of the two International Courts, Article 53 of their Statutes provides practically with identical paragraphs.[12] That provision was included in the Statute of the Permanent Court on the basis of a draft of the 1920 Advisory Committee of Jurists.[13] When formulating Article 53, the framers of the Statute anticipated such situations which are well known in municipal laws and they provided the course as to how to proceed in such cases and excluded the default judgment. Thus both Courts 'in harmony with modern procedural law does not treat a party in default as guilty, and is far from regarding failure to appear as *a ficta confessio*'.[14] As for the reasons with regard to rejecting the default judgment, the Committee of Jurists stated that before the Permanent Court of International Justice:

> the contesting parties are States, and that it is a particularly serious matter to pronounce sentence against them, in the event of their denying the Court's right to try them. To make the Court's judgments, even in the event of a refusal to appear, acceptable to the sensitiveness of sovereign States, the sentence pronounced on the State at fault must rest upon all desirable guarantees to give it moral force, and consequently to ensure that it is respected and more easily put into execution.[15]

A closer look at Article 53 of the Statute of the International Court of Justice shows that it contains two provisions clearly separable in substance. Paragraph 1 essentially puts at some disadvantage the state failing to appear as it entitles the state which appears to call upon the Court to decide in favour of its claim. Paragraph 2 of Article 53, on the other hand, is an instruction for the Court, before deciding on the request of the

---

12 Art. 53. of the Statute of the International Court reads as follows:

1. Whenever one of the parties does not appear before the Court, or fails to defend its case, the other party may call upon the Court to decide in favour of its claim.
2. The Court must, before doing so, satisfy itself, not only that it has jurisdiction in accordance with Article 36 and 37, but also that the claim is well founded in fact and law.

13 See: Advisory Committee of Jurists. Procés-Verbaux of the Proceedings of the Committee. 16 June–24 July 1920. The Hague, (1920) 779.

14 *Fisheries Jurisdiction Case* (United Kingdom v. Ireland) (Merits), Judgment of 25 July 1974, Separate opinion of Judge de Castro, *ICJ Reports 1974*, 94.

15 Advisory Committee of Jurists. Procés-Verbaux, Rosenne (2001) 740.

party which appears, to satisfy itself that the claim is well founded in fact and law. Article 53 does not at all make the task of the Court easier in considering the request of the party which appears, since in the absence of one of the parties, the Court must act as if both parties had taken part in the proceedings. Thus paragraph 2 of Article 53 of the Statute practically weakens the provision of paragraph 1 and protects the interests of the party which does not appear, trying to secure the process as if both parties participated in the proceedings before the Court.

(a) The Court on Non-appearance

It happened in several contentious cases brought before the two International Courts, submitted either on a treaty provision, or under declarations of acceptance, that one of the parties, in particular the respondent did not take part in the proceedings. In that respect one could differentiate between two situations, namely that when the respondent state did not take part in *any stage of the proceedings*, and that when one of the parties was absent from *a certain phase of the proceedings.*

From the time of the Permanent Court one could refer to two cases where obviously non-appearance has happened; however, in these cases the provisions of Article 53 were not applied.[16]

From the jurisprudence of the International Court one can mention 11 cases where one of the parties failed to appear before the Court either at any phase of the proceedings or only at certain phases.[17,18] Among these

---

[16] These were the *Denunciation of the Treaty of November 2, 1865, between China and Belgium case*, in which the respondent, China, appointed no agent, nor did it at any time take part in the proceedings. The other was the *Electricity Company of Sofia case*, where in December 1939 the public hearing was held in the absence of the Bulgarian agent and Bulgaria did not file a written rejoinder within the period set, nevertheless the Court adopted an order fixing a date for the commencement of the oral proceedings. On the non-appearence in these cases, see Elkind (1984) 31–7.

[17] Thus, in the two *Fisheries Jurisdiction cases*, the two *Nuclear Tests cases*, the *Trial of Pakistani Prisoners of War case*, the *Aegean Sea Continental Shelf case*, the *United States Diplomatic and Consular Staff in Tehran case*, the respondent states failed to appear in any phase of the proceedings. However, in the *Corfu Channel case*, the *Anglo-Iranian Oil Company case*, the *Nottebohm case* and the *Military and paramilitary activities in and against Nicaragua case*, one of the parties was absent only from certain phases of the proceedings.

[18] It should be added that James Fry, using a much wider definition of non-appearance and equating non-participation with non-cooperation, states that 'non-participation is the failure to do whatever is expected to be done by a

cases there were five instances (the two *Nuclear Tests cases,* the *Anglo-Iranian Oil Company case,* the *Nottebohm case* and the *Military and Paramilitary Activities in and against Nicaragua case*) in which the Court's jurisdiction was based either exclusively, or subsidiary on declarations of acceptance made under Article 36, paragraph 2 of the Statute. Thus, the cases of non-appearance under optional clause declarations were not numerous; however, as will be discussed later, some of these instances had considerable influence on the evaluation of that practice. However, what is fortunate is that since in the *Nicaragua case* there was no single instance of real non-appearance.

It should be noted that Article 53 of the Statute was not applied in the *Anglo-Iranian Oil Co. case* nor the *Nottebohm case*, with all probability because, although the respondents failed to participate in the first phase of the proceedings, they later appointed their agents and took part in the proceedings before the Court. Article 53 was also not mentioned in the Court's judgment delivered in the two *Nuclear Tests cases*, where in both cases the respondent, France, refused to take part in any stage of the proceedings and had not appointed its agent. In all other cases of non-appearance, including those where the Court's jurisdiction was founded on compromissory clauses, Article 53 was applied. In these cases the Court expressed its regret that the respondent states did not take part in the proceedings instituted by the applicants; and by reference to Article 53, the Court held that, in accordance with the Statute and its settled jurisprudence, it must examine *proprio motu* the question of its own jurisdiction and should consider also the objections which might be raised against the Court's jurisdiction.[19]

---

disputant at any point in a procedure'. He refers to three other proceedings as non-participation instances: the case concerning the *Request for an Examination of the Situation in Accordance with Paragraph 63 of the Court's Judgment of 20 December 1974 in the Nuclear Tests* (New Zealand *v.* France), the *Maritime Delimitation and Territorial Questions between Qatar and Bahrain* (Qatar *v.* Bahrain), and even an advisory opinion, the *Legal Consequences of the Construction of a Wall in the Occupied Palestinian Territory.* Cf. James D. Fry, 'Non-Participation in the International Court of Justice Revisited: Change or Plus Ça Change?' (2010), 49. *Colum J Transnat'l Law*, 38–9, 43, 44.

[19] See *Fisheries Jurisdiction* (United Kingdom v. Iceland) (Jurisdiction of the Court), Judgment of 2 February 1973, *ICJ Reports 1973*, 7–8; *Fisheries Jurisdiction* (Germany v. Iceland), *Jurisdiction of the Court,* Judgment of 2 February 1973, *ICJ Reports 1973*, 54; *Nuclear Tests* (Australia v. France), Judgment of 20 December 1974, *ICJ Reports 1974*, 257; *Nuclear Tests* (New Zealand v. France), Judgment of 20 December 1974, *ICJ Reports 1974*, 461; *Aegean Sea Continental Shelf,* Judgment of 18 December 1978, *ICJ Reports*

There is no question that from the non-appearance cases, the *Nicaragua case* has excited the greatest world-wide interest. That could be explained among other factors not only because this time the non-appearing state was a big power and one of the most powerful states of the world, but that respondent ceased to take part in the proceedings after the judgment rendered by the Court on 26 November 1984 on the questions of the jurisdiction of the Court (to entertain the dispute) and the admissibility of Nicaragua's application, and in that judgment the World Court declared that the application was admissible and the Court had jurisdiction to decide on the merits of the case.[20]

In the judgment on the merits, the Court, by referring to its previous statements on non-appearance in other instances, stated that it:

> regrets even more deeply the decision of the respondent State not to participate in the present phase of the proceedings, because this decision was made after the United States had participated fully in the proceedings on the

---

1978, 7–8; *United States Diplomatic and Consular Staff in Tehran*, Judgment 24 May 1980, *ICJ Reports*, 1980, 9.

It is interesting to mention that in the *Nuclear Tests cases*, where France failed to take part in any stage of the proceedings, the Court didn't refer to Art. 53, however, in its 1974 judgments delivered in these cases the Court's statements regarding the failure of the respondent to take part in the proceedings were almost identical with what were said in the cases when Art. 53 was applied. Cf. *Nuclear Tests* (Australia v. France), Judgment of 20 December 1974, *ICJ Reports 1974*, 257 and *Nuclear Tests* (New Zealand v. France), Judgment of 20 December 1974, *ICJ Reports 1974*, 461.

20 Not long after the Court's judgment on 18 January 1985, the agent of the United States in its letter stated

> 'that the judgment of the Court was clearly and manifestly erroneous as to both fact and law. The United States remains firmly of the view, for the reasons given in its written and oral pleadings that the Court is without jurisdiction to entertain the dispute, and that the Nicaraguan application of 9 April 1984 is inadmissible. … the United States intends not to participate in any further proceedings in connection with this case, and reserves its rights in respect of any decision by the Court regarding Nicaragua's claims.'

Letter of the Counsellor for Legal Affairs of the Embassy of the United States of America to the Registrar, 18 January 1985. *Military and Paramilitary Activities in and against Nicaragua* correspondence. 408 http://www.icj-cij.org/docket/files/70/9635.pdf (accessed 28 August 2013).

request for provisional measures, and the proceedings on jurisdiction and admissibility.[21]

In connection with the cases of non-appearence the question emerges whether states have a legal duty to appear before the Court and participate in the proceedings before the Court and whether non-appearance before the Court could be considered as an action contrary to international law. According to a well-known scholar, Fitzmaurice,[22] states have a duty to appear before the Court; other experts, thus Rosenne,[23] Gros,[24] Thirlway,[25] Elkind[26] maintain that there is no such duty. One could say that not only were authors rather divided on this issue but even the opinions of the members of the Institute of International Law varied[27] when discussing its resolution on "Non-Appearance Before the International Court of Justice" at its session of 1991 held in Basel.[28]

After the Court's decision on the merits of the *Nicaragua case* one could say that the above-mentioned dispute could be considered as resolved, since the Court, although it expressed its regret at the non-appearance of the United States of America, recognized that a state party to the proceedings before the Court may decide not to participate in them[29] and didn't declare a non-appearing state as acting contrary to its duties under international law.

---

[21] *Military and Paramilitary Activities in and against Nicaragua* (Nicaragua v. United States of America) (Merits), Judgment of 27 July 1986, *ICJ Reports 1986*, 23.

[22] Sir Gerald Fitzmaurice 'The problem of the Non-Appearing Defendant Government' (1980) 51, *BYIL*, 89, 106–15.

[23] Rosenne (2006), 1360.

[24] Cf. *Fisheries Jurisdiction Case* (United Kingdom v. Iceland) (Merits), Judgment 25 July 1974, Dissenting opinion of Judge Gros, *ICJ Reports 1974*, 126.

[25] Cf. H.W.A. Thirlway, *Non-Appearance before the International Court of Justice* (CUP 1985) 64–82.

[26] According to Elkind, states cannot be compelled to appear before the Court; however, both the opposing party and the Court have a right to insist that the respondent state appear. See Jerome B. Elkind, 'The Duty to Appear before the International Court of Justice' (1988) 37, *ICLQ*, 674, 681.

[27] On the discussion, see Stanimir A. Alexandrov, 'Non-Appearance before the International Court of Justice' (1995) 33, *Colum J. Transnat'l L*, 41, 45.

[28] Resolution of the Institute of International Law, Session of Basel, 1991, on *'Non-Appearance Before the International Court of Justice'*.

[29] *Military and Paramilitary Activities in and against Nicaragua* (Merits), Judgment of 27 July 1986, *ICJ Reports 1986*, 23.

The Court's findings in the *Nicaragua case* regarding the non-appearance of a party could be summarized as follows:

- the case will continue without the participation of the non-appearing state;
- the non-appearing state remains a party to the case;[30]
- the non-appearing state is bound by the eventual judgment in accordance with Article 59 of the Statute;
- there is no question of a judgment automatically in favour of the party appearing; and
- the Court is required to 'satisfy itself' that the appearing party's claim is well founded in fact and law.[31]

Comparing what was said by the Court in the *Nicaragua case* to its previous statements regarding non-appearance, one should underline the passage stating that the non-participation of a party in the proceedings at any stage of the case cannot affect the validity of the Court's judgment. The importance of that pronouncement lies in the fact that although, even before the *Nicaragua case* there was a sound understanding that the non-appearance of a party had no effect on the validity of the Court's judgment, however, as Alexandrov pointed out, there is a strong link between non-appearance and non-compliance of international judgments,[32] and in most cases the unarticulated motivation of the non-appearing party was to separate itself from the Court's future judgment. Thus, it is not accidental that the United States in its letter of 18 January 1985, stated not only that it intended not to participate in the proceedings of the *Nicaragua case* before the Court, but reserved 'its rights in respect of any decision by the Court regarding Nicaragua's claims'. It is obvious that the Court had to react to that statement and had to make it clear that the non-appearing state would be bound by the future judgment of the Court. Some years later that Court's statement was reaffirmed by the resolution of the Institute of International Law by pronouncing that 'Notwithstanding the non-appearance of a State before the Court in proceedings to which it is a party, that State is, by virtue of the Statute,

30 On the question whether a non-appearing state is a party to the proceedings of the Court, see Thirlway (1985) 46–63.

31 Cf. *Military and Paramilitary Activities in and against Nicaragua* (Merits), Judgment of 27 July 1986, *ICJ Reports 1986*, 24.

32 Alexandrov (1995) 68.

bound by any decision of the Court in that case, whether on jurisdiction, admissibility, or the merits.'[33]

(b) The Real Cause of Non-appearance – the Lack of Confidence

Regarding the causes of non-appearance, one could agree with those views which mention a certain distrust and lack of confidence in the impartiality of the Court, whenever a state refuses to participate in a case.[34] However, instead of alluding any distrust, in most cases states are in fact contesting the jurisdiction of the Court, or arguing on the non-justiciability of the case, and quite often give a detailed analysis of treaties, reservations, or the legal situation. As examples, one could refer to the *Fisheries Jurisdiction cases*, the *Nuclear Tests cases* or the *Aegean Sea Continental Shelf case*.

Thus in the *Fisheries Jurisdiction case* (United Kingdom v. Iceland) in different documents Iceland was claiming that the 1961 Exchange of Notes had taken place at a time when the British Royal Navy had been using force to oppose the 12-mile fishery limit; the compromissory undertaking for judicial settlement by the parties was not of a permanent nature; the object and purpose of the provision for recourse to judicial settlement had been fully achieved; the Icelandic Government had also alluded to 'the changed circumstances resulting from the ever increasing exploitation of the fishery resources in the seas surrounding Iceland'; and as a conclusion in its letter of 29 May 1972, it was stated that an agent will not be appointed to represent the government of Iceland.[35]

In connection with the *Nuclear Tests cases*, it should be mentioned the communication of 16 May 1973 sent to the Court by the French Ambassador to The Hague contained a rather detailed legal analysis of the lack of the Court's jurisdiction in these cases. France argued that neither the 1928 General Act, nor Article 36, paragraph 2 of the Statute could serve as the basis of the Court's jurisdiction for the French nuclear essays introduced by Australia and New Zealand, since the 1928 General Act is no longer in force, and the declaration of acceptance of the Court's jurisdiction made by the French Government on 20 May 1966, excludes from the Court's jurisdiction 'disputes concerning activities connected

---

33 Art. 4. Resolution of the Institute of International Law, Session of Basel, 1991 on *'Non-Appearance Before the International Court of Justice'*.

34 On the willingness of states and the causes of lack confidence in the impartiality of the Court, see Elkind (1984) 171–206.

35 See *Fisheries Jurisdiction Case* (United Kingdom v. Iceland) Correspondence 374–6. www.icj-c.i.j.org/docket/files/55/9401.pdf. (accessed 13 September 2013).

with national defence.'[36] According to the French Government, the Court was manifestly not competent in these cases and it could not accept the Court's jurisdiction, and accordingly, the French Government did not intend to appoint an agent.

In the *Aegean Sea Continental Shelf case*, Turkey in its communications to the Court of 25 August 1976, 24 April 1978 and 10 October 1978[37] expounded its legal position that the General Act of 1928, invoked by Greece, was no longer in force. Even assuming that the General Act was still in force and applicable as between Greece and Turkey, it would be subject to a reservation made by Greece that would exclude the Court's competence.[38]

The *Case concerning United States Diplomatic and Consular Staff in Tehran* differed from the above-mentioned four cases since in that instance Iran argued on the non-justiciability of the case at hand. In its notes addressed to the Court, the Iranian Government stated that the dispute was not one of interpretation and application of the treaties upon which the American Application is based and 'the Court cannot examine the American Application divorced from its proper context, namely the whole political dossier of the relations between Iran and the United States over the last 25 years.'[39]

The *Nicaragua case* was again different, because in the first phase of that case the United States made use of all the possibilities in a normal procedure to challenge the jurisdiction of the Court, nevertheless the Court pronounced that it had jurisdiction. Thus, in the second phase of the proceedings, from which the United States was absent, the Washington Government had not much to say on the question of jurisdiction except that in its 1984 judgment the 'Court was clearly and manifestly

---

36 See *Nuclear Tests* (Australia v. France), Correspondence 347–57, the same communication was sent in the case between New Zealand v. France. www.icj-c.i.j.org/docket/files/58/11007 (accessed 13 September 2013).

37 The last-mentioned communication was received in the Registry on the morning of the second day of the public hearings.

38 The communication of 25 August 1976 was submitted at the provisional measures stage and since it was precisely the procedural document required by the Rules, and at the appropriate time, according to Thirlway it seems impossible to contend that Turkey at the relevant time was failing to appear and defend its case. Cf. Thurlway (1985), 79. But no pleadings were filed by the government of Turkey, it was not represented at the oral proceedings and no formal submissions were made.

39 Cf. Notes of Iran of 9 December 1979 and 16 March 1980.

erroneous as to both fact and law'.[40] Thus in that phase of the proceedings, almost nine months after the termination of its declaration of acceptance and pronounciation that it would not take part in the phase of the merits of the *Nicaragua case*, the United States in an unofficial communication bearing the title of the 'Document Informally Made Available to Members of the Court by the United States Information Office in the Hague' treating the political aspects of its conflict with Nicaragua, and interpreting the political situations and events in Central-America, thus practically trying to defend its position.[41]

One could see that states non-appearing before the Court tried to explain their conduct either on the non-justiciability of the dispute or by challenging the jurisdiction of the Court on legal grounds, even with respect to reservations to their declarations of acceptance as happened in the *Nuclear Tests cases* and the *Aegean Sea Continental Shelf case*. These arguments appeared in letters, communications, notifications, etc., sent to the Court, or were made public. For these documents there are no rules or time limits and the states are presenting these documents at any time. Nevertheless one could say that when states absent from the proceedings of the International Court of Justice object, as expressed in their various documents, to the jurisdiction of the Court, *their action to some extent fulfils a function similar to a preliminary objection relating to lack of jurisdiction of the Court*, but without observing the provisions on these objections in the Rules.[42] The International Court of Justice, for its part, examined these pleas of the non-appearing states, with the exception of the *Nuclear Tests cases* and the *Trial of Pakistani Prisoners of War*.[43]

Non-appearing before the Court instead of filing a preliminary objection is always a demonstrative action, and, irrespective of the arguments advanced by the non-appearing state, it expresses in a very strong manner the dissatisfaction of a state with the Court and the whole mechanism of third-party settlement of international disputes.

---

40 See the letter of 18 January 1985 of the Counselor for Legal Affairs of the Embassy of the United States of America to the Registar.

41 See http://www.icj-cij.org/docket/files/70/9633.pdf (accessed 13 September 2013).

42 According to Thirlway if the communication from the non-appearing state raises questions of jurisdiction or admissibility, it should be treated by the Court as a preliminary objection. Cf. Thirlway (1985) 174.

43 This happened because in the cases concerning the French nuclear tests, the Court dealt with the object of the applications and not the question of jurisdiction. The *Trial of Pakistani Prisoners of War* was removed from the Court's list before the expiry of the time limits set for the submission of written memorials.

(c) The Consequences of Non-appearance

Having examined the cases of non-appearance the question emerges as to what the consequences are of the non-appearance of respondent states. These consequences relate first of all to the proceedings before the Court, but affect in some degree also the position of the parties to the dispute.[44]

As regards the proceedings, a consequence of the attitude of the defaulting states is that the proceedings before the Court actually divide in two, and first of all the Court has to consider and satisfy itself as to its own jurisdiction. As a consequence of the non-appearance, therefore, the proceedings have some similarities to those cases where one of the parties is raising preliminary objections, since, in view of the provisions of Article 53 of the Statute, the Court first should be satisfied of its jurisdiction in the case at hand.

Another consequence of non-appearance is that it deprives the proceedings before the Court of their contradictory character, since the real debate is missing from these proceedings as a consequence of the absence of one of the parties. The situation remains the same even if the non-appearing states in letters, telegrams and other documents are expressing their observations, arguments, etc. regarding the dispute, especially because the non-appearing party submits such documents upon the opening of the proceedings, usually in reply to the application, thus depriving itself of the possibility of challenging the arguments put forward by the applicant later in the written or oral proceedings. Thus a withdrawal from a case might have an unfortunate product with respect to the non-appearing state, as happened according to some authors – in the merits of the *Nicaragua case*, the United States view was not adequately considered by the Court.[45]

In cases of non-appearance, particularly as regards the merits of the disputes, the character of the Court's task changes to a certain extent, since in such cases a considerable part of the work of the Court consists, aside from examining the more or less well-founded and very subjective arguments of the non-appearing party appeared in letters and other documents, but also in deducing the arguments, or at least parts of the arguments which might be raised by the non-appearing party.

---

[44] It should be added that the non-appearing state divests itself also of the possibility of nominating a judge ad hoc.

[45] Cf. Jonathan I. Charney, 'Disputes Implicating the Institutional Credibility of the Court: Problems of Non-Appearance, Non-Participation, and Non-Performance' in Dambrosch (1987) 291.

There is no question that the non-appearance before the Court either in the whole or only in a phase of the proceedings is a tactical decision of a state. The real motivations behind such steps are much more political than legal, and such an attitude of a state, as it was already said, is nothing else than a certain kind of demonstrative political action.

As one could see, the failure to participate by one of the parties at the Court's proceeding hinders the good administration of justice. Although, there is no duty for the states to take part in the proceeding before the Court, there is however a duty to cooperate with the Court. Exactly that was referred by the Institute of International Law in its resolution of 1991 by stating that: 'In considering whether to appear or to continue to appear in any phase of proceedings before the Court, a State should have regard to its duty to co-operate in the fulfillment of the Court's judicial functions.'[46]

The duty of cooperation is the consequence of the legal principle of good faith which has a legal foundation in Article 2, paragraph 2 of the United Nations Charter integrating that principle into both the law of the Charter[47] and the Statute forming, under Article 92 of the Charter an integral part of that. Thus states are bound to fulfil their obligations deriving from the Statute in good faith which includes also the obligation, not to hinder, but to act so as to enable the Court in fulfiling its tasks connected with the good administration of justice.

[46] Art. 2. Resolution of the Institute of International Law, Session of Basel, 1991 on *'Non-Appearance Before the International Court of Justice'*.

[47] Jörg P. Müller, 'Article 2(2)' in Bruno Simma in collaboration with Hermann Mosler, Albrecht Randelzhofer, Christian Tomuschat, Rüdiger Wolfrum (ed.) *The Charter of the United Nations.* A Commentary (C.H. Beck, 1994) 92.

11. Reconsidering the optional clause system

I NINETY YEARS OF PARTIAL OBLIGATORY ADJUDICATION

With the establishment of both the Permanent Court and the optional clause in its Statute a good framework seemed to be created for the introduction of compulsory international adjudication.

Although a great deal of controversy surrounded the elaboration of the provisions of the optional clause, the hopes of the founding fathers were not without justification, that being a new system of partial obligatory adjudication, having strong roots in the documents adopted at the very successful Hague Peace Conferences and based on the voluntary acceptance of the Court's jurisdiction, thus fully observing the sovereignty of states.

Those who were the partisans of generally obligatory international adjudication were convinced that with the establishment of the Permanent Court an important step had been taken towards a regime of generally obligatory international adjudication. Mankind was in the aftermath of an unprecedented terrible war lasting more than four years, and there was the expectation that the idea of peaceful settlement of international disputes would find more supporters than ever before. That was upheld also by the fact that, after the entry into force of the Statute of the Permanent Court of International Justice, states had started to deposit declarations of acceptance under Article 36, paragraph 2. The fact that in most cases, declaring states had renewed their fixed-term declarations or even replaced them with ones for an unlimited period was a further encouraging phenomenon.

However, one could witness another development as well. Namely that there appeared limitations and reservations in the declarations of acceptance and already in the early years of the Permanent Court some states introduced limitations to their declarations. As one could see from the previous chapters, over the course of time the reservations to declarations of acceptance have grown in complexity, with states 'inventing' new reservations drafted with great legal skills, which, in some cases, were the result of a Court's decision. Thus more and more limitations appeared in the declarations of acceptance over and above both the reciprocity and time limitations which were mentioned in the Statute itself.

Thus the states' practice diverged from what was expected and, instead of an end to the 'provisional solution' reflected in the optional clause[1] and the growth of a system of general international obligatory adjudication, a very complicated and fragmented network of declarations of acceptance developed.

The international community of states consented to the acceptance of the Court's compulsory jurisdiction with different reservations. Although states party to the optional clause system could challenge the reservations to declarations of acceptance, the instances were scarce. In most cases the parties disputed the permissibility of certain reservations only in concrete disputes before the Court. Thus one could say that states were reluctant and there were very few instances where a state objected against a reservation that was included in a declaration of acceptance of a state newly adhering to the optional clause system. That passivity of the international community of states was due to two facts. First, as has already been said, the network of optional clause declarations does not form a treaty-like bond between states and the states that are party to the optional clause system are in reality confronting with a declaration of another declaring state – in that case where a concrete dispute with that state is submitted to the Court's decision. As the second reason, one could mention that several states – although having concerns regarding some reservations in a newly declaring state's declaration of acceptance – didn't want to poison their relations with that state, and in most cases they kept silent regarding a rather disputed reservation.

If states would be more active and more often challenged some reservations added to the newly declaring states' declarations of acceptance, it is not clear what the result would be of such objections. In the case of declarations of acceptances, in contrast to the law of treaties, there are no rules or established practices that are the consequences of objections to a reservation added to a declaration of acceptance and also it is not clear what the consequences might be if a state were to introduce in its declaration of acceptance a reservation which contradicted the object and purpose of the optional clause. The jurisprudence of the Court shows us that the World Court avoided deciding on the permissibility of

1 Torres Bernárdez called the system as provisional. Cf.Torrres Bernárdez (1992) 293, footnote 2.

any reservation to declarations of acceptance or the compability of a reservation with the object and purpose of the optional clause system in all cases whereby a disputed reservation came into question. It gave effect to the reservations as they stood and as parties adopted them.[2] Taking into consideration all the circumstances, one could say that, it was a wise decision of the Court to refrain in concrete cases from ruling on the permissibility of certain reservations to declarations of acceptance, since any decision would have adversely affected the Court's compulsory jurisdiction. Any decision on the admissibility of certain reservations would have given some sort of 'encouragement' to the inclusion of such reservations in the declarations of acceptance; while any decision on the inadmissibility of certain rather disputed reservations might have considerably influenced the outcome of the concrete case before the Court. Not to mention that it might have led other states party to the optional clause system to withdraw those declarations of acceptance containing similar reservations to that being declared by the Court as inadmissible.

During the 1950–60s the optional clause system had as Waldock called a 'period of decline'. Rather few cases were submitted to the Court's decision, more and more so-called destructive reservations appeared in declarations of acceptance, in concrete cases before the Court the parties referred to these reservations in order to evade the Court's decision in their dispute and, later on, it became widespread practice for the respondent to fail to appear before the Court.

One could say that the dark years are now gone. The hands of the Court are full with work, more and more cases are submitted to the Court's decision[3] and the optional clause was never before so popular as nowadays.

At the end of 2013 there were 80 states' declarations of acceptance in force, thus more than 41 per cent of the United Nations member states had valid declarations of acceptance. It is true that at the time of the Permanent Court there was a year, 1935, when from the 58 member

---

[2] Cf. *Case of Certain Norwegian Loans,* Judgment of 6 July 1957, *ICJ Reports 1957*, 27.

[3] That is also thanks to the Secretary-General's Trust Fund to Assist States in the Settlement of Disputes through the International Court of Justice established in 1989, see http://www.un.org/law/trustfund/trustfund.htm (accessed 17 October 2013). On the Fund, see Mary Ellen O'Connell, 'International Legal Aid: The Secretary General's Trust Fund to assist States in the Settlement of Disputes through the International Court of Justice' in Janis (1992) 235–44.

Several developing states with the help of the Fund submitted their disputes to the Court's decision.

states of the League of Nations, 42 states made declarations of acceptance. However, one should not forget that the League of Nations was less universal than the United Nations and between the two world wars there was great instability in the membership of the League of Nations, since after some years of membership several states left the organization. The same holds true for the optional clause system, at that time some states were party to the system only for a rather short period. In contrast to that, the United Nations is really universal, but what is even more important for our subject is that there is a great stability in the composition of the states party to the optional clause system. That can be proved by the fact that since 1946, thus in almost 70 years only seven states' – Bolivia (1953), Brazil (1953), El Salvador (1988), Guatemala (1952), Nauru (1998), Thailand (1960) and Turkey (1972) – declarations of acceptance have expired without submitting a new one, and eight states – China (1972), Columbia (2001), France (1974), Iran (1951), Israel (1985), South Africa (1967), Serbia (2008) and the United States of America (1986) – have withdrawn their declarations of acceptance.

Regarding the actual states that are party to the optional clause system what is important is that since 1990, 28 declarations of acceptance were deposited, and among them there were several states which either had never before made a declaration of acceptance or now returning to optional clause system.[4] It is also a welcome change that several former socialist states, breaking the policy of their governments in more than 40 years, made declarations of acceptance and even submitted their disputes to the Court's decision.

But what is even more important, is that the declarations of acceptance are not dead letters, and states are using the possibilities provided by the optional clause system. More and more cases are submitted to the Court's decision under optional clause declarations – this can be proved by the fact that since 2005 until the end of 2013 proceedings were instituted before the Court in 22 contentious cases and in more than one third of the cases the Court's jurisdiction was based among others on declarations of acceptance.[5]

---

[4] Among the recently adhering states, one could mention Cyprus (2002), Djibuti (2005), Commonwealth of Dominica (2006), Germany (2008), Ireland (2011), the Ivory Coast (2001), the Marshall Islands (2013), Slovakia (2004) and Timor-Leste (2012).

[5] See *Dispute regarding Navigational and Related Rights* (Costa Rica v. Nicaragua), *Status vis–à–vis the Host State of a Diplomatic Envoy to the United Nations* (Commonwealth of Dominica v. Switzerland), *Questions relating to the Obligation to Prosecute or Extradite* (Belgium v. Senegal), *Jurisdiction and*

No question that one of the weakest points of the system is that the United Kingdom is the only great power having a declaration of acceptance in force, and two other great powers, France and the United States after withdrawing their declarations in 1974 and 1986 respectively, didn't deposit new declarations of acceptance. The People's Republic of China and the Russian Federation (or its predecessor the Soviet Union) have always stood aside from the optional clause system.

The majority of the writers of international law are recognizing the importance of the optional clause system in the settlement of international disputes and in that connection some of them have drawn conclusions from the link between compliance and jurisdiction and tried to conclude that the willingness of the states to execute the Court's decisions has been bigger in cases brought under compromissory clauses or under special agreements than in cases under declarations of acceptance.[6] In an article analysing 129 cases between 1947 and 2003, the authors came to the conclusion that the compliance rate with the Court's judgment was 85.7 per cent in cases submitted by special agreement, 60 per cent in cases brought under compromissory treaty clause and only 40 per cent in cases submitted under declarations of acceptance.[7] Without entering into detail it should be mentioned that the situation is much more complicated than is reflected in that study because well-founded conclusions regarding the compliance rate of the Court's decisions should

Enforcement of Judgements in Civil and Commercial Matters (Belgium v. Switzerland), *Whaling in the Antarctic* (Australia v. Japan: New Zealand intervening), *Certain Activities carried out by Nicaragua in the Border Area* (Costa Rica v. Nicaragua), *Construction of a Road in Costa Rica along the San Juan River* (Nicaragua v. Costa Rica), *Questions relating to the Seizure and Detention of Certain Documents and Data* (Timor-Leste v. Australia) *cases*. It should be added that the two proceedings between Nicaragua and Costa Rica were joined by two separate Orders of the Court dated 17 April 2013.

[6] See Tom Ginsburg and Richard H. McAdams, 'Adjudicating in Anarchy: An Expressive Theory of International Dispute Resolution' (2004) *Wm & Mary L. Rev*, 1229–339. http://scholarship.law.wm.edu/wmlr/vol45/iss4/2 (accessed 13 August 2013); Eric A. Posner and John C. Yoo, 'Judicial Independence in International Tribunals' (2005) 93, *Cal L R*, 1–74; Aloysius P. Llamzon, 'Jurisdiction and Compliance in Recent Decisions of the International Court of Justice' (2008) 18, *EJIL*, 815–52.

[7] See Ginsburg and McAdams (2004).

be made only after very careful analyses of all the details of each case as well as the events following the Court's judgments even after years of the decision.[8]

Since the adoption of the Permanent Court's Statute in 1921, the optional clause system has been unchanged, with the exception of the provisions introduced in the Statute at the San Francisco Conference accommodating and transferring the declarations of acceptance in force to the new Court. In the different rounds of UN reforms the questions connected with the Court's jurisdiction were not on the agenda, and the reform documents made suggestions in most cases regarding the composition of the Court, the election of judges and the access to the Court.[9] Apart from this, already at the time of the Permanent Court, in different documents of the League of Nations, resolutions of United Nations' organs and international scientific associations, there appeared statements that states should adhere to the optional clause system or add

---

[8] One could only regret that in Tom Ginsburg's and Richard McAdams's very valuable article there are errors regarding the jurisdictional bases of several cases (see table at 1330–39). Thus, for example, in the *Certain Norwegian Loans case* the Court's jurisdiction was based not on a treaty provision but on the parties' declarations of acceptance; the same holds for the *Case concerning the Temple of Preah Vihear*, which was also a dispute submitted to the Court's decision under Art. 36. para. 2 of the Statute. On the other hand, the *South-West Africa cases* (Ethiopia v. South Africa and Liberia v. South Africa) were not cases under the optional clause but disputes referred to the Court on the basis of the Mandate's compromissory clauses concluded at the time of the League of Nations. The situation regarding the *Fisheries Jurisdiction cases* (United Kingdom v. Iceland and Federal Republic of Germany v. Iceland) is the same; these were disputes brought under compromissory clauses, and the applications based on the Court's jurisdiction on Art. 36, para. 1 of the Statute and the 1961 Exchange of Notes between the parties. Another major error one could find regards the ten *Legality Use of Force cases* between the former Yugoslavia and the NATO states, since only in six of these cases was the Court's jurisdiction based not only on Art. IX of the *Convention on the Prevention and Punishment of the Crime of Genocide* but on the parties' declarations of acceptance as well.

[9] Cf. 'Reforming the United Nations: What About the International Court of Justice? ABILA Committee on Intergovernmental Settlement of Disputes' (2006) 5, *Chinese J I L*, 39, 42. doi:10.1093/chinesejil/jml001 (accessed 19 October 2013).

fewer limitations to their declarations of acceptances,[10] but the essence of the existing system of compulsory jurisdiction was not addressed.[11]

One could think that after more than 90 years of states' practice and the jurisprudence of the two International Courts it is high time to reconsider the optional clause system, especially the system of reservations to declarations of acceptance, not only because the actual wide spread of reservations is a phenomenon that was not envisaged by the founding fathers, but because some of the reservations undermine the optional clause system.

II A POSSIBLE SOLUTION

As has already been mentioned the Court has never contested the admissibility of reservations to declarations of acceptance, although the need has been felt in several instances to disallow certain reservations or to place a limitation on making them.

In the literature of international law, Leo Gross was one of the authors who dealt with the question of how to resolve the problem of reservations

---

[10] Here, one should refer to UN Res. No. 3232 (XXIX) on 'Review of the Role of the International Court of Justice', http://www.un.org/en/ga/search/view_doc.asp?symbol=A/RES/3232(XXIX)&Lang=E&Area=RESOLUTION; and UN Doc. No. A/47/277 'Report of the Secretary General Pursuant to the Statement adopted by the Summit Meeting of the Security Council on 31 January 1992', http://www.un.org/ga/search/view_doc.asp?symbol=A%2F47%2F277&Submit=Search&Lang=E. (accessed 23 October 2013). See also Manila Declaration on the Peaceful Settlement of International Disputes, adopted by the UN General Assembly on 15 November 1982, (37/10) stating in II. Part para. 5 that:

> States should bear in mind …
>
> (b) That it is desirable that they:
>
> (ii) Study the possibility of choosing, in the free exercise of their sovereignty, to recognize as compulsory the jurisdiction of the International Court of Justice in accordance with Article 36 of its statute.

[11] See, 'The International Court of Justice Efficiency of Procedures and Working Methods'. Report of the Study Group established by the British Institute of International and Comparative Law as a contribution to the UN Decade of International Law by D.W. Bowett, J. Crawford, I. Sinclair, A.A. Watts. (1996) 45, *ICLQ* Supplement. On different reform suggestions, see also Kolb (2013) 1205–06.

to declarations of acceptance.[12] According to Gross the General Assembly could eventually adopt a resolution on the subject of reservations *ratione temporis*;[13] or, it may be desirable to consider, in connection with the revision of the Statute, whether the Court itself should not have been able to rule on the conformity of some declarations of acceptance within the optional clause system, either *ex officio* or at the request of any state being a party to the system of compulsory jurisdiction.[14]

One could agree with the American author that taking into consideration the importance and central position of the General Assembly in the United Nations Organization any decision of that organ on reservations to declarations of acceptance would have great authority. However, the General Assembly is a political organ and the problem of reservations to declarations of acceptance and the compatability of certain reservations with the optional clause system is a very complicated legal problem which necessitates a decision by experts of international law and not political organs, it not being a political decision or compromise.

By the amendment of the Statute it might be possible to introduce some limitations regarding making reservations. However, taking into consideration the reluctance of states to amend either the Charter, or the Statute, which according to Article 69 could be amended by the same procedure as the Charter, one should admit that any amendment of the Statute doesn't have much chance in the foreseeable future.

Thus, problems of reservations to declarations of acceptance should be resolved by the Court itself and within the framework of the exisiting legal rules. According to the present author the problems connected with reservations to declarations of acceptance could be the subject of an advisory opinion given by the Court.

The appropriateness of an advisory opinion on the question of reservations to declarations of acceptance might not be questioned. The international community of states has established a system which has been functioning for more than 90 years and although it has had some dark years, at present it is flourishing to the satisfaction of the international community of states. Nevertheless, the system is faced with the problem of a growing number of reservations to declarations of acceptance which are making illusory the acceptance of the Court's compulsory jurisdiction. One should also not forget that, although now the problems

---

12 Leo Gross, 'The International Court of Justice: Consideration of Requirements for Enhancing its Role in the International Legal Order' (1971) 65, *AJIL*, 253.

13 *Id.* 314–15.

14 *Id.* 316.

connected with some of the disputed reservations seem to be slipping, one can never know when a state could come forward again by formulating either its declaration of acceptance, or a concrete dispute with a reservation or limitation being destructive to the optional clause system.

In connection with an advisory opinion on reservations to declarations of acceptance the first question which emerges is who should request that opinion. It would be self-evident that the most appropriate institution would be the Secretariat of the United Nations or the Secretary-General himself being the depository of declarations of acceptance. However, as it is well known, with that issue being raised on several occasions, that right was not accorded either to the Secretariat or the Secretary-General,[15] although the Secretariat, with the Secretary-General as its head, is the only principal organ not empowered to make requests for advisory opinions.

The other appropriate organ might be the General Assembly, since the General Assembly may request advisory opinions *ex lege* on the basis of Art. 96, para. 1 of the Charter on any legal question within the scope of its activities. The problems of reservations to declarations of acceptance include questions connected with the peaceful settlement of disputes covered by Art. 2, para. 3 of the Charter which formulates one of the main principles of the Organization, which, 'is a cornerstone of the contemporary world order.'[16] The jurisprudence of the Court shows us that in its advisory opinions the Court had to examine the implications of the requirement whether the matters of the requested opinion were 'arising within the scope' of the requesting organ's acitivities, thus whether the requesting organ had not acted *ultra vires*.[17] In the case of the General Assembly that issue could not be raised since the General Assembly has the power to discuss and deal with any matters within the scope of the Charter. Thus, the question of reservations to declarations of acceptance is in the purview of the General Assembly.

The motion to the General Assembly for the request of an advisory opinion from the Court might come either from a delegation or any Committee of the General Assembly. There are no special rules regarding the preparation of a request or the majority required to pass a resolution

---

[15] Cf. Rosalyn Higgins, 'A comment on the current health of Advisory Opinions' in Lowe-Fitzmaurice (1996), 568–71; Kolb (2013), 1049–50.

[16] Cf. Christian Tomuschat, 'Article 2(3)' in Simma-Mosler-Randelzhofer-Tomuschat-Wolfrum (1994), 99.

[17] Cf. Chittharanjan F. Amerasinghe, *Jurisdiction of Specific International Tribunals* (Martinus Nijhoff 2009) 215.

on an advisory opinion from the Court.[18] The only requirement that one can find in the Rules of Procedure of the General Assembly is that if any Committee contemplates recommending the General Assembly to request an advisory opinion it may refer the matter to the Sixth Committee for advice and the drafting of the request.[19] The voting record on some of the relevant advisory opinions in the General Assembly show us that these resolutions were passed by a majority.[20] One could hope that a recommendation regarding the request of an advisory opinion on the reservations to declarations of acceptance might reach the necessary majority in the General Assembly.

The subject matter of a request of an advisory opinion concerning reservations to declarations of acceptance would be a request on a legal question of a general nature which is unrelated to a concrete problem awaiting a practical solution. Thus, it would have some similarities to the advisory opinion of the *Legality of the Threat or Use of Nuclear Weapons*, which was the first advisory opinion of a general nature not having a specific dispute regarding the subject matter at question. Since according to Art. 65 of the Statute, the Court has discretion whether to give an advisory opinion or not;[21] in connection with the advisory opinion of the *Legality of the Threat or Use of Nuclear Weapons*, some states and members of the Court tried to persuade the Court that in the exercise of its discretionary power it should decline to render the opinion requested by the General Assembly; nevertheless the Court met the request. According to the Court it might not be an obstacle for giving the

---

18 Cf. Hermann Mosler, 'Article 96' in Simma-Mosler-Randelzhofer-Tomuschat-Wolfrum (1994) 1011.

19 Cf. *Rules of Procedure of the General Assembly* (embodying amendments and additions adopted by the General Assembly up to September 2007) A/520/Rev.17 ANNEX II. Methods and procedures of the General Assembly for dealing with legal and drafting questions http://www.un.org/en/ga/search/view_doc.asp?symbol=A/520/rev.17&Lang=E (accessed 20 October 2013).

20 The voting records of the General Assembly on the resolutions requesting advisory opinions in some relevant cases were the following: *Reservations to Multilateral Conventions* on 16 November 1950 (47 votes in favour, 5 against, 5 abstentions, 3 non-voting: total voting membership; 60); *Legality of the Threat or Use of Nuclear Weapons* adopted on 15 December 1996 (78 votes in favour, 43 against, 38 abstentions, 26 non-voting: total voting membership; 185); *Legal Consequences of the Construction of a Wall in the Occupied Palestinian Territory* adopted on 8 December 2003 at the Tenth Emergency Special Session (90 votes in favour, 8 against, 74 abstentions: total voting membership; 172).

21 Cf. Jochen Abr. Frowein – Karin Oelers-Frahm, 'Advisory Opinions' in Zimmermann -Tomuschat – Oellers-Frahm (2006) 1411.

requested opinion if the request does not relate to a special dispute.[22] Repeating his statement made 45 years before in the advisory opinion of the *Interpretation of Peace Treaties with Bulgaria, Hungary and Romania*, the Court stated that 'The purpose of the advisory function is not to settle at least directly disputes between States, but to offer legal advice to the organs and institutions requesting the opinion.'[23] It added that 'The fact that the question put to the Court does not relate to a specific dispute should consequently not lead the Court to decline to give the opinion requested.'[24] One could expect that in the case of an advisory opinion regarding reservations to declarations of acceptance the Court would follow the same reasoning.

One of the advantages of deciding on the problems connected with reservations to declarations of acceptances in an advisory opinion, rather than a contentious case, might be that the opinion of the Court would not influence directly the outcome of a concrete dispute under consideration by the Court.

Regarding the question to be put to the Court, there might be two variants. The first one involves formulating to the Court a very general question as it was in the *Legality of the Threat or Use of Nuclear Weapons*, the second possibility is to draft several more detailed questions as was done in the request of the advisory opinion of the *Reservations to the Convention on the Prevention and Punishment of the Crime of Genocide*.

As a general question it is possible to formulate the following 'are there any limitations to joining reservations to declarations of acceptance'.

Or these questions might be put to the Court:

- are there any limitations in the number and scope of reservations to declarations of acceptance
- which reservations might be considered as unpermitted and being in contradiction with the object and purpose of the optional clause
- what are the consequences of an invalid reservation, and would the invalidity affect the whole declaration of acceptance or only the reservation itself.

---

22 *Legality of the Threat or Use of Nuclear Weapons*, Advisory Opinion of 8 July 1996, *ICJ Reports 1996*, 236.

23 Cf. *Interpretation of Peace Treaties with Bulgaria, Hungary and Romania* (First Phase), Advisory Opinion of 30 March 1950, *ICJ Reports 1950*, 71.

24 *Legality of the Threat or Use of Nuclear Weapons*, Advisory Opinion of 8 July 1996, *ICJ Reports 1996*, 236.

The problem of the number and scope of limitations or reservations to declarations of acceptance is a rather complicated one. No question that thanks to the permissibility of reservations to declarations of acceptance the optional clause system is more flexible and offers the opportunity for more states to join and it is also generally admitted that states are free in making their declarations of acceptance and to join limitations or reservations on their own will. However, one could expect that, if there is a real wish to join the optional clause system by a declaring state, then that state should act bona fides and should not add so many reservations to its declaration of acceptance which make only in name the acceptance of the Court's compulsory jurisdiction. According to the present author there should be a reasonable limit to the reservations and limitations to declarations of acceptance and that should be determined by the Court itself.

It would be premature to predict how the Court will evaluate the rather disputed reservations, but one could suppose that it will declare unpermitted and invalid some of these reservations. In that case the Court may state that the invalidity affects the whole declaration of acceptance or only the reservation which might be severed from the declaration itself. Therefore the question emerges as to what should happen with those declarations in force which contain such invalid reservations. Regarding the future of these declarations the solution might be found in the 'Guide to Practice on Reservations to Treaties' adopted by the International Law Commission in 2011.[25] Although, as was said before, the reservations to declarations of acceptance differ from the reservations to multilateral treaties, but the solutions in the Guide regarding invalid reservations might have relevance. Thus, following the Guide, it might be stated that a declaring state making an invalid reservation might have some time, for example, one year, to either withdraw the reservation, thus maintaining its declaration of acceptance without the benefit of the invalid reservation, or leave the optional clause system.

The Court's advisory opinion on reservations to declarations of acceptance wouldn't resolve all the problems connected with the optional clause system and would not terminate the provisional solution created

---

[25] See, *Yearbook of the International Law Commission*, 2011, vol. II, Part Two. Sixty-third session (26 April–3 June and 4 July–12 August 2011). That instrument put an end to a long dispute between the International Law Commission and the Human Rights Committee and recognized the competence of that Committee to assess the permissibility of reservations. http://legal.un.org/ilc/texts/instruments/word_files/english/commentaries/1_8_2011. (accessed 13 August 2013).

by the clause nor introduce compulsory international adjudication, but it will increase the credibility of the whole system, create a clear situation and possibly encourage some states, which were reluctant especially due to some uncertainties connected with the Court's compulsory jurisdiction, to deposit their declarations of acceptance under Art. 36, para. 2 of the Statute. Thus, the Court's advisory opinion would contribute to increasing the role of the optional clause system in the settlement of international disputes.

Appendix

Declarations of acceptance made between 1921 and 2013

State	Date of deposition	Duration	Reservations, limitations
ALBANIA	17. 09.1930 (ratification 17.09.1930)	5 years, from ratification	– ratification – reciprocity – excluding retroactive effect (double formula) – excluding disputes relating to territorial status of Albania – objective reservation of domestic jurisdiction – reservation concerning other method of pacific settlement
	renewed 07.11.1935	5 years, as from 17.09.1935	
ARGENTINA	28.12.1935[1]	10 years, from ratification	– ratification – reciprocity – excluding retroactive effect (double formula) – reservation concerning other method of pacific settlement – excluding questions already settled, or by international law belonging to local jurisdiction, or constitutional questions
AUSTRALIA	20.09.1929 (ratification 18.08.1930)	10 years, thereafter until denunciation	– ratification – reciprocity – excluding retroactive effect (double formula, critical date 18.09.1930) – reservation concerning other method of peaceful settlement – Commonwealth reservation – objective reservation of domestic jurisdiction – reservation to request suspending proceedings, in the case of disputes under consideration by the Council of LoN
	modification 07.09.1939		– excluding disputes arising out of events occurring during present crises
	02.09.1940	5 years, as from 21.08.1940, thereafter until	– reservation concerning other method of peaceful settlement – Commonwealth reservation

State	Date of deposition	Duration	Reservations, limitations
		notice of termination	– objective reservation of domestic jurisdiction – reservation concerning events occurring at the time of hostilities – reservation to request suspending proceedings, in the case of disputes under consideration by the Council of LoN
	06.02.1954	until notice of termination	– reciprocity – excluding retroactive effect (double formula, critical date 19.08.1930) – reservation concerning other method of peaceful settlement – Commonwealth reservation – objective reservation of domestic jurisdiction –reservation concerning events occurring at the time of hostilities –reservation concerning natural resources of seabed, subsoil of continental shelf, including products of sedentary fisheries – reservation concerning jurisdiction or rights in respect of Australian waters, within the meaning of the Australian Pearl Fisheries Acts – reservation to request suspending proceedings in respect of disputes under consideration by the UN Security Council
	17.03.1975	until notice of withdraw	– reciprocity – reservation concerning other method of peaceful settlement
	22.03.2002	until notice of withdraw	– reciprocity – reservation concerning other method of peaceful settlement – excluding disputes concerning delimitation of maritime zones, and on exploitation of any disputed area of or adjacent to any such maritime zone – reservation preventing surprise applications
AUSTRIA	14.03.1922	5 years	
	renewed 12.01.1927 (ratification 13.03.1927)	10 years	– ratification – reciprocity
	renewed 22.03.1937 (ratification 30.06.1937)	5 years, as from 13.03.1937	– ratification – reciprocity
	19.05.1971	5 years, thereafter until notice on termination	– reciprocity – reservation concerning other means of peaceful settlement

State	Date of deposition	Duration	Reservations, limitations
BARBADOS	01.08.1980	until notice of termination	– reciprocity – excluding retroactive effect – reservation concerning other method of peaceful settlement – Commonwealth reservation – objective reservation of domestic jurisdiction – disputes concerning conservation, management or exploitation of the living resources of the sea, or in respect of prevention or control of pollution or contamination of marine environment in marine areas adjacent to the coast of Barbados
BELGIUM	25.09.1925 (ratification 10.03.1926)	15 years	– ratification – reciprocity – excluding retroactive effect (double formula) – reservation concerning other method of pacific settlement
	10.06.1948 (ratification 22.06.1948)	5 years	– ratification – reciprocity – excluding retroactive effect (double formula) – reservation concerning other method of pacific settlement
	03.04.1958 (ratification 17.06.1958)	5 years, thereafter until termination	– ratification – reciprocity – excluding retroactive effect (double formula, critical date 13.07.1948) – other method of pacific settlement
BOLIVIA	07.07.1936	10 years	– reciprocity
	05.07.1948 (ratification 16.07.1948)[2]	5 years	– reciprocity
BOTSWANA	16.03.1970	no time limitation	– reciprocity – reservation concerning other means of peaceful settlement – objective reservation of domestic jurisdiction – reserving the right to amend at any time with immediate effect
BRASIL	01.11.1921	5 years	– reciprocity – on condition that compulsory jurisdiction is accepted at least two of the Powers permanently represented on the Council of the LoN[3]
	renewed	10 years	– reciprocity

State	Date of deposition	Duration	Reservations, limitations
	13.07.1926 (ratification 26.01.1937)		– excluding questions which by international law fall exclusively within the jurisdiction of the Brazilian Courts of law or which belong to the constitutional regime of each state
	renewed 12.02.1948[4] (ratification 12.03.1948)	5 years	– reciprocity
BULGARIA	29.07.1921 (ratification 12.08.1921)	no time limitation	– reciprocity
	24.06.1992	5 years, thereafter until termination (6 months period of notice)	– reciprocity – reservation preventing surprise applications – excluding retroactive effect – reserving the right to amend at any time within 6 months period of notice
CAMBODIA	19.09.1957	10 years, thereafter until notice of termination	– reciprocity – reservation on other method of peaceful settlement – objective reservation of domestic jurisdiction – disputes relating to any matter excluded from judicial settlement or compulsory arbitration by any treaty or international instrument
CAMEROON	03.03.1994	5 years, thereafter until notification on termination	– reciprocity
CANADA	20.09.1929 (ratification 28.07.1930)	10 years, thereafter until notice of termination	– ratification – reciprocity – excluding retroactive effect (double formula) – reservation concerning other method of peaceful settlement – Commonwealth reservation – objective reservation of domestic jurisdiction – reservation to request suspending proceedings, in the case of disputes under consideration by the Council of LoN
	modification 07.12.1939		– excluding disputes arising out of events occurring occurring during hostilities under way
	07.04.1970	until notice of termination	– reciprocity – excluding retroactive effect (double formula) – reservation concerning other method of peaceful settlement

State	Date of deposition	Duration	Reservations, limitations
			– Commonwealth reservation – objective reservation of domestic jurisdiction – excluding disputes concerning conservation, management or exploitation of living resources of the sea, or in respect of prevention or control of pollution or contamination of the marine environment in marine areas adjacent to the coast of Canada – reserving the right to amend at any time with immediate effect
	10.09.1985	until notice of termination	– reciprocity – reservation concerning other method of peaceful settlement – Commonwealth reservation – objective reservation of domestic jurisdiction – reserving the right to amend at any time with immediate effect
	10.05.1994	until notice of termination	– reciprocity – excluding retroactive effect (double formula) – reservation concerning other method of peaceful settlement – Commonwealth reservation – objective reservation of domestic jurisdiction – disputes concerning conservation and management measures with respect to vessels fishing in the NAFO Regulatory Area, and the enforcement of such measures – reserving the right to amend at any time with immediate effect
CHINA	10.05.1922	5 years	– reciprocity
	26.10.1946[5]	5 years, thereafter until notice of termination (6 months period of notice)	– reciprocity
COLOMBIA	06.01.1932	no time limitation	– reciprocity
	30.10.1937[6]		– reciprocity – excluding retroactive effect (double formula, critical date 06.01.1932)
COSTA RICA	28.01.1921[7]	no time limitation	
	05.02.1973	5 years, thereafter tacitly renewed for 5 years, if not denounced	– reciprocity

State	Date of deposition	Duration	Reservations, limitations
		before expiration of any 5 year period	
COTE D'IVOIRE	29.09.2002	unlimited duration	– reciprocity – reservation concerning other method of pacific settlement – objective reservation of domestic jurisdiction – reserving the power of denunciation or modification
CYPRUS	29.04.1988	no time limitation	– reciprocity – objective reservation of domestic jurisdiction – reservation preventing surprise application – reserving the right to amend at any time with immediate effect
	03.09.2002	until notification of withdraw	– reciprocity – excluding interpretation of treaties concluded before 16.08.1960, or binding on Cyprus by succession – reservation preventing surprise application – objective reservation of domestic jurisdiction – reserving the right to amend at any time with immediate effect
CZECHOSLO-VAKIA	19.09.1929[8]	10 years, from ratification	– ratification – reciprocity – excluding retroactive effect (double formula) – reservation concerning other method of pacific settlement – reserving the right of either party to a dispute to submit it, before any recourse to the Court, to the Council of LoN
DEMOCRATIC REPUBLIC OF CONGO	08.02.1989	until notice of revocation	– reciprocity
DENMARK	before 28.01.1921 (ratification 13.06.1921)	5 years	– ratification – reciprocity
	renewed 11.12.1925 (ratification 28.03.1926)	10 years, as from 13.06.1926	– ratification – reciprocity
	renewed 04.06.1936	10 years, as from 13.06.1936	– ratification – reciprocity
	10.12.1946	10 years, as from	– reciprocity

State	Date of deposition	Duration	Reservations, limitations
	10.12.1956	10.12.1946 5 years, thereafter further periods of 5 years if not denounced 6 months before any 5 year period	– reciprocity
DJIBOUTI	02.09.2005	5 years	– reciprocity – reservation concerning other method of settlement – objective reservation of domestic jurisdiction – reservation concerning hostilities – multilateral treaty reservation – excluding disputes with states not having diplomatic relation or not recognized – excluding disputes with non-sovereign states – excluding disputes with the Republic of Djibouti – excluding disputes concerning status of territory, boundaries, etc., different marine zones, status of islands, bays, gulfs, maritime boundaries – excluding disputes concerning airspace, superjacent to its land and maritime territory – reserving the right to terminate or amend with immediate effect
DOMINICA, COMMON-WEALTH OF	31.03.2006	no time limitation	
DOMINICAN REPUBLIC	30.09.1924 (ratification 04.02.1933)	no time limitation	– reciprocity
EGYPT	30.05.1939[9]	5 years, as from ratification	– ratification – reciprocity – excluding retroactive effect (double formula) – reservation concerning other method of pacific settlement – excluding disputes relating to the rights of sovereignty of Egypt – objective reservation of domestic jurisdiction

State	Date of deposition	Duration	Reservations, limitations
	18.07.1957		– reciprocity – excluding retroactive effect – declaration covering only disputes arising under para. 9 (b) of the 1957 Declaration of Egypt on 'the Suez Canal and the arrangement of its operation'
EL SALVADOR	19.12.1930 (ratification 29.08.1930)	5 years	– excluding disputes concerning questions which cannot be submitted to arbitration in accordance with the political constitution of Salvador – excluding disputes which arose before the signature, and pecuniary claims made against the nation – reciprocity only in regard to states which accept the arbitration in that form
	26.11.1973	5 years	– reciprocity – excluding retroactive effect (double formula) – reservation concerning other means of peaceful settlement – objective reservation of domestic jurisdiction – reservation concerning disputes on status of El Salvador's territory, frontiers, etc. – excluding disputes concerning territorial sea, continental slope, continental shelf, etc. islands, bays, gulf, etc., airspace superadjacent to lands and maritime territory, – reservation concerning disputes connected with hostilities – multilateral treaty reservation – reserving the right to amend at any time
	26.11.1978[10]	extended for 10 years from 26.11. 1978	
ESTONIA	02.05.1923	5 years	– reciprocity – excluding retroactive effect – reservation concerning other method of pacific settlement
	renewed 25.06.1928	10 years, as from 02.05.1928	
	renewed 06.05.1938	10 years, as from 02.05.1938	
	21.10.1991		– reciprocity – excluding disputes entrusted to other tribunals

State	Date of deposition	Duration	Reservations, limitations
ETHIOPIA	12.07.1926 (ratification 16.07.1926)	5 years	– reciprocity – excluding retroactive effect – reservation concerning other method of pacific settlement
	renewed 15.04.1932	prolongation for 5 years, as from 16.07.1931	
	renewed 18.09.1934	extension 2 years, as from 18.09.1934, with retrospective effect covering period 18.07.1933–19.09.1934	
FINLAND	1921 (ratification 06.04.1922)	5 years	– ratification – reciprocity
	renewed 03.03.1927	10 years, as from 06.04.1927	– reciprocity
	renewed 09.04.1937	10 years, as from 06.04.1937	– reciprocity
	25.06.1958	5 years, as from 26.06.1958, tacitly renewable for same duration, unless denounced not later than 6 months before the expiry of 5 years	– reciprocity – excluding retroactive effect (double formula, critical date 25.06.1958)
FRANCE	02.10.1924[11]	15 years	– ratification – reciprocity – reservation excluding the Court's proceedings during the attempt to settle the dispute by conciliation, as provided in Art. 15. para. 3 of the Covenant – reserving the right to terminate the declaration if the 1924 Protocol on arbitration, security and disarmament cease to be in effect
	19.09.1929 (ratification 25.04.1931)	5 years	– ratification – reciprocity – excluding retroactive effect (double formula)

State	Date of deposition	Duration	Reservations, limitations
			– reservation concerning disputes which cannot be settled by conciliation or by the Council according to Art. 15, para. 6 of the Covenant – reservation concerning other method of arbitral settlement
	renewed 11.04.1936	5 years, as from 25.04.1936	
	amended 10.09.1939		– reservation excluding disputes arising out of events occurring during hostilities under way
	18.02.1947 (ratification 03.02.1947)	5 years, from 01.03.1947, thereafter until termination	– ratification – reciprocity – excluding retroactive effect (double formula) – reservation concerning other method of peaceful settlement – subjective reservation of domestic jurisdiction
	10.07.1959	3 years, thereafter until termination	– reciprocity – excluding retroactive effect (double formula) – reservation concerning other method of peaceful settlement – objective reservation of domestic jurisdiction – reservation concerning disputes arising out of any war, hostilities, or of a crisis affecting the national security – excluding disputes with any State which, at the date of occurrence of the facts or situations giving rise to the dispute, has not accepted the Court compulsory jurisdiction for a period at least equal to that specified in the 1959 French declaration
	16.05.1966[12]	until termination	– reciprocity – excluding retroactive effect (double formula) – reservation concerning another mode of pacific settlement – objective reservation of domestic jurisdiction – reservation concerning disputes arising out of war, international hostilities, or of crisis affecting national security, and disputes concerning activities connected with national defence – excluding disputes with a state which, at the time of occurrence of the facts or situations giving rise to the dispute, had not accepted the Court's compulsory jurisdiction – reserving the right to amend at any time with immediate effect

State	Date of deposition	Duration	Reservations, limitations
GAMBIA	22.06.1966	until termination	– reciprocity – excluding retroactive effect – reservation concerning other settlement of disputes – Commonwealth reservation – objective reservation of domestic jurisdiction
GEORGIA	20.06.1995	no time limitation	– reciprocity
GERMANY	23.09.1927 (ratification 29.02.1928)	5 years	– ratification – reciprocity – excluding retroactive effect (double formula) – reservation concerning other method of pacific settlement
	renewed 09.02.1933 (ratification 05.07.1933)	5 years, as from 01.03.1933	
	30.04.2008	until withdrawing with immediate effect	– reciprocity – excluding retroactive effect (double formula) – reservation concerning other method of peaceful settlement – any disputes relating or connected with deployment of armed forces abroad, involvement in such deployments or decisions thereon – reservation concerning disputes connected with the use for military purposes of the territory of Germany, including its airspace and maritime areas subject to German sovereign rights and jurisdiction – reservation preventing surprise applications
GREECE	12.09.1929	5 years	– reciprocity – excluding disputes relating to the territorial status of Greece, including its rights of sovereignty over its ports and lines of communication – disputes relating to the application of treaties accepted by Greece and providing another procedure
	renewed 12.09.1934 (ratification 19.07.1935)	5 years	
	renewed 08.09.1939 (ratification 20.02.1940)	5 years, as from 12.09.1939	

State	Date of deposition	Duration	Reservations, limitations
	10.01.1994	5 years, thereafter until termination	– reciprocity – excluding disputes relating to defensive military action taken by the Hellenic Republic for reasons of national defence
GUATEMALA	17.12.1926[13] 27.01.1947[14] (ratification 10.02.1947)	no time limitation 5 years	– ratification – reciprocity – reciprocity – excluding disputes with the United Kingdom regarding the territory of Belize
GUINEA, REPUBLIC OF	04.12.1998	until withdrawal	– reciprocity – excluding retroactive effect (critical date 12.12. 1958) – reservation concerning other method of settlement – objective reservation of domestic jurisdiction – reserving the right to amend at any time
GUINEA-BISSAU	07.12.1989	unlimited 6 months of notice of termination	– reciprocity
HAITI	04.10.1921	no time limitation	
HONDURAS	02.02.1948 (ratification 10.02.1949)	6 years, as from 10.02.1948	– reciprocity
	renewed 19.04.1954	6 years, as from 24.05.1954	
	renewed 10.03.1960	for indefinite duration	– reciprocity
	06.06.1986	until notice of withdrawal	– reciprocity – reservation concerning other means of the pacific settlement – objective reservation of domestic jurisdiction – reservation concerning armed conflicts affecting the territory of Honduras – reservation concerning disputes referring to: (i) territorial questions with regard to sovereignty over islands, shoals and keys; internal waters, bays, the territorial sea and the legal status and limits thereof (ii) sovereignty regarding contiguous zone, exclusive economic zone and continental shelf and the legal status and limits thereof (iii) airspace over the territories, waters and zones referred above – reserving the right to amend by notice at any time

State	Date of deposition	Duration	Reservations, limitations
HUNGARY	14.09.1928 (ratification 13.08.1929)	5 years, as from ratification	– ratification – reciprocity
	renewed 30.05.1934 (ratification 09.08.1934)	5 years as from 13.08.1934	– ratification – reciprocity
	renewed 12.07.1939[15]	for the period from 13.08.1939 to 10.04.1941	
	22.10.1992	until notice of withdrawal 6 months period of notice	– reciprocity – excluding retroactive effect (double formula) – reservation concerning other method of peaceful settlement – objective reservation of domestic jurisdiction – reservation concerning hostilities – reservation preventing surprise applications – reserving the right to amend at any time, 6 months period of notifice
INDIA	19.09.1929 (ratification 15.02.1930)	10 years, thereafter until termination	– ratification – reciprocity – excluding retroactive effect (double formula) – reservation concerning other means of pacific settlement – Commonwealth reservation – objective reservation of domestic jurisdiction – reserving the right to request suspending proceedings, in the case of disputes under consideration by the Council of LoN
	amended 27.09.1939		– reservation excluding disputes arising out of events occurring during hostilities under way
	28.02.1940 (ratification 07.03.40)	5 years, as from 28.02.1940, thereafter until notice of termination	– reciprocity – excluding retroactive effect (double formula, critical date 05.02.1930) – reservation concerning other method of peaceful settlement – Commonwealth reservation – objective reservation of domestic jurisdiction – reservation concerning disputes connected with hostilities – reserving the right to suspend proceedings in case of disputes under consideration by the Council of LoN

State	Date of deposition	Duration	Reservations, limitations
	07.01.1956 (ratification 09.01.1956)	until termination	– reciprocity – excluding retroactive effect (double formula, critical date 26.01.1950) – reservation concerning other methods of peaceful settlement – Commonwealth reservation – subjective reservation of domestic jurisdiction – reservation concerning disputes regarding war events, military occupation, etc.
	14.09.1959	until termination	– reciprocity – excluding retroactive effect (double formula, critical date 26.01.1950) – reservation concerning other methods of peaceful settlement – Commonwealth reservation – subjective reservation of domestic jurisdiction – excluding disputes concerning belligerent or military occupation or discharge of any functions pursuant to any recommendation or decision of anyUN organ – reservation preventing surprise applications – excluding disputes with states not having diplomatic relations with India
	18.09.1974	until termination	– reciprocity – reservation concerning other method of settlement – Commonwealth reservation – objective reservation of domestic jurisdiction – reservation regarding disputes where the jurisdiction of the Court founded on the basis of a treaty concluded under the auspices of the LoN, unless India agrees to jurisdiction in each case – multilateral treaty reservation – excluding retroactive effect (double formula) – excluding disputes with states not having diplomatic relations with India or which has not been recognized by India – reservations concerning disputes relating to (i) territorial status, boundaries, etc.; (ii) the status of its territory or the modification or delimitation of its frontiers or any other matter concerning boundaries; (iii) territorial sea, continental shelf and margins, exclusive fishery zone, exclusive economic zone, and other zones of national maritime jurisdiction including for the regulation and control of

State	Date of deposition	Duration	Reservations, limitations
			marine pollution and the conduct of scientific research by foreign vessels; (iv) condition and status of islands, bays and gulfs and that of the bays and gulfs that for historical reasons belong to India; (v) the airspace superjacent to its land and maritime territory; and (vi) the determination and delimitation of its maritime boundaries
IRAN	02.10.1930 (ratification 19.09.1932)[16]	6 years, thereafter until notification of termination	– reciprocity – ratification – excluding retroactive effect (double formula) – reservation concerning disputes relating to territorial status of Persia, including rights of sovereignty over island, ports – reservation concerning other method of peaceful settlement – objective reservation of domestic jurisdiction – reserving the right to suspend proceedings in case of disputes submitted to the Council of LoN
IRAQ	22.09.1938[17]	5 years from ratification	– reciprocity – excluding retroactive effect (double formula) – reservation concerning other method of peaceful settlement – excluding disputes with Arab states – objective reservation of domestic jurisdiction – excluding disputes affecting territorial status of Iraq including rights of sovereignty over its waters and communications – reserving the right to require suspending proceedings in respect of disputes submitted to the Council or Assembly of LoN
IRELAND /IRISH FREE STATE	14.09.1929 (ratification 11.07.1930) 15.12.2011	20 years	– ratification – reciprocity – excluding disputes with the United Kingdom in regard to Northern Ireland – reserving the right to amend or to withdraw the declaration at any time with immediate effect

State	Date of deposition	Duration	Reservations, limitations
ISRAEL	04.09.1950 (ratification 25.01.1951)	5 years from ratification	– reciprocity – excluding retroactive effect (double formula) in particular, which do not involve a legal title created or conferred by a Government or authority other than the Government of the State of Israel or an authority under the jurisdiction of that Government – reservation concerning other means of peaceful settlement – objective reservation of domestic jurisdiction – excluding disputes between Israel and another state which refuses to establish or maintain normal relations with it
	17.10.1956 (valid from 25.10.1956)	until notice of termination	– reciprocity – excluding retroactive effect (double formula, critical date 25.10.1951), provided that such dispute does not involve a legal title created or conferred by a government or authority other than the government of Israel or an authority under the jurisdiction of that government – reservation concerning other means of settlement – subjective reservation of domestic jurisdiction – excluding disputes between Israel and another state which refuses to establish or maintain normal relations with Israel – excluding disputes arising out of events occurring between 15.05.1948 and 20.07.1949 – excluding disputes connected with any war events, hostilities, etc. breach of armistice agreement or belligerent or military occupation in which involved Israel at any time
	amended 28.02.1984[18]		– reservation preventing surprise applications
ITALY	09.09.1929 (ratification 07.09.1931)	5 years	– ratification – reciprocity – reservation concerning other method of settlement, and in any case where a solution through the diplomatic channel or further by the action of the Council LoN could not be reached

State	Date of deposition	Duration	Reservations, limitations
JAPAN	15.09.1958	5 years, thereafter until notice of termination	– reciprocity – excluding retroactive effect (double formula, critical date 15.09.1958) – reservation concerning other means of peaceful settlement – reservation concerning arbitration and judicial settlement
	09.07.2007	5 years, thereafter until notice of termination	– reciprocity – excluding retroactive effect (double formula, critical date 15.09.1958) – reservation concerning arbitration and judicial settlement – reservation preventing surprise applications
KENYA	19.04.1965	until notice of termination	– reciprocity – excluding retroactive effect (double formula, critical date 12.12.1963) – reservation concerning other method of settlement – Commonwealth reservation – objective reservation of domestic jurisdiction – excluding disputes concerning belligerent or military occupation or the discharge of any functions pursuant to any recommendation or decision of a UN organ – reserving the right to amend at any time with immediate effect
LATVIA	11.09.1923[19]		– ratification
	10.09.1929 (ratification 26.02.1930)	5 years	– ratification – reciprocity – excluding retroactive effect (double formula) – reservation concerning other method of peaceful settlement
	renewed 31.01.1935 (ratification 26.02.1935)	5 years, thereafter until notice of abrogation	– ratification – reciprocity – excluding retroactive effect (double formula, critical date 26.02.1930) – reservation concerning other method of peaceful settlement
LESOTHO	06.09.2000	until notice of termination	– reservation concerning other means of peaceful settlement
LIBERIA	1921[20]	no time limitation	– ratification – reciprocity
	20.03.1952	5 years, thereafter until notice of termination	– reciprocity – subjective reservation of domestic jurisdiction – reservation concerning settlement of disputes by other tribunals

State	Date of deposition	Duration	Reservations, limitations
LIECHTEN-STEIN	29.03.1939	5 years	– excluding retroactive effect – other method of pacific settlement
	29.03.1950	until revoked, subject to one year's notice	– reciprocity
LITHUANIA	05.10.1921 (ratification 16.05.1922)	5 years	
	renewed 14.01.1930	5 years, as from 14.01.1930	
	renewed 12.03.1935	5 years, as from 14.01.1935	– reciprocity
	21.09.2012	until notice of termination	– excluding retroactive effect (double formula) – reservation concerning other method of peaceful settlement – reservation concerning matters excluded from compulsory arbitration – excluding disputes connected with military operation carried out in accordance with a decision taken by international security and defence organisation or organisation implementing common security and defence policy – reserving the right to amend at any time with immediate effect – reservation preventing surprise applications
LUXEMBOURG	1921[21]		–ratification
	15.09.1930	5 years, thereafter tacitly renewed for 5 years, if not denounced before 6 months before the expiration	– reciprocity – excluding retroactive effect (double formula) – reservation concerning other method of peaceful settlement
MADAGASCAR	02.07.1992	until notice of termination	– reciprocity – reservation concerning other means of settlement – objective reservation of domestic jurisdiction – reserving the right to amend at any time with immediate effect

State	Date of deposition	Duration	Reservations, limitations
MALAWI	12.12.1966	no time limitation	– reciprocity – excluding retroactive effect (double formula) – subjective reservation of domestic jurisdiction – reservation concerning other method of peaceful settlement – reservation concerning disputes relating to or arising out of belligerent or military occupation – reserving the right to amend at any time with immediate effect
MALTA	06.12.1966	until notice of termination	– reciprocity – reservation concerning other method of peaceful settlement – Commonwealth reservation – objective reservation of domestic jurisdiction – excluding disputes connected with military occupation or the discharge of any functions pursuant to any UN recommendation or decision – multilateral treaty reservation – reservation concerning matters excluded from compulsory arbitration – excluding disputes in respect of which arbitral or judiciary proceedings have taken place with any state which, at the date of the commencement of the proceedings, had not accepted the Court's compulsory jurisdiction – reservation preventing surprise applications – reserving the right to amend at any time with immediate effect
	amended 02.01.1981 (suppl. to the 1966 declaration)		– stating 'accepting as compulsory without the condition of reciprocity and without reservation the jurisdiction of the International Court of Justice in respect of any disputes concerning the delimitation of areas of the continental shelf in the Mediterranean Sea'
	02.09.1983 (completing the 1966 declaration)		– reservation excluding disputes concerning its territory, including the territorial sea, and the status thereof – reservation excluding disputes concerning continental shelf or any other zone of maritime jurisdiction, and resources thereof – reservation excluding disputes concerning the determination or delimitation of any of the above-mentioned zones

State	Date of deposition	Duration	Reservations, limitations
			– reservation excluding disputes concerning prevention or control of pollution or contamination of the marine environment in marine areas adjacent to the coast of Malta
MARSHALL ISLANDS	23.04.2013	until notice of termination	– reciprocity – reservation concerning other method of peaceful settlement – reservation excluding disputes with states accepting the Court's compulsory jurisdiction in relation or for the purpose of the dispute – reserving the right to amend at any time with immediate effect
MAURITIUS	23.09.1958	until notice of termination	– reciprocity – other method of peaceful settlement – Commonwealth reservation – objective reservation of domestic jurisdiction – excluding disputes connected with military occupation or the discharge of any functions pursuant to any UN recommendation or decision – reservation concerning matters excluded from compulsory arbitration – excluding disputes in respect of which arbitral or judiciary proceedings have taken place with any state which, at the date of the commencement of the proceedings, had not accepted the Court's compulsory jurisdiction – reservation preventing surprise applications – reserving the right to amend at any time with immediate effect
MEXICO	28.10.1947	5 years, thereafter until termination, taking effect after 6 months	– reciprocity – excluding retroactive effect (double formula) – subjective reservation of domestic jurisdiction
MONACO	22.04.1937 (ratification 22.04.1937)	5 years	– excluding retroactive effect (double formula) – reservation concerning other method of pacific settlement
NAURU	29.01.1988	5 years	– reciprocity – reservation concerning other method of pacific settlement
	renewed 09.09.1992[22]	5 years, as from 29.01.1993 5 years	– reciprocity – reservation concerning other method of pacific settlement

State	Date of deposition	Duration	Reservations, limitations
NETHERLANDS	06.08.1921	10 years, as from 06.08.1926	– reciprocity – excluding retroactive effect – reservation concerning other method of pacific settlement
	renewed 02.09.1926	10 years, from 06.08.1936	– reciprocity – excluding retroactive effect – reservation concerning other method of pacific settlement, agreed after the Statute's entry into force
	renewed 05.08.1936	10 years, thereafter until notice of denunciation	– reciprocity – reservation concerning other method of pacific settlement, agreed after the Statute's entry into force
	05.08.1946	5 years, renewable tacitly for 5 years, unless notice of termination given not less than 6 months before the expiry of 5 years	– reciprocity – reservation concerning other method of pacific settlement, agreed by the parties after entry into force of the Statute
	01.08.1956		– reciprocity – excluding retroactive effect (critical date 05.08.1921) – reservation concerning other method of pacific settlement
NEW ZEALAND	19.09.1929	10 years, thereafter until notice of termination	– ratification – reciprocity – excluding retroactive effect (double formula) – reservation concerning other method of pacific settlement – Commonwealth reservation – objective reservation of domestic jurisdiction – reservation to request suspending proceedings, in the case of disputes under consideration by the Council of LoN
	modification 07.09.1939		– excluding disputes arising out of events occurring during hostilities under way
	01.04.1940	5 years, thereafter until notice of termination	– reciprocity – excluding retroactive effect (double formula, critical date 29.03.1930) – reservation concerning other method of pacific settlement – Commonwealth reservation

State	Date of deposition	Duration	Reservations, limitations
			– objective reservation of domestic jurisdiction – reservation concerning hostilities – reservation to request suspending proceedings, in the case of disputes under consideration by the Council of LoN
	22.09.1977	5 years, thereafter until expiration of 6 months after notice of termination	– reciprocity – reservation concerning other method of peaceful settlement – reservation preventing surprise applications – reservation concerning disputes relating to exploitation, conservation, etc. of the living resources in marine areas within 200 nautical miles from the baselines – reserving the right to amend at any time, in the light of the results of Third UN Conference on the Law of the Sea in respect of the settlement of disputes
NICARAGUA	24.09.1929	unconditionally	
	amended 24.09.2011		– excluding disputes regarding any matter or claim based on interpretations of treaties or arbitral awards that were signed and ratified or made, prior to 31.12.1901
NIGERIA	03.09.1965	no time limitation	– reciprocity
	amended 30.04.1998		– reservation preventing surprise applications – subjective reservation of domestic jurisdiction – reservation concerning other method of peaceful settlement – reservation concerning hostilities – excluding disputes with states not having diplomatic relations – excluding disputes concerning, allocation, delimitation, demarcation of territory (whether land, maritime, lacustrine or superjacent air space) – excluding retroactive effect regarding disputes before independence (double formula) – reserving the right to amend at any time, with immediate effect
NORWAY	06.09.1921 (ratification 03.10.1921)	5 years	– ratification – reciprocity
	renewed 22.09.1926	10 years, as from 03.10.1926	– reciprocity

State	Date of deposition	Duration	Reservations, limitations
	renewed 29.05.1936	10 years, as from 03.10.1936	– reciprocity
	16.11.1946	10 years, as from 03.10.1946	– reciprocity
	17.12.1956	5 years, as from 03.10. 1956 thereafter tacitly renewed for period of 5 years, unless notice of termination given not less than 6 months before expiration	– reciprocity
	02.04.1976	5 years, from 03.10. 1956, thereafter tacitly renewed for periods of 5 years, unless notice of termination given not less than 6 months before expiration	– reciprocity – reserving the right to amend at any time, in the light of the results of Third UN conference on the Law of the Sea in respect of the settlement of disputes
	25.06.1996 (amending the 1976 declaration)	5 years, from 03.10.1956, thereafter tacitly renewed for periods of 5 years, unless notice of termination given not less than 6 months before expiration	– reciprocity – providing that the UN Convention on the Law of the Sea and the 1995 Agreement relating to straddling fish stocks and highly migratory fish stocks shall apply to all the disputes concerning to the law of the sea
PAKISTAN	22. 06.1948 (ratification 09.07.1948)	5 years, thereafter until expiration of 6 months after notice of termination	– reservation concerning other tribunals – subjective reservation of domestic jurisdiction – multilateral treaty reservation
	23.05.1957	until notice of termination	– reservation concerning other tribunals – subjective reservation of domestic jurisdiction – multilateral treaty reservation

State	Date of deposition	Duration	Reservations, limitations
	13.09.1960	until notice of termination	– excluding retroactive effect (critical date 24.06.1948) – reservation concerning other tribunals – objective reservation of domestic jurisdiction – multilateral treaty reservation
PANAMA	25.10.1921 (ratification 14.06.1929)		– reciprocity
PARAGUAY	11.05.1933[23]	unconditionally	
	25.09.1996		– reciprocity – excluding retroactive effect
PERU	19.09.1929 (ratification 29.03.1932)	10 years, from ratification	– ratification – reciprocity – excluding retroactive effect (double formula) – reservation concerning other method of settlement by arbitration, or to submit the dispute previously to the Council of LoN
	07.07.2003	until notice of withdrawing	– reciprocity – reservation concerning arbitration or other judicial settlement – reserving the right to amend at any time with immediate effect
PHILIPPINES	12.07.1947 (ratification 21.08.1947)	10 years, as from 04.07.1946, thereafter until notice of termination	– reciprocity
	18.01.1972	notice of termination until	– other method of peaceful settlement – subjective reservation of domestic jurisdiction – reservation preventing surprise application – multilateral treaty reservation – reservation concerning disputes arising out of or concerning jurisdiction or rights claimed or exercised by the Philippines – reservation concerning disputes in respect of the natural resources, including living organisms belonging to sedentary species of the sea–bed and subsoil of the continental shelf, or its analogue in anarchipelago
POLAND	24.01.1931[24]	5 years	– ratification – reciprocity – excluding retroactive effect (double formula) – reservation concerning other method of peaceful settlement

State	Date of deposition	Duration	Reservations, limitations
			– objective reservation of domestic jurisdiction – excluding disputes with states refusing to establish normal diplomatic relations with Poland – excluding disputes connected with World War I or with Polono-Sovietic War – excluding disputes resulting from the Treaty of Peace of 18.03.1921 – excluding disputes relating to internal law connected with the above-mentioned war events
	25.09.1990	5 years, thereafter automatically prolonged for one year; 6 months of notice of termination	– reciprocity – excluding retroactive effect (double formula, critical date 21.09.1990) – reservation regarding disputes with regard to the territory and state boundaries – reservation excluding disputes regarding the pollution of the environment, unless the ICJ jurisdiction results from Poland's treaty obligations – reservation concerning disputes with regard to foreign liabilities or debts – reservation preventing surprise application – reservation concerning other method of peaceful settlement – objective reservation of domestic jurisdiction – reserving the right to amend at any time, taking effect after 6 months
	25.03.1996	until notice of withdraw, taking effect after 6 months	– excluding retroactive effect (double formula, critical date 25.09.1990) – reservation regarding disputes with regard to the territory and state boundaries – reservation excluding disputes regarding environmental protection – reservation concerning disputes with regard to foreign liabilities or debts – reservation preventing surprise application – reservation concerning other method of peaceful settlement – objective reservation of domestic jurisdiction – reserving the right to amend at any time, taking effect after 6 months
PORTUGAL	28.01.1921 (ratification 08.10.1921)		– reciprocity

State	Date of deposition	Duration	Reservations, limitations
	19.12.1955	1 year, thereafter until notice of denunciation	– stating that declaration applies to all disputes arising before or after 16.12.1920 – reserving the right to exclude any dispute at any time, with immediate effect
	25.02.2005	until notice of termination	– reservation concerning other method of peaceful settlement – reservation preventing surprise applications – excluding retroactive effect (double formula, critical date 26.04.1974), unless it refers to territorial titles or rights or to sovereign rights or jurisdiction – excluding any dispute with a party to a treaty regarding which the jurisdiction of the Court has been explicitly excluded – reserving the right to amend at any time with immediate effect
ROMANIA	08.10.1930 (ratification 09.06.1931)	5 years	– ratification – reciprocity in respect of governments recognized by Romania – excluding retroactive effect (double formula) – excluding matters for which special procedure has been provided – reserving the right to submit the dispute to the Council of LoN before having recourse to the Court – excluding questions which might cause the existing territorial integrity of Romania and of her sovereign rights, including rights over ports and communications, to be brought in question – objective reservation of domestic jurisdiction
	renewed on 04.06.1936	5 years, as from 09.06.1936	
SENEGAL	02.12.1985	no time limitation	– reciprocity – excluding retroactive effect – reservation concerning other method of settlement – objective reservation of domestic jurisdiction –reserving the right to amend at any time with immediate effect
SERBIA/ YUGOSLAVIA	16.05.1930 (ratification 24.11.1930)	5 years from ratification	– ratification – reciprocity in relation to any government recognized by Yugoslavia – excluding retroactive effect – objective reservation of domestic jurisdiction

State	Date of deposition	Duration	Reservations, limitations
			– reservation concerning other method of peaceful settlement
	26.04.1999[25]	until notice of termination	– reciprocity – excluding retroactive effect (double formula) – reservation concerning other procedure or method of pacific settlement – objective reservation of domestic jurisdiction
SIAM see THAILAND			
SLOVAKIA	28.05.2004	until notification of withdrawal	– reciprocity – excluding retroactive effect (double formula) – reservation concerning other method of peaceful settlement – reservation preventing surprise applications – excluding disputes with regard to the protection of environment – objective reservation of domestic jurisdiction – reserving the right to amend at any time with immediate effect
SOMALIA	11.04.1963	until notice of termination	– reciprocity – reservation preventing surprise applications – reserving the right to amend at any time with immediate effect
SOUTH AFRICA	29.09.1929	10 years, thereafter until notice of termination	– ratification – reciprocity – excluding retroactive effect (double formula) – reservation concerning other method of peaceful settlement – Commonwealth reservation – objective reservation of domestic jurisdiction – reservation to request suspending proceedings, in respect of any dispute under consideration by the Council of LoN
	modification 18.09.1939		– excluding disputes arising out of events occurring during hostilities under way
	07.04.1940	until notice of termination	– reciprocity – excluding retroactive effect (double formula) – reservation concerning other method of peaceful settlement – Commonwealth reservation

State	Date of deposition	Duration	Reservations, limitations
			– objective reservation of domestic jurisdiction – reservation concerning hostilities – reservation to request suspending proceedings, in respect of any dispute under consideration by the Council of LoN
	13.09.1955[26]	until notice of termination	– reciprocity – excluding retroactive effect (double formula) – reservation concerning other method of peaceful settlement – Commonwealth reservation – subjective reservation of domestic jurisdiction – reservation concerning hostilities
SPAIN	21.09.1928	10 years	– reciprocity – excluding retroactive effect (double formula) – reservation concerning other method of peaceful settlement
	29.10.1990	until withdrawal, with 6 months of period of notice, in respect of states establishing a period of less than 6 months, the withdrawal of the declaration become effective after such shorter period	– reciprocity – reservation concerning other method of peaceful settlement – reservation preventing surprise applications – excluding retroactive effect (double formula) – reserving the right to amend at any time with immediate effect
SUDAN	02.01.1958	until notice of termination	– reciprocity – excluding retroactive effect (double formula, critical date 01.01.1956) – reservation concerning other method of peaceful settlement – subjective reservation of domestic jurisdiction – reservation concerning hostilities
SURINAME	31.08.1987	5 years, then shall continue in force after that period until 12 months after giving notice of termination	– reciprocity – excluding retroactive effect (critical date 07.08.1987) – reservation concerning other method of settlement

State	Date of deposition	Duration	Reservations, limitations
SWAZILAND	26.05.1969	until notification of withdraw	– reciprocity – reservation concerning other means of peaceful settlement – objective reservation of domestic jurisdiction – reserving the right to amend at any time with immediate effect
SWEDEN	16.08.1921	5 years	– reciprocity
	renewed 18.03.1926	10 years, as from 16.08.1926	– reciprocity
	renewed 18.05.1936	10 years, as from 16.08.1936	– reciprocity
	05.04.1947	10 years	– reciprocity – excluding retroactive effect (double formula)
	06.04.1957	5 years, then renewing by tacit agreement for the same duration, unless notice of abrogation, at least 6 months before the expiration of any such period	– reciprocity – excluding retroactive effect (double formula, critical date 06.04.1947)
SWITZER-LAND	before 28.01.1921 (ratification 25.07.1921)	5 years, from ratification	– ratification – reciprocity
	renewed 01.03.1926 (ratification 24.07.1926)	10 years, from ratification	– ratification – reciprocity
	renewed 23.09.1936 (ratification 17.04.1937)	10 years, from ratification	– ratification – reciprocity
	28.07.1948	until abrogation subject to one year's notice	

State	Date of deposition	Duration	Reservations, limitations
THAILAND / SIAM	20.09.1929 (ratification 07.05.1930)	10 years	– ratification – reciprocity – reservation concerning other means of pacific settlement
	renewed 09.05.1940	10 years, as from 07.05.1940	– ratification – reciprocity – reservation concerning other means of pacific settlement
	renewed 20.05.1950[27]	from 03.05.1950	– ratification – reciprocity – reservation concerning other means of pacific settlement
TIMOR-LESTE	21.09.2012	until notice of termination	– reserving the right to amend at any time with immediate effect
TOGO	25.10.1979	unlimited period subject to denunciation	– reciprocity – reserving the right to amend
TURKEY	12.03.1936[28]	5 years	– reciprocity – excluding retroactive effect – excluding disputes relating to the application of treaties or conventions providing for some other method of peaceful settlement
	22.05.1947 (ratification 06.06.1947)	5 years, as from 22.05.1947	– reciprocity – excluding retroactive effect (double formula) – reservation concerning a different method of settling disputes
	renewed 08.06.1954	5 years, as from 22.05.1952	
	renewed 07.08.1958	5 years, as from 23.05.1957	
	renewed 19.03.1964	5 years, as from 23.05.1962	
	renewed 31.08.1967[29]	5 years, as from 23.05.1967	
UGANDA	03.10.1963		– reciprocity
UNITED KINGDOM	19.09.1929 (ratification 05.02.1930)	10 years until notice of termination	– ratification – excluding retroactive effect (double formula) – reservation concerning other method of peaceful settlement – Commonwealth reservation – objective reservation of domestic jurisdiction – reservation to require suspending proceedings, in the case of disputes under consideration by the Council of LoN

State	Date of deposition	Duration	Reservations, limitations
	modification 11.09.1939		– excluding disputes arising out of events occurring during hostilities under way
	28.02.1940	5 years, thereafter until notice of termination	– reciprocity – reservation concerning other method of peaceful settlement – Commonwealth reservation – objective reservation of domestic jurisdiction – reservation concerning hostilities – reservation to require suspending proceedings, in the case of disputes under consideration by the Council of LoN
	13.02.1946 limited acceptance	5 years	– reciprocity – accepting the jurisdicition of the Court 'in all legal disputes concerning the interpretation, application, or validity of any treaty relating to the boundaries of British Honduras, and over any questions arising out of any conclusion which the Court may reach with regard to such treaty.'
	02.06.1955	until notice of termination	– reciprocity – excluding retroactive effect (double formula, critical date 05.02.1930) – other method of peaceful settlement – Commonwealth reservation – objective reservation of domestic jurisdiction – excluding disputes arising out of events occurring between the 03.09.1939, and 02.09.1945 – reservation concerning hostilities, military occupation, etc. – disputes relating to any matter excluded from compulsory adjudication or arbitration
	31.10.1955	until notice of termination	– reciprocity – excluding retroactive effect (double formula, critical date 05.02.1930) – other method of peaceful settlement – Commonwealth reservation – objective reservation of domestic jurisdiction – excluding disputes arising out of events occurring between 03.09.1939, and 02.09.1945 – reservation concerning hostilities, military occupation, etc. – reservation concerning disputes relating to any matter excluded from compulsory adjudication or arbitration – excluding disputes in respect of which arbitral or judicial proceedings are taking, or have taken place, with any state which, at the

State	Date of deposition	Duration	Reservations, limitations
			date of the commencement of the proceedings, had not accepted the Court's compulsory jurisdiction
	18.04.1957	until notice of termination	– reciprocity – excluding retroactive effect (double formula, critical date 05.02.1930) – reservation concerning other method of peaceful settlement – Commonwealth reservation – objective reservation of domestic jurisdiction – excluding disputes arising out of events occurring between 03.09.1939 and 02.09.1945 – excluding disputes relating to hostilities, military occupation, etc. or relating to any question which, in the opinion of the Government of the United Kingdom, affects the national security of the United Kingdom or of any of its dependent territories – disputes relating to any matter excluded from compulsory adjudication or arbitration – excluding disputes in respect of which arbitral or judicial proceedings are taking, or have taken place, with any state which, at the date of the commencement of the proceedings, had not accepted the Court's compulsory jurisdiction – reservation preventing surprise applications – reserving the right to amend at any time with immediate effect
	26.11.1958	until notice of termination	– reciprocity – excluding retroactive effect (double formula, ritical date 05.02.1930) – reservation concerning other method of peaceful settlement – Commonwealth reservation – objective reservation of domestic jurisdiction – excluding disputes arising out of events occurring between 03.09.1939 and 02.09.1945 – excluding disputes relating to hostilities, military occupation, etc. – disputes concerning questions connected with events occurring before the date of the Declaration which, had been the subject of proceedings brought before the Court previous to that date, would have been excluded from the Court's compulsory jurisdiction under the second part of the

State	Date of deposition	Duration	Reservations, limitations
			reservation numbered (v) in the 1957 UK declaration – disputes relating to any matter excluded from compulsory adjudication or arbitration – excluding disputes in respect of which arbitral or judicial proceedings are taking, or have taken place, with any state which, at the date of the commencement of the proceedings, had not accepted the Court's compulsory jurisdiction – reservation preventing surprise applications – reserving the right to amend at any time with immediate effect
	27.11.1963	until notice of termination	– reciprocity – excluding retroactive effect (double formula, critical date 05.02.1930) – reservation concerning other method of peaceful settlement – Commonwealth reservation – objective reservation of domestic jurisdiction – excluding disputes arising out of events occurring between 03.09.1939 and 02.09.1945 – excluding disputes relating to hostilities, military occupation, etc. – disputes relating to any matter excluded from compulsory adjudication or arbitration – excluding disputes in respect of which arbitral or judicial proceedings are taking, or have taken place, with any state which, at the date of the commencement of the proceedings, had not accepted the Court's compulsory jurisdiction – reservation preventing surprise applications – reserving the right to amend at any time with immediate effect
	01.01.1969	until notice of termination	– reciprocity – excluding retroactive effect (double formula, critical date 24.10.1930) – reservation concerning other method of peaceful settlement – excluding disputes already submitted to arbitration by agreement with any state which had not at the time of submission accepted the compulsory jurisdiction of the Court – Commonwealth reservation – reservation preventing surprise applications

State	Date of deposition	Duration	Reservations, limitations
	amending 05.07.2004		– reserving the right to amend at any time with immediate effect – reciprocity – excluding retroactive effect (double formula, critical date 01.01.1974) – reservation concerning other method of peaceful settlement – Commonwealth reservation – reservation preventing surprise applications – reserving the right to amend at any time with immediate effect
UNITED STATES OF AMERICA	26.08.1946[30]	5 years, thereafter until the expiration of 6 months after notice of termination	– reservation concerning other tribunal – subjective reservation of domestic jurisdiction – multilateral treaty reservation
URUGUAY	before 28.01.1921 (ratification 27.09.1921)		– reciprocity
YUGOSLAVIA See SERBIA			
ZAIRE See DEMOCRATIC REPUBLIC OF CONGO			

NOTES

1 No ratification has been deposited.
2 After 5 years the declaration was expired.
3 That condition was met on 5 February 1930.
4 After 5 years the declaration was expired.
5 On 5 September 1972 the Government of the People's Republic of China indicated that it did not recognize the statement of 1946 concerning the acceptance of the Court's compulsory jurisdiction.
6 By a note registered on 5 December 2001 Colombia terminated its declaration of acceptance.
7 Costa Rica withdrew from the League of Nations even before the ratification of the Protocol of Signature, thus her signature of the Protocol and the optional clause has lapsed.
8 No ratification has been deposited.
9 No ratification has been deposited.
10 The declaration expired in 1988.
11 No ratification has been deposited.
12 The declaration was terminated on 2 January 1974.

13 No ratification has been deposited.
14 After 5 years the declaration was expired.
15 No ratification has been deposited.
16 On 9 July 1951 Iran terminated its declaration of acceptance.
17 No ratification has been deposited.
18 By a note of 21 November 1985, Israel terminated its declaration of acceptance.
19 No ratification has been deposited.
20 No ratfication has been deposited.
21 No ratification has been deposited.
22 After 5 years the declaration was expired.
23 By a note of 26 April 1938 Paraguay withdrew the declaration of acceptance.
24 No ratification has been deposited.
25 On 13 May 2008 Serbia stated that it did not recognize the declaration of 26 April 1999.
26 In a communication dated 12 April 1967, the Government of South Africa gave notice of withdrawal and termination of the declaration of 12 September 1955.
27 The declaration expired in 1960.
28 No ratification has been deposited.
29 After 5 years the declaration was expired.
30 In a notification received by the UN Secretary-General on 7 October 1985, the Government of the United States of America gave notice of the termination of its declaration of 26 August 1946.

Selected bibliography

BOOKS

Abi-Saab, G., *Les exceptions préliminaires dans la procédure de la Cour Internationale* (Editions A. Pedone, 1967) 279.

Alexandrov, S.A., *Reservations in Unilateral Declarations accepting the Compulsory Jurisdiction of the International Court of Justice* (Martinus Nijhoff Publishers 1995) 176.

Amerasinghe, F., *Jurisdiction of Specific International Tribunals* (Martinus Nijhoff Publishers 2009) 574.

Anand, R.P., *The Compulsory Jurisdiction of the International Court of Justice* (Hope India Publications 208) 364.

Ando, N., McWinney, E., Wolfrum, R. (eds), *Liber Amicorum Judge Shigeru Oda* (Kluwer Law International 2002) vol. I–II 1633.

Anghie, A., Sturgess, G. (eds), *Legal Vision of the 21st Century: Essays in Honour of Judge Weeramantry* (Kluwer Law International 1998) 791.

Arend, A.C. (ed), *The United States and the Compulsory Jurisdiction of the International Court of Justice* (University Press of America 1986) 209.

Aust, A., *Modern Treaty Law and Practice* (University Press 2000) 224.

Benis, S.F., *Jay's Treaty* (Yale University 1962) 526.

Bustamante y Sirvén, A.S. de, *La Cour Permanente de Justice International* (Paul Goulé, tr.), (Librairie Recueil Sirey 1925) 262.

Cheng, B., *General Principles of Law as Applied by International Courts and Tribunals* (Stevens 1953) 490.

Collier, J., Lowe, V., *The Settlement of Disputes in International Law: Institutions and Procedures* (OUP 1999) 395.

Constantopoulos, D.S., Eustathiades, C.Th., Fragistas, N.C. (Hrsg), *Grundprobleme des Internationalen Rechts: Festschrift für Jean Spiropoulos* (Schimmelbusch & Co. 1957) 471.

Damrosch, L.F. (ed), *The International Court of Justice at a Crossroads* (Transnational Publishers 1987) 511.

Decaux, E., *La Réciprocité en Droit International* (LGDJ 1980) 374.

Deuxième Conférence Internationale de la Paix: Actes et Documents. (Martinus Nijhoff Publishers 1908, 1909) vol. I–III.

Dinstein, Y. (ed), *International Law at a Time of Perplexity: Essays in Honour of Shabtai Rosenne* (Martinus Nijhoff Publishers 1989) 1056.

Dreyfus, F., *L'Arbitrage International* (Calmann Levy 1892) 395.

Dubisson, M., *La Cour Internationale de Justice* (LGDJ 1964) 470.

Elkind, J.B., *Non-appearance before the International Court of Justice. Functional and Comparative Analysis* (Martinus Nijhoff Publishers 1984) 233.

Fachiri, A.P., *The Permanent Court of International Justice* (Reprint of the 2nd Edition 1932, Scientia Verlag 1980) 416.

Farmanfarma, A.N., *The Declarations of Members accepting the Compulsory Jurisdiction of the International Court of Justice* (Imprimerie Gauguin & Laubscher S. 952) 192

Gross, L. (ed), *The Future of the International Court of Justice* (Oceana Publications 1976) vol. I–II 862.

Guillaume, G., *La Cour internationale de Justice à l'aube du XXIème siècle: Le regard d'un juge* (Pedone 2003) 331.

Guyomar, G., *Lé défaut des Parties à un différend devant les Juridictions Internationales* (LGDJ 1960) 242.

Guyomar, G., *Commentaire du Réglement de la Cour internationale de Justice* (A. Pedone 1983) 760.

Harley, J.E., *The League of Nations and the New International Law* (Oxford University Press 1921) 127.

Hoijer, O., *La solution pacifique des litiges internationaux* (Editons Spes 1925) 570.

Hudson, M.O. (ed), *The World Court Reports, 1920–1942* (Carnegie Endowment of International Peace 1943) vol. I–IV 513, 549, 777 870.

Hudson, M.O., *The Permanent Court of International Justice, 1920–1942* (Arno Press 1972) 807.

Janis, Mark W. (ed), *International Courts and Tribunals for the Twenty-First Century* (Kluwer Academic Publishers 1992) 261.

Jenks, C.W., *The Prospects of International Adjudication* (Stevens and Sohns Ltd., Oceana Publications 1964) 805.

Kamarowsky, L., *Le tribunal international* (Serge de Westman (tr.), G. Pedone-Lauriel 1887) 528.

Kelsen, H., *The Law of the United Nations* (Stevens and Sons Limited 1951) 994.

Kolb, R., *The International Court of Justice* (Hart Publishing 2013) 1307.

Lauterpacht, E., *Aspects of the Administration of International Justice* (The Grotius Publications Limited 1991) 166.

Lauterpacht, Sir H., *The Development of International Law by the International Court of Justice* (Reprint) (Grotius Publications Limited 1982) 408.

Lindsey, E., *The International Court* (Thomas Y. Crowell Company, 1931) 98–9.

Lowe, V., Fitzmaurice, M. (eds), *Fifty years of the International Court of Justice: Essays in honour of Sir Robert Jennings* (Grotius Publications, Cambridge University Press 1996) 640.

Martens, F. de, *Traité de Droit International* (A. Marescq 1883) 567.

Maus, B., *Les Réserves dans les Déclarations d'Acceptation Obligatoire de la Cour Internationale de Justice* (Librairie E. Droz 1959) 215.

Lord McNair, A., *The Law of Treaties* (Clarendon Press 1961) 789

Mérignhac, A., *Traité Théorique et Pratique de l'Arbitrage International* (Paris 1895) 479.

Merrilis, J.G., *International Dispute Settlement* (Grotius 1991) 288.

Miller, D.H., *The Drafting of the Covenant* (G.P. Putman 1928) vol. I–II 555, 857.

Mosler, H., Bernhardt, R. (eds), *Judicial Settlement of International Disputes* (Springer Verlag 1974) 572.

Rajan, M.S., *United Nations and Domestic Jurisdiction* (Orient Longmans 1958) 679.

Rauschning, D. (hrsg), *The Vienna Convention on the Law of Treaties: Dokumente* (Alfred Metzner Verlag 1978) 543.

Reibstein, E., *Völkerrecht, Eine Geschichte seiner Ideen in Lehre und Praxis* (K. Alber 1963) 640.

Revon, M., *L'Arbitrage International. Son Passé – Son Présent – Son Avenir* (A. Rousseau 1892) 540.

Rosenne, S., *The Time Factor in the Jurisdiction of the International Court of Justice* (A.W. Sythoff 1960) 75.

Rosenne, S., *The World Court* (4th revised edition) (Martinus Nijhoff Publishers 1989) 320.

Rosenne, S., *Intervention in the International Court of Justice* (Martinus Nijhoff Publishers 1993) 207.

Rosenne, S. (ed), *The Hague Peace Conferences of 1899 and 1907 and International Arbitration. Reports and Documents* (T.M.C. Asser Press 2001) 457.

Rosenne, S., *The Law and Practice of the International Court 1920–2005* (4th edition with the assistance of Yaël Ronen, Martinus Nijhoff Publishers 2006) vol. I–IV 1982.

Russel, R.B., Muther, J.E., *A History of the United Nations Charter* (The Brookings Institution 1958) 1140.

Shany, Y., *The Competing Jurisdictions of International Court and Tribunals* (OUP 2004) 348.

Shihata, I.F.I., *The Power of the International Court to Determine its own Jurisdiction* (Martinus Nijhoff Publishers 1965) 400.

Simma, B., Mosler, H., Randelzhofer, A., Tomuschat, C., Wolfrum, R. (eds), *The Charter of the United Nations: A Commentary* (Beck C.H. 1994) 1258.

Spiermann, O., *International Legal Argument in the Permanent Court of International Justice: The Rise of the International Judiciary.* Cambridge Studies of International and Comparative Law (CUP 2005) 538.

Stuyt, A.M., *Survey of International Arbitrations 1794–1970* (Sijthoff 1976) 572.

Szafarz, R., *The Compulsory Jurisdiction of the International Court of Justice* (Martinus Nijhoff Publishers 1993) 189.

Taracouzio, T.A., *The Soviet Union and International Law* (The MacMillan Company 1935, Kraus Reprint Co. 1972) 530.

Ter Meulen, J., *Der Gedanke der Internationalen Organisation in seiner Entwicklung 1300–1800.* (M. Nijhoff 1917, 1929) vol. I–II 397, 371.

Thirlway, H.W.A., *Non-appearance before the International Court of Justice* (CUP 1985) 184.

Zimmermann, A., Tomouschat, Ch., Oellers-Frahm, K. (eds), *The Statute of the International Court of Justice. A Commentary* (Oxford University Press 2006) 1577.

ARTICLES

Alexandrov, S.A., 'Non-Appearance before the International Court of Justice' (1995) 33 *Colum J Transnat'l L* 41–72.

Alexandrov, S.A., 'The Compulsory Jurisdiction of the International Court of Justice: How Compulsory Is It?' (2006) 5 *Chinese J I L* 29–38.

Bindschindler, R.L., 'La délimitation des compétences des Nations Unies' (1963) 108 *RCADI* vol. I. 307–424.

Bleichert, M.A., 'The Effectiveness of Voluntary Jurisdiction in the ICJ: El Salvador v. Honduras, A Case in Point' (1992) 16 *Fordham Int'l L J* 799–830.

Bowett, D.W., 'Reservations to Non-restricted Multilateral Treaties' (1976–77) 48 *BYIL* 67–92.

Briggs, H.W., 'Reservations to the Acceptance of Compulsory Jurisdiction of the International Court of Justice' (1958) 93 *RCADI* 224–366.

Briggs, H.W., 'The International Court of Justice Lives up to its Name' (1987) 81 *AJIL* 78–86.

Buffet-Tchalakoff, M.F., 'La compétence de la Cour internationale de Justice dans l'affaire des "Actions Frontalières et Transfrontalières"' (Nicaragua–Honduras) 1989 93 *RGDIP* 1989 623–653.

Cot, J.P., 'La bonne foi et la conclusion des traités' (1968) 3 *Rev B D I* 140–59.

Crabb, J.H., 'On Judging the Connally Amendment' (1962) 50 *Geo L J* 529–45.

Crawford, J., 'The Legal Effect of Automatic Reservations to the Jurisdiction of the International Court' (1979) 50 *BYIL* 63–86.

D'Amato, A., 'Modifying U.S. Acceptance of the Compulsory Jurisdiction of the World Court' (1985) 79 *AJIL* 385.

Dreyfus, S., 'Les déclarations souscrites par la France aux termes de l'Article 36 du Statut de la Cour internationale de la Haye' (1959) 5 *AFDIP* 258–73.

Eisemann, P.M., 'Les effets de la non-comparution devant la Cour internationale de Justice' (1973) 19 *AFDI* 351–75.

Elkind, J.B., 'The Duty to Appear before the International Court of Justice' (1988) 37 *ICLQ* 674–81.

Enriques, G., 'L'acceptation sans réciprocité de la juridiction obligatoire de la Cour Permanente de Justice' (1932) 13 *RDILC* 834–60.

Fitzmaurice, G.F., 'The Law and Procedure of the International Court of Justice, 1951–54' Part I. 31 (1954) *BYIL* 371–429.

Fitzmaurice, G.F., 'The Law and Procedure of the International Court of Justice, 1951–54' Part II. 32 (1955–56) *BYIL* 20–96.

Fitzmaurice, G., 'The problem of the Non-Appearing Defendant Government' (1980) 51 *BYIL* 89–122.

Fry, J.D., 'Non-participation in the International Court of Justice Revisited: Change or Plus Ça Change?' (2010) 49 *Colum J Transnat'l L* 35–74.

Ginsburg, T. and McAdams, R.H., 'Adjudicating in Anarchy: An Expressive Theory of International Dispute Resolution' (2004) 45 *Wm & Mary L Rev* 1229–339.

Gray, Ch., 'The Use and Abuse of the International Court of Justice: Cases concerning the Use of Force after Nicaragua' (2003) 14 *EJIL* 867–905.

Greig, D.W., 'Nicaragua and the United States: Confrontation over the Jurisdiction of the International Court' (1992) 62 *BYIL* 123–65.

Gros, A., 'La recherche du consensus dans les décisions de la Cour internationale de Justice' in R. Bernhardt, W.K. Geck, G. Jaenicke, H. Steinberger, (hrsg), *Völkerrecht als Rechtsordnung, Internationale Gerichtsbarkeit, Menschenrechte: Festschrift für Hermann Mosler.* (Springer Verlag 1983) 351–8.

Gross, L., 'Bulgaria Invokes the Connally Amendment' (1962) 56 *AJIL* 357–82.

Gross, L., 'The International Court of Justice: Consideration of Requirements for Enhancing its Role in the International Legal Order' (1971) 65 *AJIL* 253–326.

Guerrero, G., 'La qualification unilaterale de la compétence nationale' in D.S. Constantpoulos, C.Th., Eustathiades, N.C., Fragistas (hrsg), *Grundprobleme des Internationalen Rechts: Festschrift für Jean Spiropoulos* (Schimmerbusch & Co. 1957) 207–12.

Hambro, E., 'Some Observations on the Compulsory Jurisdiction of the International Court of Justice' (1948) 25 *BYIL* 133–57.

Hambro, E., 'The Jurisdiction of the International Court of Justice' (1950) 76 *RCADI* vol. I 121–214.

Highet, K., 'Evidence, the Court, and the Nicaragua Case' (1987) 81 *AJIL* 1–56.

Howell, J.M., 'The Commonwealth and the Concept of Domestic Jurisdiction' (1967) 5 *Can YB Int'l L* 14–44.

Hudson, M.O., 'The twenty-fifth year of the World Court' (1946) 40 *AJIL* 1–52.

Hyde, C.C., 'The United States accepts the Optional Clause' (Editional Comment) (1946) 40 *AJIL* 778–81.

Iglesias Buigues, J.L., 'Les déclarations d'acceptation de la juridiction obligatoire de la Cour internationale de Justice: Leur nature et leur interprétation' (1972) 23 *ÖzöR* 255–88.

Jennings, Y.R., 'Recent Cases on "Automatic" Reservations to the Optional Clause' (1958) 7 *ICLQ* 349–66.

Jennings, Y.R., 'The United Nations at Fifty: The International Court of Justice after Fifty Years' (1995) 89 *AJIL* 493–505.

Jessup, P.C., 'Acceptance by the United States of the Optional Clause of the International Court of Justice' (Editorial Comment) (1945) 39 *AJIL* 745–51.

Jessup, P., 'The International Court of Justice Revisited' (1971) 11 *VJIL* 299–309.

Kelsen, H., 'Compulsory Adjudication of International Disputes' (1943) 37 AJIL 397–406.

Kooijmans, P.H., 'Who Tolled the Death-Bell on Compulsory Jurisdiction' in A. Bos, H. Siblesz (ed.) Realism in Law-Making, Essays on International Law in Honour of Willem Riphagen. T.M.C. Asser Instituut (Brill 1986) 71–87.

Lauterpacht, H. 'The British Reservation to the Optional Clause' (1930) 10 *Economica* 137–72.

Lawson, R.C., 'The Problem of the Compulsory Jurisdiction of the World Court' (1952) 46 *AJIL* 219–38.

Lémonon, E., 'La Cour permanente de Justice internationale' (1922) 49 *JDI* 761–73.

Llamzon, A.P., 'Jurisdiction and Compliance in Recent Decisions of the International Court of Justice' (2008) 18 *EJIL* 815–52.

Lloyd, L., 'A Springboard for the Future': A Historical Examination of Britain's Role in Shaping the Optional Clause of the Permanent Court of International Justice' (1985) 79 *AJIL* 28–51.

Loder, B.C.J., 'The Permanent Court of International Justice and Compulsory Jurisdiction' (1921–1922) 2 *BYIL* 6–26.

Merrills, J.G., 'The Optional Clause Today' (1979) 50 *BYIL* 87–116.

Merrills, J.G., 'The Optional Clause Revisited' (1993) 64 *BYIL* 197–244.

Oda, S., 'Reservations in the Declarations of Acceptance of the Optional Clause and the Period of Validity of those Declarations: The Effect of the Schultz Letter' (1988) 59 *BYIL* 1–30.

Oda, S., 'The Compulsory Jurisdiction of the International Court of Justice: a Myth?' (2000), 49 *ICLQ* 251–77.

Oellers-Frahm, K., 'Probleme und Grenzen der obligatorischen internationalen Gerichtsbarkeit' (1989) 27 *AVR* 442–54.

Owen, H.J., 'Compulsory Jurisdiction of the International Court of Justice: A study of its Acceptance by Nations' (1968–1969) 3 *Ga L Rev* 704–26.

Oxman, B.H., 'Complementary Agreements and Compulsory Jurisdiction' (2001) 95 *AJIL* 277–312.

Pastor Ridriejo, J.A., The Spanish Declaration of acceptance of the Compulsory Juridiction of the ICJ (1990), 1 *Spanish Yb of IL* 19–35.

Posner, E.A. and Yoo, J.C., 'Judicial Independence in International Tribunals' (2005) 93 *Cal L R* 1–74.

Preuss, L., 'The International Court of Justice, the Senate and Matters of Domestic Jurisdiction' (1946) 40 *AJIL* 720–36.

Preuss, L., 'Article 2, paragraph 7 of the Charter of the United Nations and Matters of Domestic Jurisdiction' (1949) 74 *RCADI* vol. I 547–653.

Reisman, W.M., 'Has the International Court Exceeded its Jurisdiction?' (Editorial Comments) (1986) 80 *AJIL* 128–34.

Rogers, W.P., 'The United States "Automatic" Reservation to Optional Clause Jurisdiction of the I.C.J' (1958) 7 *ICLQ* 758–62.

Romano, C.P.R., 'International Justice and Developing Countries: A Quantitative Analysis' (2002) 1 *Law & Prac Int'l Courts & Trib* 367–99.

Scott, G.L. and Carr, G.L., 'The ICJ and Compulsory Jurisdiction: The Case for Closing the Clause' (1987) 8 1 *AJIL* 57–76.

Sohn, L.B., 'The Role of International Law in the 21st Century' in *The Compulsory Jurisdiction of the International Court of Justice: A Turning Point?*' Proceedings of the Roundtable in honour of Louis B. Sohn (Vrije Universiteit Brussel 1991) 3–50.

Sohn, L.B., 'The Limited Acceptance of the Compulsory Jurisdiction of the International Court of Justice by the United States' in *The Compulsory Jurisdiction of the International Court of Justice: A Turning Point?*' Proceedings of the Roundtable in honour of Louis B. Sohn (Vrije Universiteit Brussel 1991) 66–72.

Soubeyrol, J., 'Validité dans le temps de la déclaration d'acceptation de la juridiction obligatoire' (1959) 5 *AFDI* 232–57.

Spiermann, O., 'Who Attempts too Much Does Nothing Well: The 1920 Advisory Committee of Jurists and the Permanent Court of International Justice' (2002) 73 *BYIL* 187–260.

Taube, M. de, 'Les origines de l'arbitrage international. Antiquité et Moyen Age' (1932) 42 *RCADI* vol. IV 3–115.

Thévenaz, H., 'La nouvelle Cour internationale de Justice' (1945) 20 *Die Friedens-Warte* 406–13.

Thirlway, H.W.A., 'Reciprocity in the Jurisdiction of the International Court' (1984) 15 *NYIL* 97–137.

Verdross, A., 'The Plea of Domestic Jurisdiction before an International Tribunal and a Political Organ of the United Nations' (1968) 28 *ZaöRV* 33–40.

Verhoeven, J., 'Le droit, le juge et la violence' (1987) 91 *RGDIP* 1159–202.

Virally, M., 'Le principe de réciprocité dans le droit international contemporaire' (1967) 122 *RCADI* vol. III 5–105.

Waldock, C.H.M., 'The Plea of Domestic Jurisdiction before International Legal Tribunals' (1954) 31 *BYIL* 96–142.

Waldock, C.H.M., 'Decline of the Optional Clause' (1955–56) 32 *BYIL* 244–87.

Watson, J.S., 'Autointerpretation, Competence, and Continuing Validity of Article 2(7) of the UN Charter' (1977) 71 *AJIL* 60–83.

Widdows, K., 'The Unilateral Denunciation of Treaties Containing No Denunciation Clause' (1982) 53 *BYIL* 83–114.

Wilcox, F.O., 'The United States Accepts Compulsory Jurisdiction' (1946) 40 *AJIL* 699–719.

Williams, Sir J.F., 'The Optional Clause, The British Signature and Reservation' (1930) 11 *BYIL* 63–84.

Wyler, E., 'Les rapports entre exceptions préliminaires et fond du litige à la lumière de l'arrêt de la CIJ du 11 juillet 1996 dans l'affaire du génocide' (2001) 105 *RGDIP* 25–54.

Index